MW00329405

'An outstanding contribution to our understanding of Iraqi and Saudi foreign policy following the 2003 U.S. invasion. Harvey's extensive research, including interviews with senior figures on all sides, is exceptionally valuable. Her arguments are original and compelling.'

Kristian Coates Ulrichsen, Fellow for the Middle East, Rice University

'A rare, incisive analysis of the Saudi approach to Iraq's momentous post-invasion shift towards Iran. Illuminating the impact on regional rivalries, and their devastating effect inside Iraq, Harvey's book is of seminal value to policymakers grappling with Saudi–Iranian tensions and state-building in Iraq.'

Vali Nasr, Majid Khadduri Professor of International Affairs and Middle East Studies, Johns Hopkins University, and author of *The Shia Revival*

'A major contribution to the literature regarding Saudi Arabia's relations with Iraq in the period following the 2003 U.S. invasion. Deploying multiple tools of social science, Harvey meticulously explores the mindset of Saudi King Abdullah toward Iraqi Prime Minister Nouri al-Maliki.'

Robert W. Jordan, former U.S. ambassador to Saudi Arabia

'A timely, persuasive and original text that fills a much-needed gap—on Saudi–Iraqi relations, the role of Iraq in the Saudi–Iranian rivalry, and the Kingdom's involvement in Iraq's domestic politics since 2003. This promises to be an important book.'

Simon Mabon, Professor of International Politics, Lancaster University, and author of *Houses Built on Sand: Violence, Sectarianism and Revolution in the Middle East*

'Shows how King Abdullah's flawed perception of Prime Minister al-Maliki as an Iranian agent drove the kingdom's disengagement and weakened its foreign policy. Harvey's account of the missteps helps to explain Saudi difficulties today in navigating Iraq, highlighting the role of human error in international relations. Informative and insightful.'

Renad Mansour, Director of the Iraq Initiative, Chatham House

'An interesting, original and historically grounded study, throwing light on key actors in the Gulf's balance of power. This important book has clear relevance for understanding recent developments in these fraught relationships.'

Charles Tripp, Professor Emeritus of Politics, SOAS University of London, and author of *A History of Iraq*

A SELF-FULFILLING PROPHECY

KATHERINE HARVEY

A Self-Fulfilling Prophecy

The Saudi Struggle for Iraq

OXFORD
UNIVERSITY PRESS

OXFORD

UNIVERSITY PRESS

Oxford University Press is a department of the
University of Oxford. It furthers the University's objective
of excellence in research, scholarship, and education
by publishing worldwide.

Oxford   New York

Auckland   Cape Town   Dar es Salaam   Hong Kong   Karachi
Kuala Lumpur   Madrid   Melbourne   Mexico City   Nairobi
New Delhi   Shanghai   Taipei   Toronto

With offices in

Argentina   Austria   Brazil   Chile   Czech Republic   France   Greece
Guatemala   Hungary   Italy   Japan   Poland   Portugal   Singapore
South Korea   Switzerland   Thailand   Turkey   Ukraine   Vietnam

Oxford is a registered trade mark of Oxford University Press
in the UK and certain other countries.

Published in the United States of America by
Oxford University Press
198 Madison Avenue, New York, NY 10016

Library of Congress Cataloging-in-Publication Data is available
Katherine Harvey.
A Self-Fulfilling Prophecy: The Saudi Struggle for Iraq.
ISBN: 9780197631324

Printed in the United Kingdom by Bell and Bain Ltd, Glasgow on acid-free paper

CONTENTS

ACKNOWLEDGEMENTS

This book, which began its journey as a PhD dissertation, was many years in the making, and I have a number of people to thank for making it possible. Foremost, I owe a huge debt of gratitude to my supervisors at King's College London, Dr Michael Farquhar and Professor Jeroen Gunning. Mike, in particular, was an excellent first supervisor, pushing me and challenging me to engage with my research on a deeper level. Whatever strengths are contained in this book are owed in large measure to his guidance while I was working on my dissertation.

I am also grateful to a number of individuals who helped me conduct my research and provided support along the way. First of all, I am grateful to all the people who spoke to me, often very candidly, for my research. I would not have been able to write this book without them. A number of friends and acquaintances were also critical in helping me to connect with important sources, including Ali Allawi, Sami al-Askari, Eliot Cohen, Jim Jeffrey, Bob Jordan, Ann Kirschner, and Mowaffaq al-Rubaie. They have my sincere thanks. In addition, I am hugely grateful to the late Jamal Khashoggi, whom I met in Washington, DC, in spring 2018. Jamal was pivotal in connecting me to the Saudi sources known in this book as the "Saudi foreign policy adviser" and the "Saudi royal family insider." Jamal was a warm and gregarious man, and his murder at the Saudi consulate in Istanbul in October 2018 was devastating to me.

A number of friends provided significant encouragement as I was on this journey. I would like to thank Khalid al-Doori and Raad Alkadiri for their friendship and the many engaging conversations we've had on Iraq. Raad also provided feedback on not one, but two different drafts of this project at various stages. I am also grateful to Bruce Riedel for his enthusiastic support of this book. Furthermore, Heba Arafah, Nina Ashby, Stephen Billick, and Ellyn Turer are dear friends on whom I frequently leaned as I was going through the ups and downs of my PhD. Kristina Perez gave me very useful advice on my book proposal, and James Norton was my biggest cheerleader as I was going through the publication process. They all have my sincere thanks.

I want to thank the team at Hurst, particularly Lara Weisweiller-Wu, Farhaana Arefin, Daisy Leitch, and Ailie Conor, for shepherding this book through to publication. I always felt in good hands, and I'm delighted to be part of the Hurst family.

Finally, I am grateful to my parents and my sister, Alex. They are my eternal champions and most significant source of support.

FOREWORD

Bruce Riedel

A Self-Fulfilling Prophecy is a path-breaking and important book that provides a unique insight into one of the most consequential issues in modern history: the disastrous war in Iraq initiated by the United States and the United Kingdom in 2003. Virtually all observers agree that the Iraq War was among the most catastrophic foreign policy decisions in the history of the two allies. Some have called it the worst foreign policy decision in American history. Until the publication of this book, however, we have not been aware of how another actor, the Kingdom of Saudi Arabia, helped to make a bad situation much worse through its own inept handling of the Iraq government after the downfall of Saddam Hussein.

Dr. Harvey's book shows that Saudi Arabia's King Abdullah had a deeply prejudiced view of Iraq's Shi'a community that warped the kingdom's policy toward the post-Saddam government led by Nuri al-Maliki. The king's view was the result of decades of Saudi interaction with its two northern neighbors, Iraq and Iran. The Islamic Revolution in Iran, the Iran–Iraq War, and the invasion of Kuwait reinforced a Saudi world view that all Shiʿa were enemies of the kingdom. But Abdullah's view was extreme even for the royal family. He had come to believe that Maliki was a pawn of the Iranians, and thus a man to be shunned. Their one and only face-to-face meeting in 2006, shortly after Maliki was elected and on his first foreign visit as prime minister, cemented Abdullah's enmity for the Iraqi, whom he accused of failing to live up to promises made in the meeting.

Another factor that was crucial in setting the king's distaste for the new Iraqi government involves the United States. The Saudis had opposed the invasion of Iraq in 2003 behind the scenes, warning that ousting Saddam would hand Iran control of Iraq on a "golden platter," a phrase they never tired of using. Then Saudi ambassador to the United Kingdom, Prince Turki al-Faisal used the same phrase with me in 2002. Abdullah and Faisal already distrusted President George W. Bush for doing too little to attend to Palestinian concerns in the Second Intifada, which the Saudis blamed on Israel and on Bush's tilt toward Israel. The distrust and distaste for the American administration was a backdrop to the Saudi shunning of Maliki and his government.

As this book brilliantly sets out, Maliki was in fact an Iraqi nationalist who did not want to do the bidding of any foreign state, but he needed outside support to face the many domestic enemies of the new Iraqi state, especially Al-Qaʿida in Iraq, which morphed into the Islamic State of Iraq. The Arab world's richest nation, Saudi Arabia, had the potential to offer that help by opening an embassy, dispersing assistance, and providing diplomatic support.

Instead, Abdullah refused to embrace the Maliki government, kept out of Baghdad, and in effect helped hand Iraq to Iran on another "golden platter." Baghdad had no option but to lean toward Tehran with Riyadh refusing to play ball. Thus, Abdullah's policy was self-fulfilling. Ignored by this prominent leader in the region, Maliki and his regime moved into Iran's orbit. Other Arab leaders, most notably King Abdullah II of Jordan, tried to fill the gap but lacked the resources for the job.

Barack Obama had won the nomination for the presidency as an opponent of Bush's war and, upon election, he was determined to get American troops home. He put Vice President Joseph Biden in charge of the disengagement, and Biden made twenty-four trips to Iraq as he managed the process between 2009 and 2013. The policy was the right one, in my view, but it also had the effect of moving Iraq and Maliki closer to Iran.

By the Arab Spring in 2011, Iraq was very much in the orbit of Iran, part of what the Jordanian King Abdullah II had called a "Shi'a crescent" that ran from Beirut through Damascus and Baghdad to Tehran. Through the unthinking help of its bitterest enemies, the United States and Saudi Arabia, Iran had emerged as a major regional power after years of isolation. The major unrest in Bahrain in 2011, a majority Shi'a state with a Sunni monarchy, only reinforced Saudi concerns about both Tehran and Baghdad, which the Saudis believed were fueling the demonstrations on the island, which is linked to the kingdom by a causeway. The Shi'a politicians in Maliki's government very much sympathized with the Shi'a in Bahrain. The Saudis, however, were deeply concerned when Obama pressed the Sunni monarch for wide-ranging reforms, and their response was to send troops across the causeway to back up the monarchy.

This book explains why Saudi Arabia pursued such a foolish and ultimately self-damaging policy toward Iraq, and the author is well placed to tell the story. After a career as an intelligence officer in the United States Navy, including service in the Fifth Fleet in Bahrain, she added a master's degree from the John's Hopkins School of Advanced International Studies and a PhD from King's College London to her undergraduate studies at Yale University. Her government service during the Iraq War gives her an insider view of American national security decision-making in the Middle East, while her academic accomplishments underscore her deep knowledge of the region and its leaders.

This book is an important and timely addition to our understanding of Saudi decision-making and the complex interactions between the three big players in the Persian Gulf. The issues that Dr. Harvey analyzes are still critically important today. The United States has drawn down its military presence in the Gulf, but it still has a force there numbering in the tens of thousands. There is no reason to believe that will end any time in the foreseeable future. Americans and their allies will need to understand better the complexities of Gulf politics, and the views and prejudices of its leaders for years to come. Dr. Harvey has provided us with a unique and insightful account of how a poor decision by President Bush and British Prime Minister Tony Blair was made much worse by King Abdullah's equally poor decision to shun Iraq.

Washington, D.C.
October 2020

LIST OF ABBREVIATIONS

AMS   Association of Muslim Scholars
CERP   Commander's Emergency Response Program
CIA   Central Intelligence Agency
CPA   Coalition Provisional Authority
EFP   explosively formed penetrator
FBI   Federal Bureau of Investigation
FBIS   Foreign Broadcast Information Service
GCC   Gulf Cooperation Council
ICG   International Crisis Group
IIP   Iraqi Islamic Party
INA   Iraqi National Alliance
ISCI   Islamic Supreme Council of Iraq
ISIS   Islamic State of Iraq and Syria
KDP   Kurdistan Democratic Party
KRG   Kurdistan Regional Government
OIC   Organization of the Islamic Conference
OPEC   Organization of the Petroleum Exporting Countries
PMF   Popular Mobilization Forces
PUK   Patriotic Union of Kurdistan
SCIRI   Supreme Council for the Islamic Revolution in Iraq
UAE   United Arab Emirates

LIST OF ABBREVIATIONS

UIA   United Iraqi Alliance
WMD weapons of mass destruction

GLOSSARY

Arba'in	a Shi'a holiday that falls forty days after Ashura and features a pilgrimage to Karbala
Ashura	a Shi'a holiday commemorating the death of the Prophet's grandson, Imam Hussein, in 680 CE in Karbala
ayatollah	honorific title for senior Twelver Shi'a clerics
Hajj	annual Islamic pilgrimage to Mecca
hawza	short for *al-hawza al-ilmiyya*, literally the territory of scholarship, meaning the Shi'a religious establishment
jihad	holy war
marji' (pl. *maraji'*)	a cleric who has attained the highest authority in the Twelver Shi'a religious hierarchy. The full title is *marji' al-taqlid* (literally, source of emulation)
Shi'a (sing. Shi'i)	short for *shi'at Ali*, literally partisans of Ali, who believe that the Prophet designated his cousin, Ali bin Abi Talib, as his successor

GLOSSARY

shuʿubi   derived from the Arabic word for "peoples"; in the Abbasid period, the *shuʿubiyya* movement consisted of the non-Arab communities that sought equality with the dominant Arabs; in the twentieth century, a derogatory term for the Shiʿa that implied that they were loyal to Iran

Sunni   literally "orthodox," Sunni Muslims believe that the Prophet did not designate a successor and consider Abu Bakr the first caliph

thalweg   deepest channel of a river; for countries with a riverine border, the *thalweg* is often recognized as the international border

ulama   scholars of Islamic law, whether Sunni or Shiʿa

wilayat al-faqih doctrine of the guardianship of the Islamic jurist as devised by Ayatollah Ruhollah Khomeini, also known in Farsi as *velayat e-faqih*

NOTE ON TRANSLITERATION

This book employs the transliteration system put forth by the *International Journal of Middle East Studies*, with a few exceptions. I have omitted the letter *ayn* at the beginning of words, as well as *hamza* at the end of words. Place names appear in accordance with their common spelling in English. In addition, for those people whose names have a common spelling in English, that common spelling has generally been used.

INTRODUCTION

The U.S. invasion of Iraq in 2003 led to the wholesale reconstruction of Iraq's political order. In the years following the invasion, what had been a power structure dominated by members of the country's Sunni Arab minority was replaced with one led by Shiʿa Islamists. Yet despite a widespread perception that Iraq's new Shiʿa-led government was automatically aligned with its Shiʿa neighbor, Iran, the new Iraqi government strove to reintegrate itself into the Arab fold. To do so, it prioritized engagement with Saudi Arabia, considered by many to be the most influential Arab state. Nevertheless, Saudi Arabia rejected the Iraqis' outreach. In doing so, Saudi Arabia paradoxically helped push Iraq into the arms of its regional rival, Iran.

Efforts taken, especially in 2007 and 2008, by a range of Iraqi leaders to establish a positive relationship with Saudi Arabia are revealed in an examination of news reporting. For instance, Iraq's Kurdish foreign minister, Hoshyar Zebari, told the Saudi-owned pan-Arab newspaper *al-Sharq al-Awsat* in September 2007, "We are interested in relations with Saudi Arabia because of its Arab, Islamic, and international standing, and it is important for us to have continuous contact."[1] The Iraqis particularly wanted the Saudis to send an ambassador to Baghdad, and thus Iraq's Shiʿa national security adviser, Mowaffaq al-Rubaie, told *al-Sharq al-Awsat* at this time that the Iraqi government would take "exceptional" measures to provide security to a Saudi embassy in Baghdad, stressing that a Saudi presence was "important to fill the Arab vacuum in Iraq."[2] For his part, Ammar al-Hakim, a leading member of the Islamic Supreme Council of Iraq, a Shi'a Islamist party originally established in 1982 as Iran's principal Iraqi client, told *al-Sharq al-Awsat* in May 2007, "The Shi'a of Iraq are Arabs, and their first and last loyalty is to Iraq and their Arab identity." He added, "We seek to establish good and developed relations with all our Arab brothers," and noted that his group had "good relations" with Jordan and the Gulf states and was "working to develop" ties to Saudi Arabia.[3]

The Saudi leadership did not, however, open an embassy in Baghdad at this time, or make any other public gesture to reciprocate the Iraqis' outreach. An examination of U.S. diplomatic cables from this period, which have been released by WikiLeaks, reveals that Iraq's top leaders from its three principal ethnosectarian communities—the Shi'a, the Sunni Arabs, and the Kurds—were voicing concern about the Saudis' standoffish attitude and communicating their desire for a better relationship. This was the perspective of Iraq's Shi'a prime minister, Nuri al-Maliki, who had himself traveled to the kingdom on his first trip abroad as premier in July 2006, and indeed, Jalal Talabani, Iraq's Kurdish president, intervened personally with King Abdullah of Saudi Arabia, whom he encouraged to engage with the new Iraq.[4] For his part, Sunni Arab Vice President Tariq al-Hashimi asked U.S. officials for help to alter the Saudi leadership's standoffish approach to Iraq, and was reported to be "[v]isibly disappointed" when he learned that an American effort to this end had failed.[5]

This situation—in which a range of Iraqi leaders attempted to engage with Saudi Arabia but saw their efforts rebuffed by the

Saudi leadership—generates the primary question addressed by this book: Why did Saudi Arabia decide not to engage with the new, Shi'a-led Iraq? Furthermore, given that prior to taking a decision, foreign policy decision-makers must define the situation confronting them, how did the Saudi leadership define the situation in Iraq following the U.S.-led invasion of 2003? In other words, what was their perception of the situation in Iraq, especially with regard to the Shi'a ascendance in the new Iraqi state? What were the ideas and beliefs, particularly about Iran and the Shi'a, that existed within the Saudi leadership prior to the invasion, and how did these beliefs inform their perception? Moreover, which actor, or constellation of actors, within the Saudi leadership took the decision not to engage, and what does this tell us about the process by which foreign policy decisions are made in the Saudi context?

Beyond the Saudis, this book also explores the perspectives of leaders in Iraq and other Arab countries, as well as the United States. In particular, how did the Maliki government respond to the Saudis' rejection of their outreach? How did Maliki's interaction with the Saudi leadership shape his own behavior, not only toward Saudi Arabia, but also toward Iran? Did the United States, Saudi Arabia's longstanding ally and the midwife of the new order in Iraq, try to broker a reconciliation between the two countries? And what were the attitudes of other Arab leaders toward the new Iraq? Were their perceptions consistent with or divergent from those within the Saudi leadership?

To answer these questions, this book offers a historical account beginning in the last decades of the twentieth century, informed by the constructivist and political psychology approaches to International Relations. It draws upon news reporting, U.S. and Saudi documents made available by WikiLeaks, and the accounts of some sixty-five people—Saudis, Iraqis, and Americans—involved in the events under investigation. It examines the beliefs that were established within the Saudi leadership about the Islamic Republic of Iran during the traumatic decade of the 1980s—a time when revolutionary Iran and Baʿthist Iraq were locked in an eight-year war—and explores how these beliefs thereafter shaped the Saudis' perceptions of regional events, foremost Iraq's post-2003 Shiʿa ascendance. The book also examines the Saudi leadership's image of Prime Minister Maliki, whom King Abdullah in particular considered to be an untrustworthy Iranian agent, even though, as will be shown, Maliki had never been particularly close to the Iranian regime and indeed sought to pursue an independent course from it through 2009. Moreover, the book explores the Iraqi government's failed attempts to engage with the Saudi leadership in 2007 and 2008, its more successful efforts to engage with other Arab states in the same period, and Maliki's turn to Iran in the aftermath of Iraq's 2010 parliamentary elections. The final chapter examines the Maliki government's gravitation toward an Iranian regional axis in the years after the Arab Spring.

The book argues that King Abdullah, operating as the ultimate foreign policy decision-maker in the Saudi system, refused to engage with the Maliki government because of his mistaken belief that the Iraqi prime minister was an Iranian agent and therefore an enemy to Saudi Arabia. In adhering to this belief, King Abdullah discounted the considerable evidence that existed to disprove it. Furthermore, and as the title of this book suggests, in so persistently refusing to engage with Maliki and his government, King Abdullah ended up creating a self-fulfilling prophecy. On a basic level, the Saudi decision to shun the Maliki government constrained the Iraqis' freedom of maneuver. The Maliki government wanted positive relations with both Iran and its Arab neighbors, but the Saudis' isolation of Iraq hindered its access to the Arab world, which made it reliant on Iran. In addition, the Iraqis began to feel threatened. Maliki perceived in the

Saudis' hostile attitude an intention to undermine Iraq's new Shi'a-led order, as well as his own premiership. Feeling thus threatened by the Saudis, he ended up abandoning his earlier, more independent approach to Iran and began to align with it. Meanwhile, other Arab leaders, who initially shared the Saudis' belief that the Shi'a of Iraq were loyal to Iran, appeared more inclined than King Abdullah in this period to revise and update their beliefs—in short, to change their mind—about the Iraqi Shi'a. That Abdullah's image of the new Iraq, and of its prime minister, was so rigid, paradoxically ended up compelling Maliki to behave in ways that confirmed Abdullah's image of him. Indeed, the principal argument of this book is that the Maliki government aligned with Iran in the years after the Arab Spring not out of some affinity its leaders professed for Iran, but because they felt threatened by Saudi Arabia.

Why should readers in the West, particularly the United States, care about the interaction that took place between two Arab countries in the years after 2003? First of all, this book reveals new information that is critical to understanding what went wrong in Iraq following the U.S.-led invasion. Despite the voluminous literature on the Iraq War, no previous book substantially addresses the Saudis' hostility to the new Iraq. In filling this gap, the book also explores a significant contradiction in the U.S. decision to undertake regime change in Iraq, a contradiction that has not hitherto been brought to light. George W. Bush and his principal advisers sought to replace Saddam Hussein's regime with a democracy, which naturally allowed the country's Shi'a majority to rise to power. Their objective was antithetical to Saudi interests, yet the success of their project was contingent on Saudi acquiescence: absent the Saudis' acceptance of the new Iraq, Iraq would be isolated and weak in the Arab world. As the following chapters reveal, the Bush administration expended considerable effort to compel King Abdullah to engage with

Iraq's new government. Their efforts, however, were unsuccessful. No amount of U.S. pressure could compel Abdullah to embrace something he regarded as threatening. In short, Bush and his advisers midwifed a new Iraqi order to which their closest Arab ally was antagonistic, a situation that hindered the American project to stabilize Iraq for years to come. In telling this story, this book explores one of the great unintended consequences of Bush's decision to invade Iraq.

On a broader and more theoretical level, this book also constitutes a case study that demonstrates how decisions taken on the basis of misperception may result in self-fulfilling prophecies. At the heart of this book lies a story about how a foreign policy decision-maker, in this case King Abdullah of Saudi Arabia, helped to create a very real conflict by acting on his mistaken belief that a foreign counterpart was an enemy. A theoretical basis for this situation is elaborated later in this introduction. Suffice it to say here that in holding a rigid image of his counterpart—one that was unresponsive to new or contradictory information—Abdullah ended up taking a decision that was self-defeating. The story that follows may therefore be considered a cautionary tale for today's policy-makers. To formulate sound policy, we must attempt to see the world as it is, not as we expect it to be, or as we might want it to be. We must strive to update our beliefs when new information becomes available. To do otherwise is potentially to find ourselves in calamities of our own making.

Iran, Iraq, and Saudi Arabia: Diverse Countries in a Diverse Region

Iran, Iraq, and Saudi Arabia, the three countries that, along with the United States, dominate the story that follows, are the most populous of the Persian Gulf region. Nevertheless, it is Iran that is by far the most populous. In 1971, where the narrative of this study begins, the population of Iran stood at 29 million people, in comparison to Iraq and Saudi Arabia, whose populations were then 10 million and 6 million, respectively. As of 2019, the Iranian, Iraqi, and Saudi populations amounted to 83 million, 39 million, and 34 million, respectively.[6] Iran's large demographic size has traditionally stoked Saudi anxiety toward its neighbor. From a Saudi point of view, as articulated by a Saudi foreign policy adviser to the royal family in an interview, Iran sees itself as the "biggest" Gulf state and therefore believes that it should be "in charge" of the region.[7]

The Persian Gulf is also a region of tremendous ethnic and religious diversity. While Iran is predominantly Persian and overwhelmingly Shi'a, subscribing to the Twelver school of Shi'a Islam, Saudi Arabia is overwhelmingly Arab and Sunni. Since the mid-eighteenth century, the House of Saud, known in Arabic as the Al Saud, has been associated with the Wahhabi school of Sunni Islam, and today Wahhabi Islam constitutes the Saudi state religion. An austere version of the faith, Wahhabi Islam is also stridently anti-Shi'a. In fact, as Toby Matthiesen contends, "The Wahhabi clergy has from the mid-eighteenth century onwards seen Shia Islam as one of its main, if not *the* main, enemy"[8] [italics in original]. Nevertheless, a sizeable Shi'a minority is found in Saudi Arabia, at perhaps 10 to 15 percent of the population. In the oil-rich Eastern Province, which abuts the Persian Gulf and is where most Saudi Shi'a reside, the Shi'a subscribe to the Twelver School; in addition, a smaller community of Isma'ilis—also known as Sevener Shi'a—is located in Saudi Arabia's Najran region on the Yemeni border. Given Wahhabi antagonism toward Shi'a Islam, the Saudi Shi'a are treated as second-class citizens inside the kingdom.[9]

Meanwhile, Iraq is the most diverse country in this already diverse region. Since the Sunni–Shi'a split in the seventh century, the area has been home to the most important shrines of the Shi'a faith. Today, some of the highest-ranking clergy of the Twelver Shi'a school are found in the Iraqi shrine cities of Najaf, Karbala, Samarra, and Kazimain, and Najaf rivals the Iranian holy city of Qom as a center of religious learning. From the eighteenth to early twentieth centuries, the Shi'a clergy located in the Iraqi shrine cities converted the local Arab tribesmen, who were nominally Sunnis, to Twelver Shi'ism.[10] Today, as a result, the Shi'a constitute a majority of the Iraqi people, at about 60 percent of the population, concentrated in Baghdad and the south of the country. However, in the twentieth century, members of the country's Sunni Arab minority, amounting to some 15 to 20 percent of the population, dominated successive Iraqi regimes. Following a 1968 coup d'état, the Arab nationalist Ba'th Party came to power. The 1968 coup elevated a faction within the Ba'th composed of clansmen from the town of Tikrit in the predominantly Sunni Arab province of Salahuddin. In the 1970s, Saddam Hussein became the dominant figure within the Ba'thist regime, and he would remain as such until his overthrow in 2003. Beyond Iraq's Shi'a and Sunni Arab communities, the Kurds, who are mostly Sunnis, constitute the country's third principal ethno-sectarian group. They also amount to about 15 to 20 percent of the population and are concentrated in the mountainous north of the country. In addition, Iraq has smaller ethnic and religious minorities, at about five percent of the population, composed of Turkmen, Persians, Christians, Yazidis, and Sabaeans, among others. Until the early 1950s, a significant Jewish population was also found in Iraq.[11]

A Word about Sunni–Shi'a Relations

Beyond the ethno-sectarian demographics of the Gulf region outlined above, a look at the demographic balance between

INTRODUCTION

Sunnis and Shiʿa across the Muslim world, along with the power relations entailed by this balance, will help put the story that follows into greater context. The Sunni–Shiʿa split resulted from disagreement within the early Muslim community over who was the rightful successor to the Prophet Muhammad; a member of his companions, as Sunnis believe, or of his family, as put forth by Shiʿa. This early disagreement ultimately generated important doctrinal differences between the two groups, which are more or less pronounced depending on the variants of Sunni and Shiʿa Islam in question. However, the deep demographic disparity between the two sects is vastly more important to understanding the relations between them than these doctrinal differences. In sum, Sunnis, who have occupied the dominant political position in most Muslim lands since the Prophet's death 1400 years ago, make up about 85 percent of Muslims worldwide; the Shiʿa make up almost all of the remainder, with most Shiʿa subscribing to the Twelver school.[12] Also notable is the concentration of Shiʿa Islam in the Persian Gulf region. As we have seen above, Iran is overwhelmingly Shiʿa, at about 90 percent of the population. Moreover, a Shiʿa majority exists not only in Iraq, but also in the Arab Gulf state of Bahrain. A little further away, the Shiʿa form a plurality of the population of Lebanon.[13] Nevertheless, the Shiʿa account for a small minority across the Arab world. According to one estimate, of the total population of the twenty-two countries that make up the Arab League, no more than about 11 percent are Shiʿa.[14]

Two important considerations flow from these demographic imbalances. First, Sunnis possess a profound sense of occupying the majority position within global Islam. Even if forming a minority in a specific country context, they remain, as Fanar Haddad notes, "cognizant of the normative role that conceptions of Sunnism play in how Muslims and Islam are imagined."[15] In short, Sunnis form the mainstream in a global Islamic context, and view themselves as the mainstream. By contrast, the Shi'a have typically been seen by the dominant Sunnis as something of a deviant outgroup, and indeed Shi'a Muslims themselves, even if they form the majority on a local level, retain deep feelings of marginalization from the Sunni mainstream.[16] This majority–minority dynamic has played out in a theological context, where leading Sunni religious institutions have frequently balked at recognizing Shi'ism as a legitimate school of Islam.[17] Wahhabis, as well as some Sunnis with Salafi leanings, go so far as to call the Shi'a non-Muslims. Furthermore, in the Arab world, Shi'a feelings of marginalization have been compounded by the fact that even in places where they have formed a majority, such as Bahrain and pre-2003 Iraq, Sunni Arabs have typically held the reins of state power. In this sense, as Haddad observes, the Shi'a have often been "artificially minoritiz[ed]": despite their superior demographic weight in places like Bahrain and pre-2003 Iraq, they have occupied inferior positions in state power hierarchies.[18] In fact, as we shall see, many Sunni Arabs in pre-2003 Iraq did not actually acknowledge that the Shi'a formed a majority of their country. A frequent but erroneous Sunni Arab refrain held that between Iraq's Sunni Arabs and Sunni Kurds, a Sunni majority existed in Iraq, a belief to which some Sunni Arabs continue to subscribe.[19]

A second consideration flowing from the demographic imbalances between Sunnis and Shi'a is that many Sunnis associate Shi'ism with Iran. In fact, Laurence Louër contends that "for many Sunnis, every Shi'a is necessarily Iranian or at least an agent in the service of Iran's expansionist intrigues."[20] This view, common among Sunnis, that imputes Iranian loyalty to non-Iranian Shi'a can be traced back to the emergence of the Safavid Empire in the early sixteenth century and its subsequent rivalry with the Ottoman Turks. In 1501, the Shi'a Safavids established a new political dynasty in Iran, with Shi'a Islam as the official religion to which the Iranian population was gradually converted. Moreover, at the same time as the Safavids were establishing themselves in Iran, the Ottomans were consolidating their territorial control over most Arab lands. In a contest for regional supremacy lasting a century and a half, the Shi'a Safavids and Sunni Ottomans fought a series of wars, articulated as a religious struggle between Sunnis and Shi'a. In this context of Sunni–Shi'a conflict, the loyalty of Shi'a communities under Ottoman control became suspect.[21] This became a lasting legacy, with many Arab Sunnis continuing to regard their Arab Shi'a counterparts as potential fifth columnists for Iran. Thus, the Arab Shi'a have often been seen by Arab Sunnis as an "other" in two respects: first, in religious terms, as belonging to a deviant sect, and second, in ethnic terms, as professing a supposed historical allegiance to Iran. As we shall see, under Saddam Hussein, Ba'thist propaganda frequently played upon the latter theme, depicting the Iraqi Shi'a as Iranian loyalists, in order to cast aspersions on Iraq's majority community.

While the story that follows takes place during a period of deep discord between Sunnis and Shi'a, it is important to keep in mind that they have not been locked in a perpetual struggle, nor do they bear immutable antagonisms toward each other, as contemporary commentators frequently contend. Indeed, more often than not their relations have been characterized by banal coexistence.[22] Rather, conflict occurs during periods of crisis, especially when power relations are disrupted. In the context of this book, the crisis occurred with the collapse of the Iraqi state following the U.S. invasion of Iraq.[23] Amid the deep uncertainty and mounting violence in Iraq after the invasion, the Shi'a community set out to take hold of the levers of power in the new state to reverse their historic marginalization; this necessarily relegated the historically dominant Sunni Arabs to a peculiar minority position, and ultimately led to a sectarian civil war. In this context, sectarian identities, which are typically more muted during periods of peaceful coexistence, became highly inflamed, both in Iraq and the wider region.[24] Moreover, while the post-2003 cycles of conflict between Iraqi Sunnis and Shi'a were frequently articulated in religious terms—as a religious struggle between separate orthodoxies—it is important to keep in mind that what they were really fighting over was not theology, but the political direction of the new Iraqi state.[25]

Misperception, Enemy Images, and Self-Fulfilling Prophecies

This book is not, however, about Sunni–Shi'a relations as such; it is about a foreign policy decision taken by Saudi King Abdullah, a Sunni, not to engage with Iraqi Prime Minister Nuri al-Maliki, a Shi'a. The book argues that the belief forming the basis for Abdullah's decision—that Maliki was beholden to Iran, in keeping with the stereotype elaborated above—was erroneous. Indeed, Maliki took significant actions during the period of his first government that demonstrated an intention to pursue an independent course from Iran, and ample evidence exists that he had been skeptical toward the Islamic Republic since the 1980s. Nevertheless, King Abdullah remained convinced that Maliki was an Iranian loyalist. That Abdullah would adhere to an incorrect belief despite plenty of contradictory evidence highlights the subjective nature of perception. How we perceive our world is shaped—even distorted—by the cognitive barriers we naturally possess as human beings. The world we inhabit is complex and ambiguous, and we are limited in our ability to process the massive amount of incoming information we are constantly receiving about it. In order to make sense of our world, our brains must sort this information, creating in all of us cognitive, or unmotivated, biases. Such biases compel us to pay selective attention to stimuli. In particular, our brains detect stimuli that conform to our preexisting beliefs, while overlooking, distorting, or even doubting the stimuli that are discrepant. We thus have a tendency to see what we *expect* to see based on what we have previously learned. Beyond our cognitive limitations, moreover, we also display motivated biases, rooted in our interests and emotional needs, particularly the basic need to maintain self-esteem. Such biases lead us to see what we *want* to see.[26] All human beings display both types of biases, and our perception is shaped by them.

However, this book is not simply about perception, but about decision-making: King Abdullah's erroneous belief that Maliki was beholden to Iran informed his decision not to engage with Maliki's government. If the everyday situations humans find themselves in are naturally ambiguous, the foreign policy situations to which political leaders must respond are exceedingly ambiguous. Indeed, foreign policy decision-makers are charged with inferring the intentions of their counterparts in foreign countries, even though inferring others' intentions is, as Robert Jervis explains, "notoriously difficult."[27] As a result, it is not uncommon for foreign policy decision-makers to misperceive the situations they face, with their misperception leading them to take what appears to an outside observer—such as a scholar—as an inappropriate decision.[28] British Prime Minister Neville Chamberlain, who believed he could make peace with Adolf Hitler on the eve of World War Two, is a noteworthy example of a foreign policy decision-maker who took what has been judged, at least in retrospect, a terribly inappropriate decision. Yet according to Keren Yarhi-Milo, Chamberlain fell into a pattern typical of decision-makers: he paid selective attention to indicators of his adversary's intentions, focusing on the indicators that conformed to his preexisting beliefs about the adversary. Yarhi-Milo argues that given this general tendency to pay selective attention, decision-makers often overlook or even discount the validity of significant indicators that contradict their beliefs.[29] Thus, as she demonstrates, British officials like Chamberlain, who initially assessed Nazi Germany's intentions as relatively benign, continually dismissed significant indicators of its expansionist intentions over the course of the 1930s.[30]

Foreign policy decision-makers may also persist in perceiving another country as hostile, even when credible indicators exist to the contrary. Just as Chamberlain overlooked strong indicators of Hitler's aggressiveness, numerous U.S. officials of the Cold War era, adhering to the belief that Soviet intentions were hostile, doubted credible conciliatory gestures made by their Soviet counterparts. In his 1962 study of John Foster Dulles, Ole Holsti demonstrated that Dwight D. Eisenhower's secretary of state repeatedly dismissed conciliatory Soviet gestures as either insincere or temporary in nature; instead of using such gestures to inform his image of the Soviets, Dulles preserved his image of them by discounting their conciliatory signals.[31] Similarly, Ronald Reagan's secretary of defense, Caspar Weinberger, continually dismissed credible friendly gestures made by Soviet leaders like Mikhail Gorbachev at the end of the Cold War. In Weinberger's view, Gorbachev's policies amounted to "nothing more than a well-crafted public relations campaign," and he remained "unequivocal" in expressing his belief to his Reagan administration colleagues that Soviet intentions continued to be expansionist.[32] Nor does it seem that Weinberger ever changed his view of Gorbachev, despite the ending of the Cold War. In a 2002 interview, the former secretary of defense stated to a historian: "Gorbachev to this day is a committed Communist and still believes that what is necessary is to strengthen communism." By his own admission, Weinberger never developed trust in this Soviet leader.[33]

Indeed, Dulles and Weinberger fit a pattern of perceiving their adversary—in their case the Soviet Union—through the lens of an enemy image. The basic premise of such an image is that the people who hold it, who attribute malign intent to the target country, judge all its actions to be indicators proving its malign intent. The data are thus assessed to prove the theory, namely that the target country is hostile.[34] In addition, the target country may be considered inherently evil and aggressive, and it may also be seen as monolithic, highly rational, and deliberate.[35] The example of Weinberger above is particularly illuminating of the enemy image concept because while he persisted in seeing the Soviet Union as hostile, many of his colleagues in the Reagan administration did not. Yarhi-Milo demonstrates how, in contrast to Weinberger, Reagan and his secretary of state, George Schultz, gradually developed positive impressions of their Soviet counterparts through personal interactions with them, which ultimately led them to develop a more benign view of Soviet intentions.[36] In this way, Reagan and Schultz can be said to have updated their beliefs about the Soviet Union based on new information. While people are in general slow to revise their beliefs, humans are nevertheless capable of belief-updating: we are not the prisoners of our beliefs, even if they are naturally resistant to change when new information arises. Nevertheless, some people are more resistant to belief-updating than others—and some, like Weinberger, essentially never update their beliefs.[37] This is essentially the core of an enemy image: the failure to update a belief in the face of information that contradicts it.

The enemy image concept helps one to understand the Bush administration's perplexing decision to invade Iraq in 2003. As Charles A. Duelfer and Stephen Benedict Dyson contend, an enemy image of Saddam Hussein gained traction in the United States as a result of the 1990–1991 Gulf War.[38] This enemy image was particularly strong within Washington policy-making circles; one of the most vivid examples of an American policy-maker who believed Saddam Hussein possessed malign intent toward the U.S. was Paul Wolfowitz, under-secretary of defense at the time of the Gulf War who went on to serve as deputy defense secretary in George W. Bush's first administration. Not only did Wolfowitz hypothesize immediately after the Al-Qa'ida attacks of 11 September 2001 that Saddam Hussein might have been linked to them, even though there was no evidence to suggest this was the case, but Wolfowitz was also convinced that Saddam had been connected to an earlier attack inside the United States, the 1993 truck bombing of the World Trade Center. Indeed, a theory took hold in 1990s Washington that Saddam, out of revenge for the Gulf War, had supported the 1993 attack, for which six New Jersey-based Islamist extremists were later convicted. Wolfowitz was one of the strongest proponents of this theory, even though it had actually been debunked by the FBI and CIA.[39]

Following 9/11, senior Bush administration officials became fixated on the prospect that terrorist organizations might obtain weapons of mass destruction (WMD), and Saddam Hussein, who was then thought to possess WMD, was seen as the most likely culprit connecting terrorists to these weapons. Under severe U.S. pressure, Saddam allowed UN weapons inspectors into Iraq in late 2002, but his regime failed to comply fully with the UN process. According to Duelfer and Dyson, the Bush administration, consistent with how information is processed through the lens of an enemy image, interpreted the Iraqi regime's evasive actions during this period as clear-cut evidence that it was hiding its WMD capabilities.[40] But not only was the Bush administration wrong regarding whether Iraq possessed WMD—as was revealed when no such weapons were found in Iraq after the invasion—but it was also wrong about whether Saddam Hussein bore malign intent toward the United States in the first place. As Duelfer and Dyson show, the Iraqi dictator actually saw the U.S. as something of a natural ally, since he and the Americans had a mutual adversary, namely Iran.[41]

Meanwhile, as will be explored in the following chapters, the Saudis have held an enemy image of Iran since the outset of the Iran–Iraq War in the early 1980s. During that bitter conflict, the Saudi leadership could reasonably judge that Iranian leaders possessed malign intent; whether or not the Iranians in fact possessed such intent, their statements and actions provided a reasonable basis whereby the Saudis could form this perception. By contrast, in the 1990s and 2000s, the Saudis continued to perceive Iran as an enemy, even though they had a less reasonable basis to do so. In this later period, Iranian intentions were more ambiguous than they had been in the 1980s, although the Saudis, for their part, continued to interpret all Iranian actions as evidence of acute Iranian hostility. In this way, the Saudis used all indicators to bolster the image they had already formed of Iran, not to add nuance to it, consistent with how people who hold enemy images process information. It should be emphasized at this point that the purpose of this book is not to assess the validity of the Saudis' enemy image of Iran—the Saudis were not necessarily wrong about Iran's supposedly hostile intentions, although their understanding of Iranian intentions tended to be simplistic and alarmist. Rather, their enemy image of Iran powerfully shaped—to the point of distorting—their perception of Iraq's Shiʿa ascendance.

Being profoundly theory-driven, enemy images tend to be self-perpetuating; however, dangerously, they may become self-fulfilling as well. The concept of the self-fulfilling prophecy originated with sociologist Robert Merton, who defined it as "a *false* definition of the situation evoking a new behavior which makes the originally false conception come *true*" [italics in the original].[42] Constructivist scholar Alexander Wendt explores how enmity can become a self-fulfilling prophecy within the international system. According to Wendt, when one state casts another in the role of an enemy, the second is forced to "mirror back" this representation because it feels threatened by the first, creating conflict in their relationship—even if the two states were not in fact threats to each other at the start of their interaction, a "logic of enmity" may set in between them that compels them to behave in ways that are actually threatening.[43] Or, as Holsti argues in his Cold War study of Dulles: "Enemies are those who are defined as such, and if one acts upon that interpretation, it is more than likely that the original definition will be confirmed."[44]

In other words, when decision-makers believe that another state is an enemy and treat it accordingly, even if the other state has benign intentions, these decision-makers may end up producing a very real conflict in which the other state actually becomes hostile. This logic will be used to assess the conflictual relationship that developed between Saudi Arabia and the Maliki government. Saudi decision-makers, principally King Abdullah, refused to engage with Prime Minister Maliki and thus cast him in the role of an enemy. Eventually, the Iraqi prime minister, feeling threatened by Saudi Arabia due to Abdullah's isolation of him, began to mirror back this representation to the Saudis. Indeed, the following chapters will demonstrate that Maliki, who had sought to establish a positive relationship with Saudi Arabia at the outset of his premiership, became antagonistic toward it after the Saudis repeatedly rejected his outreach.

Ultimately, this book argues that the decision made by the Saudi leadership not to engage with the Maliki government not only produced a conflictual relationship between Saudi Arabia and Iraq, but, most significantly, made it more likely that Maliki would align with Iran. The Saudis' decision not to engage derived from their inaccurate and stereotypic image of Maliki as an Iranian client, and in fact a core argument in social psychology is that inaccurate social stereotypes may become self-fulfilling prophecies through the interaction of perceivers and targets. Indeed, experiments in social psychology have demonstrated that perceivers, treating targets in line with an inaccurate stereotype of the targets' social group, often elicit a change in targets' behavior consistent with the stereotype.[45] While these experiments have typically focused on the interactions of perceivers and targets on an individual level—reflecting, for instance, the interaction between King Abdullah and Prime Minister Maliki—Merton, in his formulation of the self-fulfilling prophecy concept, provides an example of an inaccurate social stereotype coming to fruition on a larger scale. In the United States in the early twentieth century, he explains, African Americans were typically excluded from joining labor unions because white union members perceived them as strikebreakers. However, Merton observed that African Americans, having few job opportunities, often took any work they could: rather than being strikebreakers because they wanted to be, they broke strikes because their exclusion from labor unions forced them to be. White Americans held a stereotypic image of their African American counterparts, but African Americans only conformed to this image because they were treated as such. Merton further points out that once African Americans were permitted to join unions, they stopped breaking strikes in large numbers.[46]

This logic will be employed to argue that the Saudi leadership, by treating Maliki in line with the stereotypic image of the Arab Shiʿa as loyal to Iran, elicited a change of behavior on the part of Maliki consistent with the stereotype. Maliki did indeed pursue a closer relationship with Iran starting in 2010, which fulfilled the Saudis' image of him as an Iranian client. Nevertheless, this change in Maliki's behavior took place because of the isolation he faced from the Saudis. Maliki began his premiership desirous of a positive relationship with Saudi Arabia and intent to pursue an independent course from Iran. That he ended up hostile to Saudi Arabia and in alignment with Iran was the result of a self-fulfilling prophecy created by the Saudis.

A SELF-FULFILLING PROPHECY

Threat Perception vs. Enemy Image

The analysis above elaborated the concept of the enemy image; before proceeding, it may be useful to clarify how this concept differs from threat perception. Stephen Walt's classic realist text, *The Origin of Alliances*, is particularly useful for understanding threat perception. The realist school of International Relations has traditionally argued that states align to balance more powerful states, with power defined in terms of material variables like military capability. Walt, by contrast, argues that a balance-of-threat model proves more empirically accurate than a balance-of-power one in understanding how states align. According to Walt, states do not seek to balance power alone; they form alliances to balance the most threatening state in the system. Walt identifies four variables to determine the degree to which a state is considered a threat: its aggregate power, in terms of its economic, military, and demographic capabilities; its geographic proximity; its offensive power capability; and its intentions—whether benign or aggressive—as perceived by its neighbors. Walt emphasizes that states' perceptions of each other's intentions are ultimately more important than their relative power positions for understanding how threat is assessed, and therefore how regional alignments form, as "even states with rather modest capabilities may prompt others to balance if they are perceived as especially aggressive."[47]

As we have seen above, political psychologists, drawing on cognitive psychology, have elaborated on how human decision-makers form perceptions of adversaries' intentions: namely, through the lens of their own preexisting beliefs, as well as their interests and desires. However, in a constructivist response to Walt, Michael Barnett points to identity as a critical variable to understand how intentions are perceived. According to Barnett, states that consider themselves to share an identity in contradistinction to another state they all consider different, are likely to be potential alliance partners.[48] As an example, the Gulf Arab states, which share a similar history, culture, and political economy, established the Gulf Cooperation Council (GCC) in 1981. Their grouping pointedly excluded the other Arab states, which either had different systems of government or did not possess significant oil resources; the GCC states therefore saw them as "different" and as "potential threats."[49] Building on this constructivist argument, David Rousseau invokes the principle that people possess not one single identity, but multiple identities. For instance, the members of the Al Saud are simultaneously Arab, Muslim, and the leaders of an oil-exporting state; they therefore have points of commonality with fellow Arab states, fellow Muslim states, and fellow oil-exporters. According to Rousseau, people use such points of commonality to construct identities for both their own state and other states, and they perceive the other state as non-threatening to the extent that they believe a shared, overlapping identity exists.[50] Nevertheless, the key realist variable of relative power remains important in Rousseau's model. He observes that the participants in his study perceived little threat if their hypothetical country was more powerful than another hypothetical country, even if the two countries had no overlapping identity.[51]

In short, each of these schools—realism, constructivism, and political psychology—illuminates an important aspect of threat perception: one state perceives another to be threatening if it is considered to be different, if its intentions are perceived as aggressive, and if it possesses greater relative power.[52] These three variables will be employed throughout this book to assess threat perception. So, to bring us back to the main point, what is the difference between threat perception and an enemy image? According to the political psychology school, from which the concept came, an enemy image forms when a perceiver systematically discards information that might mitigate his assessment of his adversary's intentions. There might be a sound basis whereby a perceiver judges that an adversary possesses malign intent, leading him to perceive threat. An enemy image takes shape, however, when the basis for that judgment begins to appear less sound, leading to an inflated sense of threat.

How Are Foreign Policy Decisions Made in Saudi Arabia?

The findings presented in this book demonstrate that King Abdullah dominated the Saudi decision not to engage with Iraq. Indeed, Abdullah even quashed proposals initiated by other senior royals to establish a Saudi presence in Iraq. Yet this view of Abdullah as an omnipotent decision-maker within the Saudi system stands in contrast to much of the academic literature on Saudi Arabia. While some scholars of Saudi Arabia emphasize the central role of the Saudi monarch in the decision-making process, many others have argued that the senior members of the royal family have traditionally sought to take decisions by consensus.[53] A third camp, meanwhile, points out that the relations within the upper ranks of the royal family have often been competitive, leading to a fragmentary decision-making process.[54] Given this debate within the academic literature on Saudi Arabia, the present study focusing on a specific Saudi foreign policy decision—not to engage with Iraq—also seeks, more broadly, to shed light on the process by which decisions have traditionally been made in the Saudi context.

What scholars of Saudi Arabia agree on is that institutions within the Saudi state are weak—the Saudi state is, at bottom, the domain of the personalities at the upper echelons of the royal family.[55] Today, Crown Prince Muhammad bin Salman, the powerful son of King Salman, who assumed the Saudi throne upon Abdullah's death in 2015, is widely considered to be the dominant figure and principal decision-maker within the Saudi system. However, as the debate mentioned above attests, it remains unclear exactly who within the senior royal family took decisions prior to Muhammad bin Salman's ascendance. That this question remains contentious is a result of the traditionally—and very deliberately—opaque nature of Saudi foreign policy decision-making. Some forty years ago, William Quandt remarked, "Saudi foreign policy decisions are made by a small group in private and with little public discussion or explanation ... Quite simply, Saudi leaders believe it is no one's business how decisions are made."[56] Toward the end of Abdullah's reign, scholars of Saudi Arabia continued to lament the lack of transparency surrounding the decision-making process.[57]

A theoretical framework advanced by political psychologist Margaret Hermann is of considerable help in conceptualizing the process by which foreign policy decisions are made in Saudi Arabia.[58] According to Hermann, there exists within each state an "authoritative decision unit," which has the authority to take foreign policy decisions. She argues that the authoritative decision unit has three possible configurations. First, the unit may be a "predominant leader," such as a president or monarch, who has the authority to take decisions alone and stifle dissent. Drawing upon this concept, I argue that Abdullah operated as a predominant leader with regard to Saudi policy toward Iraq—the research findings indicate that he took this decision alone, while suppressing opposing views. Hermann points out that to be a predominant leader, the state's chief executive must not only be vested with the authority to control decision-making, whether by law or general custom, but must also exert this authority. With respect to Saudi decision-making today, King Salman is considered to be vested with the authority to control Saudi decision-making, but instead of exerting this authority himself, he has, for the most part, transferred it to his son Muhammad. Thus, in contrast to King Abdullah, who asserted his authority as a predominant leader, at least with regard to the decision of whether to engage with Iraq, King Salman generally has not.

The second type of authoritative decision unit Hermann identifies is that of a "single group," which is composed of members of the same government body and takes decisions collectively. However, in the absence of a predominant leader or single group, according to Hermann, the decision-making process becomes the preserve of "multiple autonomous actors" from different government bodies. In situations where decision-making is diffused across multiple actors, the process in effect becomes dependent on the ability and willingness of different actors with different political loyalties to come together to resolve foreign policy problems. Moreover, in the absence of established rules to govern a decision-making process conducted by multiple actors, the state may effectively dissolve into anarchy, with actors using decision-making to score political points against each other. Such situations are most typical of states like Saudi Arabia, where institutions are weak.[59] Hermann considers that these three types of decision-making unit—a predominant leader, a single group constituted of actors from the same government body, and a coalition of autonomous actors from different bodies—are exhaustive of the possible decision-making constellations within a state.[60]

The strength of Hermann's model, for the purposes of this book, is its correspondence to the three views of Saudi decision-making advanced by scholars of Saudi Arabia. While I argue that King Abdullah operated as a predominant leader with respect to the decision not to engage with Iraq, the research findings indicate that at different points in the period under examination—from the 1970s to 2015—all three decision-making constellations became manifest within the Saudi state. Fahd, Abdullah's predecessor, became king in 1982, and for the next thirteen years he took decisions in consultation with his full-brothers, Princes

Sultan and Nayef, then the minister of defense and aviation and the minister of interior respectively. Fahd, Sultan, and Nayef were members of the Sudairi line within the Al Saud, and during this thirteen-year period the Saudi decision-making process may be considered to have been dominated by the small group constituted of the senior Sudairi princes. The more notable finding is that during this period, Fahd marginalized actors outside the Sudairi group, principally his half-brother Abdullah, then crown prince, and Foreign Minister Prince Saud al-Faisal, the son of a half-brother.[61] With regard to Prince Saud, a Saudi royal family insider interviewed for this book recounted that Fahd mistrusted his foreign minister, who, considered to be the leading prince of his generation, displayed latent ambitions to assume the throne. Fahd therefore tended to rely on personally chosen emissaries, not his foreign minister, to carry out foreign policy decisions. In fact, the royal family insider recounted that, as a result, Saud was considered within the royal family to have been "insulted" by Fahd; according to this source there was even the expectation that Prince Saud would resign, although the source observed, using an Arabic analogy, that he was able to withstand the pressure Fahd placed upon him "like a camel."[62]

Then, in 1995, Fahd suffered a debilitating stroke, from which he never recovered. Fahd's incapacitation unleashed a fierce struggle between Crown Prince Abdullah and Fahd's full-brothers for dominance within the Saudi state. This struggle will be examined in Chapter 1. During this period, the decision-making process became fragmented across multiple autonomous actors who sought to gain leverage against each other in the vacuum created by Fahd's stroke. The findings further indicate that this power struggle came to some degree of resolution after the 11 September attacks in 2001; hostility in the United States toward Saudi Arabia in the wake of 9/11 caused the senior Saudi princes to feel highly threatened, compelling them to unite behind a single leader, in this case Crown Prince Abdullah. Abdullah's dominant position within the Saudi state was further consolidated upon his formal assumption of the throne in 2005, which, in turn, allowed him to dictate Saudi policy toward Iraq during the period of his reign.

What thus becomes notable about the decision-making process in the Fahd and Abdullah period is not that one of the three constellations to which Hermann points was in play, but that at different times *all three constellations* were. What is distinctive, therefore, about the Saudi decision-making process is its fluidity across time,[63] underscoring the low institutionalization of the Saudi state and the salience of its key personalities. Ultimately, this is the contention upon which scholars of Saudi Arabia agree—that personalities dominate the Saudi decision-making process—and indeed this book will reflect the centrality of King Abdullah to the decision not to engage with Iraq.

Plan of the Book

The following six chapters tell the story of how Saudi Arabia paradoxically pushed post-2003 Iraq into an Iranian embrace. Chapter 1 explores the Saudis' perception of an Iranian threat in the last three decades of the twentieth century. As seen above, the intentions of other states, particularly those considered adversaries, are ambiguous, and in ambiguous situations the perceptions humans form are typically a function of their preexisting beliefs. Furthermore, past traumatic events such as wars may create a powerful prism through which subsequent events are perceived; given the trauma of the earlier event, foreign policy decision-makers may be resistant to assimilating new information which indicates how the present is different from the past. Chapter 1 contends that the Iranian Revolution of 1979 and the eight-year Iran–Iraq War that followed constituted a traumatic event for the Saudi leadership, establishing a powerful belief among them about an inherent Iranian expansionism. During this decade, the Saudi leadership even began to view Iran through the lens of an enemy image. In turn, the beliefs established within the Saudi leadership in the 1980s would continue to shape their perception of an Iranian threat in the 1990s and 2000s. Beyond the Saudis' threat perception, this chapter also explores the repression of the Iraqi Shiʻa community by the country's Baʻthist authorities before and after the Iranian Revolution and the Saudis' response to the Iraqi invasion of Kuwait in 1990 to provide additional context to understand Saudi policy toward post-2003 Iraq.

Chapter 2 begins the analysis of the Saudi leadership's response to the Shiʻa ascendance in Iraq. The chapter focuses primarily on the Saudis' perception of what was taking place in Iraq in the period from the U.S. invasion in early 2003 through the end of 2005. It argues that in this period, the Saudi leadership perceived that the U.S., by virtue of the policies it was implementing in Iraq, was allowing Iran to establish its predominance there. In Chapter 3, the discussion turns to the decision by the Saudi leadership, especially King Abdullah, not to engage with the government of Iraqi Prime Minister Maliki, which was seated in spring 2006. Chapter 3 demonstrates that Abdullah in particular perceived Maliki to be an untrustworthy Iranian agent, and therefore refused to engage with him. Indeed, Abdullah came to see Maliki as an enemy, as he viewed Iran to be. The chapter argues that, in contrast to Abdullah's image of him, Maliki had never been particularly close to the Iranian regime. Nevertheless, the Saudi leadership appeared to become more invested in maintaining the image they had formed of Maliki than in gathering more information about him in order to add nuance to their image.

The purpose of Chapter 4 is to examine the dynamic between Saudi Arabia and Iraq in the period from late 2006 to early

2009. During this period, the Maliki government attempted to forge a diplomatic opening to the Saudi leadership, which was consistently rebuffed by King Abdullah. In addition to the Iraqis, many third parties, including George W. Bush and Arab leaders such as President Hosni Mubarak of Egypt and King Abdullah II of Jordan, tried to urge Abdullah to adopt a different approach to the new Iraq, and it appears that even Abdullah's own principal foreign policy advisers counseled him to establish a Saudi presence there. For their part, the Iraqis, foremost Maliki, perceived that the Saudi leadership opposed Iraq's Shiʻa ascendance and therefore began to feel threatened by them. In contrast to Saudi Arabia, many other Arab states began to engage meaningfully with the Maliki government during this period, especially after Maliki initiated a confrontation with Iranian-backed Shiʻa militias in spring 2008, an action that demonstrated for many that he genuinely intended to pursue an independent course from Iran.

Chapters 5 and 6 demonstrate the self-fulfilling prophecy created by Saudi Arabia, whereby Maliki ended up aligning with Iran. Chapter 5 focuses on the lead up to and aftermath of Iraq's 2010 parliamentary elections. As seen above, experiments in social psychology have demonstrated how a perceiver, treating a target in line with an inaccurate stereotype, often elicits new behavior on the part of the target that conforms to the stereotypic image. In a reflection of this logic, Chapter 5 shows that prior to the 2010 elections, Maliki resisted pressure from Iran to join an Iranian-backed Shiʻa Islamist electoral coalition, preferring to establish his own nationalist-oriented list. The Saudi leadership, however, backed a predominantly Sunni Arab coalition headed by Ayad Allawi, a secular Shiʻi politician; in the eyes of Maliki, and of the Shiʻa more broadly, Allawi's list represented a Saudi-backed effort to restore Sunni Arab power in Baghdad. When Allawi's list won a narrow victory over Maliki's in the election, Maliki, in a reversal of his pre-election behavior, won the support of Iran and joined with the Iranian-backed Shi'a Islamists to retain the premiership and safeguard Iraq's new order. In this way, the chapter argues, the self-fulfilling prophecy began to come to fruition. Perceiving Maliki to be an Iranian agent and therefore an enemy to Saudi Arabia, Abdullah refused to engage with Maliki and backed Allawi's bid for the premiership. However, in doing so he compelled Maliki to feel threatened by Saudi Arabia and to align with Iran.

Maliki's alignment with an Iranian regional axis became even more pronounced after the onset of the Arab Spring, as explored in Chapter 6. At this time Saudi Arabia, as well as other Sunni countries such as Turkey and Qatar, started to provide material support to rebels in Syria. The Saudis, in particular, sought to undermine the Assad regime, a longstanding ally of Iran, to roll back what they regarded as Iran's unacceptable regional influence. For their part, members of the Maliki government perceived that the Saudis were interfering not only in Syria to undermine the Assad regime, but also in Iraq to undermine *them*. They therefore started to turn toward Iran for defense. The chapter argues that whether or not it was accurate, their perception that Saudi Arabia was seeking to topple their government, derived from the Saudis' hostile attitude to the new Iraq, compelled them to pursue a closer relationship with Iran. The final section of the chapter addresses new developments in the Saudi–Iraq relationship since Maliki's ouster from the Iraqi premiership in summer 2014 and King Abdullah's death in early 2015. Since that time, Saudi Arabia, appearing to accept Iraq's Shi'a ascendance as a *fait accompli*, has pursued a rapprochement with Iraq.

In sum, it was not inevitable that a Shi'a-led Iraq would end up in an Iranian regional alignment. Following the travails of the Saddam period, Iraq's new leaders wanted positive relations with all of their neighbors, including Saudi Arabia. Maliki himself wanted, above all, to ensure that the new Iraq would be an independent state, beholden to no outside power. Nevertheless, Saudi Arabia refused to engage with Maliki's government. The Saudi decision hindered Iraq's access to the Arab world, and, in time, Iraq's Shi'a leaders came to fear that the Saudi leadership sought to reverse Iraq's post-2003 Shi'a ascendance. The consequence was that the Maliki government became ever more reliant on Iran. The chapters that follow tell this story.

1

IRAN, IRAQ, AND SAUDI ARABIA IN THE LATE TWENTIETH CENTURY

As seen, a state is considered threatening by another if it is perceived as different, if its intentions are perceived as aggressive, and if it possesses greater power than the first. These variables—namely identity, an estimate of intentions, and relative power—elucidate the sense of threat Saudi Arabia has perceived from Iran since the 1970s. Being by far the largest state of the Persian Gulf region, Iran has traditionally stoked the anxiety of its neighbors. Moreover, in the 1970s, the Saudi leadership exhibited concern over a massive military build-up Iran was then pursuing, although the threat the Saudis perceived at that time was mitigated by the fact that both states were conservative monarchies allied to the United States.

By contrast, following the 1979 Iranian Revolution, when the Shah's conservative regime was replaced by Shiʿa revolutionaries, Iran appeared to become highly threatening to the Saudis. The Iranian revolutionaries not only stated their intention to export the revolution abroad, but also became embroiled in an eight-year war with Iraq. During this period, Saudi leaders began to view their neighbor through the lens of an enemy image, inferring that revolutionary Iran harbored malign intent, namely to impose its hegemony on the region at the expense of the existing Gulf regimes, including the Kingdom of Saudi Arabia. This episode is of the utmost importance, as the beliefs that were established among the Saudi leadership during this period—specifically, that the Islamic Republic was expansionist—would continue to shape their perception of it thereafter. The second half of this chapter reveals that Saudi leaders continued to assess Iranian intentions as hegemonic in the 1990s, and subsequent chapters will demonstrate that they adhered to this view in the 2000s, which in turn shaped their perception of Iraq's post-2003 Shiʿa ascendance. Indeed, the beliefs established among the Saudis in the 1980s about Iranian expansionism have continued to shape their perception of Iran to the present day.

But the Saudi leadership regarded not only revolutionary Iran as highly threatening during the tumultuous 1980s; they also felt threatened by their ostensible ally in the war with Iran—Baʿthist Iraq. The Saudis had suspected since before the Iranian Revolution that Saddam Hussein himself sought to project his dominance onto the region, and their fears were realized when two years following the conclusion of the Iran–Iraq War, Iraq invaded and annexed its tiny neighbor, Kuwait. Having considered Iran as the bigger threat in the 1980s, the Saudis saw Saddam Hussein as their primary enemy following the invasion of Kuwait. Indeed, during the Gulf War of 1990–1991, the Saudis sought Saddam's removal from power. Critically, however, what they wanted to take place in Iraq was a palace coup, not the empowerment of the country's Shiʿa majority, as would occur after 2003.

Saudi Perceptions of Iran in the 1970s

Saudi anxieties about Iran predate the Iranian Revolution of 1979. In 1968, Britain, which had been the predominant power in the Persian Gulf since the nineteenth century, announced its plan to withdraw from the Gulf by 1971. Iran, then under the leadership of Muhammad Reza Shah Pahlavi, immediately sought to fill the power vacuum that would thereby be created. The Shah's ambition was supported by the Nixon administration, which was itself concerned about Soviet penetration into the region following the British departure.[1] In order to establish Iran's regional primacy, the Shah invested heavily in developing his military capabilities, with Iran's defense expenditure increasing more than tenfold over the course of the 1970s, from $779 million in 1970 to $7.9 billion seven years later.[2] The Shah, with the support of the Nixon administration, also purchased American weapons on an enormous scale: Iranian arms imports, amounting to $264 million in 1970, rose to $2.6 billion in 1977.[3] At this time, Iran's armed forces stood at more than five times the size of those of Saudi Arabia.[4]

Identity, however, actually mitigated the sense of threat the Saudis perceived from Iran in this period. Although Iran was predominantly Persian and Shi'a, in comparison to predominantly Sunni Arab Saudi Arabia, its "otherness" in the eyes of Saudi leaders was tempered by the fact that both states were conservative, pro-U.S. monarchies. Iran and Saudi Arabia generally regarded themselves as aligned, therefore, against their radical, pro-Soviet neighbors, such as Iraq, which had fallen under the control of the Arab nationalist Ba'th Party as a result of a 1968 coup. In fact, the Ba'thists were then providing support to subversive groups in the Gulf monarchies, leading the Saudis to regard Iraq as more threatening than Iran at this point.[5] As the British were preparing to depart the Gulf region, the Shah and King Faisal of Saudi Arabia therefore reached an accommodation over the new regional order, whereby the Shah recognized the Arab side of the Gulf, including the newly independent states of Bahrain, Qatar, and the United Arab Emirates (UAE), as Saudi

Arabia's sphere of influence, while Faisal recognized Iran's role as guardian of Persian Gulf waters.[6]

Nevertheless, Iran's massive military buildup still produced significant concern within the Saudi leadership over its intentions, especially after the Shah began to deploy his power in the Gulf. Most significantly, Iran occupied the strategic Gulf islands of Abu Musa and Greater and Lesser Tunb, located near the Strait of Hormuz and claimed by the UAE, in 1971. Such maneuvers created anxiety on the part of the Saudi leadership, as well as in the ruling circles of the smaller Gulf Arab states.[7] According to a 1975 U.S. diplomatic cable, Saudi Defense Minister Prince Sultan bin Abd al-Aziz reported that the Saudi leadership was "increasingly disturbed by the Iranian arms build-up," which he said was provoking "suspicion" among them that "Iran really did have aggressive intentions on the Arab side of the Gulf."[8] Iranian intervention on the Arab littoral would violate the Shah's agreement with Faisal, whereby he had recognized this zone as the Saudi sphere of influence. During the Shah's reign, therefore, the Saudi leadership cooperated with him, but remained wary that he harbored intentions to expand into what they regarded as their own backyard.[9]

Thus, the Saudi leadership began to perceive threat from an increasingly powerful Iran following Britain's departure from the Persian Gulf, even though the identities that the two states shared as conservative monarchies and allies of the U.S. reduced, for the time being, the degree of threat they detected. Nevertheless, with the fall of the Shah in 1979 and the rise of an anti-U.S., revolutionary Shi'a regime in Tehran, Iran would truly become the "other" in Saudi eyes. Moreover, the new Iranian regime would explicitly assert an intention to export its revolution abroad and even to overthrow Iraq's Ba'thist regime. From 1979, therefore, the sense of threat the Saudi leadership perceived from Iran would rise dramatically.

THE LATE TWENTIETH CENTURY

The Iranian Revolution and the Iran–Iraq War

In early 1979, the Shah fled Iran as a result of popular protests that had escalated over the previous year, and Ayatollah Ruhollah Khomeini, who would become the foremost leader of the Iranian Revolution, returned to the country in triumph after fourteen years in exile. During his period of exile in the Iraqi shrine city of Najaf, Khomeini had formulated an Islamist political philosophy known as *velayat e-faqih* in Farsi, or *wilayat al-faqih* in Arabic, meaning guardianship of the Islamic jurist and calling for a government under the supreme authority of the leading Islamic scholar. In late 1979, the Iranian public voted to adopt a constitution enshrining Khomeini's doctrine for the newly established Islamic Republic of Iran. Moreover, from early 1980, Khomeini declared that Iran would export its revolution throughout the world; he proclaimed that the revolution was not meant for Iran alone, but was intended for all peoples everywhere.[10] These events had significant repercussions throughout the Gulf region. In Iraq, the Ba'thist authorities responded by initiating a severe crackdown on the Iraqi Shi'a religious community in the spring of 1979. Brutally suppressed by the Ba'thists, members of this community would take positions of power in post-2003 Iraq. Then, in September 1980, Iraq invaded Iran, leading to a devastating eight-year war between the two countries. For their part, the Saudi leadership blamed the Iran–Iraq War on Iran, even though it had been initiated by Iraq. During this period, the Saudi leadership even began to perceive revolutionary Iran through the lens of an enemy image, inferring that it sought to expand throughout the Gulf at the expense of Iraq and the Gulf Arab monarchies. Iraq's response to the Iranian Revolution is addressed first, before turning to that of Saudi Arabia.

A SELF-FULFILLING PROPHECY

Iraq and the Iranian Revolution

Saddam Hussein, who formally took power as president of Iraq in 1979, regarded the revolution in Iran as a source of both threat and opportunity, and his fear and ambition impelled him to order the invasion.[11] Identity lay at the heart of the new Islamic Republic's threat, as perceived by the Ba'thists, while a momentarily favorable balance of power between the two countries informed the sense of opportunity they detected. The Ba'thists perceived threat from revolutionary Iran principally because of its "otherness"—as well as its apparent commonality with Iraq's own restive Shi'a religious establishment. Indeed, the revolution took place at a time when the Ba'thist regime's relations with the Shi'a religious community were already fraught. Relations had deteriorated since the Ba'thists took power in 1968. The following year, in the wake of a crisis with Iran over the Shatt al-Arab, the waterway that separates southern Iraq from its neighbor, the Ba'thist regime sought to exploit the tensions with Iran to implement measures to constrict the clerical community's traditional independence, for instance expelling some 20,000 members of the community from Iraq, alleging they were Iranian.[12] Five years later, detecting the growth of Shi'a Islamist opposition, the regime executed five members of the Da'wa Party, an organization of Shi'a *ulama* and educated laymen established in Najaf in the late 1950s. In 1977, a massive confrontation took place between the Ba'thist authorities and the Shi'a religious establishment during a religious procession from Najaf to Karbala. Some 30,000 pilgrims, defying an official ban on the procession, were intercepted on their way to Karbala by Iraqi army units; some 2,000 pilgrims were arrested, 16 were reported killed, and 8 of the participants were later sentenced to death.[13]

The revolution in Iran then led to an escalation in the ongoing crisis between the Ba'thists and the Iraqi Shi'a Islamists.

Days after Khomeini's return to Iran, Ayatollah Muhammad Baqr al-Sadr, a leading Iraqi cleric based in Najaf, declared a public holiday to celebrate the revolution. Al-Sadr had helped establish the Da'wa Party and served as its principal ideologue, and that spring al-Sadr's followers in the party traveled to Najaf and openly pledged their allegiance to him. In response, the Ba'thist authorities initiated a harsh crackdown on the Da'wa Party, arresting some 5,000 members, of whom about 200 were executed or killed under torture. A substantial number of the Da'wa members who were released fled abroad.[14] Nevertheless, the domestic crisis continued to escalate. While the remnants of the Da'wa Party left inside Iraq were no longer able to stage any sort of mass challenge to the Ba'thists, in early 1980, they began to instigate a series of small-scale bombings to continue their resistance.[15] That March, Da'wa Party membership was made a capital offense, and the following month a Shi'a militant made an assassination attempt on Deputy Prime Minister Tariq Aziz. In the wake of that incident, the Ba'thists executed Ayatollah al-Sadr, which sent shock waves through the wider Shi'a population of the Gulf. A massive popular protest was mounted in Bahrain to protest the execution, while the Iranian revolutionaries called for a "jihad" against the Iraqi regime.[16] Following al-Sadr's execution, Khomeini himself exhorted Iraqis to take up arms against Saddam Hussein to overthrow his regime.[17] Thus, the Iranian Revolution began to undermine the basis of the Ba'thists' power. The revolution in Iran impelled the Iraqi Shi'a Islamists to mobilize, which in turn impelled the Ba'thists to crack down on them, although in doing so, the Ba'thists triggered a confrontation with the Iraqi Shi'a's co-religionists in revolutionary Iran.

Meanwhile, a temporarily favorable balance of power informed the sense of opportunity Saddam Hussein detected. While the Iranian armed forces had been the largest in the Gulf region, in 1979 and 1980 Iran's new leaders sought to dismantle these forces, which were associated with the reviled Shah, and widespread desertions were also taking place in the midst of the turmoil of the revolution.[18] With Iran's military arsenal thus incapacitated, Saddam Hussein sensed an opportunity to project Iraqi power into the Gulf.[19] His primary objective was to reverse an agreement over the Shatt al-Arab, which he had concluded with the Shah in 1975 at Algiers. Prior to 1975, the entire Shatt had been under Iraqi control, but in the Algiers Agreement Saddam had agreed to recognize Iran's claim to ownership of the waterway up to its *thalweg*, or deep-water mark. Saddam had concluded the deal under Iranian pressure: the Shah had been supporting an Iraqi Kurdish rebellion against the central Iraqi state to gain leverage in his dispute over the Shatt with the Ba'thists.[20] Thus, as Iran descended into disarray from 1979, Saddam aimed to retake control of the entire waterway, which would give him better access to the Persian Gulf. Indeed, on 17 September 1980, five days prior to the Iraqi invasion of Iran, Saddam abrogated the Algiers Agreement. Moreover, by invading Iran, Saddam also intended to portray himself as the Arabs' chief protector, thereby positioning himself as leader of the Arab world. His stated objectives for the invasion, therefore, included the longstanding Arab nationalist goals to "liberate" the Arab population of the Iranian province of Khuzestan—known as Arabistan in Arab discourse—as well as the islands of Abu Musa and the Tunbs, claimed by the UAE.[21]

While bold, Saddam Hussein's plan for the invasion had envisioned a limited strike just over the Iranian border. Nevertheless, the invasion resulted in an eight-year war fought mostly on Iraqi territory. Within days of the invasion, the United Nations called for a ceasefire, and Saddam offered his peace terms. The Iranians, by contrast, refused to negotiate, and indeed, for the next eight years the Iranians rejected negotiations.[22] The first year of the war consisted largely of stalemate, but in fall 1981, Iranian forces began an offensive to push the Iraqis out of Iran. By the follow-ing June, the Ba'thists, with their forces in disarray, ordered a withdrawal from Iranian territory and proposed to the Iranians a return to the 1979 status quo.[23] Nevertheless, that summer, Khomeini rejected the Ba'thists' proposal and decided instead to carry the war into Iraq. Iranian intentions, as articulated by the Iranians themselves, appeared unambiguously aggressive in the summer of 1982, not only toward Iraq, but also toward the Gulf Arab states. The Iranian media was awash at this time with calls by revolutionary leaders for a "final offensive" into Iraq to topple Saddam's regime, and Khomeini himself even proclaimed that after the Ba'thists' anticipated defeat, "Iraq will be annexed to Iran."[24] Khomeini elaborated that Iraq would establish its own Islamic government, and even projected, "If Iran and Iraq can merge and be amalgamated, all the diminutive nations of the region will join them."[25] Moreover, Iranian actions for the remainder of the war buttressed their declarations of aggressive intentions. While their initial invasion of Iraq, begun in July 1982, quickly stalled, they would launch repeated offensives into Iraq, for instance with two further ground campaigns taking place in late 1982 and five in 1983 along the entire length of the Iran–Iraq border. In total, the Iranians would launch some twenty-five ground offensives into Iraq between 1982 and 1987, while rejecting all ceasefire proposals.[26] Khomeini would only agree to accept a ceasefire in the summer of 1988, once Iraqi forces had finally pushed the Iranians out of Iraq and the U.S. had established a massive naval presence in the Gulf. Nevertheless, Khomeini likened the decision to drinking a "poi-soned chalice."[27]

Meanwhile, throughout the war the Ba'thists continued to repress Iraq's Shi'a community. In 1980, the Iraqi regime resumed its deportations of members of the Iraqi Shi'a *ulama*, whom it alleged were Iranian; some 40,000 members of the clerical community were deported to Iran that year, and indeed as many as 200,000 were expelled from Iraq over the course of the decade.[28] In addition, the Ba'thist authorities sought to cast aspersions on the Iraqi Shi'a in Ba'thist propaganda of the 1980s. Such anti-Shi'a propaganda had deep roots in Sunni Arab-dominated Iraq, and was consistent with the widely held Sunni stereotypes of the Shi'a. Long before the onset of the Iran–Iraq War, or even the Ba'thists' assumption of power, Iraqi polemicists of Arab nationalist persuasion, typically Sunni Arabs, had sought to cast doubt on the Arabism of the Iraqi Shi'a, thus stigmatizing them in the eyes of their compatriots and thereby marginalizing the country's majority community. The Iraqi Shi'a had thus periodically been linked to the *shu'ubiyya* movement of the early Islamic period—the term being derived from the Arabic word for "peoples"—when non-Arab communities of the Umayyad and Abbasid Empires sought equality with the dominant Arabs.[29] Soon after the establishment of modern Iraq, Arab nationalist writers had exhumed this historical episode, distorting it to establish a connection between the *shu'ubis*, portrayed as Persian and anti-Arab, and the Iraqi Shi'a. For instance, in a 1993 treatise one writer claimed: "The Shi'a are *shu'ubis* in their entirety; Persians in their entirety. They are the remnants of the Sassanids in Iraq," a reference to the Persian empire that fell to the Arab Muslims in the seventh century.[30] The implication of this argument was that the Iraqi Shi'a owed their allegiance not to the Arabs, but to Persia, or Iran in the modern context. Moreover, twentieth-century Arab nationalist propaganda alleged that the *shu'ubis* of the Abbasid period had posed a dangerous internal threat to the empire because while they pretended to assimilate, they in fact sought to undermine its Arab culture and values by reasserting their own Persian practices.[31] According to Eric Davis, such narratives were deployed to send two messages: Sunni Arabs were taught that their Shiʿa compatriots were "untrustworthy and duplicitous," while the Shiʿa were encouraged to renounce their cultural heritage in favor of Arab nationalism.[32]

During the Iran–Iraq War, the Baʿthists revitalized the *shuʿubiyya* narrative. Their propaganda, however, no longer focused on the distant Abbasid period, but rather asserted that Iran had been hostile toward Iraq throughout history.[33] One leading polemicist claimed in a 1983 treatise, for example, that "Iran covets Iraq" due to the latter's cultural superiority.[34] Interestingly, King Abdullah of Saudi Arabia would utter this same phrase two decades later in a conversation with U.S. officials, as recorded in a U.S. diplomatic cable from 2006; according to the cable, Abdullah told the Americans that "Iran covets Iraq," although he did not elaborate, or possibly his elaboration was not captured in the cable.[35] Furthermore, Saddam Hussein himself expressed his view on the imagined *shuʿubiyya* phenomenon in a 1989 treatise published under his name. In it, Saddam effectively argued that Iraq's "historical problem"—the predicament it had experienced throughout time—consisted of internal conspiracies that had been fueled by an outside Persian power, and Eric Davis contends that Saddam thereby sowed suspicion not only toward Iran, but also toward the entire Iraqi Shiʿa community.[36] Saddam's claim is highlighted here because it fundamentally contributed to how many Sunni Arabs, both inside and outside Iraq, would perceive Iraq's post-2003 Shiʿa ascendance. Indeed, as we will see in the next chapter, an allegation would become widespread, including among the Saudi leadership, that a Shiʿa Islamist coalition prevailed in Iraq's first free elections of January 2005 because millions of Iranians had infiltrated the country to vote for it. In this view, consistent with Saddam's contentions, an internal conspiracy had apparently taken place in Iraq, fueled by Iran, to bring the Shiʿa to power.

A SELF-FULFILLING PROPHECY

Saudi Arabia and Revolutionary Iran

Following the Iranian Revolution, and especially the onset of the Iran–Iraq War, the Saudi leadership considered revolutionary Iran to be highly threatening. Indeed, all the variables that inform threat perception pointed to an Iranian threat, as seen by the Saudis: Iran's new leaders—Persian Shi'a revolutionaries—truly appeared to be the "other" and its principal leader had stated his intention to replace the Iraqi Ba'thists with an Iranian-aligned Islamic republic, which, he said, would put pressure on the other states of the region to follow; moreover, the country, regardless of its change of regime, was still considerably more powerful than Saudi Arabia. By late 1981, at the time of a failed coup attempt in Bahrain, Saudi leaders would come to view Iran through the lens of an enemy image, inferring that it possessed malign intent toward Saudi Arabia.

Nevertheless, in the first years of the revolution, the Saudi leadership sought to conciliate the new regime. Indeed, their attempt to conciliate revolutionary Iran flowed from the power differential between them: the Saudi leadership, then possessing limited military capabilities, typically sought to avoid direct conflict with superior powers.[37] Thus, after the fall of the Shah, the Saudis signaled accommodation toward the Iranian revolutionaries, with Saudi leaders emphasizing the common identity of the two countries, namely a shared adherence to Islamic principles.[38] A year and a half later, on the heels of the Iraqi invasion of Iran, the Saudi leadership maintained this conciliatory stance, officially adopting neutrality toward the war and calling for mediation between the two sides.[39] At the same time, they sought to balance the threat emanating from revolutionary Iran by strengthening their longstanding security partnership with the United States, which deployed a small military contingent to the kingdom days after the Iraqi invasion.[40] Moreover, by early 1981, the

Saudi leadership began to tilt toward Iraq in the war, providing financial assistance to the Ba'thists, although they officially maintained their neutral façade. In fact, the Saudi leadership still regarded Iraq as threatening—particularly as its Ba'thist leader, Saddam Hussein, appeared to be making his own bid to project hegemony over the Arab world—but the Saudis now viewed it as the lesser threat. Even though Iraq had been the one to invade Iran, the Saudi leadership perceived Iran as the greater threat due to its refusal to negotiate an end to the war.[41]

In December 1981, however, the Saudi leadership, perceiving that Iran had become a direct threat to the kingdom, dropped its neutral stance and began overtly to align with Iraq. That October, Iranians on the annual Hajj pilgrimage to Mecca had demonstrated in support of Ayatollah Khomeini, leading the Saudi authorities to deport some eighty Iranian pilgrims.[42] In the wake of the incident, the Saudi leadership, in a letter written by King Khalid to Khomeini, maintained their conciliatory tone, suggesting that the Iranian pilgrims had "defied" Khomeini's instructions.[43] Nevertheless, in his reply to Khalid, Khomeini publicly attacked the Saudi leadership, denouncing its security partnership with the United States, the Shah's former ally whom Khomeini reviled as the "Great Satan."[44] Two months later, in December 1981, a more spectacular incident set the region on edge, when the Bahraini government uncovered a coup plot that was to have been carried out three days later, which it attributed to an Iranian-based group called the Islamic Front for the Liberation of Bahrain. While the Bahraini authorities estimated that as many as 150 people could have been involved in the plot, 73 people were arrested and convicted, comprising 60 Bahrainis, 11 Saudis, 1 Kuwaiti, and 1 Omani.[45]

The Bahrain coup plot galvanized the Saudi leadership to publicly denounce Iran and overtly align with Iraq. Days after the plot's discovery, Saudi Interior Minister Prince Nayef bin Abd al-Aziz, then the most outspoken member of the Saudi leadership, declared that the Iranians had become "the terrorists of the Gulf."[46] A week later, Prince Nayef traveled to Baghdad, where he stated that the kingdom stood with Iraq in the war with Iran.[47] At this time, Prince Nayef contended that Iran was the aggressor in the war and declared that Iraq was acting "not only in defense of Iraq's territory and sovereignty but also in defense of the entire Arab nation"; he asserted that, therefore, "our stand must be an Arab stand in support of Iraq."[48] Similarly emphasizing a confrontation between Iran and an imagined Arab nation, then-Crown Prince Abdullah stated in the Arabic press in 1983 that an Iranian victory against Iraq would provoke "an all-out Arab war with Iran."[49] Such statements indicated that the Saudi leadership considered the war at this point to be a conflict waged by Iran, a non-Arab outsider, against an Arab ingroup. As they regarded Iraq as the principal defender of this ingroup, they began to provide it with substantial support from 1982, for instance constructing a pipeline across their territory to export Iraqi oil and increasing their own crude production, of which the excess was sold on Iraq's behalf in order to prop up its economy.[50] Nevertheless, the kinship the Saudi leadership felt toward the Iraqi Ba'thists was still limited. Most particularly, in 1981, Saudi Arabia led the establishment of the GCC, grouping together the six Arab monarchies of the Gulf region, from which both Iran and Iraq were deliberately excluded.[51] Thus, the Saudi leadership may have pointed to a symbolic boundary that separated all the Arab states from Iran, but they established a very real one that further separated the Gulf Arab monarchies from the Iraqi Ba'thists. Even if the Saudis regarded the Ba'thists as less threatening than the Iranian revolutionaries at this point, they still considered them to be threatening.

By contrast, however, the Saudi leadership began to view revolutionary Iran through the lens of an enemy image following the discovery of the Bahrain coup plot. As seen in the introduction, a country perceived as an enemy is assumed to possess malign intent, and the enemy image becomes a lens through which all its actions are judged as indicators of its malign intent. The enemy country may also be seen as monolithic, highly rational, and deliberate. Thus, while the Bahrain coup plot was in fact an amateurish operation planned by disaffected Shiʿa citizens of the Gulf Arab states who had been given refuge in the Islamic Republic, a Saudi think tank analyst named Mansur Hasan al-Utaibi wrote in 2008 that the plot had constituted "an Iranian conspiracy to overthrow the ruling regime in Bahrain."[52] For his part, Prince Nayef even declared in December 1981 that the failed operation in Bahrain "was engineered by the Iranian Government and was directed against Saudi Arabia."[53] Thus, what was actually a clumsy affair was seen by Saudi leaders as a deliberate act by an Iranian enemy to harm the kingdom. Furthermore, by the following spring, as Iranian forces were gaining momentum toward their invasion of Iraq that summer, Prince Nayef explicitly expressed the view that Iran's true aim in the war was to assert hegemony over the entire region. In response to a question about the Bahrain coup plot incident, Nayef stated to the press:

> [T]he conflict with Iran is not merely a war between Iran and Iraq, but ambitions that are aimed at controlling the Arab side, that is, opposite the Iranian coast starting with Bahrain and ending with all the region's states. This is aimed at creating regimes loyal to Iran ... The Iranian side thinks that the region's states will one day belong to it, like the islands near the Strait of Hormuz and other Arab territories.[54]

In this analysis, Iran's objective appeared to be the imposition of control over the Gulf at the expense of the existing regimes, including Saudi Arabia. This view appeared to be the prevailing one within the Saudi leadership: U.S. diplomats based in the kingdom at the time wrote in a 1985 cable that the principal figures of the Saudi state—King Fahd, Crown Prince Abdullah, Prince Sultan, and Prince Nayef—"appear to be in complete agreement" about what they regarded as the Islamic Republic's "basic hostility" toward the Al Saud regime, and the U.S. diplomats further assessed that these leaders' "worst fears" comprised the prospect of a "triumphant revolutionary Iran looming menacingly over Kuwait and Saudi Arabia itself."[55] From this point, and continuing into the present day, the Saudi leadership would evince demonstrable concern over what they considered to be Iranian expansionism in the Gulf, and eventually in the wider Arab world as well.

In fact, by virtue of Iranian leaders' continuation of the war and stated intention to export the revolution, many Gulf Arabs, not only the Saudis, inferred malign intent on the part of Iran toward the Gulf monarchies. A 1985 Kuwaiti editorial, for instance, declared that Iran's incessant offensives into Iraq provided "definite proof" that the Iranian campaign was "not aimed at Iraq alone, but that Iran looks with greed toward all the GCC countries in order to control them."[56] This perception—that Iran's objective in the war was to dominate the region—would endure. Al-Utaibi, the Saudi think tank analyst, wrote in 2008 that the Iranian leadership pursued the war in order "to weaken the biggest Arab power in the Gulf region, and from there to threaten the rest of the regional states."[57] The Saudis' apprehension toward Iran was further exacerbated by their view of *wilayat al-faqih*. In the Saudi interpretation of Khomeini's doctrine, the Islamic Republic projected itself as the leader of Shi'a Islam, and thus as the guardian of all Shi'a communities of the Muslim world, including those inside Saudi Arabia.[58] In fact, al-Utaibi contends that Khomeini sought to mobilize the Shi'a communities of the Gulf against the Gulf states in order to replace those monarchies with Islamic republics along the model of revolutionary Iran.[59] In this analysis, revolutionary Iran indeed appeared to harbor malign intent toward the Gulf Arab states.

At the same time, Iranian leaders fed the Saudis' perception of Iranian hostility. Indeed, whether or not Khomeini in fact possessed malign intent toward the Saudi leadership, his rejection of their conciliation had established their perception of an Iranian threat in the first place. Ironically, the Saudi leadership would do the same to Nuri al-Maliki's government from 2006, with their refusal to engage putting it on the defensive with regard to Saudi Arabia. Nevertheless, in the 1980s, Iranian leaders at times made statements and took actions that appeared unambiguously hostile to Saudi Arabia. For instance, in 1982, following another incident between Iranian pilgrims and Saudi authorities at the Hajj, Iranian leaders called for Mecca and Medina to be placed under international supervision, and in 1984 Iranian forces began to attack Saudi oil tankers in the Gulf in response to Iraqi attacks on Iranian shipping, in what became known as the Tanker War.[60] Saudi–Iran relations then deteriorated to their lowest point during the war years as a result of the 1987 Hajj, when Saudi security forces, overreacting to an Iranian demonstration, fired into the crowd, resulting in the deaths of 402 mostly Iranian pilgrims.[61] Within days, Ayatollah Khomeini condemned the Saudis as "traitors to the two holy shrines," while Ayatollah Hussein-Ali Montazeri, then Khomeini's designated successor as supreme leader, called for the "liberation" of Mecca and Medina "from the hands of the criminals of Al Saʿud."[62] For his part, Prince Nayef publicly declared his belief following the incident that "the Iranian Government harbors hatred for the Kingdom of Saudi Arabia."[63] The following spring, the Saudi leadership severed diplomatic relations with the Iranian regime, partly as a result of the 1987 Hajj.

Nevertheless, the Saudi leadership still took clear steps to conciliate the Islamic Republic during the war, given its inclination at that time to avoid conflict with superior powers. At bottom, they did not want to remain on openly hostile terms with Iran.[64] Thus, in 1984, the Saudis made a goodwill gesture toward Iran, increasing its Hajj quota by 50 percent from the previous year. When a relatively moderate Iranian leader, Speaker of Parliament Akbar Hashemi Rafsanjani, reciprocated this goodwill gesture by stating Iran's acknowledgement of the Saudis' rightful guardianship of the holy sites, the Saudis invited him to attend that year's pilgrimage. Although he declined, the clearest indication of a relative thaw in Saudi–Iran relations came a year later, when Saudi Foreign Minister Saud al-Faisal made a surprise trip to Tehran.[65] This thaw continued until the 1987 Hajj conflagration. Nevertheless, at the 1988 Hajj, which coincided with the ending of the war, Saudi leaders again signaled conciliation toward Iran: King Fahd publicly expressed his sorrow during that pilgrimage that Iranian pilgrims were absent, a result of the events the year before.[66] Thus, the Saudi leadership sought to convey to their Iranian counterparts during the war years that although they would stand by Iraq as long as the war continued, they would pursue better relations with the Islamic Republic once it agreed to end hostilities.[67] Khomeini, for his part, however, continued to reject the Saudis' conciliation following the war's conclusion. In fact, at the time of his death in 1989, Khomeini singled out Saudi leaders for opprobrium, calling them "conspirators against the House of God," and intoning, "May God's curse go to them."[68] Such a statement on the part of the Iranian Revolution's primary leader would understandably compel the Saudis to question Iranian intentions toward them.

According to Robert Jervis, traumatic events such as wars may create a powerful prism through which foreign policy decision-makers judge other states' intentions. Given the trauma of an earlier event, decision-makers may be unreceptive to assimilating new information demonstrating how the circumstances that previously led to war have changed; they may therefore continue to assess the intentions of formerly hostile countries as hostile.[69] The analysis above has demonstrated that during the period of the Iran–Iraq War, the Saudi leadership judged revolutionary Iran's intentions to be hostile and expansionist, a judgment for which Iranian revolutionaries, particularly Khomeini, provided a reasonable basis through their statements and actions. Moreover, this period was one of great trauma for Saudi leaders. As a result, the beliefs that were established among them at this time— namely, that Iran was inherently expansionist—became particularly ingrained, producing an image of Iran as an enemy that has perpetuated itself to the present day. Indeed, the second half of this chapter will demonstrate that the Saudi leadership continued to assess Iranian intentions as expansionist in the 1990s, an assessment to which they adhered, as we shall see, in the 2000s. Nevertheless, in contrast to their view, Iranian intentions appeared less obviously expansionist in the post-revolutionary period, and actually it could be argued that Iranian intentions were primarily defensive at this time. Before assessing the Saudis' perception of Iran in the 1990s, their response to the Iraqi invasion of Kuwait is addressed below.

Saudi Arabia and the Gulf War

While the Saudi leadership had perceived revolutionary Iran as far more threatening than Iraq during the Iran–Iraq War, by the end of the war, Iraq—at this point a country under arms with one million men purported to be in its armed forces— appeared to be the greater threat. Then, in 1990, Saddam Hussein ordered the invasion of Kuwait. From that point on, the Saudi leadership regarded Saddam Hussein as an enemy and prioritized his removal from power. Moreover, as their relations with Iraq collapsed, the Saudi leadership's relations with Iran improved, even though Saudi–Iran relations would again deteriorate in the 1990s.

Following the conclusion of the Iran–Iraq War, Iraq appeared to be a growing threat in Saudi eyes. Not only did Saddam Hussein command an enormous army, but his intentions also appeared increasingly belligerent toward the smaller Gulf states. At the end of the war, Iraq faced a severe economic crisis: having financed the war through foreign loans, it had accrued a massive foreign debt it was unable to pay. By 1990, Iraq's debt burden had become untenable, and Saddam Hussein insisted that the Gulf Arab states not only forgive their previous loans to Iraq, but also extend a new loan of $30 billion. Then, on top of the existing crisis, oil prices fell 30 percent in the first six months of 1990, with Saddam Hussein blaming the oil price drop on OPEC members Kuwait and the UAE, which were exceeding their oil-production quotas.[70] In June 1990, Saddam publicly declared that Kuwait and the UAE were undermining Iraqi interests, and in late July Iraqi forces began to mobilize along the border with Kuwait.[71]

During this period, the Saudi leadership sought to conciliate Saddam Hussein, signaling a willingness to accommodate his demand for new loans and pressing Kuwait and the UAE to abide by their oil-production quotas.[72] Moreover, as Iraqi forces began to mobilize along the Kuwaiti border, King Fahd made an attempt to mediate between the two sides, hosting representatives from Iraq and Kuwait in Jeddah on 31 July. Reflecting how exceedingly ambiguous other leaders' intentions can be—even when they are mobilizing their armed forces—the Saudi leadership still did not believe at this point that Saddam Hussein actually intended to invade Kuwait. Fahd, who had received an assurance from the Iraqi leader that he would not order an invasion, believed he was mobilizing his forces to gain leverage in the negotiations.[73]

Nevertheless, the Saudis' assessment was proved wrong and their attempt to conciliate Saddam a demonstrable failure when, on 2 August 1990, Iraqi forces seized Kuwait in its entirety. From this point, King Fahd regarded Saddam Hussein as an enemy, inferring that the Iraqi leader possessed malign intent toward Saudi Arabia as well as Kuwait. Indeed, by 3 August Iraqi forces had massed along the Saudi–Kuwait border, and even began to conduct patrols some 25 kilometers inside the kingdom itself.[74] Fahd would later state his belief to a domestic audience that Saddam Hussein had intended to "swallow" not only Kuwait, but a portion of Saudi Arabia as well.[75] Thus, on 6 August Fahd accepted a U.S. proposal to deploy American troops to the kingdom, with the first units arriving the next day.[76] That fall, the George H.W. Bush administration assembled a large UN-authorized, Saudi-based international coalition to liberate Kuwait, and, by January 1991, almost 800,000 foreign troops, the majority of whom were American, were located on Saudi soil.[77]

While this massive U.S. military intervention in Saudi Arabia would provoke a significant domestic backlash against them, the Saudi leadership's overriding objective at this point was Saddam Hussein's removal from power.[78] Moreover, they felt reasonably assured that the Iraqi dictator would fall as a result of the operation to liberate Kuwait. Indeed, the general expectation within the U.S.-led coalition was that Saddam would not be able to survive a humiliating defeat and that a coup was therefore likely to take place.[79] Like the Saudi leadership, George H. W. Bush and his advisers also desired Saddam's ouster through a military coup, although in the absence of a coup they did not intend to invade Iraq to depose him.[80] Preoccupied throughout the conflict with Iraq's potential to fragment, they wanted to ensure that a unified Iraq remained strong enough to continue as a regional counterweight to Iran.[81] By contrast, the Saudi leadership evinced less concern about the Islamic Republic than the U.S. administration did, and instead prioritized the need to undercut Iraq's power.[82] The Saudis' position toward Iran stemmed from the Islamic Republic's cautious behavior throughout the crisis. Following Khomeini's death, Iran came under a new, more moderate leadership, which sought to reintegrate Iran into the international order. During the Gulf Crisis, therefore, the Islamic Republic officially condemned the Iraqi invasion and supported the UN action, and by thus demonstrating a new pragmatism, it was able to improve relations with many Arab states, including Saudi Arabia, with whom it reestablished full diplomatic relations in March 1991.[83] Indeed, an editorial in the Saudi newspaper *Okaz*, explaining the official Saudi decision to restore relations, pointed to Iran's "pragmatic stance" during the Gulf War, as well as the emergence of "moderate and sensible leaders" in Tehran.[84] Although Saudi Arabia's relations with Iran improved considerably at the end of the Gulf War, the rest of this chapter will explore how the Saudi leadership continued to harbor deep suspicions toward it.

Meanwhile, to Saudi leaders, the opportunity to topple Saddam appeared to materialize upon the liberation of Kuwait. By the time the U.S.-led coalition moved into Kuwait in late February 1991, Iraqi forces, having faced five weeks of air strikes, were in disarray and had begun a disorderly retreat back to Iraq. The Ba'thists announced their willingness to accept a ceasefire, and one was signed by the U.S. and Iraqi commanders in the Iraqi town of Safwan on 3 March. Nevertheless, at the same time, popular, spontaneous uprisings broke out across Iraq. The rebellion began on 1 March, initiated by Iraqi soldiers retreating from Kuwait; the following day Basra fell to the rebels, and within days the revolt spread rapidly through southern Iraq. On 4 March, the Iraqi Kurds also began to rebel. In sum, in early March, Saddam Hussein's regime lost control of fourteen of

Iraq's eighteen provinces, concentrated in the Shiʿa south and Kurdish north.[85]

The Saudi leadership, for their part, regarded the uprisings as the key moment to put pressure on Saddam Hussein's weakened regime to precipitate his fall.[86] In an interview, Chas Freeman, the U.S. ambassador to Saudi Arabia during the Gulf War, observed, "The Saudis were all over me and anybody else they could talk to, to please arm the Shiʿa, please support the Shiʿa." Freeman elaborated that the Saudi objective was not to empower the Shiʿa rebels as such, but to use the rebellion as a means to destabilize the regime, thus sending a signal to the Iraqi military to overthrow Saddam.[87] In fact, Prince Turki al-Faisal, then the Saudi intelligence chief, confirmed in an interview that the Saudi leadership pushed the U.S. to support the uprisings at this time, and still lamented the president's decision not do so.[88] George H. W. Bush and his advisers, for their part, chose not to back the rebellion out of fear that assisting the Iraqi Shiʿa would benefit Iran, even though it seems that Iran, itself fearing a U.S. response, did not actually support the uprisings at this time.[89] Whatever the case, with the U.S. standing on the sidelines during the rebellion in southern Iraq, the Baʿthist regime was able to brutally suppress the Iraqi Shiʿa rebels by the end of March 1991.

Overall, during the Gulf War, the Saudi leadership considered the threat coming from Iraq to take precedence over that coming from Iran. As a result of the Iraqi invasion of Kuwait, the Saudi leadership desired Saddam Hussein's removal from power and wanted to support the Iraqi uprisings of March 1991 to that end. However, in wanting to support the rebellion, they appeared to view the Iraqi Shiʿa merely as an available tool to assert leverage against Saddam. In the post-2003 period, the Saudis would similarly assess that Iraqi Shiʿa groups served as a tool for Iran to carry out its regional objectives. Indeed, the Saudis never appeared to consider that these groups might be actors in their own right, with their own interests and objectives. In this way, they would end up conflating Iraqi Shiʻa leaders with Iran in the post-2003 period. Having looked at the Saudi response to the Iraqi invasion of Kuwait, we return to the theme of Saudi perceptions of Iran. Although the Saudi leadership had reconciled with the Islamic Republic during the Gulf War, they still believed it harbored intentions to assert regional hegemony.

Saudi Perceptions of Iranian Expansionism after the Gulf War

At the end of the Gulf War, Saudi Arabia restored diplomatic ties with Iran, whose new, more moderate leaders had demonstrated their pragmatism during the conflict. Over the following years, the kingdom's relations with Iran were often tense, although the two states avoided open confrontation.[90] However, the purpose of the analysis below is not to explore Saudi–Iran relations in the 1990s as such, but to examine the ongoing skepticism that the Saudi leadership showed toward Iran's regional intentions.[91] In the 1990s, Iran took actions that can be reasonably construed as provocative toward the Gulf Arab states, for instance expelling Emirati citizens from the island of Abu Musa in 1992 and even backing the bombing of the Khobar Towers housing complex in Saudi Arabia's Eastern Province in 1996. The latter incident led to the escalation of regional tensions, which were ultimately defused by a notable Saudi–Iranian reconciliation initiated by Crown Prince Abdullah—an initiative that not only reflected a Saudi effort to calm regional tensions but also pointed to a power struggle then unfolding at the upper echelon of the Saudi royal family. While the Iranians may have themselves regarded their actions as defensive in this period, the Saudi leadership tended to view them as indicators that the Islamic Republic retained hegemonic objectives. Moreover, beyond the actions Iran actually took, the Saudi leadership also appeared to detect an Iranian link to crises even when there did not appear to be substantial evidence of their involvement. In particular, Saudi leaders' preexisting beliefs about Iranian expansionism colored their perception of two specific episodes: the imposition of a no-fly zone over southern Iraq in 1992 and unrest in the Bahraini Shi'a community in the mid-1990s. By thus assessing all indicators as evidence of Iran's hegemonic intentions, even when they had a less reasonable basis to do so, the Saudi leadership's image of Iran as an enemy perpetuated itself, consistent with the beliefs that had been established among them in the 1980s.

By late 1991, the Saudi leadership again seemed suspicious of Iran's regional intentions. In fact, as recorded in a November 1991 U.S. diplomatic cable, Foreign Minister Saud al-Faisal expressed his belief to U.S. diplomats in Riyadh that Iran's objective remained, as before, "regional hegemony and intervention in Arab affairs." As a result, he told the U.S. officials, all the GCC states viewed their neighbor "as a threat not an ally."[92] To substantiate his estimate of Iranian intentions, Prince Saud pointed to Iranian actions since the end of the Gulf War, particularly its military build-up and its strident opposition to U.S. efforts to mediate a solution to the Arab–Israeli conflict.[93] Indeed, Iran was then launching a military rearmament program, with its defense expenditure nearly doubling in 1991 over the previous year as it purchased ballistic missile technology from places like China and North Korea.[94] Iran also sought in late 1991 to stymie the Middle East peace process overseen by the George H. W. Bush administration by hosting Palestinian factions opposed to peace at a conference in Tehran.[95] However, the intentions that lay behind these actions were more ambiguous than had been the case in the 1980s. In contrast to Prince Saud's assessment of November 1991, it can be argued that Iran's actions at this time pointed to a defensive, not offensive, mindset on the part of its leaders, who felt threatened by the continued U.S. military presence in the Gulf after the liberation of Kuwait and its attempt to establish a new, post–Gulf War regional order.[96] However, it is not a surprise that only three years after the conclusion of the Iran–Iraq War, behavior that Iran itself may have thought defensive would be interpreted by its neighbors as evidence of an ongoing offensive posture.

Moreover, conflict set in between Iran and the Gulf Arab states from 1992, and tensions thereafter escalated for much of the decade. In late summer 1992, Iran provoked a crisis with the GCC when it expelled Emirati residents from Abu Musa, the Gulf island claimed by both Iran and the UAE, which the two countries had been co-administering since 1971. This action provoked the Gulf Arab press to assert that Iran retained expansionist objectives,[97] and its refusal to negotiate a compromise solution with the UAE continues to undermine its relations with the GCC to the present day. Pointing to an unwillingness to compromise, an Iranian official went so far as to declare in 1995 that Iran was willing to fight "an 80-year war" to defend Abu Musa and the Tunbs; in response, a Saudi newspaper close to the government asserted that this official's remark revealed Iran's "hegemonic aims."[98] In addition to the conflict over the Gulf islands, the Hajj remained a particular irritant in the Saudi–Iran relationship, to the extent that it provoked a new Saudi–Iranian media war in 1994. That year, Iranian Supreme Leader Ali Khamenei claimed that the Saudi leadership had mistreated Iranian pilgrims; in the following months, Iranian news outlets went so far as to predict the "imminent fall" of King Fahd, while the Saudi media denounced the Iranian regime's "strange thirst for chaos, war, and destruction."[99]

Furthermore, two particular episodes in the 1990s indicate the extent to which the Saudis' perception of regional events was shaped by their preexisting beliefs about Iranian expansionism, both of which show the Saudis perceiving dangerous Iranian meddling, even though there was little evidence even to support the contention that Iran was involved. The first episode concerned the imposition by the U.S., France, and Britain of a no-fly zone over southern Iraq in August 1992 to protect the Iraqi Shiʿa from the Baʿthist state. In April of the previous year, the U.S. and its allies had imposed a no-fly zone over northern Iraq to protect the Kurds, who were then rebelling against the Iraqi regime. Given that the northern no-fly zone had, by 1992, allowed the Kurds to begin to establish their own autonomous government, the Saudi leadership were reportedly "alarmed" at the prospect that imposition of the second no-fly zone would create a Shiʿa autonomous region in southern Iraq.[100] As observed above, while the Saudis had appeared intent on using the Shiʿa uprisings of March 1991 as a lever against Saddam, it had not been their aim at that time to empower the Iraqi Shiʿa. In August 1992, they reportedly feared a Shiʿa autonomous region would ally with Iran, providing it with a platform to expand its influence through the region.[101] In fact, officials in Riyadh were then recounting to the Western press that Iran was already taking steps to exploit the southern no-fly zone—allegedly sending weapons and agents into southern Iraq—to establish "a pro-Tehran state" in the area, although the journalist reporting this story noted that there was no independent verification of these claims.[102] This relatively minor episode is noteworthy because it foreshadows the Saudi response to events in Iraq in 2003. As seen in the introduction, a fundamental principle of cognitive psychology is that humans tend to see what they expect to see, and indeed, the Saudi leadership would anticipate in 2003, and then immediately detect indicators, that Iran was trying to fill the vacuum in Iraq created by the U.S. invasion.

The second and more significant episode relates to the Bahraini Shiʿa uprising of the mid-1990s. The roots of the unrest were socio-economic: by the 1990s, Bahrain had depleted its relatively limited oil resources, but had experienced a huge increase in population.[103] The Bahraini authorities, however, openly accused Iran of fomenting the turmoil.[104] No significant evidence has ever materialized to substantiate this claim. Nevertheless, the Saudi leadership, for their part, appeared to credit the Bahrainis' version of events. Indeed, as recorded in a U.S. diplomatic cable from 1995, Foreign Minister Saud al-Faisal expressed his opinion to U.S. officials in Riyadh that Iran's interference in Bahrain was "very serious," although he observed that Iran denied its involvement.[105] Interestingly, Saud al-Faisal remarked that the Iranians had conveyed to the Saudi leadership their desire to try to prove they were unconnected to the unrest in Bahrain, although the Iranian claims appeared unconvincing to the Saudi foreign minister.[106] This last remark is consistent with the perception of another country through the lens of an enemy image: in such a scenario, the perceiver is more inclined to believe that the other country possesses malign intent than to credit gestures it might make to try to prove its goodwill. Furthermore, as seen in the introduction, humans tend to see not only what they expect to see, but also what they *want* to see according to their interests and emotional needs. Beyond the Saudis' tendency to see indicators of Iranian expansionism consistent with their preexisting beliefs, it is plausible that Saudi leaders, in attributing the turmoil in Bahrain to an external actor rather than to the Bahraini Shiʿa's socioeconomic grievances, may have implicitly preferred not to acknowledge the domestic roots of an uprising in a fellow Gulf Arab monarchy. Both types of biases on the part of Saudi leaders could have contributed to the perception that Iran was meddling in Bahrain in the 1990s.

While tensions with Iran had already simmered for a number of years by the mid-1990s, they escalated significantly as a result of a 1996 attack on the Khobar Towers housing complex in Dhahran, Saudi Arabia. Nineteen U.S. airmen were killed when a massive truck bomb exploded outside the complex.[107] In the aftermath of the attack, Iran became a prime suspect, and by 1998 the FBI formed a determination that the bombing had been carried out by members of Hizballah al-Hijaz, a Saudi Shi'a militant group, at the direction of the Iranian Revolutionary Guards.[108] In late 1996, tension between the U.S. and Iran escalated, with the Clinton administration coming under increasing domestic pressure to retaliate against Iran.[109] For its part, Iran threatened to strike U.S. Gulf Arab allies if attacked, leaving Gulf Arabs with the sense of being caught in the middle of the U.S.–Iran confrontation.[110]

In this context, a Saudi–Iranian rapprochement began to take shape in early 1997. In the mid-1990s, Iranian emissaries to Saudi Arabia had repeatedly attempted to improve the bilateral relationship, but had been rebuffed by the Saudi side.[111] The Khobar Towers attack then appeared to lead to a Saudi reassessment of their policy toward Iran.[112] At the March 1997 summit of the Organization of the Islamic Conference (OIC) in Islamabad, Crown Prince Abdullah, leading the Saudi delegation in place of King Fahd who had suffered a debilitating stroke at the end of 1995, initiated the reconciliation: on the sidelines of the summit, Abdullah met with Iranian President Rafsanjani, whom he invited to attend the Hajj the following month.[113] Then, with the election that summer of reformist Iranian politician Muhammad Khatami to Iran's presidency, the Saudi–Iran rapprochement picked up pace.[114] In the following years, prior to the 2003 invasion of Iraq and the 2005 presidential election of hardline Iranian politician Mahmud Ahmadinejad, Saudi–Iranian relations experienced a notable period of détente. Landmark visits were made on both sides, with Crown Prince Abdullah visiting Tehran in late 1997 and President Khatami traveling to Saudi Arabia in 1999, and a security agreement was signed by the two countries in 2001.[115]

The initiation of the rapprochement by the Saudi side in early 1997 was motivated not only by realpolitik, but also by domestic political considerations. In terms of realpolitik, the Saudi leadership undoubtedly sought to defuse the tensions that were escalating in the region following the Khobar Towers bombing; in Prince Turki's recollection, the rapprochement took place because both Saudi Arabia and Iran "wanted to get over negative issues."[116] Nevertheless, it appears that another significant factor propelling the reconciliation from the Saudi side was a fierce power struggle then unfolding between Crown Prince Abdullah and Fahd's full-brothers, which had been unleashed by Fahd's incapacitation.[117] The roots of the rivalry between Abdullah, on the one hand, and the Sudairi princes—Fahd, Sultan, and Nayef—on the other, had deep roots—a Saudi royal family insider interviewed for this book observed that this rivalry was what primarily motivated Abdullah throughout his adult life.[118] The rivalry started to become apparent under King Khalid, Fahd's predecessor, when Abdullah and Sultan, who were the heads of two rival security organizations, the National Guard and Ministry of Defense respectively, were seen as competitors to succeed Fahd, Khalid's designated heir apparent. As second deputy prime minister under Khalid, Abdullah was considered to be Fahd's likely successor, although the mechanism by which he would move from this post to crown prince was not automatic, and there were rumors that the ambitious Sultan aimed to move ahead of Abdullah in the line of succession.[119] Although Abdullah did become crown prince upon Khalid's death, it appears that the matter of the succession remained contentious: in 1992, Fahd decreed a new law that allowed the Saudi monarch to unilaterally choose his successor, which Abdullah reportedly viewed as a potential obstacle to his assumption of the throne.[120]

During this period, the research findings indicate that rival decision-making centers emerged at the top of the Saudi hierarchy, with the leaders of these rival centers seeking to assert their authority within the state, reflective of, in Margaret Hermann's foreign policy decision-making framework, a quasi-anarchical decision-making constellation in which decision-making is fragmented among multiple actors operating without rules. These rival decision-making centers revolved around Crown Prince Abdullah, still the head of the Saudi Arabian National Guard, Fahd's full-brothers Princes Sultan and Nayef at the Ministries of Defense and Interior respectively, and Fahd's son Abd al-Aziz, who controlled the Royal Court during his father's incapacitation.[121] In the vacuum created by Fahd's ill health, it appears that these senior princes struggled fiercely against each other. For instance, Abdullah was intensely concerned throughout the late 1990s, according to a royal family insider, that Prince Abd al-Aziz would force him to relinquish his command of the National Guard and thus deprive him of his pathway to the throne. Abdullah therefore sought to buttress his position within the family by undertaking policy initiatives that would enhance his prestige, with one such initiative being the rapprochement he set into motion with Iran at the 1997 OIC summit in Islamabad.[122] Moreover, it was reported at this time that President Hafez al-Assad of Syria, a longstanding personal friend of Abdullah as well as an ally of Iran, supported Abdullah's claim to the throne and was mediating between him and the Iranians.[123]

Thus, the Saudi decision to initiate the rapprochement with Iran may be considered to have been not only a means to tamp down the regional tensions that had escalated in the wake of the Khobar Towers bombing, but also a way for Abdullah, as an autonomous actor within the Saudi state, to gain leverage over a rival group of autonomous actors, namely the Sudairis. Furthermore, the research findings indicate that Abdullah undertook at least two other noteworthy initiatives in the late 1990s and early 2000s to curtail the power of Interior Minister Prince Nayef. The first was to empower Nayef's own son, Muhammad, at the Ministry of Interior. For his part, Muhammad bin Nayef is said to have aligned with Abdullah because his father favored a different son, Saud, who served as his chief of staff. In the second initiative, Abdullah cultivated closer relations with the Saudi Shi'a elite in 2003, which thereby allowed him to encroach on a security file—namely, the management of relations with the Shi'a of the Eastern Province—that had traditionally been Nayef's responsibility.[124]

Regardless of the machinations then unfolding within the upper echelons of the Saudi royal family, it should be pointed out that in seeking to defuse tensions with Iran and even pursue greater cooperation with it, Abdullah, and his brothers more broadly, did not necessarily see Iran as less of a threat. Rather, by this point, as pointed out by a foreign policy adviser to the Saudi royal family, they viewed their U.S. ally, with its large military presence in the Gulf, as a "security guarantor" to balance the Iranian threat.[125] At bottom, the Saudi initiative to reconcile with Iran reflected the Saudi leadership's pragmatic preference to coexist peacefully with their larger neighbor, rather than be locked in a dangerously escalating confrontation, while relying on the U.S. to balance it.

Indeed, what the analysis above has demonstrated is that in the 1990s, the Saudi leadership continued to assess Iranian intentions as expansionist, consistent with the beliefs that had been established among them in the 1980s, even though the nature of Iranian intentions was actually much more ambiguous during this period than in the decade before. The Iranians themselves may have had a defensive mindset, although their actions—for instance, the 1992 Abu Musa incident and the 1996 Khobar Towers bombing—would have understandably been seen by the GCC states as provocative. Often, however, another state's intentions are inherently ambiguous: what that state may consider to be its own defensive behavior may be seen as offensive by others. This point is made to elucidate the inherent ambiguity of another state's intentions; typically, there are no black-and-white answers. Furthermore, in ambiguous situations such as these, foreign policy decision-makers become even more reliant on their preexisting beliefs to form perceptions, with those perceptions then becoming the basis for their decisions.

Conclusion

As a result of the Iranian Revolution, and particularly the Iran–Iraq War, the Saudi leadership came to regard Iran as highly threatening. Indeed, during the war years Saudi leaders began to see the Islamic Republic as an enemy, inferring that it intended to impose hegemony over the region at the expense of the existing regimes, including the Kingdom of Saudi Arabia. In the 1980s, the Iranians, through their actions and statements, provided a reasonable basis whereby the Saudis could form this perception, but Iranian actions became more ambiguous in the post-revolutionary period. Nevertheless, in the 1990s, Saudi leaders adhered fairly rigidly to the perception they had formed of Iran in the previous decade, continuing to assess it as harboring expansionist objectives. Further pointing to the self-perpetuating dynamic behind the Saudis' enemy image of Iran, they tended to detect indicators of Iranian expansionism in the 1990s in situations where significant Iranian involvement was never substantiated, such as the Bahraini uprising of the mid-1990s. This tendency to see Iran as expansionist, and then to detect indicators that bolstered their view, would in turn shape how they regarded the Shi'a ascendance in Iraq in the aftermath of Saddam Hussein's overthrow, the subject of the next chapter.

2

A NEW IRAQ WITH A PERSIAN FLAVOR?

In the spring of 2003, the U.S. invaded Iraq and toppled Saddam Hussein. Over the next three years, three successive, short-lived political entities came and went in Iraq: the Coalitional Provisional Authority (CPA) under the leadership of American diplomat L. Paul Bremer III; the Interim Government headed by Ayad Allawi, a secular Shiʿi member of the Iraqi opposition to Saddam Hussein; and the Transitional Government led by Daʿwa Party member Ibrahim al-Jaʿfari. The Interim Government, led by secularists, was broadly reflective of Iraq's old order, while the Transitional Government, dominated by Shiʿa Islamists, was reflective of the new one. Meanwhile, throughout this period Iraqi resistance mounted to the U.S. occupation, and by spring 2005, Baghdad also found itself mired in a sectarian civil war.

The Saudi leadership, for their part, began to perceive in the aftermath of the invasion that the U.S., by virtue of the policies it was implementing in Iraq, was allowing Iran to establish its predominance there. While Iran did in fact begin to intervene in Iraq as soon as Saddam Hussein fell from power, its intentions behind doing so were highly ambiguous. Nevertheless, the Saudi leadership assessed, consistent with their preexisting beliefs, that Iran harbored expansionist intentions toward post-Saddam Iraq—that it aimed to assert hegemony over the country—even though it could also be reasonably argued that Iran's intentions were more limited and defensive in nature; that it sought to ensure that the new Iraq emerged as a friend, not an enemy, for example. More to the point, in focusing so intently on Iranian intentions at this time, Saudi leaders also tended to overlook how the intentions of Iraqi Shi'a leaders could diverge from those of the Iranians. Indeed, even though Sunni Arabs, both inside and outside Iraq, tended to conflate the Iraqi Shi'a—particularly Iraqi Shi'a Islamists—with their Iranian co-religionists, there was in fact significant diversity within the Iraqi Shi'a community, as well as between them and the Iranians.

Furthermore, the Saudi leadership tended to gather information about post-invasion Iraq from Iraqi sources whose biases matched their own, particularly Sunni Arabs and secular Shi'a. Such Iraqis tended to look unfavorably upon the emergence of Shi'a Islamist power in Baghdad, often characterizing it as an Iranian ascendance in their country. Thus, the Saudi leadership's perception of Iranian expansionism into Iraq was reinforced. The Saudis' initial perceptions would become a lens through which they would process information about Iraq for the years to come, contributing to their decision not to engage with the government of Nuri al-Maliki, which was formed in spring 2006.

From 9/11 to the Invasion of Iraq

In the United States, the Al-Qa'ida attacks of 11 September 2001 quickly led to planning within the George W. Bush administration for an invasion of Iraq. Within days of 9/11, the proposal to pursue regime change in Baghdad, in addition to an intervention in Afghanistan to dismantle Al-Qa'ida, was already being discussed in Washington.[1] The principal rationale for the decision to invade Iraq was to prevent the scenario whereby Saddam Hussein, who was then believed to possess weapons of mass destruction, might pass these weapons on to Al-Qaʻida.[2] The Saudi leadership deeply opposed the U.S. plan to overthrow Saddam Hussein by means of a military intervention. Although the Saudis had continued to desire Saddam's ouster since the conclusion of the 1990–1991 Gulf War, they believed that an invasion could result in a power vacuum in Baghdad that would destabilize the wider region. Indeed, Foreign Minister Saud al-Faisal voiced this concern prior to the 2003 invasion, positing that an invasion could produce an Iraqi "political vacuum," and ultimately civil war.[3] As will be seen below, the Saudi leadership also expressed anxiety at this time that Iran would seek to exploit such a vacuum in Iraq.

Meanwhile, the 9/11 attack had immediate repercussions within the Saudi leadership itself, bringing some measure of respite to the rivalry between Crown Prince Abdullah and the Sudairis. In the wake of the attack, which had been perpetrated by fifteen Saudi citizens, hostility toward the kingdom mounted in the United States, as well as within the Bush administration.[4] This U.S. hostility caused Saudi officials to voice concern that they could become another U.S. target for regime change.[5] According to Saudi sources, the external pressure that the kingdom faced at this time compelled the royal family to unite behind a single leader, in this case Abdullah.[6] Furthermore, a Saudi royal family insider added that Nayef, who had traditionally maintained close ties to the Wahhabi religious establishment, and possibly even to Al-Qaʻida, saw his position within the family weaken as a result of 9/11. This source observed that while the Sudairis united behind Abdullah at this time, they still hoped they would ultimately be able to retain the throne, as the source claimed that everyone within the family expected

Abdullah to die before Fahd. According to this source, Abdullah, who was then in his late seventies, smoked heavily and had suffered a number of strokes, and thus it was never anticipated that he would actually live to be ninety, surviving not only Fahd, but Sultan and Nayef as well.[7] Additionally, with Abdullah's empowerment within the family, Prince Saud al-Faisal, an intra-family ally of Abdullah, also gained greater authority.[8]

With regard to Saudi policy toward Iraq, the Saudi leadership sought to walk a fine line, desiring Saddam's ouster, but in a way that would not produce a power vacuum in Baghdad that could lead to regional upheaval, as a massive military invasion threatened to do. Indeed, since the conclusion of the Gulf War, Iraq's weakening state had been a central preoccupation of Saudi leaders, who feared that the country's disintegration could unleash a civil war that would also embroil its neighbors.[9] Thus, if the Bush administration was determined to take out Saddam, they counseled the Americans to remove Saddam, as well as his top lieutenants, while keeping his regime and the country's Sunni Arab power structure in place.[10] Above all, the Saudis preferred to see Saddam removed via covert action.[11] In the 1990s, the U.S. and Saudi Arabia, in addition to other regional states such as Jordan, had repeatedly endeavored to foment a coup in Baghdad, although the various attempts had failed. As a result, the U.S. had lost faith in the coup option, even though the Saudi leadership, according to Prince Turki al-Faisal, had for its part continued to regard a coup as "doable."[12] Then, at a Saudi–U.S. summit in April 2002, Crown Prince Abdullah sought to redirect the Bush administration away from military intervention in Iraq and back toward covert action, when he presented a proposal for a new $1 billion joint covert program.[13] A month before the Saudi–U.S. summit, Abdullah had publicly embraced Izzat Ibrahim al-Duri, one of Saddam's principal lieutenants, at an Arab summit in Beirut, leading some observers to hypothesize over a possible rapprochement between Saudi Arabia and Iraq.[14] However, given the Saudis' continued support for a coup in Baghdad, it seems more likely that Abdullah's public embrace of al-Duri was intended as a signal to the Arab world of his opposition to the proposed U.S. invasion.

Furthermore, the Saudis' fear that an invasion could lead to an Iraqi power vacuum revived their concerns about Iran's intentions toward its former adversary. Indeed, as seen in Chapter 1, Crown Prince Abdullah was of the opinion that "Iran covets Iraq."[15] Robert Jordan, then the U.S. ambassador to Saudi Arabia, recounts in his memoirs that the Saudi leadership communicated to the Americans, prior to the invasion, their concern that Iran would seek to expand into an Iraqi vacuum.[16] Compounding their anxiety, the Badr Brigade, an Iranian-based Iraqi paramilitary organization, prepositioned its forces in southern Iraq and Iraqi Kurdistan in advance of the invasion.[17] The Badr Brigade formed the military wing of the Supreme Council for the Islamic Revolution in Iraq (SCIRI), an organization of Iranian-based Iraqi Shi'a Islamists that the Iranians had helped establish in 1982, and which had originally been formed as an Iraqi transitional government in the event the Iranians captured significant Iraqi territory.[18] In light of the Badr mobilization in early 2003, Prince Turki al-Faisal observed in an interview that "it was clear to us that the Iranians would take advantage" of the impending invasion.[19] Thus, as had become typical of the Saudi leadership since the traumatic experience of the Iran–Iraq War, they expressed concern over Iranian expansionism as the Bush administration prepared to invade Iraq.

The rest of this chapter demonstrates that Iran did begin to intervene in Iraq in the wake of the U.S. invasion; nevertheless, the nature and the extent of its intervention at this time were highly ambiguous. It has generally been argued that Iran aimed to empower the Iraqi Shi'a after Saddam Hussein's overthrow, as well as to compel a U.S. withdrawal from Iraq.[20] However, a more fundamental question revolves around its broader objectives: did Iran intend simply to ensure that the new Iraqi regime would be a friend, not an enemy, as the Iraqi Ba'thists had been, or did it desire to turn the new Iraq into a client state? Stated another way, were its actions evidence of a defensive mindset—to forestall a situation in which Iraq could again threaten it, as it had done in 1980—or evidence, at an extreme, of an objective to transform Iraq into a platform from which it would impose regional hegemony? At bottom, the inherent ambiguity of this period naturally lends itself to many alternative assessments of Iranian intentions, and it also seems plausible that some Iranian leaders could have had relatively limited objectives while others were more maximalist. As for the Saudi leadership, they assessed, consistent with their preexisting beliefs, that it was Iran's goal to assert hegemony over Iraq, and ultimately over the region. Their assessment was not necessarily invalid, given the inherent ambiguity of Iranian intentions, although it did tend toward a more extreme reading.

Ultimately, however, it is not the purpose of this book to examine the validity of the Saudi leadership's assessment of Iran's post-2003 objectives. What it aims to accomplish, in this and subsequent chapters, is to argue that the Saudis' view of Iran, which did not admit much room for ambiguity, in turn shaped their perception of Iraq's new Shi'a leaders. In focusing so intensely on Iran's supposedly hegemonic intentions, the Saudis tended to overlook how Iraqi Shi'a leaders' interests could diverge from those of the Iranians.

The U.S. Hands Iraq to Iran on a Golden Platter?

On 20 March 2003, an international coalition led by the U.S. initiated the invasion of Iraq and, meeting little resistance on their drive to Baghdad, coalition forces quickly entered the capital. On 9 April, U.S. troops pulled down a statue of Saddam Hussein in Baghdad's Firdus Square, symbolizing the fall of his regime. However, as soon as Saddam's statue fell, it became clear that the optimistic assumptions the Bush administration had formed prior to the invasion—namely that the Iraqis would welcome the Americans as a force of liberation—had been unfounded. Most immediately, the relatively small size of the invasion force was inadequate to secure the country after the fall of the regime. Widespread looting immediately broke out in the capital, lasting three weeks and causing $12 billion worth of damage.[21] Furthermore, over the course of 2003, the U.S.-led coalition would encounter increasing resistance from both Iraq's Sunni Arab and Shi'a Arab communities, and indications of Iranian interference were also detected in the country.

The most noteworthy development that took place in Iraq following the invasion was the emergence of Shi'a power. Having been sidelined by successive twentieth-century regimes, the Shi'a community took just over half the seats on a governing council composed of prominent Iraqis that had been established by the United States and its allies in the summer of 2003. This development was shocking to the country's Sunni Arabs. Not only did Iraqi Sunni Arabs tend to reject the notion that the Shi'a constituted a majority of the Iraqi people, but many also conflated the Iraqi Shi'a with Iran. With the empowerment of the Iraqi Shi'a, Iraqi Sunni Arabs tended to see a nefarious Iranian intervention taking place in the country. However, despite Sunni Arab perceptions, significant differences had historically existed between the Shi'a of Iraq and Iran, as well as within the Iraqi Shi'a community itself, and these different orientations would mitigate the extent to which an Iraqi Shi'a regime would actually want to align with Iran. Meanwhile, the Saudi leadership believed that U.S. policy in Iraq following the invasion was allowing Iran to exert control over the country. Consistent with their preexisting beliefs about Iranian expansionism, the Saudi leadership quickly detected what they saw as indicators of Iran's intentions to establish its predominance in Iraq. This initial perception on the part of the Saudis became a lens through which they would continue to assess the situation in Iraq for years to come.

The Emergence of Shi'a Power in Iraq

Given the security breakdown in Iraq following the invasion, in early May, Bush decided to impose a U.S. occupation over the country and appointed Bremer, a retired American diplomat, to head the occupation administration—the CPA. Within days of Bremer's arrival in Baghdad on 12 May, he issued two orders of inestimable impact. The first removed the top four ranks of Ba'th Party members from government service. In the second, Bremer disbanded Iraq's entire security apparatus and announced that new security services would be built from scratch. While the de-Ba'thification policy had been advocated by some Bush administration officials, Bremer's first two orders had not been formally reviewed by the administration, nor was Bush himself aware of them prior to their promulgation.[22] Thus, Bremer's first two orders, which removed close to 800,000 public-sector employees from their positions, were issued without warning, and to the surprise of many in Iraq, the United States, and around the world. Bremer's first order dismissed some 30,000 civil servants, and the second put an estimated 750,000 Iraqis out of work.[23] Sunni Arabs, who had predominated in the upper echelons of the Ba'thist regime and the officer corps, were disproportionately affected.

Indeed, Bremer, following Bush's guidance, aimed to establish a new political order that, in his words, was "fully representative of all Iraqis."[24] Within the Bush administration, a secondary rationale for the decision to overthrow Saddam Hussein had taken shape: to establish an Iraqi democracy so as to trigger what the administration believed would be a democratic transformation across the Middle East.[25] Bremer thus sought to empower the Iraqi Shi'a community, which necessarily demoted Sunni Arabs to a status commensurate with their demographic weight as a minority. In July, Bremer announced the formation of the Iraqi Governing Council to advise the CPA and make appointments to Iraq's ministries, and he filled the council's twenty-five seats with prominent Iraqis according to an ethno-sectarian quota.[26] Thus, the council was composed of thirteen Shi'a Arabs, five Sunni Arabs, five Kurds, one Christian, and one Turkmen. Of the thirteen Shi'a members, five were Islamists, including Ibrahim al-Ja'fari, a leading member of the Da'wa Party, and Abd al-Aziz al-Hakim, a cleric and brother of Muhammad Baqr al-Hakim, the leader of SCIRI. Most of the council members were exiles who had just returned to the country.

The Shi'a religious establishment, led by Grand Ayatollah Ali al-Sistani, Iraq's senior *marji' al-taqlid* (source of emulation) since the 1990s, cooperated tacitly with Bremer, recognizing that it was the U.S.'s objective to establish a democratic system in Iraq that would necessarily empower the Shi'a community.[27] By contrast, in 1920, the Shi'a of Iraq, at the instigation of the religious establishment, had rebelled against British forces, which had taken control of the area during World War One. Thereafter, the Shi'a had become sidelined in the twentieth-century political order that had taken shape in Iraq during the British mandate period.[28] By cooperating with the U.S. occupational authorities, the Shi'a religious establishment in 2003 was intent not to repeat their predecessors' mistake.

Nevertheless, while the Iraqi Shi'a community held a common objective to take advantage of the historical opportunity presented by the U.S. invasion to establish Shi'a power in Baghdad, an

objective further shared by their Iranian co-religionists, significant differences also existed among the Iraqi Shi'a, as well as
between them and the Iranians. First of all, the Iraqi and Iranian
Shi'a have important cultural differences, deriving from their
Arab and Persian backgrounds. The Shi'a of Iraq are mostly of
Arab tribal origin, having been converted to Shi'a Islam in the
nineteenth and early twentieth centuries as they abandoned their
nomadic lifestyle; in turn, the practice of the religion in Iraq
reflects the community's traditional tribal values, in contrast to
the more mystical characteristics of its practice in Iran.[29]
Furthermore, while Persians had predominated in the Iraqi shrine
cities prior to the establishment of the Iraqi state, large numbers
of the clerics of Persian origin left Iraq in the first half of the
twentieth century, leaving Arab *ulama* in a more dominant position.[30] Nevertheless, the Iraqi Shi'a *ulama*, in contrast to their lay
counterparts, naturally belonged to a transnational community
that transcended Iraq and encompassed the wider Shi'a world,
which included non-Arab Shi'a communities such as in Iran and
Afghanistan.[31] Thus, the Iraqi clerics' identity as men of religion
created an orientation shared by their clerical counterparts in
other Shi'a countries, in contrast to Iraqi laymen.

Meanwhile, the Da'wa Party, which in the first decades of its
existence had included both clerics and laymen, had a particular
Arab identity and an ideology that drew inspiration from Sunni
Egyptian thinkers like Hasan al-Banna and Sayyid Qutb.[32]
Moreover, the party had not been on good terms with Khomeini
during the period of his exile in Najaf, while he was developing
his own doctrine of *wilayat al-faqih*.[33] Although many Da'wa
members relocated to Iran following the Ba'thists' crackdown on
their movement starting in 1979, a cleavage had then developed
between the party's clerical and lay members. Lay members
regarded their organization as an Iraqi nationalist party in exile,
not a proxy of Iran, and moreover, many of them chose not to

embrace *wilayat al-faqih* despite Khomeini's reported displeasure.[34] Their reluctance to adopt Khomeini's doctrine seems unsurprising, given that it specifically subordinated lay leaders to clerical power. By contrast to Da'wa's lay members, clerical members were more willing to accept *wilayat al-faqih* and even to see Khomeini as a *marji'* deserving of loyalty.[35] For his part, Muhammad Baqr al-Hakim, a cleric and son of the late Grand Ayatollah Muhsin al-Hakim, had been willing to subordinate himself to the Islamic Republic from the outset of the Iranian Revolution, and had thus been given leadership of SCIRI. Iran had chosen to promote SCIRI, its preferred proxy, throughout the 1980s and 1990s, at the expense of Da'wa, and in time SCIRI became a political party under the personal control of al-Hakim, while the Da'wa Party underwent various schisms. Da'wa's clerical members had progressively integrated themselves into the Iranian regime and religious establishment, and what had remained of the party was a more Iraqi nationalist organization composed of laymen. At the end of the Iran–Iraq War, many Da'wa members left Iran and relocated to London and Damascus.[36]

Cleavages also existed between the popular movement started by the late Ayatollah Muhammad Sadiq al-Sadr in the 1990s and both the traditional religious establishment and SCIRI. Ayatollah al-Sadr, a relatively obscure member of a notable scholarly family, had gained prominence within the Shi'a religious establishment in the early 1990s as a result of Ba'thist support; Saddam Hussein had sought to promote a pliable Shi'a cleric who would command the loyalty of the Shi'a masses and be obedient to the regime.[37] Nevertheless, his choice of Ayatollah al-Sadr ultimately backfired. By contrast to Grand Ayatollah Sistani, who belonged to the politically quietist tradition within Shi'a Islam, al-Sadr had embraced the politically activist tradition.[38] Al-Sadr had attacked what he called the passivity of the traditional clerical establishment, whose silence, he asserted, had contributed to

Shi'a suffering. In contrast to what he called the *hawza sakita*, or silent clerical establishment, he had aimed to create a *hawza natiqa*, or one that was vocal.[39] Most notably, in 1998 al-Sadr had reinstituted the practice of Friday prayers, which had fallen into disfavor in the Shi'a tradition, and had tailored his sermons to appeal to Iraq's large Shi'a underclass. As a result, the attendance of his sermons had reached into the tens of thousands.[40] Nevertheless, the Shi'a middle classes were less favorably disposed to al-Sadr, regarding him as a destabilizing force.[41] Furthermore, a schism had developed between the Sadrists and SCIRI. This schism reflected the traditional rivalry of two prominent scholarly families—the Sadrs and the Hakims—but it also stemmed from the traumatic experience of the March 1991 uprisings, as the Sadrists felt betrayed by SCIRI's failure to come to the aid of the Shi'a rebels.[42]

The Ba'thist regime, threatened by al-Sadr's growing popular appeal, had him and two of his sons murdered in 1999. The Sadrist movement then went dormant, but it reemerged in the wake of the 2003 invasion under the leadership of a third son, 29-year-old Muqtada al-Sadr. The Shi'a slum of northeast Baghdad, home to two million residents, previously known as Saddam City, was renamed Sadr City at this time, with clerics loyal to the late ayatollah taking charge of the community.[43] Furthermore, the rivalries between the traditional religious establishment and exile groups, on the one hand, and the Sadrists, on the other, erupted into violent confrontation on the heels of Saddam's overthrow. On 10 April 2003, Abd al-Majid al-Khoei, a son of the late *marji'* Grand Ayatollah Abu al-Qasim al-Khoei, was murdered by a mob in Najaf thought to be composed of Sadrist followers. Al-Khoei, who had relocated to London after the Gulf War, had been recruited by the CIA to act as a channel between the Shi'a religious establishment and the U.S.-led coalition. However, al-Khoei made two mistakes after his arrival: he disparaged Muqtada, as he underestimated the power retained by the Sadrist networks, and engaged with a cleric considered to be a Ba'thist agent.[44] Al-Khoei died a few hours after being attacked by the mob; reportedly, Muqtada was at home only a short distance from where he lay dying, but chose not to come to his assistance.[45] With al-Khoei's death, the Sadrists reemerged as a potent force within the Shi'a hierarchy, and Muqtada became an antagonist not only to his intra-Shi'a rivals, but also to the Americans, who believed he was responsible for the incident.

As a result, the Sadrists were excluded from the Iraqi Governing Council formed in July 2003. For his part, Muqtada condemned the exile-dominated council, which included his intra-Shi'a rivals. Following the council's formation, Muqtada declared that the Sadrists instead desired a fully representative Islamic government, and announced the creation of a Sadrist militia known as the Mahdi Army.[46] Muqtada also established connections to the Iranian regime at this time. In June, he had traveled to Iran, where he had reportedly met with Iran's supreme leader, Ayatollah Ali Khamenei, and Qasim Soleimani, head of the Iranian Revolutionary Guards' Qods Force, which was responsible for operations in Iraq.[47] That fall, Sadrist militiamen clashed with coalition forces for the first time.[48] Thereafter, the Sadrists sought to assert greater control in the areas where they predominated and deepen their connections to Iran's Revolutionary Guards.

Meanwhile, Ayad Allawi, a secular Shi'i figure and prominent member of the Iraqi opposition in exile, also took a seat on the Iraqi Governing Council formed in July 2003. Allawi had from an early age been a Ba'thist, and as an Iraqi oppositionist from the late 1970s, he had associated mainly with other dissident Ba'thists and Arab nationalists while projecting distance toward Iran. Allawi had joined the Ba'th as a boy in 1957, at a time when most members of the Iraqi branch of the party, then numbering in the hundreds, were Shiʻa.[49] Allawi participated in the Baʻthist coup d'état of 1968, which had brought the party to power in Iraq, but three years later he relocated to London to study medicine. In London, he had remained a party member, although he increasingly opposed the ascendance of Saddam Hussein within the party and regime. In 1978, Saddam sent an assassin to murder Allawi in his London home; he survived, but unsurprisingly he broke formally with Saddam as a result.[50] Then, in the 1980s, according to Ali Allawi, his cousin and an Iraqi scholar who has held various cabinet positions in the Iraqi government, Allawi had sought to connect with other dissident Baʻthists and Arab nationalists in exile, while distancing himself from Shiʻa Islamist opposition groups and particularly Iran. Ali Allawi observes that in the 1980s, "Any hint of an Iranian connection would have been anathema to him."[51] In fact, Eric Davis argues that at the time of the Iran–Iraq War, any Iraqi Shiʻi who desired to escape the Iraqi regime's calumny, which insinuated Iranian loyalty to them, needed "to become more Baʻthist than the Baʻthists."[52] In this interpretation, Shiʻa Iraqis needed to prove their loyalty to Iraq and the Arabs. Whatever Allawi's state of mind during this period, being a Baʻthist, he sought to disassociate himself from Iran entirely.

As for Iraqi Sunni Arabs, the CPA's decisions in the first months of the occupation—de-Baʻthification, the disbanding of the army, and the formation of the Iraqi Governing Council—represented the overthrow of the longstanding political order they had dominated. Unsurprisingly, most Sunni Arabs rejected this turn of events and denounced the U.S.-led occupation that had brought it about. Very few Sunni Arabs were willing, therefore, to work with the CPA, apart from returning exiles and members of the Iraqi Islamic Party (IIP), the Iraqi branch of the pan-Arab Sunni Islamist Muslim Brotherhood that had operated underground in Iraq for decades.[53] By the summer, an insurgency, composed of some 5,000 to 10,000 fighters, had taken root in Sunni Arab areas west of Baghdad.[54] A crisis of identity on the part of Sunni Arabs—the result of their loss of power and sense of marginalization by the occupation—was the key motivating factor behind the insurgents' decision to take up arms.[55] The disproportionate force, which at this time was used by U.S. soldiers against Sunni insurgents as well as against the Sadrists, as will be seen below, also fueled these groups' desire to mount resistance to the occupation.[56] Over the course of 2003, the Sunni insurgency became increasingly lethal: while 138 soldiers had been killed in the invasion, a total of 170 coalition fatalities occurred in the period from May to August, a figure that rose to 238 in the last four months of the year.[57] By fall, coalition soldiers were withdrawn to their bases to reduce their vulnerability and insurgents began to target Iraqis who collaborated with the occupation.[58]

Many Sunni Arabs regarded the Iraqi Governing Council as a particularly alien invention, given that it was dominated by exiles and was constituted according to an explicit ethno-sectarian formula, allowing Shiʿa Iraqis to take a majority of seats. In fact, many Sunni Arabs even disputed the notion that the Shiʿa formed a majority of the Iraqi people.[59] In the twentieth century, the contention that Sunnis, not Shiʿa, constituted the majority had been a widespread belief among Sunni Arabs, many of whom claimed that between the country's Sunni Arabs, Sunni Kurds, and other smaller Sunni communities such as the Turkmen, a Sunni majority existed.[60] It can be argued that such a perception among Iraqi Sunnis derived from a motivated bias—the tendency to see what one wants to see—on their part: occupying a position of power in twentieth-century Iraq, Iraqi Sunnis had had an interest in believing that they, not the Shiʿa, formed the majority. The unveiling of the Iraqi Governing Council, with thirteen of its twenty-five members being Shiʿa, was therefore jarring to many Sunnis. For instance, Harith al-Dari, a Sunni Arab religious scholar who formed the Association of Muslim Scholars (AMS) after the fall of Baghdad, asserted in a Friday sermon, "The evil thing about this council ... is that it has made one community prevail over the others," noting that, "The [sect] that was given the majority ... does not in fact represent the absolute majority ... of the Iraqi people."[61] Al-Dari's group became notable at this time for articulating the grievances of the Sunni Arab community. Like the insurgents, with whom they sympathized, they refused to participate in Iraq's new political process and demanded the withdrawal of the occupation.[62]

Furthermore, it is widely believed that Iran began to establish a presence in Iraq following Saddam Hussein's overthrow, although the nature of its intervention was highly ambiguous. Upon the fall of the Ba'thist regime, there was an immediate upsurge in two-way traffic across the Iran–Iraq border. In late April, the Shi'a community celebrated the religious festival of Arba'in in Karbala, and some two million pilgrims converged on the shrine city, with many coming from Iran; by summer, Iranian officials estimated that every day some 10,000 people crossed into Iraq, with a similar number returning to Iran, about half of whom were estimated to be Iranian pilgrims.[63] In addition, Iranian-based Iraqi refugees—and it is estimated that as many as one million Iraqis may have been deported to Iran in the 1980s[64]—began to return to Iraq in large numbers. It was widely believed that the Iranian regime was using the masses of pilgrims crossing the border as cover to insert its intelligence operatives into Iraq, and was recruiting returning Iraqi exiles into its networks.[65] Furthermore, the U.S.-led coalition estimated in the summer of 2003 that a contingent of some 4,000 Badr personnel had entered the country. The coalition judged that this force, at Iranian direction, was carrying out assassinations of former regime loyalists and targeting an Iraqi-based Iranian opposition group, the Mujahedin-e Khalq.[66] Nevertheless, that Iran was in fact establishing a presence in Iraq at this time does not bring significantly greater clarity to the nature of its intentions: these indicators can be used to argue that Iranian intentions were fairly limited—that it aimed to protect its interests in Iraq—or that its objective was more ambitious, for instance that it was laying the groundwork by which it would ultimately be able to exert a large degree of control over the country. The Americans themselves debated the nature of Iranian intentions in late 2003 and early 2004, without arriving at a consensus.[67] In short, it was unclear to outsiders what exactly the Iranians were aiming to achieve in Iraq at this time—and perhaps it was even to the Iranians.

Regardless, many Iraqis, for their part, perceived that Iran was aiming to turn the new Iraq into a client state.[68] Such a perception was unsurprising given the beliefs that already existed among them: as seen in the last chapter, the Ba'thists had actively taught that Iran was the country's historical enemy. Furthermore, many Iraqis looked with deep suspicion toward the returning Shi'a Islamist organizations, SCIRI, Badr, and Da'wa, which were widely seen as pawns of the Islamic Republic, intent on subordinating Iraq to Iran.[69] Beyond the Shi'a Islamist organizations, however, many Sunni Iraqis looked upon their Shi'a compatriots more generally with suspicion, attributing Iranian loyalty to them consistent with the beliefs that had been inculcated by successive twentieth-century regimes. For instance, a 2005 report by the International Crisis Group noted that the term "Iranian" was indiscriminately used by many Iraqis to refer to a wide variety of their Shi'a compatriots, such as Shi'a clerics, Shi'a Iraqis of Persian origin, or even Shi'a Iraqis whose family names simply sounded Persian.[70] Similarly, in his 2006 study of the Iraqi insurgency, Ahmed S. Hashim observes that for many Sunni Arabs there was "something ineluctably non-Arab or anti-Arab—indeed, even anti-Iraqi—about the Shi'a of their country."[71] Again, it can be argued that this perception derived not only from unmotivated biases relating to preexisting beliefs, but motivated ones, relating to interests, as well. In the twentieth century, successive Iraqi regimes had taught Iraqi Sunnis to be suspicious toward the Shi'a, but Iraqi Sunnis had also had an inherent interest to hold beliefs that justified the Shi'a's marginalization from power. To rationalize their own hegemony within the twentieth-century state, Iraqi Sunnis may have implicitly preferred to believe that the Shi'a of their country were Iranian loyalists, not fellow Iraqi patriots.

Such perceptions on the part of Iraqi Sunnis have been examined here because the Saudi leadership would themselves gather information about the situation in post-Saddam Iraq from these quarters. Saudi leaders, inclined to see indicators of Iranian expansionism, relied upon the information of Iraqi Sunnis, who were themselves inclined to see indicators of Iranian meddling in their country; with Saudi leaders thus gathering information from sources whose biases matched their own, it becomes unsurprising that they would begin to perceive that Iran was taking steps to assert control over post-Saddam Iraq. It should be pointed out that Abdullah of Saudi Arabia, in particular, had significant personal connections in Iraq. His mother had been the daughter of the paramount chief of the Shammar tribe, which has a presence in both Saudi Arabia and Iraq, and at least one of his wives also came from the Iraqi branch of the Shammar.[72] The Shammar has not only a Sunni branch in Iraq, but a Shi'a one as well, and it is plausible that the Saudi leadership interacted with, and gathered information from, members of both. Indeed, as will be seen, Abdullah would meet with Iraqi Shi'a leaders during this period, even receiving Muqtada al-Sadr in January 2006.[73] Nevertheless, one Iraqi Shi'a leader with whom the Saudi leadership developed a particularly close relationship in this period was former Ba'thist Allawi, who in fact became a principal Saudi informant.[74] Like Iraqi Sunnis, Allawi and his secular Shi'a associates also tended to perceive that Iran was intervening in the country and attributed Iranian loyalty to the Iraqi Shi'a Islamists, as will be explored below. Thus, in gathering information from Allawi, the Saudis also relied upon a source whose bias matched their own.

The Saudis' Perception of the Situation in Iraq

Following the invasion, Saudi leaders frequently argued that the U.S., by virtue of the policies it was implementing in Iraq, had handed the country to Iran on a golden platter,[75] and this phrase effectively sums up their perception of what was taking place in Iraq in the wake of Saddam Hussein's overthrow. Indeed, in an interview, Robert Jordan, the U.S. ambassador to Saudi Arabia at the time of the invasion of Iraq, observed that Saudi leaders began to assert that the U.S. had handed Iraq to Iran "on a silver platter" before he left his posting in Riyadh in October 2003.[76] An Iraqi diplomat who later interacted with the Saudi leadership observed in an interview that they also frequently used this phrase when speaking to Iraqis.[77] In fact, Prince Turki al-Faisal, the former Saudi intelligence chief who also served as Saudi ambassador to the UK from 2003 to 2005 and to the U.S. from 2005 to 2007, used this phrase in an interview with me.[78] It should be pointed out that Saudi leaders would say both "silver platter" and "golden platter"; "silver" is employed in the English expression, whereas "golden" is employed in a similar Arabic expression. The Iraqi diplomat, for instance, noted that Saudi leaders would say "golden platter" in Arabic.[79]

Indeed, according to Ambassador Jordan, the Saudis had a sense of "bewilderment" at the policies Bremer implemented in 2003, questioning in particular de-Ba'thification and the dissolution of the army.[80] For his part, Prince Turki called the formation of the Iraqi Governing Council according to an ethno-sectarian formula "the worst idea ever."[81] The Saudis had counseled the Americans to preserve Saddam Hussein's regime, as well as Iraq's Sunni Arab power structure, in order to prevent the creation of a vacuum that Iran could exploit. They were then stunned, albeit powerless, when the Americans disregarded their advice entirely.

Implicit in the Saudis' view that the U.S. handed Iraq to Iran on a golden platter is the assumption that Iran retained expansionist intentions—that U.S. policy was simply providing Iran the opportunity to carry out its hegemonic objectives. In fact, an internal Saudi Foreign Ministry document, released by WikiLeaks, later made this implicit assumption explicit, assessing that Iran's post-2003 agenda in the Gulf consisted of imposing "its hegemony on the region by promoting Shi'a thought"; according to a Saudi source close to the ruling elite, "Shi'a thought" is synonymous with *wilayat al-faqih*.[82] Thus, consistent with the beliefs that had been promulgated among the Saudi leadership since the Iranian Revolution, Saudi leaders continued to assess that Iranian intentions in the post-2003 period were expansionist.

The fate of a Saudi field hospital operating in Baghdad in 2003 exemplifies how the Saudi leadership perceived the situation in Iraq at this time. Even if the Saudi leadership were troubled by the policies the U.S. was implementing in Iraq that year, they took significant steps to help alleviate the humanitarian situation there, most notably deploying a mobile field hospital to Baghdad in late April.[83] In December, however, the Saudis were asked to withdraw their hospital from Iraq for the stated reason that Iraqi hospitals had begun to operate normally.[84] According to Bremer, the previous month Saudi employees of the hospital had been detained by coalition forces after they were caught photographing coalition facilities, and other hospital employees had taken similar, but unidentified, actions that were perceived to compromise the security of coalition forces.[85] Similarly, an analyst writing in the Gulf Arab journal *Ara hawla-l-Khalij* in 2005 noted that the Saudi government had been compelled to withdraw the hospital because of "American pressure and the detention of a number of Saudi nurses working in the hospital."[86] By contrast, in the recollection of Saudi sources interviewed for this book, the withdrawal of the Saudi hospital stemmed from Iran's opposition to the Saudi presence in Iraq. According to a Saudi who has served as an adviser to the government on Gulf affairs, the "extreme Shi'a"—those who were considered to be close to Iran—pushed the Americans "to get rid of" the hospital. He gave the example of Ahmad Chalabi, a longstanding member of the Iraqi opposition to Saddam who had developed close ties to both the American and Iranian governments.[87] Furthermore, in Prince Turki's recollection, the hospital was withdrawn because it "came under threat" from the Iranians; he recounted that the hospital was specifically targeted by Iranian-backed militias because "it was doing such a wonderful job" addressing the humanitarian situation in Baghdad. When asked whether he thought the Iranians were deliberately trying to exclude the Saudi presence from Iraq, he responded, "Absolutely."[88]

While it is possible that the Saudi field hospital became a target of an Iranian-backed militia like Badr, it is also possible that Prince Turki was misrepresenting, or simply misremembering, what had actually happened. Indeed, whatever in fact took place, his and the Saudi foreign policy adviser's recollections appear consistent with how a perceiver processes information through the lens of an enemy image—namely that the perceived enemy has the will and ability to carry out deliberate actions to harm him. Furthermore, their recollections are illustrative of the Saudi leadership's perception that the U.S. was allowing Iran to become predominant in Iraq in the aftermath of Saddam Hussein's overthrow, to the point of deliberately excluding a Saudi presence there.

Moreover, their recollections point to a tendency to discount variation between the Iranian regime and Iraqi Shiʿa groups. For his part, the Saudi foreign policy adviser, in his account of the field hospital's fate, conveyed the sense that Iraqis perceived to be close to Iran were manipulating the Americans to carry out Iran's bidding. While Iraqis such as Chalabi may have indeed been manipulating the Americans at this time, it is not at all clear that they were carrying out Iran's agenda as opposed to their own.[89] Moreover, in the view of Prince Turki, Iran at this time was generally "push[ing] back into Iraq" those Iraqis previously based in Iran who, he said, "were very much under the control of the Iranians."[90] Again, this view obscured how the interests of Iran, on the one hand, and Iraqi Shiʿa leaders, on the other, could not only converge, but also diverge. Indeed, in Prince Turki's account, Iraqi Shiʿa figures, at least those previously based in Iran, appeared as little more than puppets. It should also be observed that by associating Khomeini's doctrine of *wilayat al-faqih* with some monolithic Shiʿa thought, as mentioned above, the Saudi foreign policy establishment demonstrated an inclination to overlook the considerable diversity within the Shiʿa faith, which they essentially equated with Iran. Such examples point to a tendency among the Saudis to portray the Arab Shiʿa as loyal to Iran, consistent with the stereotype that is widespread among Sunni Arabs.

In general, human beings have a tendency to form conclusions quickly, long before adequate information exists to support them, because, at bottom, we dislike uncertainty.[91] Iran began to establish a presence in Iraq in 2003, although its motivation behind doing so—whether it intended simply to defend its interests, aimed to exert hegemony, or had other objectives along this continuum—was highly ambiguous. Nevertheless, instead of acknowledging the inherent ambiguity of the situation and waiting for more information that might clarify it, the Saudi leadership formed a conclusion in 2003. They assessed that due to the deficiencies of U.S. policy, Iran was gaining the upper hand in post-Saddam Iraq, which assumed, consistent with their preexisting beliefs, that Iran had expansionist intentions. Their view also tended to discount the particular interests of Iraqi Shiʿa groups. The danger, however, in forming a conclusion too quickly is that it becomes a lens through which subsequent information is filtered; additional information is generally used to bolster the conclusion already formed, rather than to challenge or add nuance to it.[92] Indeed, the Saudi leadership would never deviate from their belief that Iran was taking steps to exert hegemony over Iraq, even though there were plausible alternative explanations for Iran's behavior. In turn, their rigid beliefs about Iran would shape their perception of the new Iraq, and contribute to their decision not to engage with the first permanent post-Saddam government under Maliki's leadership.

Mounting Resistance

The situation in Iraq was ambiguous, and only becoming more so because of the increasingly complex landscape of Iraqi resistance. In August 2003, three large-scale suicide attacks took place in the country, which were later attributed to a group led by Abu Musʿab al-Zarqawi. The first two struck the Jordanian embassy and the UN headquarters in Iraq, and the third and most devastating took place in Najaf, killing about one hundred people including Muhammad Baqr al-Hakim of SCIRI.[93] Thereafter, al-Hakim's brother, Abd al-Aziz al-Hakim, took leadership of the organization. Then, in the first months of 2004, even more devastating suicide bombings struck Irbil, the capital of Iraqi Kurdistan, and the Shiʿa shrine cities of Karbala and Kazimain during the Shiʿa holiday of Ashura.[94] In February 2004, the CPA released a letter that had been recovered in a raid, attributed to Zarqawi and addressed to the Al-Qaʿida leadership in Afghanistan. In it, Zarqawi singled out the Shiʿa as "the most evil of mankind" for siding with the occupation against Iraqi Sunnis, and elucidated his strategy, namely to launch a wholesale attack on the Shiʿa in order to foment a sectarian civil war, thereby forcing the occupation authorities to withdraw from Iraq and allowing the Sunnis to retake power in Baghdad.[95] In 2004, Zarqawi affiliated with the global Al-Qaʿida network, renaming his organization Al-Qaʿida in Iraq. Most of the jihadists fighting with Zarqawi were foreign fighters who traveled to Iraq from across the Arab world, many of them Saudi citizens.[96]

In spring 2004, the coalition forces initiated significant confrontations with both the Sunni insurgency and the Sadrists. That April, in response to the murder of four American civilian security guards in Fallujah, a Sunni Arab town 50 kilometers west of Baghdad then the epicenter of the insurgency, U.S. Marines initiated an assault on the city, which, within days, had killed over 600 Iraqis without actually undermining insurgent control.[97] That same month, the CPA announced that an arrest warrant had been issued for Muqtada al-Sadr in connection to the murder of Abd al-Majid al-Khoei. In response, Muqtada called for a revolt against the occupation, and thousands of Sadrists attacked coalition forces and took control of key government buildings in Sadr City and Shiʿa towns of the south.[98]

By May, the coalition had mostly regained control of these areas, except for Najaf, where Muqtada had sought refuge. Some of the Shiʿa members of the Iraqi Governing Council, in cooperation with Grand Ayatollah Sistani, sought to mediate a solution to the crisis, striking an agreement whereby Muqtada would withdraw from Najaf but his militia would not be disarmed.[99] Nevertheless, this ceasefire broke down in August after U.S. troops surrounded Muqtada's home in Najaf in a show of force. Throughout August, the Sadrist militias clashed with coalition forces in Najaf, Sadr City, and other Sadrist strongholds of the south. At the end of the month, Grand Ayatollah Sistani intervened to broker another compromise solution: as in May, the Sadrists agreed to withdraw from Najaf in exchange for retaining their weapons.[100]

According to findings by the U.S.-led coalition, the Sadrists, and particularly a faction led by Qais al-Khazali, an intra-Sadrist rival of Muqtada, chose to deepen their connections to the Iranian Revolutionary Guards following the failure of the two Sadrist uprisings. Al-Khazali would be captured by coalition forces in 2007 and interrogated extensively. Based on the information he conveyed to the coalition, al-Khazali sought the assistance of Qasim Soleimani of the Revolutionary Guards' Qods Force because he desired to fight in a more disciplined manner.[101] Thereafter, according to American sources, the Qods Force would begin to train special Sadrist units in Iran. These units were known as "Special Groups," with one of the most significant special groups being al-Khazali's faction, Asa'ib Ahl al-Haq.[102] In addition, the Revolutionary Guards began to provide a steady supply of weapons to the Sadrists, most significantly a sophisticated device known as an explosively formed penetrator (EFP), which the Sadrists deployed as roadside bombs against the coalition from 2004.[103] While an average of five EFP attacks per month took place against coalition forces through April 2005, monthly EFP attacks jumped significantly in the second half of 2005, from twenty in June to fifty-eight in October.[104]

That Iran supported the Sadrists against the U.S.-led coalition does not fundamentally bring greater clarity to the nature of its intentions at this time. It strongly appears that Iran wanted the coalition to withdraw from Iraq. However, it is unclear whether it desired the coalition's withdrawal because it felt threatened by the presence of this massive U.S. military force, or because this force prevented it from exerting its own control over Iraq. Both scenarios can be argued based on the available data. This point is made simply to point out that there was no definitive answer to the nature of Iran's intentions toward Iraq in the period after 2003, and in the absence of a definitive answer, observers' perceptions were mostly a function of their preexisting beliefs about Iran.

A Brief Return of the Old Order and the January 2005 Elections

In 2004, the CPA transferred governing authority to a new Iraqi government. In late 2003, the CPA and the Iraqi Governing Council had agreed on a timeline for the power transfer: an appointed interim government would be inaugurated in June 2004, elections would be held by January 2005 for a transitional government that would oversee the drafting of a constitution, and finally, parliamentary elections would take place by December 2005 for Iraq's first permanent post-Saddam government. During the transition, the Bush administration would compel the Iraqis to stick to this timeline, resisting calls that would be made to delay the process.

The Interim Government of 2004 would be broadly reflective of Iraq's pre-2003 political order, albeit now with a secular Shi'i—Allawi—at the helm. Composed of a number of former Ba'thist officials, the Allawi government sought to reconcile the Iraqis who felt aggrieved by the overthrow of Saddam, while reintegrating Iraq into the Arab fold and explicitly distancing it from Iran. Indeed, the rhetoric of leading members of the Interim Government sought to reinforce the symbolic boundary between an Arab Iraq and a Persian Iran, which had been established by Iraq's successive twentieth-century regimes. Nevertheless, a Shi'a Islamist political coalition, backed by Iran, would prevail in Iraq's first free elections of January 2005. For those who had a preference for Iraq's old order, which included the leaderships of most of the Arab states, this Shiʻa Islamist coalition appeared not to be a member of the Arab ingroup, but of an Iranian, or even Persian, outgroup. Indeed, it appeared that for those who were partisan to the old order, the emergence of Shiʻa Islamist power in Baghdad was so peculiar that many could not explain it except by characterizing it as an Iranian creation.

In spring 2004, the CPA, in conjunction with the UN, nominated members of the Interim Government, which was inaugurated on 28 June. It was decided that the premiership would be held by a member of the majority Shiʻa community, and Allawi, the candidate most acceptable to the Iraqi Governing Council's Sunni and Shiʻa members, was appointed to the post.[105] Meanwhile, a Sunni Arab was appointed to the presidency, a ceremonial post, while a Shiʻi and a Kurd took the two vice president positions.

Overall, the Interim Government's composition reflected the U.S. objective to establish a new, secular order that reflected Iraq's ethno-sectarian diversity, while reconciling the country's Sunni Arabs. Thus, while the Shiʻa Islamists had been prominently represented on the Iraqi Governing Council, only two took positions in the Interim Government: al-Jaʻfari of Daʻwa became one of the two vice presidents, and Adel Abd al-Mahdi, a lay member of SCIRI and close confidant to the Hakim family, became minister of finance. Meanwhile, the formation of the Interim Government coincided with amendments made by Bremer to the de-Baʻthification policy. The previous fall, Bremer had appointed Iraqi Governing Council member Ahmad Chalabi to chair a commission to implement the de-Baʻthification policy. However, Chalabi's commission, composed mostly of returning Iraqi exiles, then dismissed not only high-ranking Baʻthist officials, as Bremer had intended, but low-ranking ones as well, in an effort to uproot Iraq's pre-2003 political order.[106] In April 2004, Bremer, seeking to reverse the purges conducted by Chalabi's commission, announced that dismissed Ba'thist officials who could prove they had joined the party for pragmatic career considerations would be reinstated in their posts. This modification also allowed the CPA to appoint former Ba'thists, many of whom were close associates of Allawi, to the Interim Government.[107]

Furthermore, upon taking the premiership, Allawi actually sought to suspend the efforts of the de-Ba'thification commission and implement a process awkwardly named de-de-Ba'thification to reintegrate some 15,000 officials who had been dismissed. He also proposed a plan to offer amnesty to Sunni insurgents, with the exception of more extreme members of the insurgency such as those fighting with Al-Qa'ida in Iraq.[108] On the regional level, Allawi sought to align the Interim Government with the broader Arab world. In fact, for years Allawi had been well known to the political elites of the Sunni Arab countries. During the Gulf War, he had formed an opposition group, the Iraqi National Accord, with financial assistance from Saudi Arabia.[109] Allawi had particularly close relations with the Jordanian regime as in the mid-1990s he had been based in Amman, where his group had attempted to stage a coup against Saddam Hussein with the assistance of Jordan and Saudi Arabia, as well as the U.S. and Britain.[110] With his close ties to the Arab states, Allawi embarked on a two-week tour that took him across the Arab world only three weeks after taking office, with the aim of reintegrating Iraq into the Arab fold.[111]

By contrast, the Interim Government's attitude toward Iran was hostile. The Iranian regime had previously sought to establish strong ties to the Iraqi Governing Council, many of whose members had longstanding connections to Iran. However, Prime Minister Allawi, according to his cousin Ali Allawi, was "a foe, and perceived to be a foe, of Iran, and frequently decried what he saw as dangerous meddling in Iraqi affairs."[112] Raad Alkadiri, another close observer of Iraq's political scene, similarly noted in an interview that Allawi could be "virulent" in his anti-Iran rhetoric.[113] While Allawi himself typically reserved this rhetoric for private audiences, the Interim Government in fact launched a public attack on Iran and its alleged machinations in Iraq only weeks after it took power. On 20 July, Defense Minister Hazim al-Sha'lan, an associate of Allawi who was also a secular Shi'i former Ba'thist, asserted, without providing details, that Iran's presence inside Iraq was "extensive and unprecedented"; he further alleged that Iranian spies, having penetrated the state, were seeking to "to upset the situation [in Iraq] socially and politically."[114] A week later, al-Sha'lan proclaimed that Iran was Iraq's "first enemy."[115]

The perception, already in existence, that Iran was interfering in Iraq was significantly amplified as a result of al-Sha'lan's statements, even though there was little evidence that actually substantiated such anti-Iranian accusations.[116] While Iraqis, especially Sunni Arab Iraqis, may have genuinely feared Iranian interference, it can also be argued that many among them more implicitly feared Shi'a empowerment; indeed, it was reported that Sunni Arabs, as well as Arabized Sunni Turkmen, generally exhibited "a palpable element of fear" that Iraq's Arab identity was eroding as the Shi'a took positions of power in the country.[117] This view could be attributed not only to Sunni Arabs and Turkmen, but more broadly to those who could be called the partisans of the old order, which also included Shi'a figures like Allawi and al-Sha'lan. From this perspective, al-Sha'lan's statements above appeared designed to establish a symbolic boundary between the partisans of the old order, who saw themselves as the Arabs of Iraq, and those who sought to establish a new order, as the Shi'a Islamists aimed to do, who were relegated to an Iranian outgroup. The creation of such a boundary naturally served to bolster the cohesion of the ingroup, and perhaps secular Shi'a figures like al-Sha'lan were particularly inclined, implicitly, to reinforce this boundary to prove their membership of the ingroup. Indeed, throughout this period secular Shiʿa figures appeared somewhat threatened by the emergence of Shiʿa Islamist power, seeking to disassociate themselves from the Islamists.[118] Regardless, whatever al-Shaʿlan's particular motivation behind drawing the symbolic boundary between the partisans of the old and new orders, in doing so he implicitly cast doubt on the Arabism of the Iraqi Shiʿa, as successive twentieth-century regimes had done.

For their part, Shiʿa Islamist leaders had acquiesced in their marginalization by the CPA during the appointment process for the Interim Government because their strategy to attain political power consisted of contesting the January 2005 elections. If they did well in the elections, they could then dominate the constitution-drafting process, which would be overseen by the Transitional Government. To maximize their prospects in the elections, the preponderance of Shiʿa candidates announced on 8 December the creation of a single electoral list, the United Iraqi Alliance (UIA), which was endorsed by Sistani. Iran also supported the creation of the UIA, reportedly providing it with substantial funding prior to the elections.[119] Composed of a range of Shiʿa Islamist parties, the UIA had also approached Allawi, but he chose instead to form his own secular, non-sectarian electoral list.[120] In the lead-up to the elections, the Shiʿa religious establishment spearheaded a comprehensive campaign to encourage Shiʿa Iraqis to vote.[121]

The Sunni Arab community, by contrast, would largely heed a call to boycott the elections. In November, U.S. forces launched a second assault on the city of Fallujah, and during seven weeks of intense fighting, 1,200 insurgents and some 6,000 civilians, in addition to 92 U.S. troops, were killed.[122] During the battle, al-Dari of the insurgent-sympathizing AMS called for a boycott of the elections, and furthermore in January, Al-Qaʿida in Iraq proclaimed that it would target Iraqis participating in the electoral process.[123] Thus, on 30 January 2005, the day of the election, the vast majority of Iraq's Sunni Arabs stayed away from the polls, the result of both their feelings of alienation and intimidation by Al-Qaʿida.[124]

Meanwhile, in fall 2004, members of the Interim Government continued to make public allegations of Iranian interference in Iraq. In October, Iraq's new intelligence chief, Muhammad al-Shahwani, another associate of Prime Minister Allawi, announced that eighteen of his agents had been killed in the previous month: ten, he alleged, by the Badr Brigade "on orders from Iran," and the rest by Al-Qaʿida, which, he speculated, had received funding from Iran.[125] Whether the Iranian regime in fact had a hand in the murder of al-Shahwani's agents, or al-Shahwani erroneously perceived this to be the case, or he was simply lying to create a public perception inimical to Iran—or some combination thereof—are open questions that reflect the inherent ambiguity of this period in Iraq. Whatever the case, as the January 2005 elections approached, Interim Government officials increasingly accused Iran of attempting to influence the upcoming vote. In December, Defense Minister al-Shaʿlan called the UIA "an Iranian list," and alleged that the Iranians "are fighting us because we want to build freedom and democracy and they want to build an Islamic dictatorship and have turbaned clerics to rule in Iraq."[126] The Sunni Arab president, Ghazi al-Yawar, asserted that the Iranian regime was pouring money into the election in order to establish a Shiʿa theocracy in Baghdad.[127]

In characterizing the UIA as an Iranian creation, these Interim Government officials aimed primarily to advance ahead of it in the upcoming polls.[128] While it seems natural that Allawi and his associates would purposefully paint their political rivals in a negative light ahead of the elections, Alkadiri pointed out in an interview that Allawi "truly believe[d]" his anti-Iranian Arab nationalist rhetoric.[129] As highlighted above, members of the Interim Government were naturally motivated to perceive their Shiʿa Islamist rivals negatively—for instance, as Iranian loyalists, not Iraqi patriots—because they had an interest in holding this belief. Whatever the case, the anti-Iranian claims being propagated inside Iraq were repeated to such an extent at this time that they snowballed into a widespread rumor that Iran was infiltrating a huge number of its citizens—a million or more—into Iraq to vote in the upcoming elections. This rumor was able to gain traction among many Iraqis, as the explosion of human traffic across the Iran–Iraq border appeared to be compelling evidence.[130] In fact, this rumor became so widespread that it even penetrated the ruling elites of the Sunni Arab world: notably, Abdullah II of Jordan recounted to the *Washington Post* in December 2004 that one million Iranians, with the support of their government, had entered Iraq to vote in the elections.[131] To U.S. officials based in Amman, Abdullah II in fact said that one million was a "conservative" estimate, and claimed that Iran was aiming to establish a client state in Iraq.[132]

Jordan had been a close ally of Iraq during its war with Iran, and further statements made by the Jordanian leadership at this time reflected the anti-Persian rhetoric Saddam Hussein's regime had propagated during that war. Indeed, the allegation that an Iranian infiltration had taken place to influence the Iraqi elections echoed the Baʿthists' propaganda of the 1980s, which contended that a Persian enemy had historically fueled internal conspiracies inside Iraq. In fact, Jordanian Foreign Minister Hani al-Mulqi publicly expounded on this Persian–Arab theme in the weeks prior to the Iraqi election. In a long interview with the pan-Arab newspaper *al-Quds al-Arabi*, published on 31 December, al-Mulqi accused Iran of "trying to meddle" with Iraq's Arabism through manipulation of the upcoming vote. Al-Mulqi said he envisioned two possible outcomes for the elections: either Sunni Arabs would forgo their boycott and the elections would produce an Iraqi government that reflected Iraq's "Arab identity," or else "a religious Shi'i regime with a Persian flavor" would emerge, which would in turn enhance Iran's regional position. Al-Mulqi noted that the Jordanian government was therefore actively encouraging Sunni Arabs to forgo the boycott, and he concluded:

> I think the next four weeks will be very important in writing the history of the region. When we suspected Iranian attempts to interfere, we had to speak out and warn. We repeat: It is in no-one's interest to have an anti-Arab Persian Shi'i religious regime in Iraq.[133]

In this view, the Shi'a Islamists of the UIA were not members of the Arab ingroup, or even political actors in their own right. Rather, in a reflection of twentieth-century Ba'thist discourse, they were seen as little more than the tools of a Persian regime that continued to harbor ill intent toward the Arabs of Iraq.

Nevertheless, on 30 January, with the Shi'a united and the Sunni Arabs boycotting, the UIA dominated the elections, winning 51 percent, or 140 of the 275 seats in the Transitional Government. Besides the UIA, the other prominent electoral blocs consisted of Allawi's Iraqi List and the Kurdistan Alliance, formed by the two principal Kurdish parties, the Kurdistan Democratic Party (KDP) and the Patriotic Union of Kurdistan (PUK). The Iraqi List and the Kurdistan Alliance won, respectively, 40 and 75 seats, or 15 and 27 percent, of the total. The remaining twenty seats went to nine different groups that reflected Iraq's diverse population: Sunni, Shi'a, Kurdish, Turkmen, Christian, and officially non-sectarian.[134] Of the 275 parliamentary seats, only 16 were occupied by Sunni Arabs.[135] Thus the Shi'a voted overwhelmingly for the Shi'a slate and the Kurds for the Kurdish one, while most Sunnis rejected the entire process, revealing that identity politics had been the critical determinant in the outcome of Iraq's first free elections. In this atmosphere, Allawi's slate had not been able to gain traction beyond a small minority of the population.

As for the Saudis, in the aftermath of the elections they argued to the Americans that the UIA electoral victory had been the result of the purported infiltration of Iranians into Iraq, claiming that some five million Iranians were present in Iraq, many of whom had voted in the elections.[136] As one former U.S. official recounted in an interview, the Saudi leadership insisted in meetings with their U.S. counterparts that the Iraqi Shi'a had had "their population flooded by millions of Iranians" in order to win the elections.[137] Another former U.S. official similarly recalled, "The Saudis, particularly the royal family and King Abdullah, had this image of Iraq being flooded with Iranians. That the Iranians came and voted in the elections ... and I think King Abdullah genuinely believed that."[138] This claim that the Saudi leadership believed some five million Iranians had infiltrated Iraq and had voted in the elections was repeated in many of my interviews with American officials, as well as with some Iraqi officials. Meanwhile, a Saudi source who has advised the government on Gulf affairs appeared reluctant to speak about this episode; while he claimed in an interview that a "huge" number of Iranians had entered Iraq after the opening of the Iran–Iraq border, when he was then asked if he was concerned some of them had voted in the elections, he declined to respond.[139] Nevertheless, it appears that the Saudi leadership continued to genuinely believe that Iranian voters had participated in the 2005 elections. In 2008, ahead of a new round of Iraqi elections, Foreign Minister Saud al-Faisal would exhort his U.S. counterparts to "make sure all the Iranians in southern Iraq do not vote like they did last time," and even proposed the use of an Arabic language test for voters to prove their Iraqi nationality.[140]

According to an American diplomat, Saudi leaders believed that the UIA had needed the assistance of Iranian voters to win the Iraqi elections because they were skeptical that the Shi'a constituted a majority of the Iraqi population.[141] This claim is very plausible. As an example, the Jordanian ruling elite seemed to believe that Iraqi Sunnis, not Shi'a, constituted the majority; as Jordanian Foreign Minister al-Mulqi had asserted in the press prior to the elections, "It is not true that Shi'is constitute a majority. Rather, the Arab Sunnis, the Kurdish Sunnis and the Turkomans constitute a majority of the composition of the Iraqi people."[142] Another former Jordanian official clarified in an interview that prior to 2003, "People always said the Sunnis, between the Arabs and the Kurds, formed 60 percent, and the Shiites 40 percent."[143] It seems that this view was widespread in Saudi Arabia as well.[144] Nevertheless, in the opinion of a Saudi source close to the ruling elite, it ultimately did not matter for the Saudi leadership whether the Shi'a constituted a majority of the Iraqi people or not. According to this source, democratic formulas were not relevant to the Saudi leadership's conception of politics: in their view, the Sunnis were supposed to be in power in the Arab world.[145]

In the twentieth century, a particular image of Iraq had been constructed in the broader Arab world: secular, Arab nationalist, and under the leadership of Sunni Arabs, even if those Sunni Arabs never explicitly advertised their sectarian identity. While Iraq was still seen to be a country of great diversity, this version of Iraq was intended to obscure the nature and extent of its diversity. Nevertheless, a new order would begin to establish itself following the January 2005 elections, which would be Shi'a-dominated and have a substantial role for the Shi'a religious establishment. Iraq's significant Kurdish minority would also be assertive in the new system. For many Arabs, both inside and outside the country, this new Iraq appeared alien, and despite the fact that the Iraqi Shi'a are mostly Arab, it seemed less Arab—even anti-Arab. As monstrous as Saddam Hussein had been, his Iraq had been seen as a member of the Arab family. For the moment, this new Iraq was not.

The Transitional Government and Descent into Civil War

The Transitional Government was dominated by the UIA, and whereas the Interim Government had oriented itself to the Arab world and distanced itself from Iran, the Transitional Government pursued close relations with Iran while appearing cold to the Arab countries. The Transitional Government's regional orientation only reinforced its image as belonging to an Iranian outgroup. Iraqi Sunni Arabs felt increasingly marginalized during this period, and indeed inter-sectarian violence escalated following the January 2005 elections to the extent that Baghdad found itself in a civil war. This section explores these developments before assessing, in the next and final section of this chapter, the Saudi leadership's perception of the new Iraqi order that was beginning to take shape in 2005.

The three principal parliamentary blocs of the Transitional Government—the UIA, the Kurdistan Alliance, and Allawi's Iraqi List—spent three months negotiating positions in the new government, and thus it was not sworn in until 3 May. Al-Ja'fari of the Da'wa Party took the premiership, while a Kurd, Jalal Talabani, leader of the PUK, became president. Al-Ja'fari was a compromise candidate: SCIRI, the dominant faction in the UIA, had originally nominated SCIRI member Adel Abd al-Mahdi, but his candidacy was opposed by the UIA's Sadrist faction.[146] Nevertheless, Abd al-Mahdi took one of the two vice president positions, and the second vice president position went to Ghazi al-Yawar, previously president in the Interim Government. Meanwhile, Allawi ultimately chose not to serve in the new government in any capacity, thus forgoing a cabinet position. Observers surmised that what Allawi had truly desired was to remain prime minister, not to take a subordinate post.[147] In sum, the new cabinet consisted of eighteen Shiʿa, nine Sunnis, eight Kurds, and one Christian.[148]

Beyond the premiership, the UIA prioritized obtaining control of the security services.[149] The CPA had begun the reconstitution of Iraq's security apparatus, a process that then accelerated under the Interim Government. During the formation period for the Transitional Government in spring 2005, SCIRI obtained control of the Ministry of Interior, which was given to SCIRI member and former Badr commander Bayan Jabr. As interior minister, Jabr integrated the Badr Brigade, estimated at 16,000 men, en masse into the security services under his control.[150] Meanwhile, the Ministry of Defense had gone to Saʿdun al-Dulaimi, a Sunni Arab former army officer who had returned to Iraq after twenty years of exile. Al-Dulaimi appeared willing to carry out the UIA agenda, and under his leadership the Ministry of Defense became populated with Kurdish and Shiʿa officers.[151]

On a regional level, the Transitional Government tilted toward Iran and away from the Arab states. Its orientation likely reflected the inflamed sectarian sentiment of this period rather than an inherent animus toward the Arab world; after all, Arab leaders, most overtly the Jordanian leadership, had recently been sounding an alarm over the Shiʿa Islamists' political ascendance, which presumably dampened the Shiʿa Islamists' enthusiasm for engagement. Other grievances evinced by the Iraqi Shiʿa toward the wider Arab world at this time included the Arab states' historic disregard for their plight under Saddam, as well as the Arab states' silence regarding the terror campaign being perpetrated against them by Sunni suicide bombers.[152] In this context, al-Jaʿfari only visited two Arab countries during his brief premiership: Kuwait in June to discuss economic and reconstruction assistance, and Saudi Arabia in November to request an expanded quota of Hajj visas for Iraq.[153] By contrast, the new government's relations with Iran appeared very warm. Two weeks after the government was sworn in, Iranian Foreign Minister Kamal Kharazi made a "landmark visit" to Iraq, being the highest-ranking Iranian official to visit since the fall of Saddam.[154] In early July, Defense Minister al-Dulaimi visited Iran, in his words, "to turn a painful page and to open another" in the relationship between the two countries.[155] Most significantly, al-Dulaimi apologized for Saddam's invasion of Iran in 1980, and announced that Iraqi soil would not be used to attack its neighbors—in effect, a pledge that the United States would not be allowed to use Iraq as a base to strike Iran.[156] A week later, Prime Minister al-Ja'fari led a delegation of ten cabinet ministers to Tehran. During the visit, the two governments announced the formation of a number of joint committees, and al-Ja'fari laid a wreath at the tomb of Ayatollah Khomeini.[157]

Meanwhile, violent conflict between Sunni and Shi'a Iraqis escalated in the wake of the January elections. On 18 February, the day before Ashura, suicide bombers attacked two Shi'a mosques in Baghdad, killing twenty-eight, and, at the end of that month, suicide bombers killed 125 more people at a police recruiting station in the Shi'a town of Hilla, constituting the single deadliest attack in post-invasion Iraq to that date.[158] In total, some 130 suicide attacks were carried out in the first six months of 2005, mostly targeting Shi'a neighborhoods.[159] Whatever the Badr Brigade's role in assassinating members of the former regime had been prior to 2005, in response to these suicide attacks, the Ministry of Interior's Special Police Commandos, populated by Badr personnel, began to act as "a major sectarian death squad" that targeted Sunnis.[160] Seeking to cleanse mixed Sunni–Shi'a neighborhoods of Sunni residents, these Ministry of Interior units kidnapped and murdered Sunni men in an effort to intimidate, and thereby expel, the Sunni population.[161] Of the Special Police Commandos, the Second Commando Brigade, more commonly known as the Wolf Brigade, became widely feared among Sunnis.[162]

Sunni–Shi'a violence escalated in the spring of 2005 to the extent that Baghdad and its environs had descended into civil war.[163] The Sunni insurgency, at this point estimated to comprise between 20,000 and 50,000 fighters, had begun to consolidate into four principal groups: the Islamic Army in Iraq, the Partisans of the Sunna Army, the Islamic Front of the Iraqi Resistance, and Al-Qa'ida in Iraq. These groups each adhered to radical Salafi ideologies and increasingly used sectarian discourse to justify their violence.[164] For its part, the Wolf Brigade became ever more aggressive over the course of 2005. In May, al-Dari of the AMS accused it of assassinating fifteen prominent Sunni religious scholars.[165] In the fall, the U.S.-led coalition received an increasing number of reports of the Wolf Brigade's abuses,[166] and that November coalition forces uncovered a "secret torture center" in the basement of a Ministry of Interior building in a Baghdad suburb, apparently run by Badr personnel affiliated with the Wolf Brigade, in which 173 mostly Sunni Arabs had been detained and brutally treated.[167]

Meanwhile, the Transitional Government's primary mandate was to oversee the drafting of a new constitution, a process dominated by the government's Shi'a and Kurdish members. The Shi'a and Kurds in effect constituted the partisans of the new order, and during the constitution-drafting process they appeared more intent to consolidate the new order than to assuage the grievances of their Sunni Arab compatriots. Indeed, Sunni Arabs had deep misgivings about the draft constitution, which was officially presented in August 2005. Their reservations centered in particular on the questions of federalism, de-Ba'thification, and Iraq's identity. Regarding federalism, the draft provided for significant decentralization, allowing any province other than Baghdad to join with any other province to form a region that would have significant autonomy. Of Iraq's communities, the Kurds most strongly advocated for this federal system, although many Shi'a, most notably Abd al-Aziz al-Hakim of SCIRI, also embraced it. By contrast, Sunni Arabs regarded federalism as a Kurdish–Shi'a plot to carve up the country. Furthermore, the draft constitution outlawed the so-called "Saddamist Ba'th," but as with Bremer's original de-Ba'thification order, the Sunni Arabs regarded this blanket prohibition as a means to marginalize them in the new political system.[168] Finally, with regard to Iraq's identity, the draft stated that the Arab people of Iraq "are part of the Arab nation," without specifying the country as a whole, which had been a Shi'a concession to a Kurdish demand.[169] For their part, Iraq's Arab neighbors appeared most outraged over this final issue. GCC Secretary-General Abd al-Rahman bin Hamad al-Attiya called the draft constitution "catastrophic" for its failure to identity Iraq as an Arab state, while Arab League Secretary-General Amr Musa called it "extremely dangerous."[170] Iraqi Sunni Arabs, having recognized that their boycott of the January 2005 elections had been an enormous mistake, voted in large numbers against the draft in the constitutional referendum of October 2005. Their numbers, however, were not enough to block its adoption, and the alienation felt by Iraq's Sunni Arabs only increased.[171]

Whereas the domestic initiatives and regional orientation of the Interim Government had been reflective of Iraq's old order, the Transitional Government moved in the opposite extreme. It established close ties to Iran, filled the security services with a paramilitary force that had been established by Iran, and oversaw the promulgation of a constitution that for many appeared to undermine Iraq's Arab identity and territorial unity. Thus, its actions only fueled the perception among Sunni Arabs that the new Shi'a-led Iraq would be a member of the Iranian outgroup.

A NEW IRAQ WITH A PERSIAN FLAVOR?

The Saudi Leadership's View of the New Iraq

In Saudi Arabia, meanwhile, the leadership had become convinced that Iran was becoming predominant in Iraq, and they also exhibited a deep sense of grievance toward the Bush administration and bafflement at its policies. U.S. and Iraqi officials, who themselves interacted with the Saudi leadership at this time, observed that the Saudis appeared to believe that the new Iraqi government was under some degree of Iranian tutelage.[172] Foreign Minister Saud al-Faisal himself articulated Saudi concerns in September 2005 to a private gathering at the Council on Foreign Relations in New York City. In Prince Saud's view, the Iranians were installing "their own people" and establishing militias in Iraq, all under the protection of the U.S.-led coalition; he declared to his American audience, "[W]e are handing the whole country over to Iran without reason."[173] Prince Saud's statement, which leaked to the press, elicited a rebuke from Iraqi Interior Minister Bayan Jabr, who memorably called the Saudi foreign minister a camel-riding Bedouin.[174] Moreover, in December 2005, Abdullah, who had finally become king in August following the death of the long-ailing Fahd, allowing him to formalize his dominance within the Saudi state,[175] expressed his view to U.S. officials in Riyadh. According to a U.S. diplomatic cable, King Abdullah "pulled no punches about ... his anger at developments in Iraq," and he argued, as recounted in the cable: "In the past ... the U.S., Saudi Arabia, and Saddam Hussein had agreed to fight Iran, to prevent Iranian infiltration in Iraq and the region. Now ... Iran has been presented with Iraq as a 'gift on a golden platter,'" using the phrase that by this point had become standard among Saudi leaders.[176]

In the evidence available from this period, Abdullah appeared deeply dismayed about the situation in Iraq, sharing Sunni Arab Iraqis' grievances over Saddam's overthrow. For instance, in an exchange with U.S. officials the king observed that, "Some people think that if Saddam were restored, there would be a return to civility," and comparing the present situation in Iraq to that under Saddam, he opined, "Now it appears worse, there is no justice, and not much hope."[177] Furthermore, Abdullah frequently expressed anger that the Bush administration had not listened to Saudi counsel. In spring 2007, Abdullah argued to U.S. officials, with reference to Iranian supremacy in Iraq: "I warned you about this ... I warned the president, the vice president, but your ears were blocked."[178] This statement attributed to Abdullah reveals the emotion he felt over what he saw as taking place in Iraq, namely that Iran had become empowered.

In 2005, a Saudi analyst, writing in the Gulf Arab journal *Ara hawla-l-Khalij*, elaborated a scenario in which the alignment of Iran and a Shi'a-led Iraq would threaten Saudi Arabia. According to the analyst, a "strategic alliance"—or even the "strategic integration"—of these two countries would transform Iran into a neighbor adjacent to Saudi Arabia, which would present "a serious threat" to the kingdom "on the political, economic, societal, and cultural levels."[179] Again, implicit in this vision, consistent with the beliefs prevalent within the Saudi leadership since 1979, was the notion that Iran actually bore malign intent toward Saudi Arabia. Nevertheless, the most revealing public testament of the Saudi government's attitude toward the ascendance of the Iraqi Shi'a came in an editorial penned by Jamil al-Hujailan, a former Saudi information minister and GCC secretary-general, in *al-Sharq al-Awsat* on the eve of Iraq's December 2005 elections. The thrust of al-Hujailan's editorial was that Iraq's Arabism was threatened by an empowered Iran. The first half of the editorial in fact recounted the history of Iran's 1979 revolution and the outbreak of the Iran–Iraq War. According to al-Hujailan, Saudi Arabia had stood with Saddam Hussein during that war not because it supported the Iraqi dictator, but because it had feared for Iraq's Arabism: "For the defeat of Arab Iraq," he wrote, "and its fall under Iranian military and political hegemony was for the Gulf countries something their interests and convictions repudiated."[180] Therefore, at the time of his writing, according to the former information minister, the Arabs had become astonished as the U.S. made repeated mistakes in Iraq, enabling Iran to strengthen its position there. As a result, he wrote, "voices were raised, inside and outside Iraq," including that of Prince Saud al-Faisal at the Council on Foreign Relations, "sounding the alarm of fear over the disappearance of its Arab face."[181]

Conclusion

On the heels of the 2003 invasion, Saudi leaders began to perceive that by virtue of the policies the Bush administration was implementing, which allowed the Shi'a community to take a position of power, the U.S. was handing Iraq to Iran. Implicit in the Saudis' view was an assumption, consistent with their preexisting beliefs, that Iran possessed hegemonic ambitions over Iraq, even though a closer examination reveals that Iran's intentions were actually very ambiguous in this period. More to the point, the Saudis' extreme view of Iranian intentions tended to obscure how the interests of the Iraqi Shi'a could diverge from those of Iran. Just as this chapter has explored the Saudis' perception of what was going on in Iraq following Saddam Hussein's overthrow, the next two examine King Abdullah's decision not to engage with the government of Maliki, who would take the Iraqi premiership in spring 2006. As will be shown, Maliki possessed a strong Arab identity, and while he was never anti-Iranian, neither was he warm toward the Islamic Republic. Nevertheless, King Abdullah would become—and remain—convinced that Maliki was an untrustworthy Iranian agent. In short, Abdullah's inaccurate view of Maliki was a natural consequence of the perception he had already formed of the new Iraq.

3

KING ABDULLAH AND NURI AL-MALIKI

Nuri al-Maliki, a longstanding member of the Da'wa Party, took the Iraqi premiership in spring 2006, and he visited Saudi Arabia that summer on his first trip abroad as prime minister. Soon after Maliki's trip, King Abdullah, for his part, concluded that the new Iraqi premier was both untrustworthy and subservient to Iran, and decided, therefore, not to engage with him further. However, in contrast to Abdullah's perception of Maliki, an examination of Maliki's background indicates that he had never been close to Iran. In fact, Zalmay Khalilzad, then the U.S. ambassador in Iraq, had decided to support Maliki's bid for the Iraqi premiership because, of the viable candidates, he had assessed that Maliki was the least susceptible to Iranian influence. Nevertheless, King Abdullah, as well as other members of the Saudi regime, appeared to become more invested in maintaining the image they had established of Maliki as an Iranian agent than in gathering more information about him to add greater nuance to their perception. In this way, the Saudi leadership's image of Maliki became self-perpetuating, even if it was largely inaccurate. Further highlighting Abdullah's antipathy toward him, in late 2006 Abdullah actually began to urge the Bush administration to replace Maliki with former Iraqi Prime Minister Ayad Allawi.

A New Iraqi Premier

In December 2005, as Iraq lay on the precipice of a full-blown civil war, parliamentary elections were held for its first permanent, post-Saddam government. By the following spring, in a twist of fate unforeseen at the time of the elections, Maliki of the Da'wa Party would take the premiership. Maliki exhibited both a strong Arab identity and skepticism toward Iran, leading Khalilzad to support his bid for the premiership. Moreover, as a condition of his support, Khalilzad required that Maliki commit to engaging specifically with Saudi Arabia.

The principal electoral blocs that ran in the December 2005 elections consisted of the Shiʿa Islamist UIA, the Kurdistan Alliance, and Allawi's Iraqi List, as well as a new Sunni Arab list called the Iraqi Accord Front, more commonly known as Tawafuq. Tawafuq's largest constituent member was the Iraqi Islamic Party (IIP), and its leader was IIP Secretary-General Tariq al-Hashimi. On election day, the UIA and Kurdistan Alliance again dominated the polls, but by a smaller margin than in January, winning 128 and 53 parliamentary seats, or 47 and 19 percent respectively. The Iraqi List, which won 25 seats, or 9 percent, also saw its share of the electorate diminish. Meanwhile, Tawafuq, the new list, won 44 seats, or 16 percent.[1] As for the United States, the Bush administration's political objective after the December elections consisted of forming a national unity government, which would include all these electoral blocs and would thereby be inclusive of all of Iraq's communities.[2]

Within the UIA, attention thereafter focused on putting forward a candidate for the post of prime minister. In early 2005,

Ibrahim al-Jaʿfari had become premier in the Transitional Government as a result of a compromise between SCIRI and the Sadrists, the principal factions of the UIA. In early 2006, SCIRI, still the UIA's dominant faction, again nominated its preferred candidate, Adel Abd al-Mahdi, for whom the Bush administration had signaled its support, as al-Jaʿfari had appeared unable, or unwilling, in 2005 to confront the Ministry of Interior over its role in the growing sectarian conflict in Baghdad.[3] However, as before, the Sadrists, the UIA's second largest faction, opposed Abd al-Mahdi's candidacy, reflecting, at bottom, the deep rivalry between the Sadrists and the Hakims of SCIRI. The Sadrists, for their part, backed al-Jaʿfari, whose weakness they appeared to favor as he was not likely to confront the growing power of the Sadrist militias. On 12 February 2006, a vote was held within the UIA for the post of premier: Abd al-Mahdi received sixty-three votes while al-Jaʿfari obtained sixty-four.[4]

Ten days later, an attack linked to Al-Qaʿida targeted the Shiʿa shrine of the Golden Mosque in Samarra; while there were no reported deaths, the shrine's golden dome collapsed in the attack. Sadrist militias immediately took to the streets, attacking Sunni mosques and abducting Sunni men in large numbers.[5] Grand Ayatollah Sistani had previously sought to restrain the Shiʿa community from seeking communal retribution against Sunni Arabs; nevertheless, in the face of the shrine's destruction even Iraq's leading *marjiʿ* could no longer contain popular Shiʿa anger.[6] Upon receiving news of the bombing, the top U.S. officials in Baghdad, Ambassador Khalilzad and coalition commander General George W. Casey, Jr., pushed Prime Minister al-Jaʿfari to take strong measures to curtail the bloodletting, but to these U.S. officials, al-Jaʿfari again appeared indifferent.[7] Given al-Jaʿfari's vacillating response to the crisis, the Bush administration broke with him, and Khalilzad began to look to advance the prospects of another candidate for the post of prime minister.[8]

The Kurds had also withdrawn their support from al-Ja'fari, and moreover they held an effective veto on his premiership, as the post required the support of a two-thirds super majority in parliament. With thus no obvious path to retain the premiership, al-Ja'fari agreed to step aside as long as the post would go to another member of Da'wa, a condition accepted by SCIRI and the Sadrists, as they considered the Da'wa Party, which did not have a militia of its own, a weak rival.[9] Two other Da'wa leaders, Ali al-Adeeb, and Maliki, were considered viable candidates for the post.

Al-Adeeb began to gain traction within the UIA, but Khalilzad, for his part, preferred Maliki's candidacy. In Khalilzad's view, the next prime minister would need to pursue national reconciliation seriously, confront the Shi'a militias, make non-sectarian appointments, particularly to the Ministries of Defense and Interior, and, in Khalilzad's words, "reach out to the Arab world, particularly Saudi Arabia."[10] Indeed, Khalilzad had traveled to Saudi Arabia in late December 2005, where he had a tense exchange with King Abdullah, who shared his apprehension about Iranian supremacy in Iraq.[11] Prior to 2003, al-Adeeb had lived in Iran, and he was believed to hold Iranian nationality; moreover, his family had remained in Iran after he had returned to Iraq.[12] As Khalilzad recounts in his memoirs, "I doubted that the leaders of the Arab world would reconcile with an Iraq led by Adeeb. If Adeeb became prime minister, the Sunni regimes of the Arab world would conclude that the United States was handing Iraq to the Iranians."[13] According to a U.S. diplomatic cable, Khalilzad assessed that Maliki, by contrast, had a more skeptical attitude toward Iran, with "deep concerns about expanding Iranian influence in Iraq."[14] Khalilzad, by his own account, decided to back Maliki's candidacy because he believed Maliki would be more acceptable to the Sunni Arab world, and Khalilzad emphasized to the future prime minister at this time that he would have to prioritize engagement with Saudi Arabia specifically.[15]

Maliki had a strong Arab and Iraqi identity. From both an Arab tribal and devout Shi'a background, he was the grandson of a Shi'a cleric who had been active in the Iraqi uprising of 1920 and was also a notable poet. Maliki lauded his grandfather's role in Iraqi history and frequently invoked his verses, as well as the verses of other Arab poets.[16] By his own account, Maliki joined the Da'wa Party in the late 1960s because he wanted to take "political action" following the Arabs' 1967 defeat to Israel, a formative experience for many Arabs in the 1960s.[17] In 1979, following the Ba'thist crackdown on Da'wa, Maliki fled to Syria. By 1981, he relocated to Iran, but apparently he did not take to life there. As Ryan Crocker, U.S. ambassador to Iraq from 2007 to 2009, recalled in an interview, Maliki asserted to him, "You don't know what arrogance is until you have been an Iraqi Arab forced to dwell with the Persians."[18] More significantly, he resisted pressure to adopt *wilayat al-faqih*, and was angered by the Iranian regime's promotion of SCIRI and repression of the more independent-minded Da'wa Party.[19] Indeed, toward the end of the Iran–Iraq War, Maliki left Iran reportedly at a time when the regime was cracking down on Da'wa, with one of his friends being executed at this time for refusing to pledge allegiance to Khomeini.[20] Maliki chose to go back to Damascus, where he headed a secret Da'wa cell until the overthrow of Saddam. A Lebanese journalist interviewed for this book observed that in a conversation he had with Maliki prior to the 2003 invasion, the future prime minister recounted how much he disliked Iran.[21] These details about Maliki's life prior to 2003 have been included here to demonstrate that he had never been particularly close, and had certainly never been loyal, to the Iranian regime.

Upon his return to Iraq in 2003, he did, however, earn a reputation as a hardline anti-Ba'thist. He became deputy chairman of the de-Ba'thification commission, and in this capacity he earned a reputation as "the arch-exponent of de-Ba'thification."[22] Indeed, Ali Allawi expressed his view in an interview that Maliki took a maximalist position on de-Ba'thification at this time both out of a desire for revenge—some sixty-five members of his family are said to have been killed by the Ba'thist regime[23]—and, more significantly, because he aimed "to destroy the basis of Ba'thist power" in Iraq.[24] Despite the Ba'thists' overthrow, Maliki remained convinced that they were plotting a return to power; the U.S. embassy assessed in early 2006 that, "His deep unease about Iranian intervention is matched only by his unease about the possibility of another Baathist coup."[25] As a result, Maliki also advocated a hardline approach to Sunni insurgents, and some Sunni Arab political leaders even alleged that he supported the targeted executions of Sunni Arabs conducted by Shi'a militias in the first years of the occupation.[26] Toby Dodge argues that the beneficiaries of regime change in Iraq, foremost the Shi'a Islamists, sought to impose "a victor's peace" on the country to secure their own dominance in the new political order,[27] and Maliki fit this pattern: his chief objective was to obliterate the old Sunni-dominated political order and consolidate a new regime with a Shi'a Arab at its head. Nevertheless, Maliki was fundamentally pragmatic, described as the "ultimate opportunist," with neither permanent friends nor permanent enemies.[28] Although he was reputed to distrust Iraq's Sunni Arab leaders, whom he regarded as probable Ba'thist sympathizers,[29] as prime minister he demonstrated a willingness to work with his Sunni Arab rivals when it suited his interests.

By May 2006, after months of negotiations, Iraq's national unity government finally took shape with Maliki at its head. Beyond Maliki, the new government reflected the ethno-sectarian diversity of the country. Jalal Talabani, a Kurd, remained president, and Abd al-Mahdi and Tariq al-Hashimi, a Shi'a Arab and Sunni Arab respectively, took the two vice president positions. Prime Minister Maliki's thirty-nine-member cabinet included deputy prime ministers from the Kurdistan Alliance and Tawafuq, in addition to six members each from the Kurdistan Alliance, Tawafuq, and Allawi's Iraqi List.[30] Allawi, however, did not himself join Maliki's cabinet, and in fact the former prime minister would spend most of his time over the next few years traveling abroad.

As for Maliki, once the government was seated, his first priority was to address the country's sectarian civil war. Following the Samarra shrine bombing of February 2006, the sectarian cleansing that had begun in Baghdad in 2005 became widespread across the capital. However, the role played by the Ministry of Interior security services decreased once Bayan Jabr, interior minister in the Transitional Government, was replaced with Jawad al-Bulani, an independent Shi'a Islamist politician with no militia ties. As interior minister, al-Bulani purged some 60,000 members of the internal security services, focusing on the most sectarian units.[31] Instead, in 2006 the civil war was fought primarily between Sadrist militias and Al-Qa'ida in Iraq, which were then competing for physical control of Baghdad through campaigns of sectarian cleansing of the city's mixed Sunni–Shi'a neighborhoods.[32] During this period, Al-Qa'ida in Iraq continued to carry out its hallmark campaign of suicide bombings, while the Sadrists conducted sectarian assassinations to intimidate and expel Sunni residents of mixed neighborhoods.[33] In 2006, at the height of the civil war, an estimated 34,452 civilians were killed and as many as 365,000 Iraqis were displaced, primarily in and around Baghdad.[34]

At the outset of his premiership, Maliki was a relatively weak figure. He lacked political experience, and was assuming power for the first time in the midst of a civil war. Nevertheless, his manner was decisive, especially in contrast to the irresolute al-Ja'fari.[35] Within weeks of sitting his cabinet, and being prodded by the Americans, he began to promote national reconciliation, shifting away from the sectarian positions he had previously taken. In early June, Maliki ordered the release of 2,500 people, mostly Sunnis, who had been detained by the coalition, and presented a plan to rebuild Iraq's war-damaged infrastructure and improve the capacity of its fledgling security forces.[36] He deployed 75,000 security personnel across Baghdad, implemented a curfew, and asserted his intention to disband the Shiʿa militias.[37] In late June, he presented a national reconciliation plan, which offered amnesty to insurgents who renounced violence and embraced the new political system.[38] Nevertheless, it was highly questionable whether Maliki would be able to execute this ambitious plan. His backing in parliament came from the Shiʿa Islamists, particularly the Sadrists, who had thwarted a SCIRI premiership, casting significant doubt on his willingness to confront the Shiʿa militias. Moreover, Sunni Arab insurgents, for their part, had made no indication they were willing to renounce violence or embrace the political process. For the time being, therefore, Iraq's descent into civil war continued.

Maliki's Failed Attempt to Engage with Saudi Arabia

A week after presenting the new national reconciliation plan, Maliki traveled to Saudi Arabia on his first trip abroad as prime minister. While the Saudi leadership actually appeared optimistic about Iraq's new premier before and immediately after the visit, by August, King Abdullah would claim that Maliki had lied to him. He would also accuse the Iraqi premier of being an Iranian agent and would refuse to meet with him ever again. Abdullah alleged that Maliki had made him various promises on which he failed to follow through. At the start of my research for this book in 2015, I took at face value that Maliki had failed to keep his promises to Abdullah, or at the very least had made promises to Abdullah in the first place. However, as I began to conduct my research, I discovered inconsistencies in the Saudi version of events, which will be explored below. Most significantly, the Saudi claim was very vague: Saudi leaders contended that Maliki made various promises, but nobody interviewed for this study, including Saudi sources, could ever tell me what specifically he had promised. By contrast, Maliki's version of events was specific. In a written exchange I had with Maliki in 2020, he identified a number of subjects he discussed with King Abdullah during their meeting, detailed below. Adding to the discrepancies surrounding the Saudi narrative, three sources I interviewed in 2015 and 2016 had very inconsistent accounts of conversations they had each had with Abdullah's intelligence chief, Prince Muqrin bin Abd al-Aziz, in the period under examination. Prince Muqrin served as Abdullah's principal aide on Iraq matters at that time. For instance, one of the three sources, an American diplomat, recalled that Prince Muqrin told him that he did not actually know what Maliki had promised Abdullah.[39] By contrast, another source, an Iraqi diplomat, recalled that Prince Muqrin told him that Maliki had put his promises to King Abdullah "in writing."[40] The third source, Sami al-Askari, a close confidant of Maliki and a fellow Da'wa member, recalled that Prince Muqrin actually acknowledged to him that the reason behind Abdullah's cold shoulder to Maliki lay with the king, not with a supposed promise Maliki had made to him.[41]

The research findings surrounding Maliki's failed attempt to engage with the Saudi leadership in 2006, as presented here, will be used to argue the following: it appears that Abdullah genuinely believed Maliki had lied to him, even though no evidence was found to substantiate his contention that Maliki had made promises to him on which he failed to follow through. Rather, it appears that Abdullah may have received information about Maliki following their meeting, which compelled him to believe that Maliki had been duplicitous. Nevertheless, Abdullah's sub-ordinates propagated his claim that Maliki had lied to him in their meeting; it appears that they did so to deflect blame away from Abdullah and onto Maliki for the failed attempt to engage. Furthermore, I present a hypothesis to account for why Abdullah began to mistrust Maliki following their meeting: it appears that he was being manipulated by a rival, or perhaps various different rivals, of the Iraqi premier. Evidence will be presented below to suggest that during this period the Saudi leadership was in fact receiving false intelligence that painted Maliki as an Iranian agent, apparently fed to them by Iraqi parliamentarian Muhammad al-Dayani of the Tawafuq coalition. The findings also point a possible finger at Allawi. As addressed in the final section of this chapter, at the time, Allawi was seeking to obtain external Arab support for his objective to return to the Iraqi premier-ship in place of Maliki; he also had a close personal relation-ship with Abdullah and obtained his backing. In general, according to a Saudi royal family insider interviewed for this book, Abdullah was susceptible to being "controlled" by close confidants. As an unsubstantiated example, this Saudi source claimed that Abdullah's Syrian hairdresser essentially dictated his Syria policy.[42] While speculative, it seems possible that Allawi similarly aimed to manipulate Abdullah, influencing Abdullah's opinion of the Iraqi premier whom he himself wanted to replace. At the very least, the research findings indicate that Allawi had a motive to do so.

For Maliki's part, while he had promised Ambassador Khalilzad that he would engage with Saudi Arabia, the new Iraqi prime minister appeared genuinely intent on establishing positive rela-tions with the Arab world, including the Saudi kingdom. In our written exchange, Maliki explained to me that, prior to his trip to Saudi Arabia, he recognized that "sectarianism" (al-ta'ifiyya) was the major problem confronting Iraq, and he believed that the symbolism of a visit by an Iraqi Shi'a prime minister to Saudi Arabia, as the center of the Sunni Muslim world, would have a beneficial effect. Maliki elaborated that he declined invitations to Iran, Turkey, Jordan, and the United States for his first trip abroad as prime minister, choosing Saudi Arabia instead, in the hope that, "I would succeed in opening a new page in [Saudi–Iraq] relations that would result in stability and the development of mutual interests for the two countries and the region."[43] Furthermore, al-Askari, Maliki's confidant whom I interviewed in 2016, provided his account of Maliki's attitude prior to the trip, in which he highlighted Maliki's desire to reintegrate Iraq into the Arab fold. Al-Askari observed that he had received two invitations after assuming the premiership, to visit Washington and to visit Tehran. However, in al-Askari's account, Maliki believed that his first trip abroad should be to an Arab country, not the U.S. or Iran, as that would send the "wrong signal." According to al-Askari, he argued to his confidants: "I want to signal that we are Arabs. Yes, we are friends with the Americans, we are friends with the Iranians, but for the Arab world, we are a family, [we are] part of this family." There were two obvious options for Maliki's first trip, according to his confidant, Egypt or Saudi Arabia, and he chose the latter.[44] The premier's attitude toward calming Iraq's sectarian conflict and reintegrating it into the Arab fold thus appeared very different from that of his predecessor, al-Ja'fari, who had appeared, for whatever reason, to be disengaged from the Sunni Arab world.

Furthermore, in the days prior to his trip to Saudi Arabia, Maliki expressed optimism to Ambassador Khalilzad. According to a U.S. diplomatic cable, the prime minister acknowledged to Khalilzad the importance of having the Saudi leadership "see him attached to the Arab identity of Iraq," and said he believed that he and the Saudis "could understand each other."[45] In addition, Iraq's senior Sunni Arab and Kurdish leaders appeared supportive of Maliki's engagement with Saudi Arabia. Tariq al-Hashimi, the Sunni Arab vice president, told Khalilzad that it was a "good sign" that Maliki was traveling to Saudi Arabia on his first trip abroad and that the Saudi leadership was willing to receive him.[46] Meanwhile, President Talabani told U.S. officials in Baghdad following Maliki's trip that he had spoken with King Abdullah. Talabani said he had "sought to assure [Abdullah] that [Maliki] was an Arab and Iraqi first and that [Abdullah] need not fear Iraq would accept Iranian leadership."[47]

Just as significantly, the Saudi leadership also appeared optimistic about Maliki at this time. Four days prior to Maliki's trip, Ambassador Khalilzad himself returned to the kingdom to brief senior Saudi officials on Iraq's new prime minister. According to a U.S. diplomatic cable, Foreign Minister Saud al-Faisal told Khalilzad that the national reconciliation plan Maliki had just presented was a "tremendous initiative," and "expressed his confidence that PM Maliki will solve many of the problems that have plagued Iraq." Prince Saud told Khalilzad that the new prime minister "is welcome here."[48]

Khalilzad also met with King Abdullah, and in his memoirs Khalilzad recalls, "I told the king that Maliki was an Arab, not a Persian. I stressed that although he led a Shia Islamist party, he was an Iraqi nationalist. I argued that Maliki could reduce Iraq's dependence on Iran if the Arab world engaged Iraq and worked with its leaders."[49] According to a U.S. diplomatic cable, King Abdullah, for his part, also appeared more optimistic about Iraq, telling Khalilzad that he "looked forward to PM Maliki's visit," and expressing his belief that "things were looking better in Iraq"; he added that "he agreed with Ambassador Khalilzad's assessment that PM Maliki was a stronger leader than his predecessor."[50] In Khalilzad's recollection of this meeting, provided in an interview, King Abdullah agreed to give Maliki a warm reception.[51] Nevertheless, the U.S. diplomatic cable observed that

Abdullah still harbored deep reservations toward Iraq, and assessed that Maliki would therefore have "his work cut out for him" during his visit.[52]

As they had promised Khalilzad, the Saudi leadership gave Maliki a warm reception during his trip, and afterward Maliki appears to have expressed satisfaction with the visit. Upon Maliki's arrival to Jeddah on 1 July 2006, a Saudi delegation led by Crown Prince Sultan and Foreign Minister Saud al-Faisal welcomed him at the airport.[53] Later that day, Sultan chaired a formal and well-publicized meeting with Maliki, in which he emphasized Saudi Arabia's "full support" for his government.[54] In addition, Maliki had a meeting with Abdullah at which Foreign Minister Saud al-Faisal was also present.[55] He then traveled on to Kuwait and the UAE. The prime minister regarded his trip to the Gulf as a success to the extent that Khalilzad writes in his memoirs, "Maliki was almost elated when he reported back to me afterward."[56] Indeed, a U.S. diplomatic cable from 9 July 2006 notes that Maliki reported to U.S. officials that "he had been extremely well-received in his stops in Saudi Arabia, UAE, and Kuwait and that overall he was very pleased with the results of these visits."[57] According to the cable, Maliki recounted that his talks with the Saudi leadership in particular were "very constructive," and that he was therefore "optimistic."[58] For their part, the Saudi leadership also appeared positive toward Maliki following the trip. A cable from the U.S. embassy in Riyadh from 5 July 2006 reports that an embassy source close to the royal family had communicated that, "King Abdullah is ready to be supportive of PM Maliki."[59] Thus it appears that Abdullah's belief that Maliki was untrustworthy did not precede their meeting.

Nevertheless, the Iraqi prime minister's relationship with the Saudi leadership very quickly soured. In August, some six weeks after Maliki's trip, Abdullah informed visiting U.S. officials that Maliki had made promises during their meeting that he had failed to carry out.[60] Furthermore, in the coming years Abdullah would become convinced that the Iraqi prime minister was an "Iranian agent."[61] There were many subsequent attempts, by the Iraqis and the Americans, for Maliki to reengage with Abdullah, but Abdullah refused to meet with him ever again, a situation that will be further explored in the next chapter. As he would later argue to U.S. officials, with reference to Maliki, "how can I meet with someone I don't trust?"[62] However, as noted above, it remains unclear what Abdullah believed Maliki had promised him. U.S. sources who interacted with Abdullah recounted that the Saudi king did not elaborate on what he believed Maliki had promised. For example, Ambassador Crocker observed in an interview, "It was very clear that King Abdullah would not deal in any way at all with Maliki, whom he accused of lying to him, but never provided specifics."[63] Similarly, another American diplomat who interacted with King Abdullah during this period recounted that he directly asked Abdullah what he believed had been promised, to which the Saudi king gave a "vague" response.[64]

The Saudis' claim remained murky. Yet another U.S. diplomat sought to investigate Abdullah's concerns, and interacted with Prince Muqrin on this subject. This official asked Prince Muqrin about the content of the promises Maliki supposedly had made, but, according to this source, Muqrin claimed, "None of us [in the Saudi leadership] really knows," although he said he believed the lie referred to a "broad promise" to pursue national reconciliation, which the king felt Maliki had failed to carry out.[65] Similarly, Prince Turki, as well as another Saudi source who has advised the royal family on foreign policy matters, told me in very general terms that Maliki's promises to Abdullah concerned national reconciliation.[66] Nevertheless, according to others who interacted with Abdullah in 2006, the Saudi king was very clear that Maliki had promised him not one broad thing, but three specific, albeit unidentified, things.[67] Moreover, the claim that

Abdullah felt Maliki had failed to keep promises regarding the national reconciliation agenda is not satisfying, given that Abdullah apparently began to assert that Maliki had lied to him within weeks of their meeting. Furthermore, even if Maliki did make a promise that he then failed to keep, it appears questionable how meaningful that promise could have been if he was expected to implement it in a matter of weeks in the midst of a civil war. When the Saudi foreign policy adviser was asked in an interview about King Abdullah's very rapid change of heart toward Maliki, he did not elaborate.[68]

By contrast to the Saudis' version of events, Maliki's version was more specific. In his written exchange with me, Maliki recounted that he and King Abdullah discussed a range of topics during their meeting. Maliki said he expressed his commitment to resolving Iraq's sectarian conflict and articulated his desire for better relations with the Arab and Muslim worlds. In this context, Maliki said he asked Abdullah to send an ambassador to Iraq. Maliki added that Abdullah, for his part, brought up two topics during their meeting: he asked questions about Grand Ayatollah Sistani and, somewhat incongruously, spoke about the discovery of oil in Saudi Arabia. Maliki recounted to me that when he later learned that Abdullah had accused him of failing to keep promises he had made, he was "astonished," and he said he thought to himself that Abdullah must not have been "mentally present" in the meeting, because, as Maliki remarked, "Why would I, as an Iraqi official responsible for Iraqis not Saudis, make him promises?" Maliki surmised that perhaps King Abdullah mistook his review of his policies as a set of promises. However, Maliki added that the Saudis added a claim to their account of the meeting that had "no truth," namely that he had written out his supposed promises for King Abdullah. Indeed, as seen at the beginning of this section, the Saudi claim that Maliki had put his promises in writing was relayed to me by an Iraqi diplomat who heard this directly from Prince Muqrin. According to Maliki, "That is something that the lowest level official cannot do with a ruler of another country."[69]

The recollections of two other sources—Ambassador Khalilzad and al-Askari—add further specificity to Maliki's account of his meeting with Abdullah. According to both Khalilzad and al-Askari, each of whom discussed the meeting with Maliki, the Iraqi prime minister claimed he and Abdullah had spoken about the need to reintegrate Saddam-era officers into the Iraqi army,[70] a policy Maliki in fact implemented in December 2006.[71] Furthermore, Khalilzad recalled that there were many rumors circulating in Baghdad about what Maliki had supposedly promised. One such rumor, according to Khalilzad, was that Maliki had promised Abdullah that he would not execute Saddam Hussein. (As will be elaborated below, the former Iraqi leader was hanged by Maliki's order in December 2006.) Khalilzad recalled, however, that Maliki repeatedly claimed that these rumors were not true.[72] Indeed, the rumor that his decision to execute Saddam constituted one of his broken promises to Abdullah could not be true, as Abdullah was already alleging that Maliki had broken his promises some four months prior to the execution.

For his part, al-Askari also approached Prince Muqrin on this topic in a 2007 meeting in London, which he arranged through a backchannel, and his account is most revealing. Al-Askari explained in an interview that his aim was to find out why Abdullah was hostile toward Maliki because he regarded this situation as "a problem for our country and for the region." Indeed, al-Askari's attempt, outside U.S. channels, to address King Abdullah's concerns is the best indicator that Maliki genuinely desired a positive relationship with Saudi Arabia. According to al-Askari's account, when he asked Prince Muqrin why Abdullah was hostile toward Maliki, the Saudi intelligence chief replied that Maliki had lied. However, al-Askari said he countered: "I am very close to al-Maliki, and he doesn't lie to me. If there's anything, he will tell me. And there is no promise. There is no promise." In al-Askari's account, Prince Muqrin, thus pressed, admitted, "The problem is the king," to which the only solution, Muqrin said, was "Allah." Al-Askari said that he interpreted this exchange to mean that Abdullah was unwilling to reconsider his opinion of Maliki.[73]

Assuming that Maliki did not actually lie to King Abdullah, a fundamental and unresolved question is why Abdullah so quickly concluded that Maliki was untrustworthy after what appeared to have been a successful meeting. An American businessman close to senior Saudi officials provided what appears to be a plausible account, although it was not corroborated by any other source. In an interview, the American businessman recounted that Maliki, in his meeting with Abdullah, had been very "agreeable," but "within a month" of the meeting, Maliki made "very incendiary anti-Sunni speeches" in Baghdad; according to this source, this "totally burned up" Abdullah, because it demonstrated that Maliki was untrustworthy.[74] This explanation is intriguing because it matches the timeline presented above; in short, it appears that something happened soon after the meeting that substantially changed Abdullah's opinion of the new Iraqi prime minister. The American businessman seemed to believe that Maliki's anti-Sunni speeches were made publicly; however, while it is plausible that he would make such statements in private, no record was found in this research that Maliki made inflammatory anti-Sunni statements in public at this time. Indeed, Maliki was then a brand new and relatively weak premier who was dependent on American patronage; he would not seem to have been in a position to make public statements derogatory to Sunni Arabs.

While few concrete conclusions can be drawn from this episode, it appears that King Abdullah received information soon after his meeting with Maliki that painted the new Iraqi prime minister in a negative light. While it is plausible that this information might have related to something Maliki actually did, it is also plausible that it could have been fabricated by rivals who sought to undermine him. For his part, Iraqi Foreign Minister Hoshyar Zebari expressed his concern to U.S. officials that the Saudi leadership "were speaking to the wrong people," namely Iraqis who did not represent the government.[75] Similarly, an Iraqi diplomat observed in an interview that many Iraqis would speak to the Saudi leadership about Maliki to advance their own personal agendas.[76] Furthermore, there is indeed evidence from this period that the Saudi leadership was being fed disinformation about Maliki that depicted him as an Iranian agent who was targeting Sunni Arab Iraqis. In early 2007, Khalilzad again met with King Abdullah and Prince Muqrin, who showed the U.S. ambassador what appeared to be official Iraqi government documents signed by Maliki, ordering the assassination of "a number of Sunni Arabs."[77] At about the same time, an online Arabic newspaper in fact published these, or similar, documents, in which Maliki allegedly informed the Iranian ambassador in Iraq that he had carried out an Iranian plan "to take vengeance" on thirteen Sunni Arab parliamentarians.[78] For his part, Khalilzad expressed his conviction to King Abdullah and Prince Muqrin that these documents were forged, and voiced his concern that somebody who sought to deter the development of a relationship between Maliki and the Saudi leadership might be seeking to manipulate them.

In fact, Ali AlAhmed, a Saudi dissident based in the Washington, D.C. area, recounted that Iraqi parliamentarian Muhammad al-Dayani of the Tawafuq coalition was circulating these documents at this time. According to AlAhmed, al-Dayani came to Washington during this period and gave the documents to CBS News, which contracted AlAhmed to assess their authenticity. AlAhmed said he judged them to be a "bad forgery" because the signature on each one appeared to be an exact replica. Moreover, later that year AlAhmed had a meeting with Prince Muqrin in northern Virginia; the Saudi intelligence chief was attempting to lure him back to Saudi Arabia. AlAhmed already knew that Prince Muqrin and King Abdullah had shown Khalilzad fake Iraqi government documents similar to the ones he had reviewed for CBS News, as it had been reported in the *New York Times*.[79] Based on a conversation he then had with Muqrin's deputy, Prince Abd al-Aziz bin Bandar bin Abd al-Aziz, at the northern Virginia meeting, AlAhmed surmised that the Saudi leadership had also received the documents from Muhammad al-Dayani.[80]

In sum, the research conducted for this book indicated that the Saudi leadership never deviated from the script that Maliki lied to Abdullah:[81] this, however, was the only aspect of their version of events that appeared to be consistent. While it is difficult to know precisely what happened, it appears that Abdullah genuinely felt Maliki had deceived him.[82] Nevertheless, it appears that Abdullah's subordinates used this narrative with their U.S. and Iraqi counterparts to deflect blame onto Maliki for their king's very rigid decision not to engage with him. Indeed, the next chapter will provide findings that Abdullah's principal foreign policy advisers, Prince Saud al-Faisal, Prince Muqrin, and Adel al-Jubeir, then the Saudi ambassador to the U.S., were themselves trying, unsuccessfully, to persuade Abdullah to engage with Iraq. However, instead of admitting to third parties that Abdullah was essentially closed to this course of action, they appeared more inclined to blame Maliki for this outcome. The analysis above has examined Abdullah's contention that Maliki was untrustworthy; the analysis below explores his belief that the Iraqi prime minister was an Iranian agent.

The Saudi Leadership's Enemy Images of Iran and Nuri al-Maliki

Whatever in fact happened following his meeting with Abdullah, it was Maliki's misfortune that he assumed the Iraqi premiership at a time when the Saudi leadership was growing even more apprehensive about Iran's regional influence, not only in Iraq but throughout the Arab east. The existence of some 1,500 diplomatic cables from the U.S. embassy in Riyadh dating from the 2005 to 2010 period, made available by WikiLeaks, facilitates an examination of the image the Saudi leadership, and particularly King Abdullah, held of Iran at that time, at least as they communicated that image to U.S. officials. While Saudi decision-makers had tended to view Iran through the lens of an enemy image since the time of the Iran–Iraq War, from 2006 they perceived that Iran's regional ambitions were becoming even more extensive. In sum, the Saudi leadership came to believe that the Islamic Republic was fueling all the crises in the region, which appeared to be a function more of their longstanding beliefs about Iranian expansionism than a considered evaluation of regional developments. However, what becomes even more notable in an examination of the WikiLeaks documents from this period is King Abdullah's particularly hardline stance on Iran, which he at times expressed in explicitly sectarian terms, as well as his categorical assessment of Maliki as an Iranian loyalist. It will be argued that Abdullah's negative feelings toward Iran and the Shi'a contributed to his unwillingness to reconsider his relationship with Maliki. In addition, findings will be presented below that, in general, Abdullah appeared to be a relatively inflexible thinker. Thus, while Abdullah's negative attitude toward Iran and the Shi'a may have rendered him less willing to rethink his relationship with Maliki, it may have also been the case that he was dispositionally inclined to impose a black-and-white judgment on a highly complex situation.

Over the course of 2006, Iran's influence in the eastern Arab world appeared steadily to increase. Beyond Iraq, the Syrian regime of President Bashar al-Assad strengthened its longstanding alliance with the Islamic Republic at this time; Syria and Iran were both facing increasing international pressure, Syria as a result of the assassination of former Lebanese Prime Minister Rafiq al-Hariri and Iran over its nuclear program. Notably, in January 2006 Assad hosted a summit attended by Iranian President Mahmud Ahmadinejad, a political hardliner elected the year before, and Hasan Nasrallah, secretary-general of Lebanese Hizballah.[83] Furthermore, that same month the Palestinian group Hamas, which also had ties to the Iranian regime, prevailed in Palestinian parliamentary elections. Hamas formed a government that spring, which caused a schism between it and Fatah, the political party of Palestinian President Mahmud Abbas. Then, in July, eleven days after Maliki's trip to Saudi Arabia, war broke out between Hizballah and Israel, leading to a thirty-four-day conflict at the end of which Hasan Nasrallah claimed a victory over the Arabs' traditional foe.[84] By late 2006, Hizballah's demand for greater representation in the Lebanese cabinet precipitated a political crisis in Beirut that would last until 2008 and be resolved in Hizballah's favor.[85]

Even before the outbreak of the 2006 Lebanon war, a U.S. diplomatic cable assessed that King Abdullah "appeared visibly worried that Iran is trying to assert itself more within the Arab and Islamic communities,"[86] while a separate cable reported that Foreign Minister Saud al-Faisal had "accused [the Iranians] of involvement in Iraq, Syria, Lebanon, and now Palestine."[87] By the end of 2006, the Saudi leadership assessed all regional crises through the lens of their enmity toward Iran. A December 2006 cable reported that in a meeting with a U.S. official, King Abdullah "stressed that Iran is currently the source of all the problems in the region, from Syria, Lebanon, Palestine, Iraq, and Afghanistan, and that the problems will get worse over time."[88] Meanwhile, in early 2007 Zebari—an Iraqi Kurd who served as Iraq's foreign minister from 2003 to 2014—expressed to U.S. officials in Baghdad his view, based on his own interaction with Saudi officials, that the Saudi leadership was "obsessed" with Iran.[89] However, the Saudi leadership's image of Iranian interference in the Arab world only increased in the period through 2010. A cable from March 2009 reported: "Prince Muqrin described Iran as 'all over the place now.' The 'Shiite crescent is becoming a full moon,' encompassing Lebanon, Syria, Iraq, Bahrain, Kuwait and Yemen among Iran's targets. In the Kingdom, he said 'we have problems in Medina and Eastern Province.'"[90] A July 2008 cable even reported that Saudi leaders argued that Iran was implementing "expansionist operations trying to convert Sunni Muslims to the Shiʿite sect."[91] In fact, a Saudi source who has advised the royal family on foreign policy matters claimed in an interview that Iran had a policy of trying to convert Sunnis to Shiʿa Islam, particularly in North Africa— he mentioned Morocco and Tunisia—as this was a way for it to assert control over the populations there.[92]

The statements above indicate that Saudi leaders assessed regional events in a very theory-driven manner. They possessed an overarching theory—that Iran was expansionist—which they applied to explain all the crises of the region. Nor did they appear to explore alternative hypotheses; for instance the notion that, on a popular level, Arab citizens felt politically disenfranchised or faced economic hardship.[93] In tying all regional crises to Iran, Saudi leaders assessed events in a way that is consistent with how information is processed through the lens of an enemy image. The question arises why the Saudis appeared so fearful of Iran. As argued in Chapter 1, the experience of the Iran–Iraq War was one of great trauma for the Saudi leadership, which created a resistance among them to assimilating new information that indicated how their past experience was different from the present. Given the trauma of the 1980s, they appeared hypersensitive thereafter to detecting apparent indicators of Iranian expansionism. However, in addition, a considerable degree of groupthink (the tendency toward conformity among the members of a group)[94] appeared to be in evidence among them. It is simply not clear that anybody within the upper echelons of the Al Saud openly challenged the existing view of Iran. In fact, political psychologist Richard Hermann observes that images of other countries as friends or enemies frequently become assumptions that are taken for granted.[95] In the apparent absence of a dissenting voice on the topic of Iran within the Saudi leadership, their highly negative image of it appeared to become deeply ingrained. It was simply assumed that Iran was expansionist, and Iranian expansionism then seemed to offer a plausible account for the problems of the region.

However, King Abdullah was particularly hardline in his perception of Iran. For instance, in 2007 Abdullah communicated to U.S. officials his view that "the Iranians are not good people," and in 2008 he declared, "Iran's goal is to cause problems ... May God prevent us from falling victim to their evil."[96] Chas Freeman, the U.S. ambassador to Saudi Arabia at the time of the 1990–1991 Gulf War, expressed his opinion in an interview that during his ambassadorship, Abdullah had been "probably the most viscerally anti-Persian" member of the senior echelons of the royal family, for instance even inquiring among the Americans about the possibility of overthrowing the Islamic Republic in the early 1990s.[97] In fact, as made clear by U.S. diplomatic cables and in the memoir of then-U.S. Secretary of Defense Robert Gates, Abdullah was similarly pressing the Bush administration in 2007 and 2008 to conduct a military strike against Iran.[98] Abdullah also at times articulated his antagonism toward Iran in explicitly sectarian language. Freeman, who developed an enduring friendship with him as a result of the Gulf War experience, observed that in general Abdullah could be "pretty anti-Shi'a."[99] In a June 2006 U.S. diplomatic cable, recording a conversation in which Abdullah expressed his anti-Iran sentiments, his aversion to Shiʻa Islam more generally becomes apparent. The author of the cable wrote that the Saudi king accused the Shiʻa of worshipping "domes, statues, and individuals," as, in his view, "worshipping anything but God was wrong."[100] Abdullah even argued, as recorded in this cable, that it was an "insult" that Shiʻa Muslims provided an income to their imams,[101] an apparent reference to the *khums* tax (a religious tax) that observant Shiʻa pay to their chosen *maraji' al-taqlid*. An Iraqi diplomat who interacted with Abdullah similarly conveyed in an interview that Abdullah held a deeply suspicious attitude toward Iran and the Shiʻa; according to this source, the Saudi king viewed *wilayat al-faqih* as a "dangerous" doctrine that "undermines the independence of states in the region," as in his view a Shiʻi who adhered to it became loyal to Iran.[102]

We will see in the next chapter that, in sharp contrast to Saudi Arabia, many Arab neighbors began to engage with Iraq in 2008. Most noteworthy is the example of Jordan. The neighbor most overtly hostile to Iraq's Shiʻa ascendance in late 2004, Jordan was among the first Arab neighbors to engage, which it began to do in 2005. In spring 2005, Abdullah II of Jordan, who only months previously had sounded an alarm over a supposed infiltration of Iranians into Iraq, publicly welcomed the formation of the Shiʻa Islamist-dominated Transitional Government, and in the fall Jordan's then-prime minister, Adnan Badran, became the most senior Arab official to visit Baghdad since the 2003 invasion.[103] While less than a year earlier, Jordanian officials had been asserting that a Shiʻa Islamist government would be "anti-Arab" and "Persian," Badran declared during his trip to Baghdad in September 2005 that, "The time has come for the Arab countries to open their hearts to Iraq despite the differences of the past."[104] In reversing course toward the new Iraq so quickly, Jordanian leaders, in contrast to their Saudi counterparts, evinced a willingness to update their thinking about Iraq and the Shiʻa. At bottom, Jordanian leaders' flexibility resulted from an economic imperative: historically, the Jordanian economy had been dependent on the supply of subsidized Iraqi oil, to which the Jordanian leadership wanted to maintain access.[105] As previously mentioned, humans tend to see not only what they expect to see, but what they want to see as well. A corollary is that humans are capable of updating their beliefs—but they have to want to do so.[106] In the Jordanian case, in seeking to maintain an economic link to Iraq, Jordanian leaders undoubtedly wanted to believe they could forge a partnership with Iraq's new Shi'a leaders, whatever their beliefs about them had previously been. They had a compelling economic interest to learn more about Iraq's new leaders and dispel their previously negative views.

By contrast, Saudi leaders, particularly King Abdullah, never appeared willing to update their beliefs about the new Iraq, and especially its new premier. In refusing to engage with Maliki following their July 2006 meeting, Abdullah appeared to be highly rigid. While people are capable of updating their beliefs if they are willing, in cases where they have negative emotions surrounding an issue, they often are *not* willing. As political psychologist David Redlawsk explains, "Feelings come first," with data typically being interpreted "in the service of those feelings."[107] Abdullah's negative attitude toward Iran and the Shi'a—as well as toward the U.S. invasion of Iraq in the first place—likely rendered him less willing to update his beliefs about Maliki and the new Iraq. Moreover, unlike Jordanian leaders, Abdullah was under no economic pressure that might have compelled him to consider a different approach to the new Iraq. Indeed, throughout this period the Saudi economy was steadily expanding due to high oil prices.[108]

However, in addition, it also appears that Abdullah was, in general, a relatively inflexible thinker with little tolerance for ambiguity. For instance, reporting in the Western press from the mid-1990s indicates that he was considered by those who knew him to see the world in "black and white."[109] Similarly, a Saudi royal family insider emphasized in an interview that Abdullah was not a "critical thinker."[110] Of course, having grown up in Saudi Arabia of the 1920s and 1930s, Abdullah had received little in the way of a modern education that would have developed critical thinking. It should also be pointed out that he was then in his early eighties, and had likely experienced some degree of cognitive decline, which is a normal part of the aging process.[111] The statements attributed to Abdullah above with reference to Iran and the Shi'a, for instance that "the Iranians are not good people" and that Shi'a practices were an "insult," provide a window onto his relatively black-and-white views. Such beliefs did not permit much room for ambiguity or nuance. Abdullah also made such black-and-white judgments with reference to Maliki. For instance, according to a U.S. diplomatic cable, he assessed that the Iraqi premier was "an Iranian 100%," and that his government had allowed "half of Iraq to become Iranian."[112] Whatever the nature of Maliki's relationship with Iran, it could not be reduced to a categorical assessment that he was 100 percent Iranian. The Saudi royal family insider, for his part, expressed the opinion in an interview that ultimately Abdullah "could not comprehend" what was going on in Iraq.[113]

Beyond Abdullah, other members of the Saudi political elite appeared inclined, as their king was, to view Maliki as an Iranian agent. An open question is whether they did so because they themselves had assessed the data in a way similar to Abdullah or because they were simply conforming to their king's assessment. Interestingly, a U.S. diplomatic cable from 2009 reported that Abdullah had argued to U.S. officials that Maliki had "opened the door" to Iranian influence in Iraq; the Saudi foreign policy adviser interviewed for this book used remarkably similar language in his interview, expressing his belief that Maliki "opened the door" for Iran to assert supremacy in Iraq.[114] This view, albeit without this same phrase, is also asserted in an internal Saudi Foreign Ministry document from 2009.[115] Such similarity of views suggests a tendency toward groupthink within the Saudi leadership; while groupthink is a fairly common phenomenon, the important point for this study is that, by suppressing dissenting views and therefore critical evaluation of a problem, groupthink may lead to suboptimal decision-making.[116] Furthermore, the view that Maliki handed Iraq to Iran is in and of itself somewhat strange, since Saudi leaders had been claiming since 2003 that the U.S. had handed Iraq to Iran on a golden platter. In appearing so intent on explaining a phenomenon they were convinced existed, it seems they overlooked the inconsistency in their own explanations.

Whatever the validity of the Saudis' image of him, Maliki took an action in late 2006 that understandably angered the Saudi leadership. Saddam Hussein, who had been captured by coalition forces in December 2003, was convicted by an Iraqi court in November 2006 for ordering a 1982 massacre on the Shi'a town of Dujail and was sentenced to death by hanging. On 26 December, an Iraqi appeals court upheld the verdict, and on the morning of the thirtieth—the day that year marking the start of Eid al-Adha for Sunni Muslims (for the Shi'a it began the next day)—the coalition transferred custody of Saddam to the Iraqi government, and the former Iraqi dictator was executed immediately by Maliki's order. A video of the hanging, which showed Saddam surrounded by cheering executioners, circulated widely inside and outside Iraq. The execution was a highly polarizing event among Iraqis, celebrated by the Shi'a and regarded as deeply vengeful by Sunni Arabs.[117] For their part, Saudi leaders were outraged by the execution, but less because of the escalation in sectarian tensions it created in Iraq than because they interpreted the execution as an indicator of Maliki's intention to undermine the kingdom's security. Eid al-Adha marks the end of the annual Hajj, and Ambassador Khalilzad recalls in his memoirs that on his next trip to Saudi Arabia, Interior Minister Prince Nayef argued to him that Saddam's execution could have triggered "a massive conflict" at the holy places and even suggested that this had been Maliki's objective.[118] While Maliki's order to execute Saddam during Eid al-Adha may have indeed been ill-considered, Saudi leaders' belief that he thereby sought to disrupt the Hajj appeared to stem more from egocentric bias—the tendency to perceive oneself as the central reference point when accounting for others' actions[119]—than a measured assessment of Maliki's decision-making calculus. What their attitude does reveal, however, is that by late 2006, the Saudi leadership assumed Maliki to be an enemy who harbored malign intent toward them.

Despite having formed a highly negative opinion of him, the Saudi leadership, or at least the Saudis interviewed for this book, did not actually appear to be particularly well informed about Maliki or the conditions of the Da'wa Party at the time. For instance, the Saudi foreign policy adviser expressed his view in an interview that the Da'wa Party was "very aggressive" and "very close to Iran," despite its reputation, at least among the Iraqi Shi'a, of relative weakness due to its lack of a militia and its historic effort to maintain independence from Iran. The Saudi foreign policy adviser gave as examples of his view the 1980 assassination attempt on Tariq Aziz by a Shi'i militant, which the Ba'thists had attributed to an Iranian plot,[120] as well as the 1985 assassination attempt on the emir of Kuwait.[121] This latter assassination attempt has actually been linked to Lebanese Hizballah operative Imad Mughniyah,[122] although a separate 1980s attack that took place in Kuwait—the 1983 bombing of the French and U.S. embassies in Kuwait City—is believed to have been carried out by a faction of Da'wa close to the Iranians, which had split from the mainstream of the party.[123] For his part, Prince Turki, when asked about his view of the relationship between Da'wa and Iran, explained that two branches of the party developed: one that took refuge in Iran and was subject to Iranian influence, and a second that took refuge in Syria and was therefore less receptive to Iran. When I replied that Maliki had chosen to live in Damascus, Prince Turki corrected me, explaining, "Well, no ... he spent more time in Iran."[124]

Humans have a natural tendency to overlook, distort, or discount information that contradicts their beliefs.[125] Whatever the validity of the Saudi foreign policy adviser's assessments of the 1980 assassination attempt on Tariq Aziz and the attacks in Kuwait during the eighties, his view that these events demonstrated Da'wa's close relationship to Iran in post-2003 Iraq assumes that the party was frozen in place in the 1980s. Furthermore, it does not take much research into Maliki's background to learn that he decided to leave Iran for Syria at the end of the Iran–Iraq War. While he was known for taking a particularly sectarian position with regard to de-Ba'thification prior to becoming prime minister, he was not known for being close to Iran. Thus, the statements made by the Saudi foreign policy adviser and Prince Turki above suggest that Saudi leaders were not really interested in learning more about him. In the research conducted for this book, nobody within the Saudi leadership appeared inclined to gather more information about Maliki in order to test their beliefs about him, although such a lack of self-criticism is not really surprising given that humans are not naturally inclined to test their hypotheses.[126] Having concluded that Maliki was an Iranian agent—or perhaps because their king had concluded he was an Iranian agent—the members of the Saudi regime appeared content to maintain this belief.

Thus, King Abdullah believed Maliki to be an untrustworthy Iranian agent, and once he had formed this perception, neither he nor anybody else in the Saudi leadership evinced any inclination to update it by gathering new information about the Iraqi premier. Further highlighting his rejection of Maliki, by late 2006, Abdullah was urging the Bush administration to replace him with Allawi, the former Iraqi prime minister widely known for his anti-Iranian views. Abdullah's support for Allawi's return to the premiership will be touched upon below and explored further in the next chapter. Below the focus is on the origin of Abdullah and Allawi's close personal relationship, as well as Allawi's ambitions, following his poor showing in the Iraqi elections of December 2005, to retake the premiership in place of Maliki.

Abdullah and Ayad Allawi

During this period, one in which King Abdullah displayed extreme skepticism toward Maliki, a close personal relationship developed between him and Allawi. In fact, Abdullah and Allawi had a significant mutual connection: Iraqi scholar Hasan al-Alawi, an associate of Allawi who was also a secular Shi'i and former Ba'thist. During the Saddam era, al-Alawi had lived in Saudi Arabia, where he had developed a close friendship with Abd al-Aziz al-Tuwaijri, then Abdullah's chief of staff. Al-Alawi and al-Tuwaijri shared a special bond over the Abbasid-era poet al-Mutanabbi, and they became so close that al-Alawi actually wrote a biography of al-Tuwaijri.[127] According to an Iraqi diplomat who interacted with Abdullah, it was al-Alawi who introduced Allawi to Abdullah, and this source added that Abdullah "loved" Allawi.[128] The Saudi royal family insider interviewed for this book similarly observed that Abdullah and Allawi had "good chemistry," particularly because Allawi was not at all religious.[129] Indeed, Allawi had never really practiced his Shi'a faith. It is not correct to say that he had no identity as a Shi'i, rather that his identity was that of a secular Shi'i distant from the Iraqi religious establishment and Iran. In fact, Ali Allawi characterized his cousin's principal base in post-2003 Iraq as "highly secular Shiʿa" who had a "hatred of Iran."[130]

Moreover, during this period Allawi appears to have been undertaking a campaign outside of Iraq to engineer a return to the Iraqi premiership. According to U.S. diplomatic cables, Allawi's electoral list had been significantly disappointed by their results in the December 2005 elections, having obtained only 25 of a total of 275 parliamentary seats.[131] Nevertheless, Allawi was assessed to harbor a "not-so-secret desire" to retake the premiership; from 2006 he spent most of his time traveling outside Iraq, and was believed to be seeking support from Arab governments "for a secular, cross-sectarian front as an alternative to the Maliki government."[132] Indeed, it appears that Allawi had long been driven by his desire to attain power, and that his primary model to do so was through external patronage. Ghassan Atiyyah, a long-time associate of Allawi, expressed his view in an interview that Allawi had been "hungry for power" since his days in the pre-2003 Iraqi opposition, while a former American diplomat observed that Allawi "focused virtually all of his energies ... waiting for outside parties to bring him to power."[133] In fact, by 2007 the amount of time Allawi was spending outside Iraq became a cause of frustration for the members of his electoral coalition who had joined Maliki's cabinet. One member of Allawi's list told U.S. officials in Baghdad that the former prime minister's objective to obtain outside Arab support for a new government was "unhelpful," while another called it "strange and weird."[134] Members of other political coalitions were less kind: they expressed the view to U.S. officials in 2007 that Allawi was "motivated solely by his ambition to be Prime Minister again."[135]

By late 2006, Allawi had won the backing of Abdullah, who at this point began to press the Bush administration to reinstall the former prime minister in power.[136] Indeed, according to the Saudi royal family insider, from 2006 Abdullah regarded Allawi as the "only" solution for the new Iraq.[137] Throughout this period, the highly secular and openly anti-Iranian Allawi was the only Iraqi Shiʻi leader toward whom Abdullah appeared enthusiastic. Abdullah's preference for Allawi further underscored his suspicion of the Shiʻa, or at least those who were more religiously oriented, and Iran more broadly.

Moreover, we find that the following was taking place: Abdullah, who was susceptible to manipulation by close confidants, as claimed by the Saudi royal family insider, was promoting for the Iraqi premiership such a confidant who was assessed to be motivated by his ambition to re-attain power in Iraq. This situation generates an obvious question: Was Allawi manipulating Abdullah to achieve his objective? This question seems particularly pertinent to the content of this chapter, as it has been demonstrated that Abdullah appeared willing to engage with Maliki in July 2006, but thereafter became hardened against any further engagement for reasons that are not clear. This question remains unresolved by this research, although, intriguingly, a U.S. diplomatic cable from 2008 indicates that Allawi himself told U.S. officials that he had recently been discussing with Arab leaders what he called "Iran's growing interference in Iraq's internal affairs."[138] Regardless, what this chapter has aimed to demonstrate is that the Saudi leadership was indeed being fed disinformation at this time, which depicted Maliki as subservient to Iran. While Muhammad al-Dayani of Tawafuq appears to have been responsible for passing the forged documents, highlighted above, to the Saudi leadership, it seems plausible that various individuals and factions antagonistic to the new Iraqi premier would have sought to influence Abdullah's opinion of Maliki.

Conclusion

In sum, King Abdullah concluded soon after meeting Maliki in July 2006 that the Iraqi premier was an untrustworthy Iranian client, and decided therefore not to engage with him further. That Abdullah refused to reconsider his position suggests that he lacked willingness to update his beliefs—for instance, as a result of his negative attitudes toward Iran and the Shi'a—and it seems that in general he was a relatively inflexible thinker with the tendency to make black-and-white assessments. In addition, Saudi Arabia faced no economic imperative, as Jordan did, that might have compelled Abdullah to reassess his decision. The next chapter will put Abdullah's decision not to engage with the Maliki government into sharper relief, because various parties—Bush administration officials, members of the Maliki government, other Arab leaders, and apparently Abdullah's own senior foreign policy advisers—would urge him, unsuccessfully, to reconsider his position. By contrast, other Arab states would begin to engage meaningfully with the Maliki government in 2008, as Jordan had begun to do in 2005. In doing so, the leaders of these states showed a greater willingness to update their beliefs, and therefore demonstrated a greater flexibility with regard to the new Iraq than did Abdullah of Saudi Arabia.

4

SAUDI ARABIA SHUNS IRAQ

Constructivist scholar Alexander Wendt argues that enmity
tends to become self-fulfilling. When one actor casts another in
the role of an enemy, the second is forced to "mirror back" this
representation, because it feels threatened by the first. Whether
or not the second actor was actually a threat to the first at the
start of their interaction, a "logic of enmity" sets in between
them, compelling them to act in ways that are actually threatening to each other.[1]

Drawing on this logic, this chapter demonstrates how King
Abdullah cast Nuri al-Maliki in the role of an enemy, which
ultimately led to the development of a conflictual relationship
between the Saudi and Iraqi governments. The Saudi king did so
by adamantly refusing to engage with Maliki or his government.
Indeed, throughout the period from late 2006 to early 2009
Abdullah rejected various attempts made by a range of parties to
compel him to engage. These attempts were undertaken by
members of the Maliki government; by senior officials in the
Bush administration, including Bush himself; by Arab leaders
like Egyptian President Hosni Mubarak and Abdullah II of

Jordan; and even by some of Abdullah's own senior foreign policy advisers. That Abdullah rebuffed all these efforts led Iraqi officials, foremost the prime minister, to suspect that the Saudi king opposed Iraq's Shi'a ascendance and desired different leadership in Baghdad. Indeed, Maliki himself would begin to feel personally threatened by the Saudis, inferring they bore malign intent toward him. In this way, the Saudis' enemy image of Maliki ended up generating an enemy image on the part of Maliki toward the Saudis—as Wendt would expect, being treated as an enemy by the Saudis, Maliki began to see the Saudis as *his* enemy. Moreover, Maliki eventually began to act in ways inimical to the Saudi leadership and, by spring 2009, he had adopted a bitter tone toward them in public. In short, a self-fulfilling prophecy was coming to fruition: Abdullah's refusal to engage with Maliki based on his perception that Maliki was an enemy of Saudi Arabia led Maliki to express an increasing degree of hostility toward the Saudis.

Nevertheless, the irony of Abdullah's perception of Maliki as an Iranian agent came into sharper relief during this period, as Maliki began to take initiatives that actually undermined Iranian influence in Iraq. Most significantly, in spring 2008 Maliki launched a campaign against Iranian-backed Shi'a militias, and the success of this campaign was considered a setback for Iran.

King Abdullah Breaks with the Bush Administration on Iraq

In late 2006, tension mounted between the Bush administration and the Saudi leadership over the changes that had taken place in Iraq. During this period, the Saudi leadership pushed the Bush administration to reinstall Ayad Allawi in power in Baghdad, while the Bush administration pressed the Saudi leadership to engage with the Maliki government. However, the two sides were deadlocked: Bush refused to reinstall Allawi, while

King Abdullah refused to engage with the Iraqi government. For his part, Abdullah appeared impervious to U.S. entreaties that he adopt a different approach to the new Iraq.

As 2006 drew to a close, there was increasing speculation that the Bush administration would order a withdrawal from Iraq, which was then in the midst of a full-blown civil war. The Saudi leadership, meanwhile, stridently opposed such a U.S. withdrawal. Bush was under significant domestic pressure to order a pull-out at this time: in the November 2006 mid-term elections, Democrats, having campaigned on the need to begin a withdrawal, won control of the House of Representatives, and, in December, a bipartisan group of prominent former U.S. officials, known as the Iraq Study Group, released a report that formally recommended a phased exit. The U.S.'s Arab allies, however, articulated to the Bush administration in late 2006 that they vehemently opposed such a withdrawal, which they feared would allow Iran to consolidate supremacy over Iraq.[2] For his part, Saudi Arabia's interior minister, Prince Nayef bin Abd al-Aziz, told U.S. officials in December 2006 that there was "no justification to leave Iraq as a playground for Iran."[3] Furthermore, according to a former American diplomat who interacted with the Saudi leadership, the Saudis not only communicated their opposition to a U.S. withdrawal, but also began to press the Bush administration at this time to "overturn everything that had happened since 2003."[4] This source recounted that while King Abdullah "reluctantly" accepted that Bush would not reinstall Iraq's Sunni Arabs to a dominant position in Iraq, he still pressed the president to take two actions at this time: to discard Iraq's new constitution and to reinstall Allawi as premier. According to this source, Abdullah argued that Iraq's leader could not be a "servant of Iran."[5] Bush, however, refused this Saudi entreaty. According to a Saudi royal family insider, Bush's refusal made Abdullah intensely upset.[6]

While the Saudi leadership actively opposed a U.S. withdrawal from Iraq, they nevertheless prepared for this scenario. In particular, they began to signal to their U.S. counterparts their intent to support Iraq's Sunni insurgency in the case of a U.S. exit; as an example, an employee of the Saudi embassy in Washington wrote in the *Washington Post* in November 2006 that "one of the consequences" of a U.S. withdrawal "will be massive Saudi intervention to stop Iranian-backed Shiite militias from butchering Iraqi Sunnis."[7] Furthermore, in October, the Saudi leadership had hosted a cross-sectarian reconciliation conference of Iraqi *ulama* in Mecca; the conference had been overshadowed, however, by a meeting King Abdullah had held at the time of the conference with Sunni Arab Iraqi scholar Harith al-Dari of the insurgent-sympathizing AMS.[8] Then, in early December, the *Daily Telegraph* reported that the Saudi leadership had informed the Bush administration that they would provide financing and weapons to Sunni insurgents in the case of a withdrawal.[9]

In January 2007, Bush, far from initiating a withdrawal from Iraq, ordered a surge of U.S. forces to the country; the Saudi leadership approved of what came to be known as "the surge," but Abdullah would still publicly distance himself from U.S. policy at this time. In late 2006, the administration had conducted, secretly, its own policy review, culminating in the president's decision to send an additional five U.S. brigades, about 20,000 soldiers, to Iraq for a one-year period. The forces would be located primarily in and around Baghdad, the site of the country's worst violence.[10] According to a senior Bush administration official, the Saudi leadership fully supported the deployment of additional U.S. forces to Iraq, as this indicated to them that the U.S. would not cede the country to Iran.[11] Nevertheless, it had become clear by this point that, having failed to convince the Bush administration to reinstall Allawi, the Saudi leadership would not be able to push the Bush administration to chart a different political course in Iraq. In March 2007, King Abdullah then took a significant step that appeared to signal that he was distancing himself from Bush administration policy in Iraq: at the 2007 Arab summit, hosted in Riyadh on 28–29 March, the Saudi king declared in his opening address that the "beloved Iraq" was under "an illegal foreign occupation."[12]

Abdullah's statement at the 2007 Arab summit impelled the Bush administration to redouble its efforts to reconcile the Saudi leadership to the new Iraq. According to a former American diplomat, "We wanted the Saudis to be engaged. We felt they had to be engaged."[13] In April, the Americans and the Iraqis made plans for Maliki to return to the kingdom to reengage personally with Abdullah. Indeed, on 19 April the Maliki government announced that the prime minister would soon travel to Egypt and Saudi Arabia "to open new relations with the Arab states."[14] A few days later, Maliki visited Cairo, but his trip to Saudi Arabia did not take place: it seems that it had been planned without in fact securing the Saudi leadership's consent, and when the time for the visit arrived, King Abdullah refused to host him.[15] Nevertheless, the Bush administration continued to press Abdullah to engage with the new Iraqi government. In May, Vice President Dick Cheney, thought by the administration to have influence with the Saudi leadership for having strongly advocated the defense of Saudi Arabia within the George H.W. Bush administration during the Gulf War, traveled to the kingdom and met with Abdullah. However, Abdullah told Cheney that he was no longer willing even to discuss the subject of Iraq with his U.S. counterparts.[16] In addition, according to a senior Bush administration official, Bush himself would press Abdullah to engage with the Maliki government whenever the two leaders would meet, albeit without success. The senior Bush administration official recalled in an interview that the effort to compel

Abdullah to engage was "a full-frontal assault from all of us."[17] In fact, Prince Turki al-Faisal pointed out in an interview that not only the Bush administration but also the Obama administration urged Abdullah to engage with Iraq.[18]

In replacing Saddam Hussein's regime with a democracy, which naturally allowed the Iraqi Shi'a to rise to power, Bush's foreign policy team had disregarded the interests of their ally, Saudi Arabia. The Saudi leadership had been highly skeptical of the Bush administration's plan to invade Iraq; however, if Bush was determined to invade, the Saudis wanted him to topple Saddam and his senior lieutenants, while keeping his Sunni Arab-dominated regime in place. This had been Saudi Arabia's objective since the Gulf War: Saddam's ouster in a manner that was least disruptive to his regime. Having completely flouted Saudi preferences, Bush and his senior advisers then sought to reconcile the Saudi leadership to the new order they had established in Baghdad. They met no success. In short, the Bush administration could not compel King Abdullah to accept something he regarded as fundamentally opposed to his interests, no matter how deep and historic the friendship between the United States and Saudi Arabia. This strange turn of events, whereby the Bush administration midwifed a new Iraqi order to which one of their closest friends in the region was adamantly opposed, constituted one of the more significant unintended consequences of Bush's decision to pursue regime change in Iraq.

Nevertheless, the rest of this chapter will demonstrate that Abdullah, in refusing to engage with Iraq, was becoming an outlier among Arab leaders. Not only did Iraq's other Arab neighbors begin to restore meaningful relations with Baghdad during this period, but many of Abdullah's Arab counterparts, as well as his own foreign policy advisers, were urging him, like the Bush administration, to reconsider his decision. Beyond his grievances toward the U.S., Abdullah's refusal to reassess his approach to

Iraq indicated a disinclination to update his beliefs, whether because of his negative attitudes toward Iran and the Shi'a, his tendency to form black-and-white assessments, or some other, unknown reason. Moreover, as highlighted above, the Saudi leadership was emitting plenty of signals of their hostility toward the new order in Iraq at this time, for instance hinting that they would support Iraq's Sunni insurgency in the case of a U.S. withdrawal and publicly breaking with U.S. policy at the 2007 Arab summit. These signals of Saudi hostility were beginning to elicit unease on the part of senior Maliki government officials about Saudi intentions.

Maliki's Growing Concern over Saudi Intentions

Having initially been optimistic about his mission to engage with Saudi Arabia before and immediately after his July 2006 trip to the kingdom, by the spring of 2007 Maliki seemed increasingly anxious that the Saudi leadership bore malign intent toward him, believing in particular that they were trying to unseat him. It seems unsurprising that Maliki would feel threatened by Saudi Arabia at this point. As seen, identity differences and an estimate of intentions are core components of threat perception. Abdullah and Maliki lay on opposite sides of the Sunni–Shi'a divide, and more to the point, by spring 2007 Abdullah had taken a number of actions that pointed to his hostile intentions to the new Iraq, as well as to Maliki personally. Abdullah's actions included calling the U.S. occupation of Iraq illegal, denouncing Maliki as a liar, and canceling Maliki's trip to the kingdom. Indeed, not only Maliki, but other Iraqi leaders, including Kurdish and Sunni Arab ones, became concerned by these Saudi actions. Moreover, it should be pointed out that Maliki's perception appears to have been basically correct, given that Abdullah was then pushing the Bush administration to replace him with Allawi. One of the principal arguments of this book is that by essentially rejecting Maliki, Abdullah cast the Iraqi leader into the role of an enemy; this in turn compelled Maliki to begin to see the Saudis as an enemy, which ultimately made a conflictual relationship between the two sides more likely.

Indeed, by early 2007 Maliki had become highly suspicious of Saudi Arabia, although, as he confided to U.S. officials at that time, he still wanted a positive relationship.[19] Even before Abdullah's statement at the March 2007 Arab summit and his canceling of Maliki's April 2007 trip, the Iraqi prime minister was expressing concern to U.S. officials that the Saudis desired new leadership in Baghdad.[20] Unsurprisingly, Abdullah's actions then reinforced Maliki's anxiety. In late April 2007, U.S. officials assessed that Maliki was "very concerned about the depth of Saudi opposition to him and his government."[21] Indeed, Maliki was of the opinion, according to a U.S. diplomatic cable, that he himself was the intended target of Abdullah's "illegal foreign occupation" statement.[22] Furthermore, Maliki knew that Bush and Cheney had both personally tried, and failed, to encourage Abdullah to adopt a different approach to Iraq. In his written exchange with me, Maliki recalled Bush's exasperation after one of his failed attempts to compel Abdullah to engage.[23] Following its formation, the Maliki government faced a series of domestic political crises, most significantly a cabinet crisis in the summer of 2007, addressed below. According to Ryan Crocker, who arrived in Baghdad as U.S. ambassador in spring 2007, in general, Maliki "firmly believed" that whatever political machinations were unfolding in Baghdad, "the Saudis were somehow involved."[24]

By thus tending to detect indicators of what he perceived to be Saudi Arabia's malign intent toward him, Maliki had himself begun to perceive his neighbor through the lens of an enemy image. It should not, however, be a surprise that he did so, as

Abdullah had fairly unambiguously expressed his hostility toward him and his government by this point. It will be recalled from Chapter 1 that the Saudis' enemy image of the Islamic Republic developed in large part as a response to the Iranian revolutionaries' continual rejection of Saudi conciliation over the course of the 1980s. In both cases—the origin of the Saudis' enemy image of Iran in the 1980s and the origin of Maliki's enemy image of Saudi Arabia in the 2000s—the image took shape because one party tried to conciliate the other, but was rebuffed. It should be reemphasized here that the core of an enemy image is a belief that another country bears malign intent to the perceiver, whether or not the perceiver reciprocates such intent. With regard to Maliki and the Saudi leadership, it is not contended that Maliki himself harbored malign intent toward Saudi Arabia at this time; rather, in line with the evidence presented above, he perceived that the Saudis did toward him.

But it was not simply Maliki, or even Iraqi leaders from the Shi'a community, who assessed the Saudi stance toward the new Iraq to be highly problematic. Leaders from Iraq's two other principal ethno-sectarian communities, the Kurds and Sunni Arabs, did as well. In general, Shi'a, Sunni Arab, and Kurdish leaders assessed Saudi Arabia's negative stance to derive from the Saudi leadership's negative attitude to the Shi'a ascendance. Indeed, in Maliki's perception, as he himself expressed it in our written exchange, King Abdullah regarded it as "impermissible" that Baghdad, the capital of the medieval Abbasid Caliphate, should be under Shi'a rule.[25] For his part, Sami al-Askari, then a close adviser to Maliki, summed up his perspective with reference to King Abdullah, stating in an interview, "The Shi'a are his enemy."[26] Kurdish leaders in the Maliki government had a similar, if less openly bitter, assessment, and in moments of candor, it appears that at least some Sunni Arab leaders did as well. Jalal Talabani, Iraq's Kurdish president who, as will be examined further below, interceded with Abdullah to try to change his attitude, expressed his opinion to U.S. officials in Baghdad that the Saudi leadership were having difficulty "accept[ing] that Iraqi Shia were, for the first time, 'on top.'"[27] This also appeared to be the assessment of Iraq's most senior Sunni Arab leader in the first Maliki government, Vice President Tariq al-Hashimi. Al-Hashimi, in a conversation with Assistant Secretary of State Jeffrey Feltman in early 2010, observed that the Saudi leadership blamed Maliki for the deterioration of Saudi–Iraq relations, but al-Hashimi asserted that this was "an excuse"; according to the vice president, the Saudi leadership were "obsessed with what they perceived to be a Shia takeover of control in Iraq."[28]

Al-Hashimi's assessment is particularly remarkable because he, like other Iraqi Sunni Arab leaders, had himself been reluctant at first to accept that the Sunnis were a demographic minority in Iraq.[29] Indeed, in the aftermath of the December 2005 election, he had argued to U.S. officials in Baghdad that the victory of the Shiʿa Islamist UIA had been the result of "massive voter fraud."[30] In the following years, however, it appears that al-Hashimi reconciled himself to the Shiʿa ascendance, because he told Assistant Secretary of State Feltman in early 2010 that he had counseled Saudi leaders that "reality had to be accepted," emphasizing to Feltman that, "This is the reality in Iraq now."[31] Thus it appears that even Iraq's senior Sunni Arab politician had urged the Saudi leadership to adopt a different approach to the new Shiʿa-led Iraq.

As an example of Maliki's perception that the Saudis bore malign intent toward him, in May 2007 he began to suspect that outside states were actively trying to unseat him; furthermore, there were indications at this time that the Saudi leadership were trying to do just that, thereby validating his perception. In May, Maliki expressed his belief to U.S. officials in Baghdad that

"Iraq's neighbors"—the cable does not further specify—were "trying to undermine his government" through support to political figures like Ayad Allawi.[32] In fact, it appears that, despite the Bush administration's refusal to reinstall Allawi, the Saudi leadership was indeed seeking to maneuver the former prime minister back into the premiership through parliamentary action. In early May, David Ignatius, foreign affairs columnist at the *Washington Post*, wrote: "The Saudis appear to favor replacing the Maliki government ... and are quietly backing former interim prime minister Ayad Allawi ... Allawi's camp believes he is close to having enough votes, thanks in part to Saudi political and financial support."[33] Ignatius' assessment, based on his own reporting, that the Saudi leadership were trying to promote Allawi through parliamentary elections would seem to validate the perception Maliki had himself formed that they sought to install new leadership in Baghdad.

That summer a severe cabinet crisis occurred, testing the durability of Maliki's government, and again there would be hints of a Saudi connection. On 26 June, the home of Culture Minister As'ad Kamal al-Hashimi, a member of the Sunni Arab Tawafuq coalition, was raided after a warrant was issued for his arrest in connection with a 2005 assassination attempt on a rival politician. The culture minister went into hiding, and four other Tawafuq ministers boycotted Maliki's cabinet.[34] In late July, Tawafuq escalated the crisis, announcing that all six of its cabinet ministers would suspend their cabinet participation in a week's time if a list of demands, such as the disbanding of militias, was not met.[35] On 1 August, the six Tawafuq ministers formally withdrew from the cabinet, and five days later, five ministers from Allawi's Iraqi List joined the boycott.[36] In the midst of the crisis, an indication of Saudi interference in Iraq came to light. On 20 July, Zalmay Khalilzad, then U.S. permanent representative at the UN, published an opinion piece in the *New York*

Times ostensibly about the UN's role in Iraq. The piece was fairly unremarkable, with the exception of a single, oblique sentence: "Several of Iraq's neighbors—not only Syria and Iran but also some friends of the United States—are pursuing destabilizing policies" in Iraq.[37] Whatever his purpose had been in writing that sentence, a week later, another *New York Times* article revealed that, according to unidentified Bush administration officials, Khalilzad "was referring specifically to Saudi Arabia," and further elaborated that the administration was "voicing increasing anger at ... Saudi Arabia's unproductive role" in Iraq due to its "financial support" of Maliki's rivals.[38] In conversations with U.S. officials, Maliki had alleged that the Tawafuq walkout had outside Arab support:[39] while this *New York Times* reporting, which appeared in the midst of the crisis, does not confirm Maliki's claim, it appears to validate his suspicions.

In sum, by early 2007 Maliki began to perceive that the Saudi leadership bore malign intent toward his government and toward him personally. He therefore began to feel threatened. Nevertheless, Maliki did not want a conflictual relationship with Saudi Arabia; following the travails of the Saddam era, he, like most of Iraq's new leaders, wanted positive relations with all of Iraq's neighbors. Indeed, the second half of this chapter will demonstrate that, in 2008, members of the Maliki government, including Maliki himself, sought to reassure the Saudi leadership that they had friendly intentions toward it—that they were not in fact an enemy, as Abdullah perceived. Nevertheless, their attempts at reassurance did not meet with success. In spring 2009, Maliki essentially gave up on trying to conciliate Saudi Arabia and would publicly articulate his frustrations with it for the first time. Thus, through the mechanism of a self-fulfilling prophecy, the Saudis' subjective perception that the Maliki government was an enemy ended up leading to objectively real tensions between Saudi Arabia and Iraq.

SAUDI ARABIA SHUNS IRAQ

Saudi Initiatives to Engage with the Maliki Government?

While nobody in the Saudi leadership appeared to have a favorable opinion of Maliki, King Abdullah's principal foreign policy advisers in fact advocated engagement with the Maliki government so as to establish a Saudi presence in Iraq that would dilute Iranian influence there. They even appeared to develop plans for engagement. King Abdullah, however, did not accept their view, and appears to have terminated their proposals. As Abdullah himself reportedly communicated to U.S. officials in 2008, he "rejected the suggestion" that Saudi engagement would empower the Maliki government to pursue an independent course from Iran, since he doubted the "willingness" of the Maliki government to do so.[40] Thus, it appears that Abdullah took the decision not to engage with the new Iraq not as a result of, but rather despite, his advisers' counsel. Furthermore, no evidence came to light in the course of my research that suggested that Abdullah's Sudairi half-brothers, Crown Prince Sultan and Prince Nayef, played any role in taking this decision. Abdullah therefore appears to have fit Margaret Hermann's definition of a predominant leader, as a single individual who had the power to quash dissent and make a foreign policy decision alone. This finding stands in contrast to the view, advanced by many scholars of Saudi foreign policy as highlighted in the introduction, that Saudi foreign policy decisions were traditionally taken through the consensus of the senior members of the royal family.

Starting in 2007, Abdullah's senior foreign policy advisers appeared to become more open to engagement with Iraq, apparently as a result not only of the Bush administration's forceful efforts to compel Saudi engagement, but of efforts undertaken by Iraqi leaders as well. Kurdish leaders in the Maliki government, specifically Foreign Minister Zebari and President Talabani, took the initiative in this respect. In early 2007, Zebari reported to

U.S. officials that on a recent trip to Saudi Arabia, he had pressed his Saudi interlocutors, Princes Saud al-Faisal and Muqrin, to engage with the Iraqi government in order to "enhance Iraqi independence from Iran," and had urged them to desist from making "antagonistic comments" that instead "push[ed] Iraqi leaders toward Iran."[41] At this time, Zebari expressed optimism to U.S. officials; he said he had "sensed a different attitude" from his Saudi counterparts, whom he believed were now "more engaged."[42] For his part, President Talabani intervened directly with King Abdullah on this topic. Talabani told U.S. officials that he had articulated to Abdullah that Iranian influence in Iraq should be "no surprise" if the Arab states isolated the country, thereby depriving it of a "counterbalance" to its Shi'i neighbor.[43]

In August 2007, indications emerged that the Saudi leadership was seriously contemplating a new approach to Iraq. On 1 August, the same day as Tawafuq's cabinet walkout, Prince Saud al-Faisal announced at a news conference that a Saudi delegation would soon travel to Baghdad to explore the possibility of reopening the Saudi embassy, which had been closed in 1990 following the Iraqi invasion of Kuwait.[44] Two weeks later, Prince Muhammad bin Faisal bin Turki al-Saud, the Foreign Ministry official who would lead the delegation, met with U.S. diplomats in Riyadh. While Prince Muhammad was no less distrustful of Prime Minister Maliki than were other members of the Saudi political elite, he reported that he had advocated within Saudi circles the reestablishment of a presence in Baghdad, as the kingdom would have no choice but to coexist with the new Iraq. He stated to the Americans, as attributed to him in a U.S. cable: "It is in our national security interests ... to help the U.S. to succeed ... We have to be in Iraq."[45] He anticipated that not only would the embassy be reopened, but that an ambassador would also be sent.[46]

The Saudi delegation indeed traveled to Baghdad in late August, but nothing would come of this initiative.[47] In April

2008, Prince Saud al-Faisal acknowledged to Ambassador Crocker, while the latter was in Saudi Arabia, that following the Saudi mission to Baghdad the previous summer, "the King simply forbade us from going any farther," an account that Abdullah himself, according to a U.S. diplomatic cable, confirmed to Crocker.[48] Nevertheless, Prince Muqrin spearheaded another plan in May 2008 to establish a presence in Iraq, this time via humanitarian assistance instead of diplomatic engagement. The Saudi intelligence chief expressed concern that, "in the future, Iraqis will ask what their large, rich neighbor did for them during the period of crisis and the answer will be nothing."[49] Therefore, according to Muqrin, the Saudi leadership was considering a provision of funds to the U.S. Commander's Emergency Response Program (CERP), a fund utilized by U.S. military commanders in Iraq to support humanitarian and reconstruction projects. Prince Muqrin stressed that the Saudi money needed to be visible in Iraq—he wanted the Iraqis to know it was coming from Saudi Arabia—and even suggested that Saudi aircraft could be used to deliver aid to outlying areas so that the Iraqi people could see the Saudi effort.[50] Nevertheless, three months later, U.S. officials were informed that Saudi money would not be committed to Iraqi reconstruction at the present time, including to the CERP program. The U.S. diplomatic cable reporting this development assessed that King Abdullah's "vehement distrust" of Maliki shaped the Saudi approach to the new Iraq.[51]

Furthermore, there is evidence that Abdullah's foreign policy advisers, like many outside parties, were trying to encourage him to adopt a different approach to Iraq. Prince Turki al-Faisal appeared reluctant, while being interviewed, to discuss differing attitudes within the Saudi leadership toward the need to engage with Iraq—asked whether anybody was urging a different course from that of King Abdullah, Prince Turki responded, "No"— likely reflecting the Saudi leadership's tendency not to discuss internal deliberations. By contrast, American sources elaborated on this subject. Ambassador Crocker explained in an interview that during his April 2008 trip to the kingdom, Princes Saud al-Faisal and Muqrin had professed their appreciation that Saudi engagement in Iraq would create a counterweight to Iranian influence there. However, both had said that the king still needed to be persuaded, and Crocker, for his part, said that he found Abdullah to be "absolutely immovable."[52] Another American source provided an even more illuminating account. This source is in private business and, having done business in the kingdom for decades, has developed personal relationships with senior Saudi officials. According to this source, Prince Saud al-Faisal and Ambassador Adel al-Jubeir recognized that Iran would "completely outmaneuver" Saudi Arabia in Iraq if the kingdom did not establish a presence there, and this source recalled, "I can't recount the number of times that I was told that one or both of them, separately or together, went to the king to say, 'We need to be present in Iraq,' and they just ran against a stone wall."[53] According to this American businessman, Abdullah's advisers, themselves being pressed by U.S. and Iraqi officials, tried to urge the king to establish such a Saudi presence, but not only would he not listen to their counsel, he would not even entertain the discussion.[54]

These research findings indicate that the Saudi leadership chose not to engage with the Maliki government because King Abdullah, perceiving Maliki as an untrustworthy Iranian agent, decided against such a course of action and then refused to reconsider his position. In turn, his negative feelings toward Maliki reflected more fundamentally a profound opposition to Iraq's new order. That he so obstinately refused to reconsider his position, despite the counsel of multiple parties, points to an unwillingness to update his beliefs, for instance because of his negative feelings toward Iran and the Shi'a, as well as a tendency to form rigid black-and-white assessments. Furthermore, that his decision prevailed, despite the views of other senior officials in the Saudi regime, indicates that he held the ultimate foreign policy decision-making authority within the Saudi state. Nobody could reverse his decision, while he himself could stifle debate. Nevertheless, the perception that lay at the heart of Abdullah's decision—that Maliki was loyal to Iran—was not well-based. The extent to which this perception was simply incorrect is elucidated below.

Maliki versus the Sadrists

Meanwhile, the landscape of Iraq's resistance had evolved. Over the course of 2007, coalition and Iraqi forces had been able to establish greater security in the Baghdad area, the epicenter of the civil war. On average, some 2,500 Iraqi civilians had been killed each month in 2006 in the civil war; civilian deaths reached 3,017 in January 2007, the month that President Bush announced the surge, but diminished to 996 by December and would continue to decline in 2008.[55] Furthermore, Al-Qaʿida in Iraq had seen a reversal in its fortunes. In June 2006, Abu Musʿab al-Zarqawi had been killed, and that fall a local tribal movement, known as the Awakening, had emerged in Anbar province to oppose Al-Qaʿida and had begun to coordinate with the coalition. By contrast, from 2006 the U.S.-led coalition found itself in an escalating conflict with Sadrist militias backed by Iran. For instance, explosively formed penetrator (EFP) attacks on coalition forces increased by 150 percent from January to December 2006, and continued to rise in 2007.[56] (The coalition assessed that EFPs were deployed exclusively by Shiʿa actors.[57]) Meanwhile, as the sectarian civil war subsided in 2007, violence within the Shiʿa community mounted, between the Shiʿa parties affiliated with the government on the one hand, and the Iranian-backed Sadrist militias on the other.

A SELF-FULFILLING PROPHECY

In the spring of 2008, Prime Minister Maliki would decide to strike back against the Sadrists, first in the southern port city of Basra and then in their Baghdad base of Sadr City. Maliki's assault on the Sadrist militias constituted a significant gamble, and his success marked a major reversal in his political fortunes. Most significantly, Tawafuq would choose to rejoin his cabinet as a result, and furthermore the next, and final, section of this chapter will demonstrate that many of Iraq's Arab neighbors would also begin to engage meaningfully with his government in the wake of the Basra and Sadr City operations. Indeed, by confronting the Sadrist militias—and by extension Iran, their chief patron—Maliki took an action that reassured many of his Sunni Arab compatriots and Sunni Arab neighbors that he intended to serve Iraq's national, as opposed to his own narrow sectarian, interests, as well as to pursue a path independent of Iran. The next section will also demonstrate that the Maliki government sought to capitalize on the goodwill generated by the Basra and Sadr City operations to reengage with Saudi Arabia, albeit without success.

Just as the Sunni Arab tribes in Anbar had begun to turn against Al-Qaʿida, the Shiʿa community began to turn against the Sadrist militias in 2007. The threat from Al-Qaʿida having receded, intra-Shiʿa violence mounted at this time. The Sadrist militias' brutality had increased during the sectarian civil war, while their discipline and internal cohesion, already low at the outset, had diminished, and fellow Shiʿa complained that the militias had become increasingly violent toward them. Iraqi bystanders were frequently unintended victims of Sadrist attacks on coalition forces, and in many cases the militias were even operating as assassins or kidnappers for hire.[58] Furthermore, the Sadrist militias had begun to target the Iraqi government, for instance launching mortar attacks on the seat of the government in Baghdad's International Zone,[59] creating a strange situation in which a militant group that received funding and supplies from Iran was fighting a government supported by Iran. In late August 2007, Sadrist-instigated violence reached a crescendo. During a Shi'a holiday, Sadrists attacked Badr militiamen who had been deployed to guard the shrines in Karbala, where a large celebration was taking place. (As previously seen, Badr was the paramilitary force affiliated with SCIRI, and rivalry between it and the Sadrist militias reflected the longstanding competition between SCIRI and the Sadrists. Moreover, in 2007 SCIRI changed its name to the Islamic Supreme Council of Iraq, and hereinafter will be referred to as ISCI.) In the Badr–Sadrist confrontation of August 2007, fifty-two people were killed, many of them pilgrims who had traveled to Karbala for the religious festival.[60] Two days of fighting ensued between the Sadrists and Badr, until Muqtada al-Sadr, in recognition of outrage in the Shi'a community against his group, announced a six-month ceasefire for the militias bearing his name. Although Muqtada had never effectively been in control of these militias, his ceasefire order was widely obeyed.[61] The factions that did not comply consisted primarily of criminal gangs, operating under the veil of Sadrist legitimacy, and the Special Groups that had been trained in Iran.[62]

Meanwhile, the southern city of Basra was in a state of chaos. British forces had been in command of the deep south since 2003, but the light British footprint, amounting to 4,000 troops in 2007, had meant that this region had been rife with violence and disorder since 2003.[63] In Basra, militias affiliated with local Shi'a political parties, such as the Sadrists, ISCI, and the Fadila Party, competed for control of the city.[64] Nevertheless, British forces transferred control of Basra province to Iraqi forces in December 2007. Thereafter, violence rose dramatically in the city of Basra, with the coalition assessing that "murder, intimidation, kidnappings, rape, and torture" had become commonplace.[65]

Violence against women was particularly dire. In 2007, 133 Basrawi women were reported to have been murdered by Shi'a militias, although the actual number was thought to be much higher. In the first three months of 2008, another thirty-eight women were known to have been killed.[66]

In late March 2008, Prime Minister Maliki made a hasty and unexpected decision to confront the Shi'a militias in Basra, informing coalition commander General David Petraeus that he would lead an operation by Iraqi forces, codenamed Charge of the Knights, on the city in two days' time.[67] The reasoning behind Maliki's hasty decision was, and still is, the subject of debate. Many observers saw it as politically motivated, intended to undermine the Sadrists, the chief target of the assault, who by this point had become his political rival.[68] By contrast, in the U.S. view, as expressed in an interview by a former U.S. diplomat, Maliki was "sickened" by the increasing reports of brutal attacks against Basrawi civilians, especially women.[69] However, in an interview in 2020, Mowaffaq al-Rubaie, a former member of Da'wa who was then Iraq's national security adviser, brought greater clarity to why Maliki initiated Charge of the Knights. According to al-Rubaie, Sistani's representative in Basra had called Maliki to tell him that, "Enough is enough," with reference to the security breakdown in Basra. Maliki interpreted this exchange with Sistani's representative as a green light from Sistani to take action.[70]

Launched in Basra on 25 March 2008, Charge of the Knights turned into a month-and-a-half-long operation against the Sadrist militias. At its outset, Maliki framed the operation as a campaign to reimpose law and order, declaring that his objective was to restore "the law of the land" in what had become a "nation of gangs, militias and outlaws."[71] The Sadrists immediately took to the streets, not only in Basra but also in Baghdad.[72] Over the coming days, fighting spread throughout the south, with

U.S. troops reinforcing the Iraqi government side. On the thirtieth, Muqtada called on the Sadrist militiamen to lay down
their weapons.[73] Maliki sent a negotiating team to Iran, where
Muqtada was located, and by the end of April, the government
announced it was in control of Basra.[74] Nevertheless, the confrontation had continued in Baghdad. On 6 April, a month-long
joint Iraqi–U.S. operation began in Sadr City, marking the first
time since 2004 that the Iraqi government had allowed the coalition to mount a major campaign in what had become a safe
haven for the Sadrist militias, including Special Groups.[75] During
the operation, Maliki again sought to project himself as a secu-
rity-minded leader for all Iraqis, asserting, "I do not negotiate
with any outlaw group, not the Mahdi Army nor the Islamic
Army"—one of the main Sunni insurgent groups—"nor any
other group because this contradicts the principles of the state."[76]
In May, the government concluded another ceasefire with
Muqtada, and Iraqi forces took control of Sadr City.[77] In their
official account of the Basra and Sadr City operations, U.S. Army
historians contend that in neither place had the militias put up
significant resistance, as had been expected; rather, they had fled
in the face of Iraqi and coalition forces.[78]

Maliki's campaign against the Sadrists had constituted a significant political and military gamble. Indeed, in the first days of
the operation in Basra, Iraqi forces had been in danger of col-
lapsing, necessitating reinforcement by the coalition, and Sadrist
parliamentarians had retaliated against him by trying to push a
no-confidence vote through parliament.[79] Nevertheless, Iraq's
main political leaders, including Vice President al-Hashimi of
Tawafuq, rallied behind the prime minister. Maliki and al-
Hashimi had been locked in an "acrimonious public quarrel"
since Tawafuq's cabinet walkout the previous summer.[80] However,
within two weeks of the start of Charge of the Knights, al-
Hashimi praised Maliki's campaign against the Sadrists, and

released a statement indicating his willingness to reconcile with him.[81] In July, following three months of negotiations over ministerial appointments, Tawafuq rejoined Maliki's cabinet. Al-Hashimi explained that Tawafuq's position on the government at that time had changed following what he called Maliki's "historic decision" to confront the militias in Basra and Baghdad, and he declared that the government had taken "an unexpected huge stride in the right direction."[82]

Prime Minister Maliki, having staked his claim to leadership on quelling the Sadrists, and having survived the ensuing confrontation, continued to project himself as a leader for all Iraqis who was, moreover, independent of Iran. Speaking at a meeting of Iraq's neighbors, convened in Kuwait in late April 2008, Maliki asserted, "The new Iraq is ... a united, democratic and multiparty country keen on establishing good relations with all countries"; he also implicitly took aim at Iran, condemning "policies of interference" in Iraq's internal affairs that "fuel[ed] violence" in the country.[83] In an interview on the pan-Arab news channel, Al-Arabiya, in late April, a news anchor remarked to the prime minister, "It is said that what happened [in Basra] was due to al-Maliki's differences with Iran ... We used to always hear that al-Maliki is Iran's closest man. Have you turned against Iran?"; Maliki responded: "By God, I will frankly say I have never been Iran's man. I also told the Americans that I am not America's man in Iraq. I tell the Arab countries that I am not the man of Saudi Arabia, Syria, Turkey, the UAE, or any other country. I am Iraq's man in Iraq."[84] In confronting the Sadrists, and by extension Iran, Maliki had taken a significant action that reassured many Sunni Arabs that he genuinely intended to pursue a path independent of his neighbor.

Maliki took a more explicit stance against Iran in private conversations with U.S. officials at this time, and in fact there is evidence that the Iranians, for their part, regarded Maliki's campaign against the Sadrists as a setback for themselves. In mid-May, Maliki reported to Ambassador Crocker and General Petraeus that Iraqi forces' operations in Basra and Sadr City had uncovered "increasing evidence" of Iranian assistance to "criminal elements" in Iraq, and he asserted that the Iraqi Shiʻa were "sick and tired" of Iranian interference in the country.[85] Following a trip to Iran in early June, Maliki told U.S. officials that he had confronted senior Iranian officials over their meddling in Iraq.[86] Whatever the truth of Maliki's claim that he had confronted his Iranian counterparts, Vice President Adel Abd al-Mahdi separately informed U.S. officials that, based on his own conversations with senior Iranian officials, the Iranian regime viewed the prime minister's operations in Basra and Sadr City as "defeats," and it was therefore "re-examining" its Iraq policy.[87] While it is also difficult to substantiate Abd al-Mahdi's claim, he was an intra-Shiʻa rival of Maliki; indeed, in late 2007, ISCI had itself attempted to engineer a vote of no confidence against the prime minister.[88] Thus, it seems unlikely that Abd al-Mahdi would speak positively about Maliki to U.S. officials if he were not sincere. Whatever the case, according to the U.S. Army's official history of the Iraq War, the operations in Basra and Sadr City "permanently reduced" the effectiveness of EFP attacks on coalition forces. In the U.S. Army's assessment, Iran's militant proxies had suffered a debilitating blow.[89]

Maliki's decision to confront the Sadrist militias in the spring of 2008 opened a new era of engagement between Iraq and its Arab neighbors. In the following months, many Arab leaders would visit Baghdad, while emphasizing Iraq's rightful place within the Arab fold. These Arab states had been reassured about Maliki's intentions by the actions he had taken. The notable exception was Saudi Arabia. Despite Maliki's campaign against the Sadrists, King Abdullah remained convinced that the Iraqi prime minister was an agent of Iran. Abdullah therefore

chose not to reciprocate renewed attempts by the Maliki government to engage in the summer of 2008.

Arab Engagement with Iraq

Following the 2003 invasion, most of the Arab states were cool
toward engagement with the new Iraq, appearing to take a wait-
and-see approach. The exception to this pattern was Jordan,
which had started to make an effort to engage in 2005. By early
2008, Iraqi leaders were expressing the opinion that it was particularly important to establish a positive relationship with Saudi
Arabia, because they feared that its standoffish attitude to the
new Iraq was keeping most other Arab states aloof as well. At
this time, Foreign Minister Zebari renewed the efforts he had
been making since 2003 to urge Iraq's Arab neighbors to establish a diplomatic presence in Baghdad, and he told U.S. officials
that Saudi Arabia was the priority. In his view, which was shared
by other senior officials such as Vice President al-Hashimi and
National Security Adviser al-Rubaie, Saudi Arabia was "the
hinge": these leaders expressed concern to U.S. officials that
other Arab states would only begin to engage meaningfully with
Iraq once Saudi Arabia had chosen to do so.[90] In this view, Iraq
could not fully rejoin the Arab fold without the acceptance, or at
least acquiescence, of Saudi Arabia. Indeed, al-Rubaie emphasized in the pan-Arab press in spring 2008 the importance of
establishing a Saudi presence in Iraq, even if it was simply "symbolic," due to what he called the kingdom's economic, political,
and religious influence in the Arab and Muslim worlds.[91] For his
part, Prime Minister Maliki was expressing increasing frustration
and anger toward the Saudi leadership for depicting him as an
Iranian agent.[92] He confided to U.S. officials in April 2008: "We
welcome relations with the Saudis and we do not want tensions,
but neither do we want to be seen as weak. We are not begging
for a relationship with them. We want a relationship of equals."[93]

Nevertheless, Maliki's campaign against the Sadrists prepared the way for a notable diplomatic opening with Iraq's Arab neighbors, with many Arab leaders publicly advocating engagement with the new Iraq. In fact, in late April 2008, an editorial in the Jordanian newspaper *al-Ra'i*, which aligned with the government and was the most widely read paper in Jordan, argued that a "pro-Arab Shi'i revolution has erupted" in Iraq, and the editorial exhorted: "Now, after al-Maliki's Government has taken such a courageous stand, Arabs must move quickly, dispatch their ambassadors to Baghdad, and reopen their embassies there. The Arabs' continued distance will only serve the Iranians."[94] The UAE was in fact the first Arab state to take a concrete step in this direction. On 5 June, Emirati Foreign Minister Shaikh Abdullah bin Zayed Al Nahyan traveled to Baghdad, where he publicly declared, "We must be frank and say that the states of the region have taken a long time to understand the new Iraq ... Iraq has suffered because its brothers failed to back it over these past years."[95] Privately to U.S. officials in Baghdad, Shaikh Abdullah acknowledged that he had been considering increased engagement with Iraq for the previous six months, but had deferred because he had not wanted "to undermine his Arab neighbors"; nevertheless, following Charge of the Knights, he said, "it was time to act."[96]

Thereafter, Arab engagement steadily increased. On 11 August, Abdullah II of Jordan visited Baghdad—the first Arab head of state to do so since the 2003 invasion.[97] Earlier that summer, Abdullah had affirmed the importance of building "bridges" between Iraq and its Arab neighbors to restore its "active and significant role" in the Arab nation.[98] Also in August, Lebanese Prime Minister Fouad al-Siniora traveled to Baghdad, proclaiming, "I believe that the return of Iraq to the Arabs ... and the return of the Arabs to Iraq, is a basic aim for which we all must work."[99] In the following months, ambassadors from the UAE,

Jordan, Bahrain, Kuwait, Syria, and the Arab League would return to Baghdad.[100] Furthermore, Egyptian Foreign Minister Ahmad Abu al-Ghait and Oil Minister Samih Fahmi traveled to Baghdad in October,[101] and the Egyptian government would appoint an ambassador to Iraq the following summer.[102] In April 2009, Palestinian President Mahmud Abbas visited Baghdad.[103] As the host of an Al-Arabiya news program commented in late summer 2008, "A new chapter of Arab–Iraq relations has been opened."[104]

The rhetoric emanating from Sunni Arab leaders such as Abdullah II of Jordan, Foreign Minister Abdullah bin Zayed of the UAE, and Prime Minister Siniora of Lebanon indicated a recognition that in order to preserve Iraq's Arabism, the Arab states themselves needed to act: instead of waiting on the sidelines while lamenting the changes that had taken place in Iraq, they needed to embrace the country's new leaders and plant an Arab flag in Baghdad. By treating the new Iraq as an outsider, the Arab states undermined its Arabism; by treating it as an insider, the Arab states instead affirmed its Arab identity. Thus, if the Arabs wanted Iraq to remain a member of their family, they themselves needed to treat it as such. In fact, at the time of the Emirati foreign minister's trip to Baghdad, an Emirati political commentator acknowledged on Al-Jazeera that Iraq had experienced an "Arab void" for the previous five years, in contrast to the significant presence Iran had established there.[105] The implication of his statement was that the responsibility for upholding Iraq's Arabism lay not only with the Iraqis—the other Arab states also needed to do their part, filling the Arab void as the Iraqis were exhorting them to do.

Furthermore, beyond these Arab states' objective to balance Iranian influence in Iraq, the prospect of increased economic opportunity there boosted their incentive to engage with Baghdad, and in turn break ranks with Saudi Arabia. Indeed, violence in Iraq reached a four-year low in May 2008,[106] which allowed the Maliki government to focus on reconstruction and the development of the energy sector. In 2009, foreign investment in Iraq would total $156.7 billion, a 241 percent increase over 2008, driven by a number of multi-billion-dollar energy deals, with smaller deals also focusing on the real estate, tourism, and transportation sectors.[107] As seen, Jordan wanted to benefit from the growth of Iraq's economy, and moreover Egypt, Lebanon, the UAE, and Syria did as well. As with Jordan, Iraq had longstanding economic relationships with Egypt and Lebanon. During the Iran–Iraq War, over one million Egyptians had worked in Iraq to fill jobs made vacant by the expansion of Iraq's armed forces, constituting Egypt's largest source of remittances, before these workers departed en masse following the invasion of Kuwait.[108] Furthermore, in the 1990s, Iraq had been Egypt's second biggest export market,[109] and after 2003 Egypt took steps to maintain this relationship.[110] As for Lebanon, before the onset of its civil war in 1975, at a time when Beirut was the banking capital of the Middle East, Iraq had been its largest trading partner.[111] Thus, in 2009, Lebanese firms would announce $10.2 billion in investment deals there, making Lebanon the fifth largest origin country of private capital into Iraq, and the second largest origin country in the Middle East after the UAE.[112] For its part, the UAE saw an investment opportunity, and in 2009 it became not only the leading source of foreign investment into Iraq from a Middle Eastern country, but the leading source of foreign investment into Iraq from any country in the world.[113] Meanwhile, Syria pursued closer ties in 2008 to boost its moribund economy, with Syrian and Iraqi officials discussing joint commercial projects such as reopening the Kirkuk–Baniyas oil pipeline, which runs from Iraq's northern oilfields to the Syrian coast.[114]

The trend that was emerging in the second half of 2008 and first half of 2009, with many Arab states establishing important economic ties to Iraq, reflected a normalization of relations that would in turn serve to increase the sense that Iraq was becoming a recognized member of the Arab family. A sense of shock had permeated the Arab world in the years following the 2003 invasion, with outrage over the destruction caused by the American occupation, as well as confusion at the wholesale overhaul of Iraq's political system, which had enabled the Shiʿa to rise to power. Iraq had been transformed, and at first the new Iraq had appeared alien—indeed, "Iranian"—to its Arab neighbors. However, the increased economic activity between Iraq and the Arab states, which followed its embrace by Arab leaders, was starting to create a sense that a new normal was being achieved; that Iraq, even if now under Shiʿa leadership, still belonged to the Arab family. In fact, following years of urging Iraq's Arab neighbors to engage, Foreign Minister Zebari was at last expressing optimism at the outset of 2009, telling U.S. officials in Baghdad following an Arab summit in Kuwait that, "[T]his time I felt really proud of my country on how far we've come, how we've been integrated into the region."[115] Publicly, Zebari professed at this time that Iraq had "returned" to the "Arab bosom."[116] Nevertheless, this emerging trend toward normalization would be disrupted in the lead-up to Iraq's 2010 parliamentary elections, the subject of the next chapter. In fact, in December 2009 President Talabani would express his belief to U.S. officials in Baghdad that "Saudi Arabia was actively working to prevent Iraq from developing relationships with its regional neighbors,"[117] and indeed a Lebanese politician aligned with Saudi Arabia recounted in an interview that his political group was being pressed by the kingdom not to engage.[118]

For their part, Iraqi officials aimed to capitalize on the increasing Arab goodwill toward the Maliki government following Charge of the Knights to improve relations with the Saudi leadership. Most significantly, in July 2008 the government invited to Baghdad Saad al-Hariri, son of former Lebanese Prime Minister Rafiq al-Hariri, who had been a close confidant to the Saudi leadership prior to his assassination in February 2005. After Rafiq al-Hariri's death, the younger Hariri inherited leadership of his father's political party, as well as his relationship with Saudi Arabia. In Baghdad, Saad al-Hariri met with political leaders from across Iraq's ethno-sectarian spectrum, and saw Prime Minister Maliki privately in a meeting that lasted over an hour.[119] In addition, on the day of Hariri's visit, Grand Ayatollah Sistani unexpectedly invited him to Najaf, where the Lebanese leader met with Iraq's senior *marjiʿ*, as well as Abd al-Aziz al-Hakim of ISCI.[120]

As Ambassador Crocker observed in an interview, by hosting Hariri, the Maliki government aimed to initiate a reconciliation with Riyadh.[121] Indeed, in his written exchange with me, Maliki recalled that in his meeting with Hariri, he asked the Lebanese leader to convey to the Saudis that he wanted nothing from them except fraternal Arab relations, expressing to Hariri that, "We are both Arab Muslim countries; it is necessary for us to have good relations."[122] Moreover, during Hariri's visit, the Maliki government spokesman, Ali al-Dabbagh, publicly pointed to its true objective, proclaiming that it constituted

a clear indication that Iraq stretches its hand to its brothers and belongs to the Arab arena. Although some are hesitant to have contacts with Iraq, I believe that Iraq's achievements, including stability and the democratic system, make it eligible for an equal relationship with all side [sic] ... The Arabs should not be late to launch contacts with Iraq. This does not serve their or Iraq's interests. Contacts will definitely serve the interests of the peoples of this region and regional security and stability.[123]

Ambassador Crocker further recounted, based on his own meeting with Hariri on the day of his trip to Baghdad, that the Lebanese leader was astonished by the warm reception he had received in Iraq.[124] In fact, Hariri's impressions, as he recounted them to U.S. officials in Baghdad, are captured in a U.S. diplomatic cable. Hariri reported that Maliki had expressed his "frustration" over King Abdullah's refusal to meet with him, but, consistent with Maliki's account above, had "stressed his desire for a better relationship." Hariri told U.S. officials that as a result of their meeting, he had "a very favorable impression of Maliki as a leader and as an Arab," and acknowledged that the Iraqi prime minister was "misunderstood" in the wider Arab world. As for his meeting with Grand Ayatollah Sistani, Hariri in fact reported that Iraq's senior *marjiʻ* had been "interested in little except the Saudi king," with whom he desired to establish a connection. As the most senior member of Iraq's Shiʻa religious establishment, Sistani's attitude toward engaging with Saudi Arabia was of supreme importance. Given his moral authority among the Iraqi Shiʻa, it is doubtful that any Shiʻa Islamist political leader would defy him. Sistani's attitude is thus the best indicator that Iraq's Shiʻa community, or at least its leaders, genuinely wanted a better relationship with Saudi Arabia. For his part, Hariri promised to U.S. officials in Baghdad that he would convey his positive impressions from his meetings to the Saudi leadership.[125]

Beyond Saad al-Hariri, there are indications that other Arab leaders were also urging King Abdullah to adopt a different approach to Iraq. According to Egyptian intelligence chief Omar Suleiman, as he observed to a U.S. official in Cairo in July 2009, President Mubarak had advised Abdullah to "accept" and "support" Maliki as Iraq's leader.[126] Similarly, Iraqi Prime Minister Barham Salih recounted to U.S. officials in May 2008 that Abdullah II of Jordan had told him that he had urged the Saudi king to "stop personalizing the Saudi–Iraq bilateral relationship."[127] For his part, Shaikh Abdullah of the UAE expressed his hope to U.S. officials in Baghdad that his June 2008 trip to Iraq would encourage the Saudi leadership to reengage. There is no evidence, however, that these Arab leaders were any more successful than the Americans, the Iraqis, or apparently even some of Abdullah's own senior advisers had been in compelling him to reimagine Saudi relations with the new Iraq. Indeed, the evidence from this period indicates that King Abdullah continued to evince no inclination to update his beliefs about Maliki or his government during this period: a July 2009 diplomatic cable from the U.S. embassy in Riyadh reported that the Saudi leadership had actually become "more unreserved with us of late about their conviction that Al-Maliki is an Iranian puppet."[128]

King Abdullah's unrelenting hostility toward Maliki continued to increase the Iraqi prime minister's frustration with the Saudi leadership, leading to a public spat between the two sides for the first time in late spring 2009. That March, Abdullah had again refused to meet with Maliki, as requested by the latter, while the two leaders were at an Arab summit in Doha.[129] Thereafter, the Iraqi prime minister expressed his belief to U.S. officials in Baghdad that reconciliation with the Saudi leadership was "impossible,"[130] and he finally aired what appears to have been his exasperation toward them in public. In response to a question on Iraqi television in May 2009 over the absence of relations with Saudi Arabia, the prime minister stated:

> We have succeeded in opening up to most countries, but Saudi Arabia has negative stances. We have initiated [attempts] to create normal and positive relations, but these initiatives were understood in a negative way as weakness. We remain ready to accept a Saudi initiative because initiatives on our side have run out, and there is no use of repeating them unless Saudi Arabia expresses its desire for a relationship.[131]

While Maliki's response to the question was blunt, it is hard to characterize it as inaccurate. Nevertheless, the Dubai-based al-Sharqiya television network, owned by Iraqi exile and former

Baʿthist Saad al-Bazzaz, called Maliki's statement an "unprece-dented attack" on Saudi Arabia,[132] and a public statement was made by the Saudi interior minister, Prince Nayef, to the effect that the kingdom would not support an Iraqi leader who worked against the interests of Iraq.[133] Sami al-Askari, in his capacity as an adviser to Maliki, then elaborated on the prime minister's statement in the Iraqi media. In fact, al-Askari had himself met with Prince Muqrin not only in 2007, but again in the summer of 2008, although the second meeting had been no more success-ful than the first in establishing an opening to the Saudi leader-ship.[134] Thus, explaining on Iraqi television that there had been many unsuccessful Iraqi initiatives to engage with Saudi Arabia, al-Askari stated, "We were hoping and we still hope that Saudi Arabia will deal with the political situation and the legal and elected government"; nevertheless, he concluded, "I believe that Iraq has done everything in its power and the Iraqi Government is not required to do more. The ball is now in the Saudi court."[135] From 2006 through 2008, Maliki, in addition to many others, had made multiple attempts to forge a Saudi–Iraqi reconciliation, all of which had proved unsuccessful. As of spring 2009, these efforts on the part of the Iraqi prime minister came to an end, and the public tone he adopted toward Saudi Arabia thereafter became increasingly less conciliatory.

Conclusion

To a casual observer, it is not self-evident why the Saudi leader-ship would decide not to engage with the Maliki government, because the decision appears self-defeating. Saudi Arabia wanted post-Saddam Iraq to remain a friend. Members of the Maliki government, including Maliki himself, also wanted to establish friendly relations with Saudi Arabia, and were continually reach-ing out to Saudi Arabia to that end. Nevertheless, the Saudis repeatedly rebuffed the Iraqis' outreach, which ultimately caused tensions to set in between the two countries. The Saudi leadership was thereby producing a situation they had wanted to avoid. The argument of this chapter, and indeed of this book as a whole, is that misperception lay at the heart of the Saudis' self-defeating decision not to engage with Iraq. The belief that formed the basis of Abdullah's decision-making—that Maliki was an Iranian agent—was simply incorrect. Indeed, Maliki's decision to confront the Sadrist militias in the spring of 2008 put the lie to that image of him.

Ultimately, however, Abdullah's image of Maliki had less to do with Maliki than with Abdullah's own attitude toward the new, Shiʿa-led Iraq. Prior to Maliki's assumption of power, the Saudi leadership had concluded that the new Iraq was dominated by Iran, and this perception then biased their perception of Maliki. Moreover, once he had concluded that Maliki was a client of Iran, Abdullah evinced no willingness to open his mind to a different view of the Iraqi prime minister. By contrast to Abdullah, other Arab leaders displayed a greater open-mindedness toward the new Iraq and took what appears to have been the more appropriate decision to engage with the Maliki government. They sought to build positive relations with Iraq's new government, and the new Iraqi government reciprocated. Furthermore, the next two chapters will put into sharper relief the self-defeating nature of the Saudis' decision to reject Maliki, as ultimately it was their rejection of him that compelled Maliki to seek the support of their adversary, Iran.

5

IRAQ'S 2010 PARLIAMENTARY ELECTIONS

The principal argument of this book is that King Abdullah of Saudi Arabia created a self-fulfilling prophecy, leading to Iraq's alignment with Iran. Iraq's new leaders, including Prime Minister Nuri al-Maliki, had sought to establish a positive relationship with Saudi Arabia and pursue independence from Iran. However, King Abdullah's refusal to engage with them, due to his belief that Maliki was an Iranian agent, led Maliki to feel threatened by the Saudis and ended up compelling him to gravitate, therefore, toward Iran. The purpose of this chapter is to examine how this self-fulfilling prophecy began to come to fruition in the aftermath of Iraq's parliamentary elections of March 2010.

As seen in the introduction, the concept of the self-fulfilling prophecy was originally defined by sociologist Robert Merton as "a *false* definition of the situation evoking a new behavior which makes the originally false definition come *true*."[1] This concept has in turn become a core theme in social psychology, used by social psychologists to demonstrate how a perceiver, treating a target in line with an inaccurate stereotype, may elicit new behavior on the part of the target that conforms to that stereotype.[2] In a reflection of this logic, this chapter argues that the Saudi leadership's support to a predominantly Sunni Arab coalition led by Ayad Allawi during the 2010 elections—interpreted by Maliki, following Abdullah's absolute rejection of him, as a Saudi attempt to undermine him personally and Shiʻa Iraqi power more broadly—elicited a change in his behavior in a way that conformed to Abdullah's stereotypic image of him.

However, that Maliki would wind up in Iran's orbit following the 2010 elections was far from a foregone conclusion before those elections. Indeed, prior to the elections, Maliki, having won broad support among Arab Iraqis, both Sunni and Shiʻa, formed a nationalist-oriented coalition called State of Law and formulated a political platform envisioning an Iraq that was independent of outside powers. Nevertheless, there was a widespread perception that both Saudi Arabia and Iran were intervening in the elections. Maliki, while resisting Iranian pressure to join a reconstituted Iranian-backed Shiʻa Islamist coalition, believed that the Saudis sought to have him removed from power in favor of their preferred Iraqi leaders. Indeed, during this period, a number of Sunni Arab politicians joined the Saudi-backed politician Allawi to form the Iraqi National Movement electoral coalition, more commonly known as Iraqiyya, for which King Abdullah publicly signaled his support in the lead-up to the elections. In the perception of Maliki, and of the Shiʻa more broadly, Iraqiyya represented a Saudi-backed effort to restore some semblance of Sunni power in Baghdad. Moreover, Maliki also experienced a significant setback in the fall of 2009, when Al-Qaʻida carried out a series of three major bombings in central Baghdad. The bombings appeared to be designed to undermine public confidence in the Maliki government ahead of the elections, and some members of the government suspected they were backed by Saudi Arabia.

The 2010 election resulted in a razor-thin victory for Iraqiyya, which won two more parliamentary seats than State of Law. At this point, Maliki changed his behavior in a way that fulfilled Saudi expectations of him. Having previously resisted pressure to join the Iranian-backed Shiʿa Islamist list, he now closed ranks with them to hold on to the premiership and safeguard Iraq's new order. In this way, King Abdullah's self-fulfilling prophecy started to come to fruition. Maliki had initially sought to maintain independence from Iran, but the Saudi leadership, believing him to be an Iranian agent, backed Allawi. The Saudi leadership thereby compelled Maliki to seek Iranian support.

Maliki's Vision for an Independent and Unified Iraq

For the first time since December 2005, Iraqis would head to the polls twice: in January 2009 for provincial elections and March 2010 for parliamentary ones. The 2010 parliamentary elections especially were considered, in the words of Foreign Minister Hoshyar Zebari, as attributed to him in a U.S. diplomatic cable, to be a "'make or break' event for Iraq," as the Iraqi people would decide whether the country would head in a sectarian or non-sectarian direction.[3] For his part, Prime Minister Maliki, having won widespread praise for spearheading the Charge of the Knights operation in spring 2008, desired to take Iraq in a non-sectarian direction. In his electoral campaign, Maliki emphasized Iraqi nationalism, calling for an independent and sovereign Iraq where its people stood united, which would, he said, further stabilize the country. Moreover, given his emphasis on unity, he sought to establish an alliance that transcended sectarian identity, and in the spring and summer of 2009 a prominent Sunni Arab leader, Ahmad Abu Risha of the Anbar Awakening, would state his intention to partner with him.

Foremost, Maliki's objective for the 2010 elections was to avoid the situation whereby Iraq turned into another Lebanon, where sectarian parties became clients of outside powers. Indeed, in the summer of 2009, Iraqi leaders were communicating to U.S. officials that interference from neighboring countries, particularly Saudi Arabia and Iran, was already underway to influence the upcoming elections.[4] In fact, Foreign Minister Saud al-Faisal had himself told U.S. officials in Riyadh that the Saudi leadership sought to encourage the formation of Iraqi electoral alliances.[5] In Maliki's perception, as he himself stated it in our written exchange in 2020, the Saudis' objective for the 2010 elections was to oust him from the premiership and install their own clients, an effort for which he said they "expended all political efforts and financial support." He observed to me that the Saudis sought to displace Iraqi leaders they perceived as beholden to Iran with the ultimate goal of asserting their own control over Iraq.[6] With regard to Iranian intervention, Maliki was under pressure from Iran at this time to join a reconstituted Shi'a Islamist alliance, discussed in further detail below. Given his objective to maintain Iraq's independence, Maliki, however, demurred. In sum, during this period both Iran and Saudi Arabia were interfering in Iraq. However, the dynamic that was underway was that Maliki wanted to remain independent of Iran; he would only choose to close ranks with it once he perceived that the Saudi effort to undermine him and impose control over Iraq had garnered success.

In late 2008, ahead of the January 2009 provincial elections, Maliki established a new political coalition called State of Law, which was officially non-sectarian, although many of its members belonged to the Da'wa Party.[7] In a major speech broadcast on Iraqi television that November, Maliki set forth his vision for Iraq, calling for a country that was sovereign and unified in terms of its territory and people, and he celebrated its diversity, declaring, "We want every citizen to be a partner in the process of construction."[8] Moreover, the actions he took at this time buttressed his call for unity and sovereignty. In fall 2008, he established Iraqi security forces' control in areas such as Khanaqin and Kirkuk, which were disputed between Iraqi Arabs and Kurds and under Kurdish *peshmerga* (militia) control. While this action enraged the Kurds, it was popular among Arab Iraqis, whether Sunni or Shi'a, who generally opposed what they regarded as Kurdish expansionism.[9] Furthermore, in the second half of 2008, Iraqi politics was dominated by negotiations between the Maliki government and the Bush administration to extend the legal basis of the U.S.-led coalition beyond 31 December 2008, when its UN mandate was set to expire. In the negotiations, Maliki refused to acquiesce in an open-ended U.S. military presence, compelling the Bush administration during months of tedious negotiations to agree to a timeline for withdrawal.[10] The agreement with the U.S. was considered a victory for Maliki's vision of an independent Iraq; he himself declared that 27 November 2008, the day it was approved by parliament, was Iraq's "day of sovereignty."[11]

On the eve of the January 2009 provincial elections, observers of the Iraqi scene noted that Maliki had won support among a broad array of Iraqis, both Sunni and Shi'a.[12] For instance, a U.S. diplomat wrote in a cable, based on conversations with Iraqis on the outskirts of the capital: "Whether Shi'a or Sunni, sheikh or shopkeeper, residents of the three rural districts [of Baghdad] praised Prime Minister Maliki's efforts to unite the country and bring an end to the sectarian violence that plagued Iraq during 2006 and 2007."[13] Thus, on election day, State of Law saw the biggest success of the various political coalitions, winning 126 of a total of 440 council seats in 12 of 14 provinces.[14] (Elections were held in fourteen of Iraq's eighteen provinces, excluding the three provinces that constituted the Kurdistan Regional Government [KRG] and the province of Kirkuk to which the KRG asserted a claim.) ISCI won the second most seats of any party, at a total of fifty-three, and the Sadrists came in third with forty-one. Meanwhile, Tariq al-Hashimi's Tawafuq coalition obtained thirty-two, and Ayad Allawi's list twenty-six.[15] In general, however, the elections had produced politically fragmented provincial councils, as in only two provinces could a single bloc govern on its own. The formation of the other provincial councils required power-sharing alliances, with many of the governing coalitions that emerged transcending sectarian affiliation; for instance, in four provinces, State of Law allied with a coalition led by Sunni Arab parliamentarian Salih al-Mutlak, which had won nineteen seats in the elections.[16]

In the wake of State of Law's January 2009 success, Maliki sought to broaden his coalition beyond its Da'wa Party base for the March 2010 parliamentary elections. To do so, he began tentative negotiations with an array of Sunni, Shi'a, and Kurdish political groups.[17] Indeed, in May 2009 Maliki articulated his belief that the upcoming elections would be held on the basis of nationalist, not sectarian, alliances.[18] In fact, Maliki was not the only politician who envisioned the formation of non-sectarian alliances: al-Mutlak told the *Washington Post* in spring 2009 that he believed three electoral blocs would coalesce in the months ahead, one led by himself, another by Maliki, and a third that would group together Sunni and Shi'a Islamist parties.[19] For his part, Maliki was more explicit in private conversations with U.S. officials about the reasoning behind his desire to avoid sectarian alliances. Asserting that efforts were already underway by Saudi Arabia and Iran to group together Iraq's Sunni and Shi'a parties, respectively, Maliki contended that the formation of sectarian alliances would be "disastrous for Iraq," turning the country into another Lebanon, with "competing identity-based groups, supported by hostile outside actors."[20] One of Maliki's closest advisers, Sadiq al-Rikabi, similarly expressed to U.S. officials his opposition to implementing the "Lebanon experiment" in Iraq, in which political parties became the "proxies" of regional powers.[21]

Indeed, a pillar of Maliki's campaign platform was the need to uphold Iraq's sovereignty and independence. Ironically, he had risen to the premiership in 2006 through the support of U.S. Ambassador Zalmay Khalilzad; while he had been opportunistic in this respect, he had nevertheless been unwilling to subordinate himself to the Americans. The Bush administration had regarded him as far from pliable; in fact, in an interview, a senior Bush administration official remembered Maliki as a "difficult person."[22] He had frequently conflicted with the U.S.-led coalition, and indeed, his major political victory in 2008 had been his success in compelling the Americans to accept a withdrawal timeline. Reportedly, Maliki had even sought to signal his unwillingness to be subservient to the United States in his initial meeting with Khalilzad at the U.S. embassy, by refusing the Americans' customary offer of tea, or even water.[23] This anecdote, even if apocryphal, spoke to Maliki's reputation for fierce independence. Indeed, Maliki did not want himself or his country to be controlled by outside powers, and he frequently invoked Iraq's sovereignty as he launched his campaign for the upcoming elections. He called for "a sovereign and strong country" in which the Iraqi people could live "proud and free," and asserted "the need to maintain unity, sovereignty, security, [and] stability" to confront what he called "foreign agendas."[24]

Of course, to form a truly non-sectarian alliance, Maliki needed a prominent Sunni partner. Many Sunni Arab political leaders, such as al-Hashimi and al-Mutlak, had expressed willingness, in private conversations with U.S. officials, to join with Maliki in a governing coalition after, but not before, the elections.[25] Nevertheless, another prominent Sunni Arab was "eager for an alliance" with Maliki: Ahmad Abu Risha, head of the Anbar Awakening.[26] Abu Risha's brother, Abd al-Sattar, had spearheaded the formation of the Awakening movement in fall 2006, before being assassinated by Al-Qaʿida in September 2007.

Upon his brother's death, Abu Risha had inherited leadership of the Anbar Awakening, which had evolved into a political party that had done well in the province's council election in January 2009.[27] Having risen to a position of power in Anbar, Abu Risha now aimed to enter the national political arena, and thus planned to join Maliki's coalition, especially as both shared a similar vision for a nationalist, unified Iraq.[28] In April 2009, Abu Risha himself told the Associated Press that he and Maliki had "agreed in principle" to run together, although they were still "laying down the foundations" for the alliance.[29] Moreover, he spoke in laudatory tones about Maliki—in late 2008, following the conclusion of the agreement with the U.S., he called the prime minister "a patriot."[30] In spring 2009, Abu Risha declared, "That man helped us save Anbar at its hour of need," as Maliki had supported the formation of the Awakening in late 2006.[31] In the summer, Abu Risha even proclaimed, with reference to the prime minister, that he intended to ally with "the one who worked towards unifying Iraq; whose work testifies that he unified Iraq, stood against the project of sectarian violence, militias, and Al-Qaʿida Organization."[32]

In the summer of 2009, Maliki reportedly faced significant pressure from Iran to join a reconstituted Shiʿa Islamist coalition.[33] Nevertheless, the prime minister declined. His main intra-Shiʿa rivals, ISCI and the Sadrists, had refused to support his return to the premiership in the next government, and moreover his camp asserted that they preferred to build a non–sectarian alliance.[34] As an adviser to Maliki told the press at this time, "Mr. Maliki wants a truly national alliance, both in its programme and composition," and "So far the [reconstituted Shiʿa] Alliance hasn't offered any guarantees that could persuade Mr. Maliki to join it."[35] In this account, what the Shiʿa alliance was offering was not sufficient to persuade Maliki to abandon his preferred strategy.

And indeed, Maliki worked hard to obtain not only a political partner, but also votes from outside the Shi'a community. The need to eschew sectarianism was a frequent theme of his campaign in the spring and summer of 2009. For instance, he declared, "I hold fast to any minister or state official who does not adopt sectarianism in any aspect. One can be Shi'i or Sunni ... One can be Kurd, Turkoman, Christian, Assyrian, Shabak, or Yazidi. This is your right, and this is the state of law and freedoms."[36] He also called upon former Ba'thists to join the political process, as long as they renounced the Ba'thist ideology, and professed, "we must sit down together as brothers."[37] Most significantly, in July he traveled to Anbar where he appeared with Abu Risha and delivered a speech to prominent Anbaris. He praised the province, as well as the late Abd al-Sattar, for turning against Al-Qa'ida, and proclaimed,

> Sectarianism must be uprooted from every mind, logic, and practice.
> We will not accept any plan that is based on a sectarian dimension.
> We accept the plan that is based on the national dimension, in which
> the Sunnis, Shi'is, Muslims, Christians, Arabs, Kurds, Turkomans,
> Shabaks, Yazidis, and all citizens of the homeland stand united ... We
> all live in dignity under the tent of Iraq.[38]

Maliki told the Anbaris at this time that their province had an important role to play in building national unity.[39]

Thus, Maliki was actively campaigning on a nationalist, nonsectarian political platform in the spring and summer of 2009. He envisioned an Iraq where its people stood united and independent of outside powers. Nevertheless, as highlighted above, he perceived that the Saudi leadership sought to remove him from power in favor of their own clients. It should be pointed out that Maliki's perception continued to be well-based. The Saudis were indeed promoting Allawi ahead of the election, as will be further discussed below, although it appeared that their primary objective was to oust Maliki. On the eve of the election, an adviser to

King Abdullah urged U.S. officials in Riyadh to "marginalize" the current prime minister, because, as ever, the Saudi official asserted that he was "an Iranian agent."[40] For his part, a Saudi royal family insider provided a more extreme assessment in an interview, stating that, in general, "Abdullah was willing to do whatever it took to get rid of Maliki," although he did not elaborate.[41] This Saudi source's perspective comports with Maliki's perception that King Abdullah was hostile to him on a basic level. But the view that the Saudis were fundamentally averse to the new Iraq had currency within the Iraqi leadership beyond Maliki: alarmingly, some members of the Maliki government even believed that the Saudis backed a series of major Al-Qa'ida bombings that took place in central Baghdad in the fall of 2009.

The Al-Qa'ida Bombings of Fall 2009

Following the January 2009 provincial elections, Maliki had appeared to be the dominant figure in Iraqi politics. Nevertheless, a series of events would occur from late summer 2009 that diminished his standing. Members of the Maliki government would perceive that Saudi Arabia was involved in these events. Most significantly, a series of three major bombings, claimed by Al-Qa'ida, targeted Iraqi government institutions in central Baghdad from August to December 2009. The Maliki government alleged that the attacks were carried out by an Al-Qa'ida–Ba'thist alliance, and moreover some officials, such as Foreign Minister Zebari, appeared to believe they were backed by Saudi Arabia and Syria to influence the upcoming elections. Some officials publicly pointed a finger to Saudi Arabia and Syria. For his part, Maliki publicly highlighted a Ba'thist role in the bombings, although he also stated obliquely that outside powers were involved.[42] That members of the Maliki government believed Saudi Arabia was connected to the bombings points to their perception, by this point, that the Saudi leadership bore malign intent toward their government, namely that the Saudis were an enemy.

Violence in Iraq had declined steeply since the sectarian civil war, but it gradually began to tick up again in early 2009.[43] That summer, Iraqi officials claimed to have intelligence of a growing alliance between Al-Qa'ida and Iraqi Ba'thists based in Syria,[44] and moreover they showed concern that both the Saudi and Syrian governments were involved with Iraqi insurgents. At the end of May, Maliki expressed his concern to U.S. officials that Saudi Arabia was attempting to foment sectarian violence, and in August two of his close advisers, Haider al-Abadi and al-Askari, reportedly claimed that Iraqi intelligence indicated that Saudi Arabia was supporting Iraqi insurgents.[45] Whatever was in fact detected by Iraqi intelligence at this time, it has been argued that Maliki perceived a Saudi threat based on his estimate of Saudi intentions. In short, King Abdullah had rejected every attempt made by the Maliki government, the U.S., and other Arab states to compel him to engage with Iraq. The Iraqi premier, suspecting that what Abdullah really wanted was new leadership in Baghdad, could reasonably perceive a Saudi threat.

Nevertheless, indications of Syrian interference in Iraq appeared more troubling to Iraqi officials in the summer of 2009. Since 2003, the Syrian regime of Bashar al-Assad had allowed foreign fighters from the Arab world to use Syria as a conduit into western Iraq, where they would then typically fight with Al-Qa'ida, often being deployed as suicide bombers; the U.S.-led coalition even assessed that senior Syrian officials were directly involved in infiltrating foreign fighters into Iraq. The Syrian regime was also assessed to have allowed senior Iraqi Ba'thists to establish a base in Syria from which to help manage the insurgency.[46] In early August 2009, Foreign Minister Zebari alleged that the Assad regime was providing increasing support to Iraqi Ba'thists and was "meddling 'significantly'" in Nineveh, then the site of the country's worst violence.[47] Evidence of Syrian support to the ongoing insurgency appeared to be compelling enough that Prime Minister Maliki traveled to Damascus on 18 August to confront Assad.[48] In advance of his trip, National Security Adviser Safa al-Shaikh communicated to U.S. officials that Maliki would take to Damascus evidence of "coordination between Syrian military intelligence and the [Iraqi] Baathists."[49] Maliki later claimed that the Iraqis had evidence, which he had presented to Assad during his trip, that Syrian intelligence had hosted a meeting of Iraqi Ba'thists and Al-Qa'ida members near Damascus on 30 July.[50] Furthermore, in an interview, al-Askari claimed that Assad, when pressed by Maliki at their meeting on 18 August, actually admitted to aiding Iraqi insurgents.[51]

On the day after Maliki's trip to Damascus, 19 August, simultaneous truck bombs struck Iraq's Ministries of Finance and Foreign Affairs in central Baghdad, killing 130 and wounding over 500, in the country's deadliest attack since 2007.[52] Al-Qa'ida claimed the attack, but Maliki publicly alleged that the bombings were carried out by an Al-Qa'ida–Ba'thist alliance.[53] Two more major attacks took place in central Baghdad in late 2009. On 25 October, a double vehicle-bombing struck the Ministry of Justice, killing 155 and wounding some 500.[54] On 8 December, five vehicle bombs targeted buildings belonging to the Interior, Finance, and Labor Ministries, killing 127 and wounding another 500.[55] These attacks were also claimed by Al-Qa'ida, and furthermore the scale of the attacks prompted an investigation by the U.S.-led coalition. In line with the Maliki government's allegations, a former senior U.S. military commander involved in that inquiry observed in an interview that the old Ba'thist intelligence service, which was "hardwired" in place in parts of Iraq and extended into Syria, was what was fueling the attacks.[56]

That fall, members of the Maliki government pointed, sometimes obliquely, other times explicitly, to the involvement of Syria and Saudi Arabia in the attacks. In fact, in the wake of the first bombing, Baghdad Governor Salah Abd al-Razzaq, a member of the Da'wa Party, explicitly stated in the press that he believed Saudi Arabia had supported the attack to undermine confidence in the Maliki government ahead of the 2010 elections.[57] For his part, days after the first attack, an irate Foreign Minister Zebari—some fifty members of his ministry had been killed in that bombing, and his own office had been badly damaged—publicly accused "neighbouring countries" of interfering in Iraq to influence the elections.[58] Furthermore, implicitly pointing a finger at Syria, the Maliki government recalled its ambassador from Damascus at the end of August, and demanded that the Syrian regime extradite two senior Syrian-based Iraqi Ba'thists, Muhammad Yunis and Sattam Farhan, to Iraq.[59] The perception that outside powers supported the bombings derived from their scale, particularly the amount and type of explosives used. In late August, Zebari told U.S. officials that, in his view, the attackers "must have had extensive support, in terms of intelligence, logistics, expertise on—and supply of—the high grade explosives," which he said amounted to "two tons of C-4"; he therefore believed that outside powers had provided assistance.[60] Similarly, close to two tons of explosives were reported to have been used in the October bombings,[61] and following the December attack, a senior Baghdad policeman and explosives expert publicly stated that the material used in the bombing "could not have been manufactured in Baghdad, it came from abroad." He added: "Neighbouring countries helped [the attackers]. The operation required lots of funding, which came from Syria or Saudi Arabia."[62] For his part, in conversations with U.S. officials, Zebari appeared comfortable explicitly accusing Syria of involvement, but hinted more obliquely at the involvement of other states. For instance, in September, Zebari expressed his belief that Syria was "actively using Iraqi Baathists and other elements to destabilize Iraq" to achieve "regime change" in Baghdad, a project that was also supported, he said, by "other neighbors."[63] Meanwhile, U.S. diplomats wrote at this time that some senior Iraqi officials made oblique references to the "malign intentions" of "some neighbors," in an effort to "[make] clear without being explicit that they are referring to Saudi Arabia."[64] The U.S. officials observed that the Iraqis appeared reluctant to overtly criticize Saudi Arabia to the Americans, given the close U.S.–Saudi relationship.[65]

In Zebari's view, again expressed obliquely to the Americans, the attacks were the result of "a convergence of interests and capabilities" among "a few" of Iraq's neighbors.[66] Indeed, fueling the perception that Syria and Saudi Arabia were both tied to the attacks was a rapprochement that had begun between the two states in January 2009. Saudi–Syria relations had deteriorated as a result of the 2005 assassination of the Saudis' chief Lebanese proxy, Rafiq al-Hariri, which was widely attributed to the Assad regime, as well as Assad's explicit alignment with Lebanese Hizballah and Iran during the 2006 war between Hizballah and Israel. Following that war, Saudi Arabia had pursued a policy of isolation toward Syria.[67] The Assad regime had made attempts to reconcile in 2007 and 2008, but the Saudis had rejected their initiatives.[68] Nevertheless, in January 2009, King Abdullah himself initiated a rapprochement, reportedly to the surprise of the Syrians.[69] Then from late 2009, concurrent with the bombings in Baghdad, a series of bilateral meetings took place between King Abdullah and Assad,[70] which apparently further stoked Iraqi suspicions. For instance, following one such meeting between Abdullah and Assad, a senior Iraqi Foreign Ministry official expressed his concern to U.S. officials in Baghdad that the Saudi and Syrian leaders were "plotting against Iraq."[71]

Furthermore, in late December, following the series of bombings in Baghdad, the Saudi leadership made a significant concession to the Assad regime, compelling Saad al-Hariri to reconcile with Assad, thus effectively ending a popular Lebanese movement against Syria, of which Hariri had been a leader since his father's murder.[72]

In fall 2009, the Maliki government pressed for a UN investigation into the bombings, but nothing would come of their efforts. The government had sent a formal request to the UN to establish an independent investigation following the first bombing in August, and continued to press for an investigation after the second.[73] With the expectation that security would continue to deteriorate prior to the elections, the government regarded the prospect of a UN investigation as a deterrent against further interference by their neighbors.[74] Nevertheless, an investigation never materialized. In the view of Hamid al-Bayati, then the Iraqi permanent representative to the UN, the Obama administration opposed the Iraqi government's attempt to involve the UN.[75]

Given that an independent investigation into the fall 2009 bombings never happened, it is impossible to know with any certainty who, beyond Al-Qa'ida, was involved in them. To an extent, however, what in fact took place is less important for the purpose of this book than the Iraqi perception of what took place. At bottom, the suspicion of some Iraqi officials that Saudi Arabia was tied to the attacks stemmed from their perception of profound Saudi hostility to the new order in Baghdad, a perception they had formed as a result of Abdullah's absolute refusal to engage with their government. Indeed, in the wake of the first bombing, Foreign Minister Zebari concluded ominously that "we will need regime change here" in Baghdad before Saudi–Iraq relations could improve.[76] By this point, Saudi Arabia appeared to members of the Maliki government as the only regional state fundamentally opposed to Iraq's new order. Therefore, if Iraqi officials conjectured that the fall 2009 bombings, given their scale, had been carried out with the assistance of an outside power, Saudi Arabia was an obvious suspect. One of the arguments of the last chapter, and of this book as a whole, is that Abdullah, perceiving Maliki to be an agent of Iran and therefore an enemy to Saudi Arabia, created a situation in which members of the Maliki government, primarily Maliki himself, perceived that the Saudi king bore malign intent toward them, and was therefore their enemy. Abdullah's perception of Maliki as an enemy compelled members of the Maliki government to mirror that perception toward the Saudi leadership. In this way, as constructivist scholar Alexander Wendt would expect, the Saudis' enmity toward the new Iraq became self-fulfilling.

Campaign Season

A wave of rising sectarian sentiment gripped Iraq in the six months ahead of the 2010 parliamentary elections. In addition to the bombings of late 2009, which appeared designed to undermine confidence in the Maliki government, Maliki's electoral campaign experienced another serious setback when the prime minister failed to attract a prominent Sunni Arab alliance partner. While Abu Risha had himself articulated his intention to join Maliki's campaign through the summer, in the fall he would join another coalition, and some in the Maliki camp would claim that his decision was the result of Saudi pressure. Furthermore, in the fall, a group of Iraq's Arab and Sunni neighbors, including Turkey, would facilitate the formation of the Iraqiyya electoral coalition, grouping together a number of prominent Sunni Arab politicians with Allawi. The Maliki camp perceived that this effort was, at bottom, a "Saudi project."[77] While King Abdullah did in fact back Allawi, what is important for the purpose of this book is the meaning this support had for

Maliki; as highlighted above, Maliki perceived that the Saudis sought to assert control over Iraq by promoting their own clients, and it was this perception that would ultimately compel him to align with Iran once Allawi's list won the most parliamentary seats in the elections. Nevertheless, in the lead-up to the elections, Maliki continued to resist Iranian pressure to join the reconstituted Shi'a Islamist alliance, believing his own nationalist coalition would win the most seats.

In conversations with U.S. officials, Maliki and his advisers, such as al-Rikabi, communicated their belief that Saudi Arabia was seeking "to align the Sunni states" in support of Iraq's Sunni politicians, and they asserted that Saudi Arabia's objective was "to prevent Iraqi Shi'a from leading the next national government."[78] In fact, Maliki claimed that the Saudi leadership had originally attempted to form an alliance of Iraq's Sunni Arabs and Sunni Kurds as a "front against the Shi'a," although the Kurds, he said, had demurred.[79] The prime minister also reported that Iran was using Saudi efforts to rally the Sunnis as "a pretext" for its own effort to rally the Shi'a.[80] Indeed, he and his advisers were critical of both Saudi Arabia and Iran at this time, accusing both states of working to inflame sectarian identities ahead of the elections.[81] The perception that Iraq's neighbors were seeking to influence the upcoming elections transcended Maliki's camp. Foreign Minister Zebari, in private conversations with U.S. officials, and President Talabani, in a public statement, both articulated their beliefs that effectively all of the regional states aimed to influence the elections.[82] For his part, Vice President Adel Abd al-Mahdi expressed his view to U.S. officials that Iraq's neighbors, particularly Saudi Arabia, were seeking "to undermine cross-sectarian cooperation" ahead of the elections in order to keep Iraq divided and weak.[83] There was also a strong perception of foreign interference on a popular level in the months leading up to the elections, but there was a polarization in views: the Shi'a generally pointed to the meddling of Syria and Saudi Arabia, while the Sunni Arabs pointed to that of Iran.[84]

In the early fall, Maliki's campaign suffered a significant setback when Ahmad Abu Risha decided not to join his coalition. As of late July, Abu Risha had been articulating in the press his intention to join Maliki, but in September he formed an alliance with Interior Minister Jawad al-Bulani instead.[85] Thus, on 1 October, when Maliki unveiled his State of Law electoral coalition, he was without a prominent Sunni partner, although more minor members of the Abu Risha and al-Dulaimi tribes from Anbar province had decided to join him.[86] Without a prominent leader from outside the Shi'a community, State of Law appeared as what it was: a predominantly Shi'a coalition with a few token Sunnis.[87] In our written exchange, Maliki expressed to me that he did not know why Abu Risha decided not to join his coalition.[88] By contrast, however, al-Askari claimed in the Iraqi press in October 2009 that Abu Risha had been under pressure by Saudi Arabia and Jordan not to join Maliki.[89] While there is no available evidence to corroborate al-Askari's allegation, Abu Risha was indeed thought to be the recipient of Saudi funds, and thus subject to Saudi pressure.[90] More significantly, in August, the governor of Anbar, an ally of Abu Risha, told the press that the Anbaris had received warnings to the effect of, "Do not ally with the Shi'ite government. Do not work with Shi'ites at all."[91] While he did not specify from whom this message had come— and there are any number of different actors to whom he could have been referring—this finding is included to demonstrate that Sunni politicians, by their own account, were under pressure not to align with Shi'a counterparts. Abu Risha still actually defied this pressure—his alliance partner, Interior Minister al-Bulani, was Shi'a—although in choosing al-Bulani over Maliki he decided to ally with a figure far less prominent than the country's Shi'a prime minister.

On 31 October, the formation of a predominantly Sunni Arab electoral coalition was announced: Iraqiyya, under the joint leadership of Allawi and al-Mutlak.[92] Their alliance was also joined by a number of prominent Sunni Arab leaders: Vice President Hashimi, Deputy Prime Minister Rafi' al-Issawi, and Usama al-Nujaifi, whose brother was the governor of Nineveh province.[93] Nevertheless, Allawi and al-Mutlak were reported to be "uneasy partners at best,"[94] and Ghassan Atiyyah, an associate of Allawi who attended at least one meeting of the Iraqiyya alliance,[95] expressed his view in an interview that Iraqiyya would never have been formed without the pressure of Turkey and the Arab states.[96] In fact, Atiyyah recounted that Allawi had even confided in him his belief that the Arab states essentially needed to select Iraq's next leader; in Atiyyah's words, paraphrasing Allawi, "The Arabs have to choose a person [to be the next premier] and force the others to follow."[97] Allawi's view, as recounted by Atiyyah, hardly seems surprising, given that the Arabs' apparent selection was Allawi himself.

While Iraqiyya was in fact a cross-sectarian coalition—grouping together one prominent Shi'i leader with four prominent Sunni leaders—in the eyes of most Iraqi Shi'a, Iraqiyya appeared as "a Sunni body with a Shi'a head."[98] Indeed, according to a Lebanese journalist who reported from Iraq in this period, most Iraqi Shi'a regarded Allawi as "Shi'i, but not Shi'a"—namely, he was seen as a Shi'i individual who did not represent the interests of the Shi'a community.[99] Similarly, in his study of Iraqi sectarianism, Khalil Osman argues that Iraqiyya represented Sunni Arab interests: according to Osman, given the unwritten convention that Iraq's premiership was reserved for a Shi'a, Sunni Arab groups coalesced around Allawi, with the backing of Turkey and Saudi Arabia, to mount an attempt to regain power.[100] In fact, Turkey had played a critical role in mediating among Sunni Arab groups since at least 2005, having facilitated the formation of the

Tawafuq alliance in advance of the December 2005 elections,[101] and evidence of its role in facilitating the formation of Iraqiyya in 2009 has come to light. For instance, Emma Sky, then the political advisor to coalition commander General Ray Odierno, recalls in her memoir that the Turkish ambassador in Baghdad was "instrumental in helping to form Iraqiya," while reportedly, then-Turkish Foreign Minister Ahmet Davutoğlu actually claimed that "he had formed Iraqiya in his own house."[102] However, stoking the perception that the creation of Iraqiyya was at bottom a Saudi project, King Abdullah would bestow upon Turkish Prime Minister Recep Tayyip Erdoğan a major Saudi award, the King Faisal International Prize for Service to Islam, two days after Iraq's March 2010 parliamentary elections, and more to the point, Allawi traveled to the kingdom in late February, on the eve of the election, where he appeared prominently in the pan-Arab press meeting with King Abdullah.[103] With Saudi Arabia having been entirely absent from the Iraqi scene for years, the publicity surrounding Allawi's trip to the kingdom in February 2010 could leave little doubt about Saudi preferences for Iraq's next government.

Meanwhile, Maliki continued to face pressure from Iran to join the reconstituted Shi'a coalition, called the Iraqi National Alliance (INA), whose formation had been announced in August.[104] According to a U.S. diplomatic cable from September 2009, the INA was reportedly "under considerable pressure from the Iranians to persuade or even threaten Maliki's Dawa party to join the alliance"; the cable further noted that the prime minister, sticking to his decision to form his own coalition, anticipated "heavy and active opposition from the Iranians."[105] Indeed, according to Iraq political observer Raad Alkadiri, Maliki remained under heavy Iranian pressure to join the INA in late 2009, although Alkadiri remarked in an interview that the prime minister continued to be "steadfast" in his refusal to comply.[106]

Nevertheless, Maliki's decision to remain separate from the INA was regarded as a significant gamble, as by doing so he was dividing the Shi'a vote: in contrast to two separate Shi'a coalitions, a united one would have been virtually assured of winning the most parliamentary seats in the election.[107] Maliki's willingness to take this gamble probably stemmed from his anticipation that, despite the setbacks he had faced in late 2009, State of Law would win the most seats in the next parliament, although he still expected to have to form a larger coalition following the election to form a government.[108] Maliki never appeared to anticipate that Iraqiyya might in fact win the most parliamentary seats in March 2010.

Meanwhile, the fall 2009 bombings and Maliki's response to them were causing an escalation in sectarian tensions. In his electoral campaign, the prime minister continued to advance a nationalist platform, calling for unity to counter sectarianism.[109] His nationalist message, however, was becoming drowned out by his rhetoric surrounding the attacks. It should be pointed out that the bombings were provoking a considerable degree of fear, not only on a popular level, but within the government as well, especially after the year and a half of relative calm.[110] That fall, the Maliki government appeared intent to try to prove to the Iraqi people that the Ba'thists were involved in the attacks, for instance televising the confessions of Ba'thists in government custody allegedly involved in the bombings.[111] Maliki's own rhetoric against the Ba'thists escalated throughout the fall, with the prime minister for instance declaring in November that they and Al-Qa'ida wanted to overthrow Iraq's democracy.[112] The government's anti-Ba'thist position, however, only stoked the grievances of Sunni Arabs, for whom de-Ba'thification remained a potent symbol of their relative loss of power since 2003. Moreover, while it appears that there was in fact Ba'thist involvement in the attacks, Maliki's allegations were rendered less credible to outside observers by the reputation he had earned, prior to becoming premier, as a leading proponent of de-Ba'thification. The effect of the government's response to the bombings was simply to alienate Sunni Arabs, re-inflaming a fault line that divided not simply Iraq's Sunnis and Shi'a, but more broadly the Shi'a and Kurdish communities on the one hand, and the Sunni Arab one on the other.[113]

In January, pre-election politicking reached a new nadir when the de-Ba'thification commission, under the leadership of Ahmad Chalabi and Ali al-Lami, both members of the INA, disqualified 500 electoral candidates, about one-sixth of the total running in the elections, for alleged ties to the Ba'th Party. A de-Ba'thification reform law had called for the creation of a new de-Ba'thification commission to replace the one headed by Chalabi and Lami, which had been established in 2003 by the CPA; however, parliament had not been able to agree on the composition of a new committee, and thus the old one continued to operate.[114] Iraqiyya was disproportionately affected by the electoral ban, and in fact al-Mutlak, a former Ba'thist who had been expelled from the party in 1977, was himself disqualified from running in the elections.[115] There was also speculation that Iran had pushed for the ban.[116] Maliki himself publicly embraced the ruling, calling for it to be implemented "without any exception."[117] In the view of then-U.S. ambassador to Iraq, Christopher Hill, while the prime minister had not initiated the measure, he sought to take political advantage of it.[118] Nevertheless, in February, under U.S. pressure, Maliki convinced an appeal panel to review the cases of 171 disqualified candidates. Of these, only twenty-six were reinstated, which did not include al-Mutlak.[119]

Thus, by the time of the election, inflamed sectarian sentiment had swamped any calls for national unity. Despite his desire to run a nationalist campaign, Maliki had himself succumbed to this sentiment, with his escalating rhetoric against the Baʿthists and his embrace of the January 2010 electoral ban. Nevertheless, according to Iraq political observer Alkadiri, Maliki and his close advisers continued to believe that their nationalist campaign had broad popular appeal.[120] Thus, the prime minister continued to refrain from joining the INA, refusing to bow to Iranian pressure to join an Iranian-backed coalition. In fact, Maliki personally remained very popular: he would win the most votes of all the candidates running in the March 2010 election.[121] Unfortunately for him, however, his State of Law coalition would not do quite as well as Iraqiyya. The victory of the Saudi-backed alliance was what would prompt him to reverse his pre-election decision to remain separate from the INA.

Post-Election Stalemate

Indeed, in a post-election stalemate that would last eight months, Maliki would eventually outmaneuver Iraqiyya, obtaining Iranian backing and aligning with the INA in order to retain the premiership and safeguard Iraq's new order. Thus, the Saudis, who wanted to oust Maliki because they considered him to be an Iranian agent, had supported Allawi, but in doing so they created a situation in which Maliki reversed his earlier behavior and aligned with Iran. The Saudis' inaccurate and stereotypic image of the Iraqi premier was thereby fulfilled. For their part, the Iranians appeared to back Maliki not because they favored him personally, but because they recognized that he was the most viable candidate for the post among the Shiʿa Islamists. The result of the election was a slim victory for Allawi's list: Iraqiyya won ninety-one parliamentary seats, out of a total of 325, in comparison to eighty-nine won by State of Law. The two other dominant parliamentary blocs were the INA and the Kurdistan Alliance, with seventy and forty-three seats, respectively. No other alliance won more than eight seats in parliament.[122] Iraq's constitution stipulated that the nominee of the largest parliamentary bloc would be charged with forming a government, and thus following the election, a jubilant Allawi declared his right to do so.[123] For his part, Maliki was shocked by the election results; he claimed that electoral fraud had taken place and demanded a recount.[124] He also called upon Iraq's Federal Supreme Court to consider whether the largest parliamentary bloc could be one that was formed after the election, not necessarily before it. The constitution was vague on this point, and the court conceded to Maliki's interpretation.[125] Thus began a race between State of Law and Iraqiyya to form the largest coalition, a competition in which Maliki ultimately prevailed. For his part, Allawi would never form a coalition larger than Iraqiyya's original ninety-one parliamentary seats.

Following the eight-month standoff, Allawi frequently articulated his account of how Maliki had prevailed, namely that Iran and the United States had blocked Iraqiyya's right to form the next government.[126] This would become the dominant narrative surrounding the resolution of the crisis.[127] As will be touched upon below, the Sadrists became the kingmaker in the post-election crisis, and at the time of their decision to support Maliki, the Sunni Arab-leaning media painted it as resulting from Iranian pressure.[128] This interpretation of the Sadrists' decision-making has also become part of the dominant narrative of this episode.[129] Nevertheless, a close examination of this period, conducted below, reveals that a more complicated process took place. Iranian support was indeed important to Maliki's ability to form an enlarged coalition, but the Iranians could not simply deliver the Iraqi premiership to him; he still needed to make deals with the Sadrists, as well as the Kurds, in exchange for their support.

For his part, Maliki appeared genuinely to believe that his loss to Iraqiyya had occurred as a result of electoral fraud—he believed the electoral results had been falsified—and moreover he told me in our written exchange that it was the United States that had falsified the results, which it did, he said, on behalf of the Saudis and their Iraqiyya clients.[130] No evidence has come to light to support Maliki's allegation, although his claim is profoundly illustrative of his mindset by this point: namely, that the Saudis expended all efforts in 2010 to have him removed, and moreover that the Americans were no longer to be trusted. Maliki's view—that Iraqiyya won the most seats in the election due to fraud—was profoundly self-serving, but it was also an indication of the extent to which he had come to view Saudi Arabia through the lens of an enemy image.

While it is beyond question that Maliki wanted to retain the premiership in 2010 out of personal ambition, his fight to hold on to power transcended his own personal aspirations and reflected more broadly his and his advisors' overriding objective to safeguard the post-2003 order. In the perception of the Shi'a, Allawi's coalition had been constructed, at bottom, to restore Sunni Arab power in Baghdad. (This perception was also shared by some U.S. diplomats then based in Baghdad, even if Maliki himself believed the Americans were aiding his rivals.[131]) For his part, al-Askari expressed his belief in an interview that Iraqiyya's ultimate objective was not really to obtain the post of premier, but rather to re-assert the Sunni Arabs' traditional control over the Iraqi army, which, al-Askari argued, constituted the true axis of power in the country.[132] Prior to the elections, Maliki adviser Sadiq al-Rikabi had articulated to U.S. officials that the Iraqi Shi'a "would naturally resist Iranian influence" so long as the Arab states "did not close the door" to them.[133] However, now Iraqiyya's victory represented, in the Shi'a perception, a Saudi-backed project to restore some semblance of Sunni Arab power. The truth is that Maliki's decision to divide the Shi'a vote had provided Allawi's list with an opening to prevail: Maliki

had taken a gamble to form his own nationalist alliance independent of Iran, but it had backfired badly. Thus, in line with
the Saudis' expectations of him, he now chose to reverse his
pre-election decision and close ranks with Iran and the other
Shi'a Islamist parties.

However, during his first government he had turned many of
those parties, such as the Sadrists, against him, and the question
remained whether they would accept his return to the premiership.
The Sadrists were by far the dominant faction within the INA
after the election, having won thirty-nine of the INA's seventy
parliamentary seats. ISCI was much diminished from its perfor-
mances in 2005 with only seventeen seats, and the remainder went
to smaller parties and independents.[134] Winning the support of the
Sadrists, who had been the target of Maliki's Charge of the
Knights campaign, was therefore crucial for him to retain the premiership. In late spring 2010, it was reported that Iran was placing
"great pressure" on Muqtada al-Sadr to accept Maliki's candidacy.[135] The Iranians, who had themselves appeared shocked by
the election results, had reportedly not favored the return of the
independent-minded Maliki to the premiership prior to the election.[136] Following the election, however, the Iranians presumably
recognized that Maliki was the most viable candidate among the
Shi'a Islamist contenders. Not only did he control eighty-nine
parliamentary seats, in comparison to the INA's seventy, but also
the INA was divided among its various factions. Reportedly, that
spring, ISCI nominated two different candidates, but, as had happened following the January and December 2005 elections, the
Sadrists vetoed both of its selections. For their part, the Sadrists
put forward Ibrahim al-Ja'fari, the weak premier of the 2005
Transitional Government, but ISCI was reported to prefer Maliki
to al-Ja'fari as "the lesser of two evils."[137]

While Muqtada was undoubtedly under Iranian pressure to
support Maliki, who was clearly not his top choice, there is evi-

dence that the Iranians did not need to force Muqtada to support the incumbent prime minister. Indeed, press reporting suggests that Muqtada and Maliki had been in negotiations since the spring, which reached a conclusion in October. For instance, in May, a Sadrist spokesman told Agence France-Presse: "The Sadr movement does not object to Nuri al-Maliki taking the position of prime minister again but we have conditions."[138] That summer, State of Law and the Sadrists were reported to be negotiating, and on 1 October it was announced that Maliki and the Sadrists had reached a deal: Muqtada would support Maliki's candidacy in return for a strong Sadrist role in his cabinet.[139] Thereafter, the Kurdistan Alliance followed suit. The Kurds' position, as articulated to U.S. officials in Baghdad, had been that the next premier needed to come from one of the Shi'a Islamist parties.[140] Nevertheless, Masoud Barzani, president of the KRG and the Kurds' chief negotiator in this process, also appeared unwilling to back Maliki without getting something in return. Indeed, Barzani and Maliki were reported to have begun negotiations in August, which appeared to reach a conclusion following Maliki's deal with Muqtada.[141]

As for Allawi, he asserted in the press following the conclusion of the crisis that the blocking of Iraqiyya's right to form the next government was "neither correct, nor constitutional, nor legal, nor democratic."[142] While the soundness of the Federal Supreme Court's post-election decision was indeed called into question, ultimately Allawi had been outmaneuvered by Maliki in the post-election period, having struggled to form an enlarged coalition. He in fact met once with Muqtada during this period, but it appeared that Muqtada's motive behind meeting with him was really to gain leverage over Maliki.[143] In the view of Iraq political observer Alkadiri, as expressed in an interview: "Everyone talks about how Maliki stole the election. Maliki didn't steal the election. Ultimately, Maliki refused to stand down and the political dynamics were that Ayad couldn't get a coalition together. People were telling Ayad that from very early on."[144] Similarly, Zaid Al-Ali, then a legal adviser to the UN in Iraq, recalls in his account of this period that Allawi "badly miscalculated" following the elections, because he failed to acknowledge that Maliki had the opportunity to form an enlarged alliance with the INA.[145]

As for the Saudi leadership, it appeared that there was not much they could do in the post-election period to promote Allawi. In April, Iraqi Kurdish and Shiʻa leaders, including Jalal Talabani, Barzani, Ammar al-Hakim of ISCI, and representatives of the Sadr trend, traveled to the kingdom, but their decision-making did not appear to be swayed by whatever entreaties the Saudi leadership made to them at this time.[146] The Saudi leadership could not really do much more than complain, as Prince Turki al-Faisal did in May 2010, when he asserted in the press that Maliki was "hijacking" the elections and "deny[ing] the Iraqi people their legitimately elected government."[147] In an interview, Prince Turki also expressed his opinion, based on Allawi's dominant narrative, that "it was really curious to see the U.S." at this time "pushing, with the Iranians," for the return of a Maliki government.[148] The Americans, however, did not really have much influence in the post-election period, given that the Sadrists, with whom they had had no relationship since 2003, were the kingmaker. Then, in late October 2010, at a point where Maliki's nomination for premier was practically assured, King Abdullah made an attempt to intervene in the Iraqi political process, inviting Iraq's leaders to convene in Riyadh to settle their crisis.[149] However, the only Iraqi who seriously embraced Abdullah's initiative was Allawi, revealing it to be little more than a last-ditch attempt to promote the Iraqiyya leader.[150] Moreover, Allawi appeared to have no strategy at this point to propel himself forward other than to rely on Abdullah's support. Thus, in November, during a conference of Iraqi leaders which brought the post-election stalemate to a final resolution, Allawi called upon his colleagues to meet instead in Saudi Arabia under the auspices of King Abdullah, a call he was still reiterating a few weeks later, even after Maliki had been formally nominated to the premiership.[151] From this point, Allawi's star began to fade in Iraqi politics.

Conclusion

As social psychologists attest, perceivers who treat targets in line with an inaccurate stereotype of the targets' social group often elicit new behavior on the part of targets that conforms to the stereotype, and indeed, the purpose of this chapter has been to highlight the change in Maliki's behavior that took place in the aftermath of the 2010 elections. Prior to the elections, Maliki sought to form his own non-sectarian, nationalist coalition, while resisting Iranian pressure to join an Iranian-backed Shi'a Islamist list. He was aware that Saudi Arabia and other Sunni states had helped form the Iraqiyya alliance under the leadership of Allawi; however, feeling confident that his coalition would win the most seats in parliament, he chose to remain independent of Iran. It was only in the aftermath of the elections, when Iraqiyya won the most seats, that Maliki changed his behavior, seeking Iranian assistance to retain the premiership. In seeking to hold on to power, Maliki was most definitely motivated by both personal ambition and the imperative to safeguard Iraq's new Shi'a-led order. But regardless of whether he was primarily motivated by personal or communal interests—and he likely conflated the two—the point is that Saudi support to Allawi ultimately compelled Maliki to seek the support of Iran. The Saudi leadership, by backing Allawi out of their conviction that Maliki was an Iranian agent, compelled Maliki to begin to act in ways that confirmed their image of him. In this way, the Saudis created a self-fulfilling prophecy.

6

SAUDI ARABIA AND IRAQ AFTER THE ARAB SPRING

In the aftermath of Iraq's 2010 parliamentary elections, the self-fulfilling prophecy created by the Saudi leadership, whereby Nuri al-Maliki began to seek Iranian assistance due to the sense of threat he felt from the Saudis, started to come to fruition. This chapter explores how this self-fulfilling prophecy became even more pronounced in Maliki's second government. Indeed, by the end of the second Maliki government in 2014, Iraq was in open alliance with Iran. The end of the chapter then looks at the rapprochement that has taken place between Saudi Arabia and Iraq since 2015, following both the ouster of Maliki and the death of King Abdullah. In recent years the two countries have begun to engage meaningfully. Whereas Abdullah isolated Iraq, today, the Saudis aim to entice it away from an Iranian orbit. For its part, Iraq seeks to tread a middle path in the region, unaligned with either Saudi Arabia or Iran.

Iraq Turns to Iran

In his first government, Maliki had taken bold actions, such as confronting the Sadrist militias in spring 2008 and refusing to join the INA in 2009, which had signaled his intention to pursue an independent course from Iran. In this period, he had attempted to establish a positive relationship with Saudi Arabia and thereby reinforce the new Iraq's membership of the Arab family. However, King Abdullah's decision not to engage with him had caused Maliki to feel increasingly threatened by Saudi Arabia, leading him, ultimately, to pursue a closer relationship with Iran.

This trend accelerated in Maliki's second government. Indeed, by the end of his second government, some three months after the fall of Mosul to the Islamic State of Iraq and Syria (ISIS) in June 2014, Maliki was publicly alleging that Saudi Arabia had declared war on his country, while Iran, for its part, took charge of the Iraqis' ground campaign against ISIS. Maliki's second government unfolded against the backdrop of tumultuous regional events—namely the Arab Spring, leading to a devastating civil war next door in Syria. The Syrian civil war unleased a new surge of inflamed sectarian sentiment in the region, as Sunni states—Saudi Arabia, Qatar, and Turkey—began to support Sunni Syrian rebels to bring down the Alawite-dominated regime of Bashar al-Assad, backed by Iran and Iranian clients like Lebanese Hizballah. Meanwhile, there was a powerful perception on the part of the Iraqi Shi'a that the Saudi leadership sought to bring down not only the Syrian regime, but also their government. Whatever the reality of the situation, this perception was a testament to how the Saudis' enemy image of Iraq had engendered an enemy image on the part of many Iraqis toward the Saudis. The Saudis, believing Maliki to be an Iranian client, had refused to engage, but their refusal to engage led the Iraqis to suspect that the Saudis desired the removal of the Maliki government. The Iraqis' perception of Saudi hostility, coinciding with ISIS's explosion onto the Iraqi scene, pushed Iraq into a firm Iranian embrace.

The start of the Arab Spring coincided almost exactly with the start of Maliki's second government. On 17 December

2010, five days before the second Maliki government was seated, a Tunisian street vendor in the Tunisian town of Sidi Bouzid set himself aflame after being harassed by the police. Muhammad al-Bouazizi's self-immolation set off dramatic protests in Tunisia that quickly ignited uprisings throughout the Arab world. Following the fall of Tunisian dictator Zin al-Abadin bin Ali in January 2011, Egyptian President Hosni Mubarak was forced to end his thirty-year rule in February. On the heels of Mubarak's resignation, massive protests broke out in Bahrain, where tens of thousands of people, initially both Shiʿa and Sunnis, took to the streets over the next month. A major theme of the Bahraini uprising was the call for greater political and social freedom for the country's Shiʿa majority. In mid-March, Saudi Arabia and the UAE initiated a military intervention in Bahrain to quell the uprising.

The Saudi leadership, for their part, fell back on their deeply ingrained beliefs about Iranian expansionism to explain the chaos that was engulfing the region. The official Saudi narrative surrounding the Arab uprisings, propagated by the Saudi media, declared that they had been instigated by Iran's sectarian and racist regime to satisfy its greedy ambitions to subjugate the region. A series of five articles by Saudi columnist Jasir al-Jasir, which appeared from 12 to 16 March 2011 in *al-Jazira*, a leading domestic Saudi newspaper, is illustrative of official Saudi discourse surrounding the uprisings.[1] Al-Jasir's articles, all appearing under headlines like, "The Plans of the Safavid Regime in Iran to Destroy the Gulf States" or "The Plans of the Safavid Regime to Destroy the Arab Countries," asserted that the Islamic Republic was the "contemporary embodiment" of the Safavid Empire, the Persian dynasty founded in 1501 that had converted the Iranian populace from Sunni to Shiʿa Islam. According to al-Jasir, the Islamic Republic, having already subjugated Iraq, was now turning its attention to Bahrain, where it sought to topple the king and annex the country. Nevertheless, al-Jasir alleged that Bahrain "was only the second stop" in Iran's expansionist plans (Iraq having been the first); he claimed that Iran had "a scheme and an initiative toward each of the Gulf Arab states."[2] He pointed out that the Iranian regime even sought to control Egypt by establishing inroads into the country via the Muslim Brotherhood and the Coptic Christian community.[3]

Al-Jasir's articles, appearing in the mainstream Saudi media, were clearly intended to cast aspersions on the popular movements fueling the uprisings for a domestic Saudi audience.[4] Nevertheless, the series also reflected, on a more fundamental level, the ideas that had existed within the Saudi leadership since the early 1980s. As seen in Chapter 1, during the Iran–Iraq War the Saudi leadership had come to the conclusion that Iran sought to impose its hegemony over the Gulf Arab states, and Chapter 3 demonstrated that in the years following the 2003 invasion of Iraq, the Saudi leadership resorted to the Iranian expansionism narrative to explain all the crises of the region, from Iraq to Lebanon to Palestine to Yemen. Given their total focus on Iran's supposedly inexorable quest to dominate the region, it is unsurprising that the Saudis failed to credit the efforts of Iraq's post-2003 leaders to establish a positive relationship with them. Indeed, the final article in al-Jasir's series is indicative of the views within the Saudi leadership toward Iraq by this point. According to the columnist, Iraq, having been subjugated, was "unable to confront Iran's greediness inside its territory," with the result being that the dignity of its citizens had become "nonexistent and without value."[5] In a similar vein, a December 2011 opinion piece in *al-Sharq al-Awsat*, the Saudi-owned pan-Arab newspaper, remarked that Iran sought to transform the Arab countries then experiencing unrest into "little Irans," or "tamed followers" as Iraq had become, it said, under Maliki.[6] What is remarkable about this Saudi view of Iraq is that there was no room even to question whether their assumptions about it were correct. It was simply an open-and-shut case that Iraq, under Shi'a leadership, had become subservient to Iran.

The Arab Spring entered a more ominous phase in 2012, when the protest movement that had begun in Syria the previous March devolved into armed conflict. The Syrian civil war pitted the country's Sunni majority, backed by Saudi Arabia, Qatar, and Turkey, against the Assad regime, backed by Iran and its regional proxies. As seen in the previous chapter, relations between the Saudi leadership and the Assad regime had deteriorated following the 2005 assassination of former Lebanese Prime Minister Rafiq al-Hariri, as well as the 2006 Lebanon War, in which Syria had supported Hizballah. In that period, King Abdullah of Saudi Arabia, according to a 2008 U.S. diplomatic cable, had been "vociferous in his condemnation" of Assad for aligning with Iran.[7] Relations had warmed up considerably in 2009 and 2010 following the rapprochement initiated by King Abdullah, but after the Assad regime initiated a brutal crackdown on protesters in the summer of 2011, Abdullah reportedly decided "to do whatever was needed to bring down" Assad, and by extension roll back Iran's influence in Syria and the wider region.[8] In late 2011, the Saudi leadership spearheaded a diplomatic initiative to compel Assad to step down, and the following year they began to arm the Syrian opposition.[9] In July 2012, Prince Bandar bin Sultan, a former U.S. ambassador to Saudi Arabia, was put in charge of the Saudis' effort to remove Assad. A Saudi royal family insider recalled in an interview that Abdullah did not in fact like Bandar, whom he had sidelined in the first years of his reign; however, following the Arab Spring, Abdullah felt he needed Bandar, who, being shrewd and intelligent, was seen as "the fix-it guy" within the royal family.[10] By the end of 2012, the Syrian rebels were on the offensive, and Assad's continuation in power was precarious.

The Syrian civil war—in particular, the perception that the Saudis were working to overthrow not only Assad in Damascus, but also Maliki in Baghdad—was what ultimately pushed the Maliki government to align with Iran. Indeed, Maliki believed that the Saudis, as well as other Sunni countries, were working to overthrow the governments in both Syria and Iraq,[11] and Maliki articulated this perception to me in our written exchange, expressing his opinion that King Abdullah and the Saudi leadership "could not bear to see a Shi'i [in power] in Baghdad, the capital of the Abbasid Caliphate, nor an Alawite [in power] in Damascus, the capital of the Umayyad Caliphate," references to two medieval Islamic empires.[12] Moreover, Maliki claimed in a 2017 interview on Iraqi television that Abdullah had at some point declared that he "would spend 100 billion to bring down the government in Baghdad."[13] Whether or not this story was accurate—and there is no evidence to substantiate that King Abdullah actually said this—it points to Maliki's strong perception that Abdullah was actively working to overthrow him, not only Assad. In this context, Maliki came to believe that the Saudis supported ISIS, the reincarnation of Al-Qa'ida in Iraq which took over one-third of Iraq's territory, including the city of Mosul, in the first half of 2014, in an effort to bring down his government.[14] While I should emphasize that I have no evidence to support Maliki's contention that Saudi Arabia supported ISIS, or any other armed group in Iraq, in writing this account of Saudi–Iraq relations I have frequently been reminded of what my Saudi royal family insider source told me in 2018, a quotation I shared in the last chapter: that "Abdullah was willing to do whatever it took to get rid of Maliki."[15] Whatever the royal family insider meant by this statement, it would appear to validate Maliki's strong suspicion that Abdullah was expending great effort to remove him from power.

However, even before the Syrian uprising devolved into civil war, Maliki was already pursuing a closer relationship with Iran.

It should be pointed out that the vociferous condemnation from within the Iraqi Shiʿa community of the Saudi-led intervention in Bahrain in March 2011—a number of Iraqi Shiʿa leaders publicly decried the intervention, while large-scale protests among Iraqi Shiʿa took place against it—contributed to the perception that Iraq was gravitating toward an Iranian regional axis.[16] Then, in July 2011, a year after Maliki had won Iran's support in the post-election crisis of 2010, the Maliki government and Iran signed a number of agreements to strengthen bilateral cooperation. During a visit by Iranian Vice President Muhammad Reza Rahimi to Baghdad to conclude the agreements, Maliki expressed great warmth toward his neighbor, calling Iran and Iraq "brethren countries," and declaring, "Our will is to establish the best [of] relations" with Iran.[17] Iraqi political analyst Sajad Jiyad recounted in an interview that Maliki was still averse to being beholden to Iran, but by this point this was the situation into which Maliki had been forced; Jiyad added that Maliki still expressed a critical attitude toward Iran at this time, but only among those close to him.[18] Maliki had indeed been forced into this relationship with Iran, as Iran was his only real friend among the regional states by this point. In Maliki's perception, the Iranians had come to his assistance in 2010, at a time when his Sunni neighbors, led by Saudi Arabia, were working to have him removed from power. It seems unsurprising that the result was that Maliki, despite his longstanding skepticism toward Iran, would seek to establish a stronger relationship with it in his second government.

Nevertheless, Iraq's alignment with Iran became starker over the course of the Syrian civil war. What is interesting is that almost as soon as the uprising began in Syria, Iraqi Shiʿa leaders were expressing concern that Assad's overthrow could pave the way for the rise of a Sunni Islamist government in Damascus, backed by Saudi Arabia, which would be antagonistic toward

Iraq's Shiʻa-led government. In April 2011, only a month after protests in Syria broke out, Khalid al-Asadi, a Shiʻi politician close to Maliki, told Agence France-Presse that Sunni Arab states were allegedly supporting the protesters, while Hamid Fadil, a political science professor at Baghdad University, expressed his view in the same article: "If the Islamists came to power [in Syria], it's clear they would have been helped by Saudi Arabia and other Sunni countries. This will impact Iraq because they will try and push Sunnis here to work against a government dominated by Shiites."[19]

While it seems that these Iraqis were projecting their own fears onto the situation in Syria—at this early stage, the Syrian protests were still overwhelmingly peaceful and democratic—their view points to how the Saudis' enemy image of Iraq had by this point produced an enemy image on the part of Shiʻa Iraqis toward the Saudis. The Saudis, inferring that the Maliki government bore malign intent toward them, had refused to engage, but their refusal to engage then prompted Shiʻa Iraqis to detect indicators of Saudi hostility toward them. And the perceptions among Shiʻa Iraqis that Saudi Arabia would seek to harm Iraq via Syria were indeed powerful. In September 2011, an unnamed Shiʻi politician told Reuters, "We don't fear Sunni rule in Syria, but we fear Wahhabi influence in Syria. We have evidence that Saudi Arabia wants to break the Shiʻite Crescent," a term first coined in 2004 by Abdullah II of Jordan to refer to a potential Iranian-led axis of Shiʻa states and non-state actors.[20] Similarly, another unnamed Shiʻi legislator recounted to Reuters, "If Saudi Arabia became influential in Syria, the Wahhabis will join forces with the people in western Iraq. There will be war inside Iraq."[21] It should be pointed out that the term "Wahhabi" has been used by Iraqi Shiʻa as a pejorative catch-all phrase referring to Sunni extremists. Meanwhile, Iraqi political analyst Ibrahim al-Sumaidaʻi expressed the view in September 2011: "Saudi Arabia and the

Sunni Arab powers will try [in the context of the Syrian conflict] to redraw the political map in Iraq to increase Sunni influence in decision-making because until now they have not made peace with Shi'ite rule here."[22] Thus, practically as soon as the Syrian conflict broke out, some Shi'a Iraqis were viewing it through the prism of the enmity that had developed between them and Saudi Arabia.

In this context, the Maliki government regarded the conflict in Syria not as the Syrians' war only, but as their war too. As Maliki later observed in an interview on Iraqi television, "My vision was that if Assad's regime fell, then the region would fall."[23] Maliki, as well as a number of Iraqi Shi'a militias backed by Iran, thus went to great lengths to prevent Assad's overthrow. As early as 2011, Asa'ib Ahl al-Haq, one of the most prominent of the Iranian-trained Special Groups, which had been established by Muqtada al-Sadr rival Qais al-Khazali in 2006, had entered Syria to fight alongside the Assad regime.[24] In early 2012, Maliki in fact invited al-Khazali's group to join the Iraqi political process; while his intention behind doing so was likely to gain leverage over Muqtada al-Sadr, Asa'ib Ahl al-Haq's entry into Iraqi politics only enhanced Iranian influence in Iraq's halls of power.[25] By 2013, members of Asa'ib Ahl al-Haq and another Iranian-backed Iraqi Shi'a militia, Kata'ib Hizballah, were entering Syria in ever larger numbers.[26] The Maliki government, for its part, not only turned a blind eye to the Iraqi Shi'a militias traveling to Syria in this period, but also routinely allowed Iranian aircraft to fly to Syria through Iraqi airspace, thereby facilitating the Iranians' delivery of military materiel to the Assad regime.[27]

On a domestic level, Maliki's second government was marked by the grave deterioration of relations between the prime minister and a number of other Iraqi leaders, primarily but not exclusively those from the Iraqiyya coalition. During his first government, Maliki had earned a reputation for concentrating power in his own hands and excluding rivals from decision-making, and he started his second term having amassed even more power. He occupied the defense and interior minister posts, in addition to the premiership, giving him control of the country's security services, and had imposed his authority over Iraq's electoral commission and central bank.[28] He also sought to weaken his rivals, including his Shi'a ones, by sowing division among them, using the powers of his post to manipulate domestic factions.[29] In sum, Maliki appeared to be turning the Iraqi government into a sort of one-man rule.

Events then started to come to a head in late 2011 as U.S. forces were preparing to leave Iraq by the end of the year, in compliance with the status of forces agreement negotiated by the Bush administration and the first Maliki government in 2008. In fall 2011, the Iraqi security forces rounded up from across the country hundreds of alleged Ba'thists, who were accused of plotting anti-government activities timed to coincide with the U.S. pullout, producing an outcry in the Sunni Arab community. In protest, the majority Sunni Arab province of Salahuddin declared itself an autonomous region in October, and Maliki inflamed the situation further by asserting that Ba'thists were trying to turn the province into a "safe haven."[30] The crisis mounted over the next two months, as Anbar, Nineveh, and Diyala provinces took their own steps to declare autonomy and Iraqiyya leaders Tariq al-Hashimi and Salih al-Mutlak, then vice president and deputy prime minister, made statements supportive of the calls for regional autonomy. Then, on 17 December, the Iraqiyya bloc, citing the prime minister's growing authoritarianism, announced a boycott of parliament. In a dramatic escalation of the crisis, Maliki ordered the house arrest of al-Hashimi and al-Multak, as well as of Rafi' al-Issawi, then finance minister. On the eighteenth, the final U.S. troops left Iraq, and the next day, an arrest warrant was issued for al-Hashimi, who fled to Iraqi Kurdistan. The charges against al-Hashimi—for allegedly running a death squad—were considered highly questionable; to Maliki's many detractors, the prime minister was simply sidelining a rival. Simultaneously, Maliki tried to remove al-Mutlak from his position as deputy prime minister, after the latter denounced him on Iraqi television as "worse than Saddam."[31]

Thereafter, the domestic political crisis only continued to grow. In spring 2012, a range of Iraqi leaders—Muqtada al-Sadr, Kurdish President Masoud Barzani, and Usama al-Nujaifi and Ayad Allawi of Iraqiyya—joined forces to try to push a no-confidence vote against Maliki through parliament. At the end of the year, the Iraqi authorities arrested a number of bodyguards employed by al-Issawi on terrorism charges. A few months later al-Issawi resigned as finance minister, and an arrest warrant was issued for him as well.

In our written exchange, I asked Maliki if he perceived that outside powers were interfering in Iraq in late 2011, coinciding with the crisis that culminated in his spectacular falling out with al-Hashimi and al-Mutlak. In his response, Maliki claimed that his Sunni rivals were then under the control of extremist Sunni groups who sought to overthrow his government, but did not mention any alleged interference by Saudi Arabia or other Sunni states. His answer somewhat surprised me, as it was reported at the time of the U.S. withdrawal that some Iraqi Shi'a were expressing fear about an alleged "Sunni coup pushed by Saudi Arabia," and al-Mutlak himself told *al-Sharq al-Awsat* in February 2012 that Maliki had accused him of being, in al-Mutlak's words, "an agent of Saudi Arabia."[32] Whatever the perception of outside interference in the December 2011 crisis, Turkey, Qatar, and Saudi Arabia revealed themselves not to be neutral in the events then unfolding in Iraq when al-Hashimi, considered a fugitive by the government in Baghdad, made high-profile visits to each of the three states in April 2012. Moreover, some ten days following al-Hashimi's arrival in Turkey, Prime Minister Recep Tayyip Erdoğan held a meeting with Kurdish President Barzani, who was leading the effort to oust Maliki at the time, prompting Maliki to declare that Turkey had become a "hostile state."[33] While Erdoğan had taken steps to cultivate good relations with the Iraqi Shiʿa—for instance, on a 2011 trip to Iraq he visited the Imam Ali shrine in Najaf and met with Grand Ayatollah Sistani—Turkey had, as seen in the last chapter, teamed up with Saudi Arabia and other Sunni countries in 2009 to form the Iraqiyya coalition; according to observers of the Turkish political scene, Ankara had believed an Iraqi government led by Iraqiyya would serve Turkish interests better than the continuation of a Shiʿa-dominated system in Baghdad.[34]

With regard to Saudi–Iraq relations, in early 2012 observers noted that there was actually cause for optimism that Saudi Arabia was adopting a new, warmer approach to its estranged neighbor. That February, an Iraqi delegation led by National Security Adviser Falih al-Fayyad traveled to the kingdom at the Saudis' invitation. The visit resulted in a security agreement between the two countries covering a range of issues, from cooperation on cross-border crime to an arrangement for prisoner exchange. (At the time, there were reported to be 387 prisoners from Arab countries in Iraqi jails, most of whom were Saudi.[35]) Also in February 2012, Saudi Arabia announced that its ambassador in Amman would take on an additional role as a non-resident ambassador to Iraq, and Maliki, perhaps seeking to build on these Saudi steps, expressed his desire for "comprehensive bilateral relations" with the kingdom in a long interview he gave to the Saudi newspaper *Okaz*.[36] But any hopes for an improvement in relations were dashed a few weeks later, at the end of March, when Saudi Arabia failed to send a high-level delegation to the 2012 Arab Summit in Baghdad, the first Arab League summit hosted by the Iraqi government since 1990. On the eve of the summit, the editorial page of the Saudi-owned *al-Sharq al-Awsat* condemned the terrorism charges brought by the Iraqi government against al-Hashimi and declared, as ever, that Prime Minister Maliki's governing coalition was a creation of Iran.[37]

The Iraqis had hoped that their hosting of the Arab Summit—for the first time in over twenty years—would be their coming-out party, finally reestablishing their country's place within the Arab fold. But not only did King Abdullah not attend the summit, a majority of Arab heads of state stayed away. The emir of Kuwait, Shaikh Sabah al-Ahmad al-Sabah, was the only notable Arab leader in attendance.[38] In 2008, Iraq's Arab neighbors had begun to engage meaningfully, reflecting recognition that they themselves diminished Iraq's Arabism when they treated it as an outsider. Four years later, amid the backdrop of a deepening civil war in Syria as well as growing domestic turmoil in Iraq, most of Iraq's Arab neighbors changed course again, treating the Maliki government with greater distance. But as before, the cold shoulder the Arabs presented to Iraq only deepened the sense of alienation many Iraqis felt toward their Arab brethren. The Arabs' standoffishness reinforced for many Iraqis that their only true friend in the region was Iran.

Iraq's domestic political turmoil, already simmering in 2012, began to boil over the following year. The arrest of al-Issawi's bodyguards in December 2012 ignited protests among Sunni Arabs in Anbar, al-Issawi's birthplace, which quickly spread to Sunni Arab communities in Salahuddin and Nineveh. Almost as soon as the protests broke out, Maliki claimed that a "foreign agenda" lay behind them.[39] In the first months of 2013, the protests evolved into a powerful "sit-in" movement, with large encampments erected in the cities and towns of Anbar, Salahuddin, and Nineveh. Sunni Arabs remonstrated against their community's marginalization by the Maliki government, on vivid display with the arrest warrants issued for al-Hashimi, who was convicted and sentenced to death in absentia in 2012, and al-Issawi. The sit-ins were, however, riven by various factions—secularists, Islamists, and tribal elements—and the most radical among them called for toppling the government in Baghdad and even reversing Iraq's post-2003 Shi'a ascendance.[40] Meanwhile, among Shi'a Iraqis, there was a strong perception that funding for the protests came from Saudi Arabia and Qatar, two of the countries most actively backing the opposition in Syria. This perception on the part of Shi'a Iraqis derived from the apparently high cost of the sit-ins. For instance, food was typically provided to the thousands of protesters every day; one protest leader estimated that the daily cost of running the encampment in his town alone amounted to $4,000–$5,000, topping $10,000 on Fridays.[41]

The protest movement coincided, more dangerously, with the resurgence of Al-Qa'ida in Iraq. Al-Qa'ida had been put on its heels by the U.S. surge of 2007 and 2008. However, following the U.S. withdrawal in late 2011 and a number of prison breaks by Al-Qa'ida militants starting in 2012, the organization, now known as ISIS, initiated a new campaign of bombings throughout the country in spring 2013. That summer, it also launched a major offensive in Nineveh designed to take the city of Mosul. By July 2013, violence in Iraq had returned to levels not seen since the end of the sectarian civil war some five years earlier, with Shi'a accounting for most of the dead.[42] Just as there was a strong perception among Shi'a Iraqis that Saudi Arabia and Qatar were backing the Sunni Arab protests, so too did many believe that financing for ISIS's terror campaign came from inside Saudi Arabia and Qatar.[43] In fact, as early as 2012 Iraqi officials were alleging that the two countries were supporting extremist groups in Iraq, while Maliki, for his part, made frequent accusations in 2013 that unnamed "Arab countries" were supporting Iraqi militants.[44] It should be pointed out that this perception also appears to be based in some degree of fact, as it has been estimated that ISIS received as much as $40 million in 2013 and 2014 from wealthy donors in the Gulf countries, not only Saudi Arabia and Qatar but Kuwait and the UAE as well.[45] Saudi Arabia was also considered to be a leading source of foreign fighters who fought with ISIS, and some Wahhabi *ulama* inside the kingdom even openly called for killing Iraqi Shi'a.[46]

Nevertheless, as the political and security situation deteriorated in Iraq in 2013, Maliki, as well as a range of other Iraqi leaders, actually appeared to make attempts to repair relations with Saudi Arabia. The first overt attempt came two weeks after a raid by Iraqi security forces on a Sunni Arab protest encampment in Hawija in late April 2013. The Hawija raid led to days of clashes between protesters and the security forces and scores of dead, increasing the alienation felt by Iraq's Sunni Arabs.[47] In early May, Maliki then gave an interview to the Saudi-owned, pan-Arab newspaper, *al-Hayat*, telling the newspaper that he sought to "sort out" his relationship with Saudi Arabia and "open the door for cooperation between the two countries." He contended that he was trying to meet protesters' demands—a month earlier, for instance, his cabinet had introduced a major reform to the de-Ba'thification law[48]—and he pronounced:

> This is our will and message to the brothers in Saudi Arabia—the leadership and the people. We want the relationship with them as brothers and neighbours, and we do not have any ambition in their land or oil, and we want to wipe out the troublemaking phenomenon against Saudi Arabia which used to be present in Iraq in the past. We are serious and we wish to be met seriously.[49]

Some months later, in November, Maliki publicly reiterated his desire to reconcile with the Saudis and even articulated his willingness to travel to the kingdom to settle their dispute.[50] At the same time, the Kuwaiti newspaper *al-Siyasa* reported that Barzani and al-Nujaifi were attempting to achieve a rapprochement between Maliki and the Saudi leadership; it was further reported that their initiative was also supported by Muqtada al-Sadr and Ammar al-Hakim, who reportedly believed that "strengthening the Iraqi–Saudi relations will lead to the establishment of balanced Iraqi–Iranian relations on equal terms."[51] In our written exchange, I asked Maliki about his efforts to reconcile with the Saudis in 2013. He responded that he had two objectives at this point, the first to deprive Saudi Arabia of "justification" for continuing "its enmity," and second, he observed on a more positive note that if the Saudis "had responded to my call, maybe we could have achieved a tour in the interest of good brotherly relations."[52] To my mind, Maliki's efforts to reconcile with the Saudis in 2013 indicated that he really did think the kingdom was fueling the turmoil in his country, and as he came under increasing pressure over the course of the year, he made a few more, almost desperate attempts to engage.

At the end of 2013, there occurred a rare instance in which the cold war between Saudi Arabia and Iraq briefly turned hot. In late November, the Mukhtar Army, a break-away faction of the Iranian-backed Shi'a militia Kata'ib Hizballah, announced that it had launched six mortar rounds across the border into an uninhabited region of Saudi Arabia. Wathiq al-Battat, leader of the Mukhtar Army, announced to the press that the strike was a "warning" to the Saudis. Condemning Saudi religious decrees that he said encouraged the killing of Shi'a Muslims, al-Battat called on the Saudis to stop "interfering" in Iraq. If they did not, he said, there would be more attacks on Saudi Arabia. Neither al-Battat nor the Mukhtar Army was considered particularly capable or credible by Iraq's security forces.[53] Nevertheless, the incident demonstrated the remarkable degree of enmity that had taken root between Iraq and Saudi Arabia. I have no evidence that members of the Maliki government ever took part in, or contemplated taking part in, an attack on the kingdom. But others in Iraq such as al-Battat were apparently willing to take this step. Saudi Arabia had cast Iraq in the role of an enemy, and as Alexander Wendt would expect, Iraq, feeling threatened by the Saudis, had by this point begun to act in ways that were indeed threatening to Saudi Arabia in return.

Meanwhile, the already considerable turmoil in Iraq was growing even worse. At the very end of 2013, Maliki proclaimed that the protest encampment in Ramadi had become an ISIS stronghold, and the Iraqi security forces moved into the city to clear the site. But the operation backfired, with ISIS taking advantage of the ensuing clashes to seize control of parts of Ramadi and Fallujah. In February, ISIS militants extended their control to the town of Sulaiman Bik in Salahuddin. In March, Maliki, having previously only made oblique accusations against the Gulf countries in public, became explicit in his meaning. In a televised interview Maliki claimed that Saudi Arabia and Qatar had "declared war on Iraq." He accused them of providing "unlimited" aid to Al-Qaʻida, and asserted: "These two countries are responsible for Iraq's sectarian, terrorist, and security crisis to the first degree."[54] In April, ISIS pushed into the Abu Ghraib area on the western outskirts of Baghdad. Then, in June, in a lightning offensive, ISIS seized Mosul; within three days, it was in control of Nineveh, as well as parts of Kirkuk and Salahuddin, including a town only about 50 miles north of Baghdad. The Iraqi security forces, by this point packed with senior officers more noted for loyalty to Maliki than for military expertise, had mostly fled in the face of the ISIS onslaught, facilitating its seizure of broad swathes of the country. Overlooking the poor showing of the security forces under his command, Maliki, for his part, blamed the fall of Mosul on Saudi Arabia. A week after the ISIS offensive, Maliki's cabinet issued a statement accusing Saudi Arabia of fueling ISIS's resurgence and charging the kingdom with crimes "tantamount to genocide."[55]

The ISIS offensive, beginning in 2013 and culminating in the fall of Mosul, finally pushed Iraq into open alliance with Iran. Toward the end of 2013, Maliki traveled to the United States to obtain assistance in the fight against ISIS, seeking in particular to purchase U.S.-made attack helicopters. Nevertheless, Maliki, having alienated Iraq's Sunni community and grown closer to Iran, had by this point lost the support he once had had in Washington, and powerful critics of his in Congress held up the sale of the helicopters.[56] The Americans tended to see Maliki's heavy-handed policies as the root cause of the new Sunni insurgency. The truth was that Maliki himself no longer bore any love for the Americans, who he believed were implicated in what he saw as the Sunni states' conspiracy to bring down his government.[57] Having failed to obtain the support he wanted from the United States, Maliki next turned to the Iranians. Less than a month after his trip to Washington, his government signed an arms deal worth $195 million with Iran—the first known instance of the Iraqis buying Iranian weapons.[58] Maliki later praised Iran for its assistance. Discounting the considerable military support the U.S. still provided to his government, Maliki declared in 2017, "We were suffering from a shortage of weapons in the confrontation against ISIS ... Iran was the only country which provided us with weapons ... We received weapons from Iran as soon as they were paid for while other countries were postponing delivery for a number of months."[59] Iran's role in the war against ISIS became even more pronounced after ISIS's seizure of Mosul. Within days of Mosul's fall, members of Iran's Revolutionary Guards deployed to Iraq, and by July, the legendary Revolutionary Guards commander Qasim Soleimani was in charge of the Iraqis' ground war against ISIS.[60] Over the following three years, Iranian-backed militias like Asa'ib Ahl al-Haq and Kata'ib Hizballah, now grouped into a state-sanctioned organization called the Popular Mobilization Forces (PMF), were integral components in the campaign to liberate ISIS-held territory. Iraq was now firmly in an Iranian embrace.

I have argued that the Iraqis' belief that Saudi Arabia sought to undermine their government ultimately pushed them into an Iranian regional alignment. Perceiving that their government would be the Saudis' next target once the Assad regime fell, they had every incentive to assist the Iranians' efforts to defend Assad. But on a more basic level, by the time ISIS took over broad swathes of Iraqi territory, there was only one country in the region the Iraqis could count on for support: Iran. Regardless of the Iraqi Shi'a's perceptions about Saudi Arabia, and regardless of whether or not their perceptions were accurate, since Maliki's failed trip to Jeddah in July 2006 the Saudis had extended little in the way of meaningful assistance to the Iraqi government. In the aftermath of the fall of Mosul, the United States came to the Iraqis' aid, sending military advisers to Baghdad in June and launching an air campaign against ISIS in August. Still, Iraq needed partners in the region—it could not only rely on the Americans—and Iran was the sole country that stepped into this void. It is true that by the summer of 2014, the Saudi leadership may have had good reasons to dislike Maliki. By this point, Maliki had lost the support of numerous critical constituencies—Iraq's Sunni Arabs and Kurds; rival Shi'a factions; the Americans, as well as the Iranians, who also regarded Maliki as divisive; and most important of all, Grand Ayatollah Sistani, who publicly urged Maliki to step down—leading to his ouster that August.[61] Nevertheless, even if the Saudi leadership's disdain for Maliki was the root cause of their decision not to assist the Iraqi government, or to engage with it in any way, their decision not to engage only enhanced the Iraqis' need to rely on the Iranians. In this way, Saudi Arabia pushed Iraq into the arms of Iran.

A SELF-FULFILLING PROPHECY

Saudi Arabia and Iraq after Abdullah and Maliki

Five months after Maliki was ousted from the Iraqi premiership, King Abdullah of Saudi Arabia, responsible for the Saudi decision not to engage with Iraq, passed away at the age of ninety. Under Maliki's and Abdullah's successors, Saudi Arabia and Iraq have begun to engage meaningfully, demonstrating that the Saudi leadership has finally accepted the reality of a Shi'a-led Iraq. In establishing improved ties with Saudi Arabia, Iraq has sought to bring balance to its relations with Iran on the one hand and the Arab countries on the other. Another important driver of the relationship on the Iraqi side has been its desire, following the defeat of ISIS, to obtain Saudi investment to aid its post-war reconstruction. Saudi Arabia, meanwhile, is motivated today by what has motivated it since 1979. Having previously isolated Iraq in order to counter the perceived Iranian threat, Saudi Arabia now sees a closer relationship with Iraq as a way to push back against Iran.

With Maliki's departure from the Iraqi premiership, the Saudis immediately signaled a potential willingness to adopt a new approach to Iraq. King Abdullah had himself always attributed his decision not to engage with Iraq to his disdain for Maliki, and within a day of Haider al-Abadi's appointment as Iraq's new prime minister, Abdullah publicly congratulated him.[62] But a true turning point was achieved with Abdullah's own passing from the scene. Two months after Abdullah's death in January 2015, the Saudi leadership sent a strong signal of a new approach, issuing an invitation to Abadi to visit the kingdom.[63] Although Abadi would not travel to Saudi Arabia until 2017, Saudi–Iraq relations continued to thaw over the course of 2015 and 2016. In June 2015, the Saudi government appointed its first resident ambassador to Iraq since 1990, and six months later it reopened its embassy in Baghdad. From George W. Bush to Barack Obama, U.S. efforts to push the Saudis to engage with Iraq never stopped, and with the departure of both Maliki and Abdullah, the U.S. redoubled its efforts. On the American side, Brett McGurk—senior U.S. envoy to the counter-ISIS coalition and an official who had been intimately involved in U.S. Iraq policy since 2004—personally took the lead in encouraging the Saudis to engage.[64] The Americans, with their deep ties to the leaderships in both Saudi Arabia and Iraq, were critical in brokering a new relationship between the two countries. Nevertheless, the Saudis' new approach to Iraq did not result simply from U.S. pressure. As seen, even under Abdullah, senior Saudi officials had recognized the value of engagement, although their efforts had been curtailed by the king.

The brokering role played by the United States is best demonstrated by a trip Adel al-Jubeir took to Baghdad in 2017. Al-Jubeir was the Saudi foreign minister at the time, following the death of Saud al-Faisal in 2015. Abadi had been invited to the kingdom in early 2015; while he was never unwilling to visit Saudi Arabia in the interest of better relations, he was reluctant to do so until he felt assured he would be appropriately received. According to a former American diplomat, Abadi wanted above all to avoid a situation where he might be "humiliated" by the Saudis, as Maliki had been.[65] Moreover, Abadi argued to the Americans that there needed to be balance in the relationship: numerous Iraqi officials had traveled to Saudi Arabia—both Iraq's new president and speaker of parliament had visited the kingdom, for instance, in fall 2014[66]—but no senior Saudi official had visited Iraq since before the 1990–1991 Gulf War. Thus, it became, in the words of an American diplomat, "a focus of U.S. diplomacy" to encourage al-Jubeir to travel to Baghdad.[67] On multiple occasions in 2016, numerous U.S. officials, foremost Brett McGurk, discussed a possible trip with al-Jubeir.[68] Nevertheless, by this point Saudi Arabia's relationship with the

Obama administration was severely strained, and al-Jubeir would not agree to a trip until Donald Trump took office in January 2017. Trump's first secretary of state, Rex Tillerson, met with al-Jubeir on 16 February 2017.[69] Prior to the meeting, McGurk ensured that Tillerson would personally ask the Saudi foreign minister to visit Baghdad; Tillerson did so, and nine days later al-Jubeir traveled to Iraq.[70] In agreeing to the visit, Saudi Arabia's new leaders—King Salman and his powerful son Muhammad bin Salman—signaled, above all, their intent to build a strong relationship with the new Trump administration.

Beyond the friction between the Saudi leadership and the Obama administration that undoubtedly delayed the Saudis' decision to send a senior official to Baghdad, al-Jubeir had exhibited a personal reluctance to travel to Iraq because of the still deeply unsettled security situation there.[71] In early 2017, the campaign to liberate Iraqi territory held by ISIS was in full swing, with the Iranian-backed PMF at the forefront. Moreover, al-Jubeir's perception of the security situation in Iraq was undoubtedly shaped by the experience of Saudi Arabia's first post-1990 ambassador to Iraq, Thamir al-Sabhan. Within days of his arrival in Baghdad in January 2016, al-Sabhan began to make public statements critical of the PMF, considered deeply offensive on the Iraqi street. Al-Sabhan continued to issue incendiary statements to the point that he came under significant threat; not only was he himself concerned for his security—he alleged that there was an Iranian plot to assassinate him—but the Americans were also deeply worried about his safety.[72] In August 2016, the Iraqi government finally requested that al-Sabhan be recalled; a Foreign Ministry official issued a statement that, "We are eager to have a good relationship with Saudi Arabia, but this ambassador is a stumbling block."[73] Summing up the episode, an American diplomat recalled that al-Sabhan was "a disaster."[74]

Nevertheless, al-Jubeir's trip to Baghdad in February 2017—the first by a senior Saudi official in almost three decades—constituted a true breakthrough in the Saudi–Iraq relationship. With the Saudis having taken a symbolic step demonstrating their commitment to a new relationship with Iraq, the Iraqis felt comfortable moving the relationship forward. Over the next eight months, Prime Minister Abadi visited the kingdom twice, aiming in particular to advance economic cooperation to support Iraq's post-war reconstruction.[75] In June 2017, Abadi traveled to Riyadh, where he and his Saudi counterparts announced the establishment of a joint Saudi–Iraqi coordination council, consisting of various committees to oversee political, economic, security, and cultural relations.[76] Four months later, Abadi returned to Saudi Arabia for the first meeting of the coordination council, attended also by an American delegation led by Secretary Tillerson.[77] At the same time that Abadi was in the kingdom in October 2017, Saudi Arabia's oil minister, Khalid al-Falih, was in Baghdad to give the opening address at Iraq's annual international trade fair. During this period, the two countries announced that the Arar border crossing—the principal crossing between Saudi Arabia and Iraq—would be reopened for the first time since 1990 for trade. Saudi Arabia also launched a new commercial air route to Iraq.[78] The Saudi leadership was now demonstrating a very different approach to Iraq from the days of Abdullah.

Since 2017, the Saudi–Iraq relationship has been sustained, although on the Iraqi side there has been disappointment that more Saudi investment has not yet materialized on the ground in Iraq. Moreover, the fluster of activity between the two countries in 2017, followed by a relative slow-down in 2018 and 2019, has contributed to a perception among Iraqis that the Saudis may not be fully engaged. The Saudis themselves have pushed back on this narrative. When asked in 2018 whether the relationship had stalled, al-Jubeir pointed to the milestones achieved in 2017 and commented, "No, there hasn't been a backing off. Quite the contrary. We're moving forward very robustly in our relationship with Iraq."[79] Still, an American diplomat observed that until recently, the Saudis had the intent to establish a presence in Iraq, but not necessarily the will or focus. According to this source, the Saudis' posture has begun to change, as of the time of writing, with the Saudi leadership now more determined to establish actual facts on the ground in Iraq.[80] A potential turning point arrived in November 2020 with the opening of the Arar border crossing, following three years of infrastructure upgrades.[81] The opening of the Saudi–Iraq border will undoubtedly enable a growth in trade. In addition, the Saudis announced in March 2021 that they would invest up to $3 billion in Iraq.[82] Time will tell whether this investment actually materializes. Nevertheless, an American diplomat observed that the Saudis, supremely focused on their Vision 2030 economic reform plan, have begun to recognize the value that Iraq could hold for the kingdom as a trade partner.[83]

While the Saudis may today see an economic opportunity for themselves in Iraq, what has propelled them to pursue a closer relationship is, above all, their desire to counter Iran. According to an American diplomat, Saudi policy remains driven by "Iran, Iran, Iran."[84] In this regard, the Saudis' apparent willingness to play a more active role in Iraq may be traced to the September 2019 attack, attributed to Iran, on their oil infrastructure at Abqaiq and Khurais.[85] In the aftermath of that incident, the Saudis have looked for new ways to push back against Iran in the region, and they see their efforts to pull Iraq away from an Iranian orbit as a means to do so. And the Saudis consider that they can be successful in this regard, as they believe they have more to offer Iraq, particularly in the economic realm, than do the Iranians, who came under mounting U.S. sanctions after

2018.[86] A Saudi editorial published in November 2020 made the Saudi point of view clear: Saudi Arabia, the editorialist wrote, aims "to extend a helping hand [to Iraq] and participate in growth and prosperity, and this is what distinguishes it from Tehran, whose policy is to support terrorism and the formation of sectarian terrorist militias that divide countries, and produce ruin and devastation."[87] In contrast to Abdullah, who isolated Iraq to perverse effect, today the Saudi leadership appears intent on offering economic enticements to Iraq to woo it away from the Iranians. In both cases, however, what has shaped their Iraq policy has been their Iran policy.

For its part, the Iraqi government appears eager to build a strong relationship with Saudi Arabia, although not necessarily at the expense of its relations with Iran. Since Abadi, Iraqi prime ministers have indicated an intention not to take sides in the ongoing Saudi–Iranian confrontation. On numerous occasions in 2017, Abadi stated that Iraq did not "want to be part of any axis," whether one led by Riyadh or by Tehran; Abadi observed that Iraqis had been the "victim" of such regional rivalries, and, signaling his intention to achieve balance in Iraq's external relations, he traveled to Iran on the heels of his first trip to the kingdom.[88] Abadi's successor, Adel Abd al-Mahdi, carried on this policy of balance, despite his longstanding ties to the Iranian regime, during his brief premiership from October 2018 to May 2020. Undertaking trips to Iran, Saudi Arabia, and Turkey in April 2019, Abd al-Mahdi expressed a desire to "boost cooperation with all neighbouring countries and avoid involvement in any regional alliances."[89]

Similarly, the current prime minister, Mustafa al-Kadhimi, who took his post in June 2020, intended to travel to Saudi Arabia, and from there on to Iran, on his first trip abroad as premier. Kadhimi was scheduled to visit Saudi Arabia in July 2020, but his invitation was revoked by the Saudis just prior to the trip. While many Iraqis suspected the Saudis canceled the trip due to their differences with Iran, an American diplomat surmised that the Saudi rationale may have had more to do with the 2020 Coronavirus pandemic.[90] Kadhimi subsequently visited the kingdom in March 2021, and in a very positive development for Iraq's policy of balance, a month later his government mediated direct talks between Saudi Arabia and Iran, thought to be the first time Saudi and Iranian officials held a significant face-to-face meeting since the two states cut relations in 2016.[91]

According to Iraqi political analyst Sajad Jiyad, most Iraqis would welcome the ability to pursue a middle path between Saudi Arabia and Iran. Jiyad observed that for most Iraqis, the experience of being forced to take sides with Iran against the Arabs "has been very, very poor." Nevertheless, most Iraqis, he believed, would also not welcome taking sides with Saudi Arabia, or for that matter with the United States, against Iran.[92] At bottom, Iraq is a country that is both predominantly Arab and predominantly Shi'a; it naturally wants strong relationships with both its Arab neighbors and its Shi'a one, and does not see a contradiction between the two. Moreover, this desire for balanced regional relations has gone hand-in-hand with the passing of inflamed sectarian sentiment in Iraq. In recent years, ISIS has been defeated, and not only have Iraq's Sunni neighbors accepted the reality of Iraq's Shi'a ascendance, but they have also acceded to the Assad regime's continuation in power in Syria. These events have lowered the sectarian temperature in the region, and have allowed the Iraqi Shi'a to feel more secure that the political gains they have made since 2003 will not be reversed. With Iraq's Shi'a-led political order having achieved a large degree of consolidation, issue politics have replaced sect-based politics as the principal focus of the Iraqi political scene.[93] Today, ordinary Iraqis are concerned most of all about their government's grave inefficiency and endemic corruption, a crisis that has little to do with sectarian conflict. In this setting, there is far less need to rely on Iran as a regional protector, and greater opportunity to engage with Saudi Arabia.

Iraq would like to tread a middle path in its region. The question remains: Will Saudi Arabia let it? For that matter, will Iran? Will the United States? To what extent will Iraq be able to follow its own course, being friends with everyone in a region frequently riven by rival axes? Furthermore, the Saudi leadership has supported Prime Minister Mustafa al-Kadhimi, who, as director of the Iraqi National Intelligence Service during the counter-ISIS campaign, established a close relationship with the Americans as well as a personal relationship with Saudi Crown Prince Muhammad bin Salman. But Kadhimi may not remain prime minister following Iraq's next parliamentary elections, scheduled for October 2021, and will Saudi Arabia be supportive of whoever might succeed him? Iraq would like to achieve balance in its regional relationships, but its success is far from guaranteed.

CONCLUSION

A PROPHECY FULFILLED

The number of scholars and analysts of the Middle East who have observed that Iran was the big winner of George W. Bush's decision to invade Iraq are too many to count. But of all the ink that has been spilled on the subject of Iraq since the 2003 invasion, remarkably little has been devoted to exploring the Saudis' hostile attitude to what took place there, most particularly its Shi'a ascendance. This book has sought to fill this glaring gap in the historical record, and in doing so bring greater clarity to the subject of why Iran came away the big winner.

Among analysts in the United States, the dominant view has been that Iran gained the upper hand in Iraq following the U.S. withdrawal in 2011. There is indeed some truth to this: the pull-out of the U.S. military presence enhanced the Iraqis' need to rely on a regional ally—and in this case, their only option was Iran. Moreover, the U.S. withdrawal afforded Nuri al-Maliki a much greater freedom of maneuver, for instance the ability to invite Qais al-Khazali's Iranian-backed group to join the Iraqi political process, which he did almost as soon as the last U.S. soldier left Iraq. But the key assumption underlying the argument that the U.S. withdrawal allowed Iran to establish its predominance in Iraq is that Iraq's Shi'a parties were willing, in effect, to do Iran's bidding in the first place. This assumption has frequently been made explicit in the mainstream media and expert commentary on Iraq in the United States.[1] Moreover, a view has taken hold among many American and other Western analysts that Maliki was, and has always been, a close friend of Iran. No less an analyst than the widely respected *New Yorker* journalist Dexter Filkins wrote in June 2014 that from 2003 on, "Maliki never stopped taking a page—and aid and direction— from his ideological brethren across the border in Iran."[2] This image of Maliki as an Iranian loyalist has endured to the point of becoming commonplace. It has been observed in leading publications like the *New York Times* and the *Wall Street Journal* that Iran was "a longtime supporter" of Maliki, and that it played "a key role" in his "rise to power."[3] The same narrative is dominant in the policymaking world. Middle East experts at think tanks in Washington and beyond have frequently made comments like Iran "carefully nurtured and backed [Maliki] since his first election in 2006," or "Nouri al-Maliki was Iran's best person."[4]

Maliki was no paragon of virtue—he had an authoritarian, manipulative view of leadership and often took highly sectarian positions—but what this book has underscored is that he was, above all, an Iraqi nationalist. What the commentary highlighted above overlooks is that although he became increasingly beholden to Iran in his second government, he had made attempts— indeed, bold attempts—to pursue an independent course from it in his first government. Moreover, the commentary in the United States and the West more generally has almost as a matter of routine overlooked the problematic relationship Iraq had with Saudi Arabia. In analysis of Iraq during the Maliki period, it may be mentioned in passing that Saudi Arabia was absent from Iraq, or that King Abdullah did not like Maliki, if the Saudis are mentioned at all. This has created a perception in the U.S. that Saudi Arabia was not much of a factor in what took place in Iraq prior to 2015. This book has sought to demonstrate, by contrast, that Saudi Arabia was indeed a very important factor in what unfolded in Iraq. On a basic level, the Saudis, in refusing to engage, deprived Iraq of an Arab counterweight that would have helped it balance its relationship with Iran. But, moreover, the Saudis' decision not to engage projected a deep hostility to the new order in Baghdad, and in time Shi'a Iraqis, whether rightly or wrongly, came to see in the Saudis' hostility an intention to reverse Iraq's Shi'a ascendance, even at the cost of destabilizing the country. In short, the Iraqi Shi'a felt deeply threatened by Saudi Arabia, and any analysis of Iraq in the period from 2010 through the rise of ISIS is incomplete without exploring this factor. Already deprived of an Arab counterweight to Iran, they became more and more reliant on their Shi'a neighbor as their fear of Saudi Arabia grew.

In telling this story, the book also illuminates a major contradiction that lay at the heart of George W. Bush's decision to pursue regime change in Iraq—his decision to replace Saddam Hussein's dictatorship with democracy, which naturally allowed the Iraqi Shi'a to rise to power. In order for the U.S. project to succeed, it was necessary for the new Iraq to be accepted by its neighbors; in the absence of regional acceptance, Iraq would be isolated and weak. But the Americans' efforts were adamantly opposed, paradoxically, by one of their closest friends in the region, Saudi Arabia. That the U.S. and Saudi Arabia were allies of long standing made no difference to the Saudis' attitude: the most senior officials within the Bush administration, including Bush himself, sought to persuade King Abdullah to engage with the new Iraq, but no amount of U.S. pressure could compel Abdullah to accept something he regarded as incompatible with his interests. To be fair to the Saudis, they themselves felt deeply betrayed by the United States. The Saudi leadership had implored the Bush administration not to invade Iraq, and then were aghast when the U.S. not only did that, but did so in a way that allowed Iran to breach its regional containment. The Saudis had every right to feel stabbed in the back, but the real point here is that in pursuing regime change in Iraq in a way that was so antithetical to Saudi interests, the Bush administration undertook a project that bore from the outset the seeds of its own failure. To sum up, the Saudis may have made a bad decision, but theirs flowed from a bad decision made by the Bush administration.

Nevertheless, the Saudis' policy not to engage with Iraq was self-defeating. Indeed, it could be said that what allowed Iran to pull Iraq into its orbit was the Saudis' decision to spurn it. Since 2003, plenty of commentators have pointed out that the Saudis have sought to roll back Iran's regional influence.[5] But what these commentators have missed is that, at least in the case of Iraq, the Saudis' policy to undermine Iranian influence paradoxically enhanced Iranian influence. Some sixty years ago, foreign policy scholars Richard Snyder, H.W. Bruck, and Burton Sapin wrote that to understand how a state behaves in the international system it is essential to understand how the decision-makers inside that state define the situations in which they find themselves; Snyder, Bruck, and Sapin argue that decision-makers do not respond objectively to a situation, but rather according to their subjective definition of it. This book reveals that the Saudi leadership—based on their ingrained beliefs about Iranian expansionism and Arab Shiʻa loyalty to Iran—subjectively defined Iraq's post-2003 Shiʻa ascendance as an Iranian ascendance, and then by acting on this definition, they caused, through the mechanism of a self-fulfilling prophecy, some semblance of it to come true. This book about Saudi Arabia and Iraq thereby demonstrates to a considerable degree the extent to which decision-makers' perceptions—in this case misperception—shape the world we live in. The Saudis believed Maliki to be an Iranian loyalist antagonistic to Saudi Arabia. Their perception of him was initially inaccurate, but in time Maliki began to behave in ways that confirmed their image of him. While it is too much to say that Maliki ever became loyal to Iran—he remains first and foremost an Iraqi nationalist—he has very much moved into the Iranian camp within Iraqi politics, and today he is outspokenly antagonistic toward Saudi Arabia. Ultimately, the Saudis' subjective perception became something of an objective fact.

Such a Saudi-created self-fulfilling prophecy seems to have been the case not only in Iraq in recent years, but also in Yemen. The Saudi leadership have long been convinced that the Houthis of northern Yemen are an Iranian client, but the Houthis' relationship with Iran seems to be driven most of all by their enmity toward Saudi Arabia. The Houthis are Zaydi Shiʿa Muslims, also known as Fiver Shiʿa, in contradistinction to the Twelver Shiʿa found in Iran and Iraq. Having been marginalized from central power in Yemen for decades, the Houthis fought six wars against the Yemeni regime of Ali Abdullah Salih between 2004 and 2010. Although the Houthis looked favorably on the Islamic Republic at that time, they received little in the way of actual assistance from Iran until, in the midst of Yemen's post–Arab Spring civil war, they seized the Yemeni capital of Sanaa in 2015 and the Saudis launched an air war against them in response. According to a 2020 RAND Corporation report: "The Saudis' intervention [in the Yemeni civil war] dramatically escalated the war and represents one of the more tragic ironies in the conflict. By all accounts, Iranian support was fairly marginal before 2015. The Saudi-led coalition, and its unpopular air campaign, may now be the greatest factor driving the Houthi–Iran relationship."[6]

But it seems that this dynamic—of Saudi Arabia alienating Shiʿa groups of the Arab world to the extent of pushing them toward Iran—is also frequently overlooked among commentators in the United States. In August 2020, Thomas Friedman of the *New York Times* wrote that Iran's "business model" has been "to hire Arab and other Shiites to fight Arab Sunnis in Iraq, Lebanon, Yemen and Syria—to project Iran's power. And what was the result of all this? Iran has helped to turn all four into failed states."[7] Whatever the intentions of the Iranian regime have been, this view substantially overlooks the motivations of Shi'a actors in places like Iraq and Yemen. Indeed, this view both reflects and reinforces the stereotype, common among Sunni Arabs, that the Shi'a of the Arab world are little more than potential pawns of Iran. Rather, an investigation into the motivations of actors like Maliki and the Houthis demonstrates that what has dictated their actions to a large degree has been the threat they have perceived from Saudi Arabia. In this respect, Saudi Arabia has also substantially contributed to state failure in Iraq and Yemen. In Yemen in particular, the Saudi contribution to state failure is rather obvious by way of an air campaign that has degenerated into quagmire.

At the center of this story about Saudi Arabia and Iraq has been the concept of the enemy image. The core of such an image is the failure to update a belief when new information comes to light. Plenty of information arose during Maliki's first government to indicate that he wanted to pursue an independent course from Iran. Many of King Abdullah's Arab counterparts, themselves initially apprehensive about a Shi'a-led Iraq, used this information to update their understanding of the new order in Baghdad, and began to engage with the Maliki government. Abdullah II of Jordan was the most noteworthy example in this regard. Openly sounding an alarm about Iraq's coming Shi'a ascendance on the eve of its first free elections, Abdullah II was the first Arab head of state to visit the new Iraq following Maliki's Charge of the Knights campaign a few years later. Abdullah of Saudi Arabia, by contrast, systematically discounted all the data that demonstrated Maliki's desire for independence. He remained convinced that the Iraqi prime minister was loyal to Iran. Abdullah's image of Maliki surely made the most sense to him, given Saudi convictions about Iran and the Arab Shi'a, but his failure to update his beliefs—to incorporate new data into them—was what led him to make the poor decision examined in this book.

May this story serve as a cautionary tale for today's decision-makers, wherever they may be. Just as Saudi leaders have long held an enemy image of Iran, so have many within U.S. policy-making circles. Indeed, an enemy image of Iran—a conviction that it only acts in bad faith—may be said to have been the impetus behind the Trump administration's decision to withdraw from the Iran nuclear deal negotiated by its predecessor and to pursue a policy of "maximum pressure" against it. Unsurprisingly, given the lessons of this book, the principal result of the Trump administration's maximum pressure campaign was a conflict spiral with Tehran. But some within U.S. policymaking circles would go even further. Some advocate regime change, arguing, as Eric Edelman and Ray Takeyh do, for instance, that, "[T]he Islamic Republic will never evolve into a responsible regional stakeholder ... It will never abandon its nuclear ambitions for the sake of commerce. And it will never recognize any U.S. interests in the Middle East as legitimate."[8]

This book has not set out to investigate what Iran actually wants in its region. What the book has done is to explore how a fairly simplistic understanding of Iranian intentions, an understanding that was unresponsive to new information, led one of Iran's neighbors to take a poor decision. The certitude of the statement above—that the Islamic Republic will never accommodate U.S. interests—rings of the certitude with which Abdullah of Saudi Arabia was convinced Maliki was an Iranian puppet. Regardless of whether or not the authors of this statement are correct in their analysis, the point is that their view prejudges a situation, and by doing so closes our minds to new information or any sort of nuance. Iran's supreme leader, Ayatollah Ali Khamenei, currently aged eighty-two, will pass from the scene in the foreseeable future, and we should not just assume that his successor will act exactly as we expect. Khamenei, as supreme leader, has been different from Khomeini, and his successor will be different from him. We should also take into account the context the Iranians find themselves in—aspects of which will necessarily evolve over the course of time, shaping how they pursue their interests. Moreover, the statement above overlooks how U.S. policy itself is a factor in Iranian behavior. The Islamic Republic may be antagonistic to the United States, but presumably a large degree of its ill will derives from the fact that some in the United States openly push for its overthrow. Iran is today an adversary of the United States, but the lesson of this book is that sweeping, categorical assumptions about our adversaries do not lead to the formulation of good policy. In short, the enemy image of Iran held by many in the U.S. does nobody any good.

As for Iraq, this book concludes by posing a question, one that is impossible to answer: What would Iraq have looked like this past decade and a half if the Saudis had made the decision to engage with it in 2006? Ask yourself for a moment: What would have been the result if, at the 2007 Arab summit, King Abdullah had welcomed the new Iraq back into the Arab fold, instead of declaring that it was living under an illegal foreign occupation? Would meaningful Saudi support to Iraq have helped end Iraq's sectarian civil war sooner? Would Saudi engagement, moreover, have helped stave off the start of a new Sunni insurgency following the Arab Spring? What about the 2010 elections? If the Saudis had not been so antagonistic toward Maliki, might Ahmad Abu Risha have joined Maliki's electoral coalition, and if Maliki and Abu Risha had prevailed in those elections, would they have formed a truly national government, instead of the increasingly sectarian one seen in Maliki's second term?

CONCLUSION

These questions cannot be answered, and no matter what, Iraqi politics is a perilous business—Saudi engagement would not have altered that reality. But it is hard to shake off the feeling that if the Saudis had decided to engage meaningfully—as many other Sunni Arab states began to do in 2008—things might have been substantially different in Iraq. We will never know. What should be clear, however, is that it was not a foregone conclusion that a Shi'a-led Iraq would be sucked into Iran's orbit. That this situation in fact came about was the result of a self-fulfilling prophecy created by the Saudis.

NOTES

INTRODUCTION

1. Mina al-Uraibi, *"Zebari: muhtammuna bi-l-'alaqat m'a al-Riyad li-thiq-liha al-'Arabi wa-l-Islami wa-l-duwali"* ["Zebari: We are interested in relations with Riyadh because of its Arab and Islamic and international standing"], *al-Sharq al-Awsat*, 2 September 2007.

2. Turki al-Suhail, *"al-Sa'udiyya tusallim al-'Iraq qa'ima bi-434 mu'taqalan"* ["Saudi Arabia hands Iraq a list of 434 prisoners"], *al-Sharq al-Awsat*, 4 September 2008.

3. Ma'd Fayyad, *"Ammar al-Hakim: hukumat al-wahda al-wataniyya hiya allati taqud al-'Iraq... wa laisa al-Shi'a"* ["Ammar al-Hakim: The national unity government is the one that leads Iraq, not the Shi'a"], *al-Sharq al-Awsat*, 16 May 2007.

4. 07BAGHDAD831_a, "Ambassador and PM: Neighbors Conference, Saudi Arabia, Kurdistan Trip," 8 March 2007 (WikiLeaks); 07BAGHDAD 3849_a, "Talabani Briefs Ambassador on Tour of Arab States," 26 November 2007 (WikiLeaks).

5. 08BAGHDAD1051_a, "Vice President Hashimi on Basra Operations, Countering Iranian Influence," 6 April 2008 (WikiLeaks); 08BAGHDAD 1256_A, "Hashemi: Olive Branch to Maliki Tentatively Bearing Fruit," 23 April 2008 (WikiLeaks).

6. The World Bank, "Population Total—Data," https://data.worldbank.org/indicator/SP.POP.TOTL, retrieved 27 October 2020.

7. Interview with a Saudi foreign policy adviser, London, 8 August 2018.

8. Toby Matthiesen, *The Other Saudis: Shiism, Dissent and Sectarianism* (Cambridge: Cambridge University Press, 2015), 8.

9. Ibid., 2–8.

10. Yitzhak Nakash, *The Shīʿis of Iraq* (Princeton: Princeton University Press, 1994), chapter 1.

11. Phebe Marr and Ibrahim al-Marashi, *The Modern History of Iraq*, fourth edition (Boulder: Westview Press, 2017), 12; CIA World Factbook—Iraq, https://www.cia.gov/library/publications/the-world-factbook/geos/iz.html, retrieved 10 June 2020.

12. Ofra Bengio and Meir Litvak, "Introduction," in Ofra Bengio and Meir Litvak (eds), *The Sunna and Shīʿa in History* (New York: Palgrave Macmillan, 2011), 1.

13. Ibid., 1.

14. Fanar Haddad, *Understanding "Sectarianism": Sunni–Shīʿa Relations in the Modern Arab World* (New York: Oxford University Press, 2020), 173.

15. Ibid., 172.

16. Ibid., 172–173. See also, Laurence Louër, *Sunnis and Shīʿa: A Political History of Discord*, trans. Ethan Rundell (Princeton: Princeton University Press, 2020), 195–196.

17. See, for instance, Rainer Brunner, "Sunnis and Shiites in Modern Islam: Politics, Rapprochement and the Role of al-Azhar," in Brigitte Maréchal and Sami Zemni (eds), *The Dynamics of Sunni–Shia Relationships: Doctrine, Transnationalism, Intellectuals and the Media* (London: Hurst, 2013).

18. Haddad, *Understanding "Sectarianism,"* 172.

19. Fanar Haddad, "Sectarian Relations before 'Sectarianization' in pre-2003 Iraq," in Nader Hashemi and Danny Postel (eds), *Sectarianization: Mapping the New Politics of the Middle East* (New York: Oxford University Press, 2017), 118, 304f.

20. Louër, *Sunnis and Shīʿa*, 2. Similarly, Geneive Abdo observes, "To listen to many Sunni in Arab states, particularly in the Persian Gulf, is to perceive all Shīʿa as iron-clad Iranian loyalists." Geneive Abdo, *The New Sectarianism: The Arab Uprisings and the Rebirth of the Shīʿa-Sunni*

Divide, The Saban Center for Middle East Policy at Brookings, Analysis Paper, Number 29 (April 2013), 4.

21. Louër, *Sunnis and Shiʻa*, 35–38; Bengio and Litvak, *The Sunna and Shiʻa in History*, 5–6.

22. In recent years, numerous scholars have pushed back against this "primordial" thesis. See, Maréchal and Zemni (eds), *The Dynamics of Sunni–Shia Relationships*; Hashemi and Postel (eds), *Sectarianization*; Frederic Wehrey (ed.), *Beyond Sunni and Shia: The Roots of Sectarianism in a Changing Middle East* (New York: Oxford University Press, 2017).

23. Haddad, *Understanding "Sectarianism,"* 8, 218.

24. Fanar Haddad, *Sectarianism in Iraq: Antagonistic Visions of Unity* (London: Hurst, 2011).

25. Haddad, *Understanding "Sectarianism,"* chapter 7.

26. Robert Jervis, *Perception and Misperception in International Politics*, new edition (Princeton: Princeton University Press, 2017), chapter 4; Jack S. Levy, "Psychology and Foreign Policy Decision-Making," in Leonie Huddy, David O. Sears, and Jack S. Levy (eds), *The Oxford Handbook of Political Psychology*, second edition (Oxford: Oxford University Press), 307–310.

27. Robert Jervis, "Perceiving and Coping with Threat," in Robert Jervis, Richard Ned Lebow, and Janice Gross Stein (eds), *Psychology and Deterrence* (Baltimore: The Johns Hopkins University Press, 1985), 14.

28. Jervis, *Perception and Misperception*, 29.

29. Keren Yarhi-Milo, *Knowing the Adversary: Leaders, Intelligence, and Assessment of Intentions in International Relations* (Princeton: Princeton University Press, 2014), chapter 1.

30. Ibid., 101.

31. Ole R. Holsti, "The Belief System and National Images: A Case Study," *Journal of Conflict Resolution* 6:3 (September 1962): 244–252.

32. Yarhi-Milo, *Knowing the Adversary*, 201, 214.

33. Ronald Reagan Oral History Project, "Interview with Caspar Weinberger," 19 November 2002, 28–29, https://www.millercenter.org/the-presidency/presidential-oral-histories/caspar-weinberger-oral-history-secretary-defense, retrieved 21 February 2019.

34. Charles A. Duelfer and Stephen Benedict Dyson, "Chronic Misperception and International Conflict: The U.S.–Iraq Experience," *International Security* 36:1 (Summer 2011): 96.

35. Richard W. Cottam, *Foreign Policy Motivation: A General Theory and a Case Study* (Pittsburgh: University of Pittsburgh Press, 1977), 65; Janice Gross Stein, "Building Politics into Psychology: The Misperception of Threat," *Political Psychology* 9:2 (June 1988): 256.

36. Yarhi-Milo, *Knowing the Adversary*, 206–215.

37. See, Philip E. Tetlock, *Expert Political Judgement: How Good Is It? How Can We Know?* (Princeton: Princeton University Press, 2005).

38. Duelfer and Dyson, "Chronic Misperception," 96–99.

39. Telephone interview with a Clinton administration official, 27 October 2015. On the theory that Iraq was linked to the 1993 World Trade Center attack, see Laurie Mylroie, *A Study in Revenge: Saddam Hussein's Unfinished War Against America* (Washington, D.C.: AEI Press, 2000). On Wolfowitz's hypothesis that Saddam was linked to 9/11, see Bob Woodward, *Plan of Attack* (New York: Simon & Schuster, 2004), 21.

40. Duelfer and Dyson, "Chronic Misperception," 98.

41. Ibid., 83–85.

42. Robert K. Merton, *Social Theory and Social Structure*, second edition (Glencoe: The Free Press, 1957), 423.

43. Alexander E. Wendt, *Social Theory of International Politics* (Cambridge: Cambridge University Press, 1999), 263.

44. David Finlay, Ole R. Holsti, and Richard R. Fagen, *Enemies in Politics* (Chicago: Rand McNally & Company, 1967), 25.

45. Stephanie Madon, Jennifer Willard, Max Guyll, and Kyle C. Scherr, "Self-Fulfilling Prophecies: Mechanisms, Power, and Links to Social Problems," *Social and Personality Psychology* 5:8 (2011): 583–584; Mark Snyder, Elizabeth Decker Tanke, and Ellen Berscheid, "Social Perception and Interpersonal Behavior: On the Self-Fulfilling Nature of Social Stereotypes," *Journal of Personality and Social Psychology* 35:9 (1977): 656–666; and Carl O. Word, Mark P. Zanna, and Joel Cooper, "The Nonverbal Mediation of Self-Fulfilling Prophecies in Interracial Interaction," *Journal of Experimental Social Psychology* 10 (1974): 109–120.

46. Merton, *Social Theory*, 424.

47. Stephen M. Walt, *The Origins of Alliances* (Ithaca: Cornell University Press, 1987), 25.

48. Michael N. Barnett, "Identity and Alliances in the Middle East," in Peter J. Katzenstein (ed.), *The Culture of National Security: Norms and Identity in World Politics* (New York: Columbia University Press, 1996.

49. Ibid., 427.

50. David L. Rousseau, *Identifying Threats and Threatening Identities: The Social Construction of Realism and Liberalism* (Stanford: Stanford University Press, 2006).

51. Ibid., 113–115.

52. In recent years, scholars of the Middle East have increasingly recognized the value of combining material and ideational variables to understand state behavior. See, for instance, Raymond Hinnebusch, "The Sectarian Surge in the Middle East and the Dynamics of the Regional States-System," *Tidsskrift for Islamforskning* 13:1 (2019): 35–61; and May Darwich, *Threats and Alliances in the Middle East: Saudi and Syrian Policies in a Turbulent Region* (Cambridge: Cambridge University Press, 2019).

53. In the first camp, see Neil Partrick, "Domestic Factors and Foreign Policy," in Neil Partrick (ed.), *Saudi Arabian Foreign Policy: Conflict and Cooperation* (London: I.B. Tauris, 2016), 12. In the second camp, see Gerd Nonneman, "Determinants and Patterns of Saudi Foreign Policy: 'Omnibalancing' and 'Relative Autonomy' in Multiple Environments," in Paul Aarts and Gerd Nonneman (eds), *Saudi Arabia in the Balance: Political Economy, Society, Foreign Affairs* (New York: New York University Press, 2005), 336; Stig Stenslie, *Regime Stability in Saudi Arabia: The Challenge of Succession* (London: Routledge, 2012), 36; René Rieger, *Saudi Arabian Foreign Relations: Diplomacy and Mediation in Conflict Resolution* (London: Routledge, 2016), 58; Anthony H. Cordesman and Nawaf Obaid, *National Security in Saudi Arabia: Threats, Responses, and Challenges* (Westport: Praeger Security International, 2005), 155–156.

54. See, Madawi Al-Rasheed, "Circles of Power: Royals and Society in Saudi Arabia" and Iris Glosemeyer, "Checks, Balances, and

Transformation in the Saudi Political System," in Aarts and Nonneman (eds), *Saudi Arabia.*

55. Al-Rasheed, "Circles of Power," 199.

56. William B. Quandt, *Saudi Arabia in the 1980s: Foreign Policy, Security, and Oil* (Washington, D.C.: Brookings Institution, 1981), 107.

57. Stenslie, *Regime Stability*, 36; Rieger, *Saudi Arabian Foreign Relations*, 58–59.

58. Margaret G. Hermann, "How Decision Units Shape Foreign Policy: A Theoretical Framework," *International Studies Review* 3:2 (Summer 2001): 47–81.

59. Joe D. Hagan, Philip P. Everts, Haruhiro Fukui, and John D. Stempel, "Foreign Policy by Coalition: Deadlock, Compromise, and Anarchy," *International Studies Review* 3:2 (Summer 2001): 169–216.

60. Hermann, "How Decision Units Shape Foreign Policy," 57.

61. Telephone interview with American diplomat based in Riyadh in the 1980s, 31 July 2015; interview with Chas Freeman, Washington, D.C., 12 April 2018; interview with Jamal Khashoggi, Washington, D.C., 24 April 2018; interview with a Saudi royal family insider, London, 17 August 2018.

62. Interview with a Saudi royal family insider, London, 17 August 2018.

63. Gregory Gause also emphasizes the fluid nature of Saudi decision-making. See, F. Gregory Gause, III, "The Foreign Policy of Saudi Arabia," in Raymond Hinnebusch and Anoushiravan Ehteshami (eds), *The Foreign Policies of Middle East States*, second edition (Boulder: Lynne Rienner Publishers, 2014), 201.

1. IRAN, IRAQ, AND SAUDI ARABIA IN THE LATE TWENTIETH CENTURY

1. Roham Alvandi, *Nixon, Kissinger, and the Shah: The United States and Iran in the Cold War* (Oxford: Oxford University Press, 2014).

2. IISS, *The Military Balance, 1970–1971* (London: The International Institute for Strategic Studies, 1970), 39; IISS, *The Military Balance, 1977–1978* (London: The International Institute for Strategic Studies, 1977), 35.

3. Marr and al-Marashi, *The Modern History of Iraq*, 115.

4. IISS, *The Military Balance, 1977–1978*, 35, 40.

5. Marr and al-Marashi, *The Modern History of Iraq*, 116.

6. Faisal bin Salman al-Saud, *Iran, Saudi Arabia and the Gulf: Power Politics in Transition* (London: I.B. Tauris, 2003); Laurie Mylroie, *Regional Security After Empire: Saudi Arabia and the Gulf*, PhD thesis (Harvard University, 1985).

7. Mansur Hasan al-Utaibi, *al-Siyasa al-Iraniyya tujah Duwal Majlis al-Taʻawun al-Khaliji (1979–2000)* [*Iranian Policy toward the States of the Gulf Cooperation Council (1979–2000)*] (Dubai: Markaz al-Khalij li-l-Abhath, 2008), 63–64.

8. From AmEmbassy Jidda to Secretary of State, Washington, D.C., "Iraq's Attempts to Stir Up Trouble in the Persian Gulf," 20 January 1975, U.S. National Archives.

9. Telegram From the Embassy in Iran to the Department of State, Tehran, 26 June 1974, *Foreign Relations of the United States, Vol. XXVII*, Doc. 62; Mylroie, *Regional Security After Empire*, chapters 3 and 4.

10. "Commentary Reviews 'Historic' Khomeyni Message," Foreign Broadcast Information Service, Daily Report, Middle East & North Africa, Supplement, 80–034-S (FBIS-MEA-80–034-S), 19 February 1980.

11. On Saddam's decision to order the invasion, see Ramazani, *Revolutionary Iran*, chapter 4; Shahram Chubin and Charles Tripp, *Iran and Iraq at War* (London: I.B. Tauris, 1988), chapter 2; Efraim Karsh, "Military Power and Foreign Policy Goals: The Iran-Iraq War Revisited," *International Affairs* 64:1 (Winter 1987–1988): 83–95; F. Gregory Gause, III, *The International Relations of the Persian Gulf* (Cambridge: Cambridge University Press, 2010), 58–64.

12. Charles Tripp, *A History of Iraq*, third edition (Cambridge: Cambridge University Press, 2007), 195; Faleh A. Jabar, *The Shiʻite Movement in Iraq* (London: Saqi, 2003), 204; Joyce N. Wiley, *The Islamic Movement of Iraqi Shiʻas* (Boulder: Lynne Rienner, 1992), 48.

13. Jabar, *The Shiʻite Movement in Iraq*, chapters 3 and 11.

14. Ibid., 230–233.

15. Ibid., 233; Tripp, *A History of Iraq*, 221.

16. Laurence Louër, *Transnational Shia Politics: Religious and Political Networks in the Gulf* (London: Hurst, 2008), 287; Edgar O'Ballance, *The Gulf War* (London: Brassey's Defence, 1988), 12.

17. "Call for Jihad Against Husayn," Foreign Broadcast Information Service, Daily Report, South Asia, 80–073 (FBIS-SAS-80–073), 14 April 1980.

18. Chubin and Tripp, *Iran and Iraq at War*, 33.

19. Ramazani, *Revolutionary Iran*, 65; Tripp, *A History of Iraq*, 223–224.

20. Marr and al-Marashi, *The Modern History of Iraq*, 120–123.

21. Ramazani, *Revolutionary Iran*, 66–67; Marr and al-Marashi, *The Modern History of Iraq*, 131–132.

22. Rob Johnson, *The Iran–Iraq War* (New York: Palgrave Macmillan, 2011), 152.

23. Ibid., 65–7; Tripp, *A History of Iraq*, 227.

24. "18 Leaders Demand 'Final Offensive' Against Iraq," FBIS-SAS-82–132, 9 July 1982; "Khomeyni: Liberate Iraq before Lebanon," FBIS-SAS-82–120, 22 June 1982.

25. "Khomeyni: Liberate Iraq before Lebanon," FBIS-SAS-82–120, 22 June 1982.

26. Efraim Karsh, *The Iran–Iraq War, 1980–1988* (Oxford: Osprey Publishing Ltd, 2002), 10–11.

27. Ibid., 79.

28. Tripp, *A History of Iraq*, 221, 225; Marr and al-Marashi, *The Modern History of Iraq*, 155.

29. Yitzak Nakash, *Reaching for Power: The Shi'a in the Modern Arab World* (Princeton: Princeton University Press, 2006), 87–88.

30. Quoted in Hasan al-Alawi, *al-Ta'thirat al-Turkiyya fi-l-Mashru' al-Qawmi al-'Arabi fi-l-'Iraq* [*Turkish Influences in the Arab Nationalist Project in Iraq*] (London: Dar al-Zawra, 1988), 144.

31. Khalil F. Osman, *Sectarianism in Iraq: The Making of State and Nation since 1920* (London: Routledge, 2015), 222.

32. Eric Davis, *Memories of State: Politics, History, and Collective Identity in Modern Iraq* (Berkeley: University of California Press, 2005), 4.

33. Ibid., 185.

34. Ibid., 185.

35. 06JEDDAH450_a, "Ambassador Khalilzad Meets with Saudi Crown Prince and King," 5 July 2006 (WikiLeaks).
36. Davis, *Memories of State*, 186–188.
37. Nadav Safran, *Saudi Arabia: The Ceaseless Quest for Security* (Ithaca: Cornell University Press, 1988), 55–56; F. Gregory Gause, III, "Saudi Arabia's Regional Security Strategy," in Mehran Kamrava (ed.), *The International Politics of the Persian Gulf* (Syracuse: Syracuse University Press, 2011), 175–177.
38. Ramazani, *Revolutionary Iran*, 87–89.
39. "Text of Foreign Minister's Speech to UN General Assembly," FBIS-MEA-80–201, 15 October 1980.
40. Ramazani, *Revolutionary Iran*, 109.
41. "Speaks on Regional Issues," FBIS-MEA-81–245, 22 December 1981.
42. "2 Million Moslems Converging on Holy Sites," *New York Times*, 8 October 1981.
43. "Letters, Statements Issued on Pilgrims in Mecca, Iran," FBIS-SAS-81–197, 10 October 1981.
44. Ibid.
45. John Vinocur, "1981 Plot in Bahrain Linked to Iranians," *New York Times*, 25 July 1982.
46. "Saudis call Iran the terrorists of the Gulf," *Guardian*, 21 December 1981.
47. "Treaty Signing Ceremony," FBIS-MEA-81–248, 28 December 1981.
48. Ibid.; "Speaks on Regional Issues," FBIS-MEA-81–245, 22 December 1981.
49. "As-Siyasah Interviews Crown Prince Abdullah," FBIS-MEA-83–057, 23 March 1983.
50. Johnson, *The Iran–Iraq War*, 98.
51. Ramazani, *Revolutionary Iran*, 102.
52. al-Utaibi, *al-Siyasa al-Iraniyya*, 141. On the 1981 Bahrain coup plot, see Louër, *Transnational Shia Politics*, 159–60; Ramazani, *Revolutionary Iran*, 131.
53. "Speaks on Regional Issues," FBIS-MEA-81–245, 22 December 1981.
54. "Interior Minister on Bahrain, Iran, Shi'ites," FBIS-MEA-82–063, 1 April 1982.

55. 85RIYADH5470_a, "Saudi Policy toward Iran," 12 June 1985 (WikiLeaks).

56. "Al-RA'Y AL-'AMM Calls for Support of Iraq," FBIS-MEA-85–120, 21 June 1985.

57. al-Utaibi, *al-Siyasa al-Iraniyya*, 148.

58. Interview with a Saudi foreign policy adviser, London, 8 August 2018; Adil bin Abdullah al-Fawzan, *al-Tahawwulat fi-l-siyasat al-kharijiyya al-Sa'udiyya ba'd 11 September* [*Transformations in Saudi Foreign Policy after September 11*], paper presented to the Institute of Diplomatic Studies at the Ministry of Foreign Affairs, 2009 (Saudi Cables doc #124421), 11–12.

59. al-Utaibi, *al-Siyasa al-Iraniyya*, 129, 147–148, 155.

60. Ramazani, *Revolutionary Iran*, 95; Johnson, *The Iran–Iraq War*, 139–141, 145; Karsh, *The Iran–Iraq War*, 50–51.

61. Thomas W. Lippman, "Iranian Participation Adds Tension to Annual Muslim Pilgrimage to Mecca," *Washington Post*, 15 June 1991.

62. "Khomeyni Sends Message to Hajj Pilgrims," Foreign Broadcast Information Service, Daily Report, Near East & South Africa, 87–148 (FBIS-NES-87–148), 3 August 1987; "Montazeri Condemns Saudi Rulers," FBIS-NES-87–148, 3 August 1987.

63. "Prince Nayif News Conference on Mecca Incident," FBIS-NES-87–166, 27 August 1987.

64. 85RIYADH5470_a, "Saudi Policy toward Iran," 12 June 1985 (WikiLeaks).

65. Ramazani, *Revolutionary Iran*, 96–97.

66. "Fahd Regrets Absence of Iranian Pilgrims," FBIS-NES-88–142, 25 July 1988.

67. 85RIYADH5470_a, "Saudi Policy toward Iran," 12 June 1985 (WikiLeaks).

68. See "Prologue," *Imam Khomeini's Last Will and Testament*, www.al-islam.org/imam-khomeini-s-last-will-and-testament/prologue, retrieved 18 November 2015.

69. Jervis, *Perception and Misperception*, 218–220.

70. Marr and al-Marashi, *Modern History of Iraq*, 170–171; "Rejuvenated Iraq Turns Wrath on Gulf Neighbours Over Oil," Reuters, 28 June 1990.

71. Youssef M. Ibrahim, "Iraq Seeks Bigger Role in OPEC," *New York Times*, 28 June 1990; "Iraq Threatens Kuwait with Tanks, Troops," Associated Press, 24 July 1990.

72. Marr and al-Marashi, *The Modern History of Iraq*, 170.

73. George Bush and Brent Scowcroft, *A World Transformed* (New York: Vintage, 1999), 310–313, 411; James A. Baker, III, *The Politics of Diplomacy: Revolution, War and Peace, 1989–1992* (New York: G.P. Putnam's Sons, 1995), 272.

74. Telephone interview with Chas W. Freeman Jr, 16 July 2015.

75. "King Fahd Gives Speech on Islamic Values," FBIS-NES-91-044, 5 March 1991.

76. Dick Cheney with Liz Cheney, *In My Time: A Personal and Political Memoir* (New York: Threshold Editions, 2011), 191.

77. Lawrence Freedman and Efraim Karsh, *The Gulf Conflict, 1990–1991: Diplomacy and War in the New World Order* (London: Faber and Faber, 1994), 203.

78. Baker, *The Politics of Diplomacy*, 289, 307.

79. Cheney, *In My Time*, 224; Bush and Scowcroft, *A World Transformed*, 411.

80. Cheney, *In My Time*, 225.

81. Powell, *My American Journey*, 516; Baker, *The Politics of Diplomacy*, 435.

82. Telephone interview with Chas W. Freeman Jr, 16 July 2015.

83. Anoushiravan Ehteshami, *After Khomeini: The Iranian Second Republic* (London: Routledge, 1995), 144–145; Henner Furtig, *Iran's Rivalry with Saudi Arabia between the Gulf Wars* (Reading: Ithaca Press, 2002), 100–103.

84. "Editor Comments on Resumption of Ties With Iran," FBIS-NES-91-060, 28 March 1991.

85. Ali A. Allawi, *The Occupation of Iraq: Winning the War, Losing the Peace* (New Haven: Yale University Press, 2007), 45–46; Andrew Cockburn and Patrick Cockburn, *Out of the Ashes: The Resurrection of Saddam Hussein* (New York: HarperPerennial, 1999), 20.

86. That the Saudis wanted to support the Iraqi uprisings of March 1991 contradicts much of the literature on the Gulf War. For instance,

Lawrence Freedman and Efraim Karsh, in their analysis of the uprisings, argued that the Saudis were reluctant to back the Shiʿa rebellion because they opposed empowering the Iraqi Shiʿa. See, Freedman and Karsh, *The Gulf Conflict*, 414.

87. Telephone interview with Chas W. Freeman Jr, 16 July 2015.
88. Interview with Prince Turki al-Faisal, Washington, D.C., 7 November 2018.
89. Baker, *The Politics of Diplomacy*, 439; Haddad, *Sectarianism in Iraq*, 77; Cockburn and Cockburn, *Out of the Ashes*, 22.
90. F. Gregory Gause, III, *Beyond Sectarianism: The New Middle East Cold War*, Brookings Doha Center Analysis Paper Number 11 (July 2014), 13.
91. For analysis of Saudi–Iran relations in the 1990s, see Shahram Chubin and Charles Tripp, *Iran–Saudi Arabia Relations and Regional Order: Iran and Saudi Arabia in the balance of power in the Gulf*, Adelphi Paper 304 (Oxford: Oxford University Press for the International Institute for Strategic Studies, 1996); Fahad M. Alsultan and Pedram Saeid, *The Development of Saudi–Iranian Relations since the 1990s: Between conflict and accommodation* (London: Routledge, 2017).
92. 91RIYADH10006_a, "Prince Saud al-Faisal Criticizes Iran," 24 November 1991 (WikiLeaks).
93. Ibid.
94. IISS, *The Military Balance, 1993–1994* (London: Brassey's, 1993), 115; James Adams, "Syria and Iran shop around for missile factories," *Sunday Times*, 13 October 1991.
95. "'Rejectionist Front' in Tehran Attacks Mideast Conference," Associated Press, 22 October 1991.
96. Anoushiravan Ehteshami and Raymond A. Hinnebusch, *Syria and Iran: Middle Powers in a Penetrated Regional System* (London: Routledge, 1997), chapter 5.
97. Youssef Azmeh, "Iran angers Gulf neighbours, undermines ties," Reuters, 10 September 1992.
98. "Paper: Islands To Stay Arab 'Despite Iranian Arrogance,'" FBIS-NES-95-237, 11 December 1995.
99. "'Source' Condemns Irresponsible Remarks by Khemeni," FBIS-

NES-94–051, 16 March 1994; "Paper Compares Position of King Fahd to Shah's," FBIS-NES-94-100, 30 September 1994; "Paper Condemns 'Wicked' Iranian Regime," FBIS-NES-94–241, 15 December 1994.

100. "Kuwait Welcomes 'No-Fly Zone;' Syria, Jordan Fear Partition," Associated Press, 26 August 1992.

101. Ibid.

102. Victoria Graham, "Iraq: No Buildup to Attack Shiites; Saddam Gives Out Medals," Associated Press, 2 September 1992.

103. Louër, *Transnational Shia Politics*, 235–237.

104. "Bahrain for the first time blames Iran for unrest," Agence France-Presse, 21 January 1996.

105. 95RIYADH712_a, "Iran: Meeting with Saudi Foreign Minister Saud al-Faisal," 8 February 1995 (WikiLeaks).

106. Ibid.

107. Steven Erlanger, "Survivors of Saudi Explosion Knew at Once It Was a Bomb," *New York Times*, 27 June 1996.

108. See, Louis J. Freeh, *My FBI: Bringing Down the Mafia, Investigating Bill Clinton, and Fighting the War on Terror* (New York: St. Martin's Griffin, 2005), chapter 1.

109. Tom Rhodes, "Pressure grows for Clinton to launch strike against Iran," *Times*, 16 December 1996.

110. "Iran warns Gulf states they will suffer if U.S. attacks," Associated Press, 9 February 1997; William Maclean, "U.S.-Iran tension, Saudi blast test Kuwait nerves," Reuters, 12 August 1996.

111. 95RIYADH712_a, "Iran: Meeting with Saudi Foreign Minister Saud al-Faisal," 8 February 1995 (WikiLeaks).

112. Anwar Faruqi, "Saudi leader's visit to Iran marks a turning point," Associated Press, 8 December 1997.

113. "Iran's Rafsanjani not decided on Saudi haj visit," Reuters, 31 March 1997.

114. al-Utaibi, *al-Siyasa al-Iraniyya*, 109.

115. Alsultan and Saeid, *The Development of Saudi–Iranian Relations*, chapter 5.

116. Interview with Prince Turki al-Faisal, Washington, D.C., 7 November 2018.

117. Marie Colvin, "Saudi Princes Vie For Crown," *Sunday Times*, 10 December 1995; Kenneth R. Timmerman, "Saudi Bombing: Iran Is a Suspect," *Wall Street Journal*, 1 July 1996.

118. Interview with a Saudi royal family insider, London, 17 August 2018.

119. Gary Samuel Samore, *Royal Family Politics in Saudi Arabia (1953–1982)*, PhD thesis, Harvard University (1983), 330; Quandt, *Saudi Arabia in the 1980s*, 82.

120. Marie Colvin, "Saudi Princes Vie For Crown," *Sunday Times*, 10 December 1995.

121. See also, in particular, Al-Rasheed, "Circles of Power."

122. Interview with a Saudi royal family insider, London, 17 August 2018.

123. Kenneth R. Timmerman, "Saudi Bombing: Iran Is a Suspect," *Wall Street Journal*, 1 July 1996; "Iran's Rafsanjani not decided on Saudi haj visit," Reuters, 31 March 1997; Dilip Hiro, "Assad's Strategy for the Golan," *Wall Street Journal*, 13 August 1997; "Saudi crown prince greeted by Iranian leader in Tehran," Agence France-Presse, 8 December 1997.

124. Interview with a Saudi royal family insider, London, 17 August 2018.

125. Interview with a Saudi foreign policy adviser, London, 8 August 2018.

2. A NEW IRAQ WITH A PERSIAN FLAVOR?

1. Woodward, *Plan of Attack*, 25–26.

2. On the U.S. decision to invade Iraq, see Woodward, *Plan of Attack*; James Mann, *Rise of the Vulcans: The History of Bush's War Cabinet* (New York: Penguin Books, 2004); Ivo H. Daalder and James M. Lindsay, *America Unbound: The Bush Revolution in Foreign Policy* (Hoboken: Wiley, 2005); Nick Ritchie and Paul Rogers, *The Political Road to War with Iraq: Bush, 9/11 and the Drive to Overthrow Saddam* (London: Routledge, 2007); Duelfer and Dyson, "Chronic Misperception and International Conflict," 73–100.

3. "Foreign minister repeats Saudi stand on Iraq war at news conference," BBC Monitoring Middle East, 8 January 2003; see also, "Saudi Arabia will not host Saddam if he decides to flee—foreign minister," BBC Monitoring Middle East, 11 March 2003.

4. See, for instance, Thomas E. Ricks, "Briefing Depicted Saudis as Enemies; Ultimatum Urged to Pentagon Board," *Washington Post*, 6 August 2002. See also, Victor Davis Hanson, "Our Enemies, the Saudis," *Commentary*, 1 July 2002, https://www.commentarymagazine.com/articles/our-enemies-the-saudis/, retrieved 31 October 2016.

5. Interview with Jamal Khashoggi, Washington, D.C., 24 April 2018.

6. Ibid.; and interview with a royal family insider, London, 17 August 2018.

7. Interview with a royal family insider, London, 17 August 2018.

8. Interview with Jamal Khashoggi, Washington, D.C., 24 April 2018.

9. Kathy Evans, "Gulf leaders back allies but fear break-up of Iraq," *Guardian*, 21 August 1992; "Unity, 'Territorial Integrity' of Iraq Stressed," FBIS-NES-92–167, 27 August 1992; "Need to Prevent Fragmentation of Iraq Seen," FBIS-NES-95–163, 23 August 1995; "Al-RIYAD Warns Against Partitioning Iraq," FBIS-NES-95–175, 11 September 1995.

10. Robert W. Jordan with Steve Fiffer, *Desert Diplomat: Inside Saudi Arabia Following 9/11* (Lincoln: Potomac Books, 2015), 145.

11. Ibid., 82; interview with a Saudi foreign policy adviser, London, 8 August 2007.

12. Interview with Prince Turki al-Faisal, Washington, D.C., 7 November 2018; Woodward, *Plan of Attack*, 69, 229; Martin Indyk, *Innocent Abroad: An Intimate Account of American Peace Diplomacy in the Middle East* (New York: Simon & Schuster, 2009), chapters 8 and 10.

13. Woodward, *Plan of Attack*, 229.

14. "Saudi crown prince and Iraqi envoy embrace at summit," Reuters, 28 March 2002.

15. 06JEDDAH450_a, "Ambassador Khalilzad Meets with Saudi Crown Prince and King," 5 July 2006 (WikiLeaks).

16. Jordan, *Desert Diplomat*, 145.

17. "Iran won't interfere with Iran-based Iraqi opposition plans to attack Saddam, says Iranian official," Associated Press, 20 January 2003.

18. Wiley, *Islamic Movement*, 60.

19. Interview with Prince Turki, Washington, D.C., 7 November 2018.

20. See, for instance, International Crisis Group, *Iran in Iraq: How Much Influence?*, Middle East Report No. 38 (21 March 2005), 10–11.

21. Marr and al-Marashi, *The Modern History of Iraq*, 208; Toby Dodge, *Iraq's Future: The Aftermath of Regime Change*, Adelphi Paper 372 (Abingdon: Routledge for The International Institute for Strategic Studies, 2005), 9.

22. Bob Woodward, *State of Denial* (New York: Simon & Schuster, 2006), 191, 197–198.

23. Marr and al-Marashi, *The Modern History of Iraq*, 211; Dodge, *Iraq's Future*, 15.

24. L. Paul Bremer III, with Malcolm McConnell, *My Year in Iraq: The Struggle to Build a Future of Hope* (New York: Simon & Schuster, 2006), 43.

25. See "Remarks on the Future of Iraq," Delivered at the Washington Hilton Hotel, Washington, D.C., 26 February 2003, in "Selected Speeches of President George W. Bush, 2001–2008," pp. 167–173, https://georgewbush-whitehouse.archives.gov//infocus/bushrecord/documents/Selected_Speeches_George_W_Bush.pdf, retrieved 31 October 2016.

26. Ibid., 93.

27. Nakash, *Reaching for Power*, 146.

28. On the Shiʿa of Iraq during the period of the British mandate, see, in particular, Yitzhak Nakash, *The Shiʿis of Iraq* (Princeton: Princeton University Press, 1994); and Pierre-Jean Luizard, *La Formation de l'Irak contemporain: le rôle politique des ulémas chiites à la fin de la domination ottomane et au moment de la construction de l'Etat* [*The Formation of Contemporary Iraq: The Political Role of the Shiʿa 'Ulama' at the End of the Ottoman Domination and at the Moment of Construction of the Iraqi State*] (Paris: Editions du Centre national de la recherche scientifique, 1991).

29. Nakash, *The Shiʿis of Iraq*.

30. Ibid., 104–105; Louër, *Transnational Shia Politics*, 82.

31. Louër, *Transnational Shia Politics*, 99–100.

32. Jabar, *The Shiʿite Movement in Iraq*, 81; Wiley, *Islamic Movement*, 31.

33. Interview with Iraqi Shiʿa Islamist, London, 4 November 2015.

34. Louër, *Transnational Shia Politics*, 199; Wiley, *The Islamic Movement*, 143.

35. Laurence Louër, trans. John King, *Shiism and Politics in the Middle East* (New York: Columbia University Press, 2012), 68.

36. Ibid., 67–68; Louër, *Transnational Shia Politics*, 199–200.

37. Allawi, *The Occupation of Iraq*, 54, 59.

38. Ibid., 54–56, 59.

39. ICG, *Iraq's Muqtada al-Sadr: Spoiler or Stabiliser?*, Middle East Report No. 55 (11 July 2006), 3.

40. Allawi, *The Occupation of Iraq*, 57–58.

41. ICG, *Iraq's Muqtada al-Sadr*, 5.

42. Cockburn, *Muqtada al-Sadr*, 68.

43. "'The Emirate of Saddam City?' Baghdad Neighborhood falls to clerical rule in post-Saddam void," Associated Press, 14 April 2003.

44. Allawi, *The Occupation of Iraq*, 92.

45. Cockburn, *Muqtada al-Sadr*, 125–126.

46. "Leading Shiite cleric denounces US-backed Iraqi Governing Council," Agence France-Presse, 18 July 2003.

47. Cockburn, *Muqtada al-Sadr*, 134.

48. Charles Clover, "US told to avoid main Shia area in Baghdad," *Financial Times*, 10 October 2003.

49. Hanna Batatu, *The Old Social Classes and the Revolutionary Movements of Iraq: A Study of Iraq's Old Landed and Commercial Classes and of its Communists, Ba'thists, and Free Officers* (Princeton: Princeton University Press, 1978), 816; Marion Farouk-Sluglett and Peter Sluglett, *Iraq Since 1958: From Revolution to Dictatorship*, third edition (London: I.B. Tauris, 2001), 108.

50. Allawi, *The Occupation of Iraq*, 52. See also, Dan Murphy, "New Iraqi leader cuts a strong figure," *Christian Science Monitor*, 20 July 2004, https:www.csmonitor.com/2004/0720/p01s03-woiq.html, retrieved 6 September 2017.

51. Allawi, *The Occupation of Iraq*, 52.

52. Davis, *Memories of State*, 188.

53. Ahmed S. Hashim, *Insurgency and Counter-Insurgency in Iraq* (London: Hurst, 2006), 21.

54. Allawi, *The Occupation of Iraq*, 176.

55. Hashim, *Insurgency and Counter-Insurgency*, 67.

56. Ibid., 275; Eric Herring and Glen Rangwala, *Iraq in Fragments: The Occupation and Its Legacy* (Ithaca: Cornell University Press, 2006), 179–85.

57. Herring and Rangwala, *Iraq in Fragments*, 18; "iCasualties—OIF—Fatalities by Month," http:icasualties.org/Iraq/ByMonth.aspx, retrieved on 21 April 2016.

58. Dodge, *Iraq's Future*, 13.

59. See, for instance, Hashim, *Insurgency and Counter-Insurgency*, 74, 387; and Haddad, "Sectarian Relations before 'Sectarianization,'" 118, 304f.

60. Interview with Ali Allawi, London, 1 October 2015.

61. "Iraqi imam calls for departure of US forces, urges national unity," BBC Monitoring Middle East, 18 July 2003; *Al-Saʿah*, 19 July 2003, p. 1 (FBIS-GMP20030722000023), quoted in Hashim, *Insurgency and Counter-Insurgency*, 75.

62. Hashim, *Insurgency and Counter-Insurgency*, 22.

63. "U.S. Prepares for Iraq Shiite Pilgrimage," Associated Press, 19 April 2003; "Iran police arrest 700 organizers of illegal pilgrimages to Iraq," Agence France-Presse, 27 August 2003; "Nearly 200 Iranian pilgrims die in five months while crossing into Iraq to go to Muslim shrines," Associated Press, 20 September 2003.

64. Osman, *Sectarianism in Iraq*, 234.

65. ICG, *Iran in Iraq*, 13.

66. Colonel Joel E. Rayburn and Colonel Frank K. Sobchak (eds), *The U.S. Army in the Iraq War*, vol. 1 (Carlisle: Strategic Studies Institute and U.S. Army War College Press, 2019), 74–75, 120, 125, 181, 269.

67. Ibid., 270.

68. ICG, *Iran in Iraq*, 2.

69. Ibid., 3; Hashim, *Insurgency and Counter-Insurgency*, 71.

70. ICG, *Iran in Iraq*, 3–6.

71. Hashim, *Insurgency and Counter-Insurgency*, 71.

72. David Holden and Richard Johns, *The House of Saud* (London: Sidgwick & Jackson, 1981), 253; telephone interview with Chas Freeman, 12 November 2015.

73. Abdullah received Muqtada al-Sadr in January 2006 while the latter was in the kingdom to perform the Hajj. Muqtada had actually been

the one to reach out to the Saudi leadership in advance of his trip, as he was then conducting a regional tour in an effort to establish a new image as a serious national leader. According to U.S. diplomatic cables, the Saudis agreed to receive Muqtada as they believed there was a slim chance he could serve as a counterweight to Iranian influence in Iraq. Nevertheless, no relationship developed between Muqtada and the Saudis at this time. In fact, a year after his meeting with the Saudis, Muqtada said it had been a "piece of play-acting." Quoted in "Iraqi Shi'i militant leader outlines terms for end to violence," BBC Monitoring Middle East, 19 January 2007. See also, "Saudi king receives firebrand Iraqi Shiite cleric," Agence France-Presse, 11 January 2006; ICG, *Iraq's Muqtada al-Sadr*, 16; 06RIYADH7_a, "Ambassador Khalilzad Seeks Post-Iraqi Elections Support from Saudi Leaders," 2 January 2006 (WikiLeaks); 06BAGHDAD79_a, "FM Zebari: Shia Far From Decision on PM Candidate, New Government Formation Also Distant," 9 January 2006 (WikiLeaks).

74. See, for instance, Saudi intelligence report, 25 April 2012 (Saudi Cables doc #9592); Saudi intelligence report, undated (Saudi Cables doc #22839); Saudi intelligence report, undated (Saudi Cables doc #20223).

75. See, for instance, 06RIYADH7_a, "Ambassador Khalilzad Seeks Post-Iraqi Elections Support from Saudi Leaders," 2 January 2006 (WikiLeaks).

76. Telephone interview with Robert Jordan, 6 January 2016.

77. Telephone interview with an Iraqi diplomat, 15 April 2018.

78. Interview with Prince Turki al-Faisal, Washington, D.C., 7 November 2018.

79. Telephone interview with an Iraqi diplomat, 15 April 2018; also telephone interview with an American diplomat, 21 May 2015.

80. Jordan, *Desert Diplomat*, 146.

81. Interview with Prince Turki al-Faisal, Washington, D.C., 7 November 2018.

82. al-Fawzan, *al-Tahawwulat fi-l-Siyasat al-Kharijiyya al-Sa'udiyya* (Saudi Cables doc #124421), 11; interview with a Saudi foreign policy adviser, London, 8 August 2018.

83. "Saudis set up field hospital in Baghdad to treat needy Iraqis," Associated Press, 29 April 2003.

84. "Mobile hospital returning to Saudi Arabia," Associated Press, 2 December 2003.

85. Email correspondence with L. Paul Bremer, III, 15 December 2015.

86. Salih al-Mani', *"al-'Alaqat al-Sa'udiyya al-'Iraqiyya fi A'qab Ihtilal al-'Iraq"* ["Saudi–Iraqi Relations in the Wake of the Occupation of Iraq"], *Ara hawla-l-Khalij*, Issue 7 (2005).

87. Interview with a Saudi foreign policy adviser, London, 8 August 2018. On Chalabi's ties to the Americans and Iranians, see, in particular, Bonin, *Arrows of the Night*.

88. Interview with Prince Turki al-Faisal, Washington, D.C., 7 November 2018.

89. On Ahmad Chalabi's relationship with the Americans, see Bonin, *Arrows of the Night*.

90. Interview with Prince Turki al-Faisal, Washington, D.C., 7 November 2018.

91. Jervis, *Perception and Misperception*, xxxvi.

92. Ibid., 187–188.

93. Dodge, *Iraq's Future*, 12; Marr and al-Marashi, *The Modern History of Iraq*, 218.

94. Allawi, *The Occupation of Iraq*, 233.

95. "Zarqawi Letter," U.S. Department of State Archive, http://2001–2009.state.gov/p/nea/rls/31694.htm, retrieved 27 April 2016.

96. For an assessment of the flow of Saudi militants to Iraq, see Nawaf Obaid and Anthony Cordesman, *Saudi Militants in Iraq: Assessment and Kingdom's Response*, Center for Strategic and International Studies, 19 September 2005. Obaid and Cordesman estimated that Saudis constituted 12 percent of the foreign fighters in Iraq. Nevertheless, Al-Qa'ida documents captured by coalition forces near Sinjar, Iraq, in September 2007 indicated that Saudis constituted 41 percent of the foreign fighters who had entered Iraq in the previous 13 months. See, Richard A. Oppel, Jr, "Foreign Fighters in Iraq Are Tied to Allies Of U.S.," *New York Times*, 22 November 2007.

97. Herring and Rangwala, *Iraq in Fragments*, 29–30.

98. Marr and al-Marashi, *The Modern History of Iraq*, 219.

99. Ibid., 219–220.

100. Ibid., 225.

101. Rayburn and Sobchak (eds), *U.S. Army in the Iraq War*, vol. 1, 391–392.

102. Ibid., 392; see also, Kimberly Kagan, *The Surge: A Military History* (New York: Encounter Books, 2009), 4–5.

103. Michael R. Gordon and General Bernard E. Trainor, *The Endgame: The Inside Story of the Struggle for Iraq from George W. Bush to Barack Obama* (New York: Pantheon Books, 2012), 151; Colonel Joel E. Rayburn and Colonel Frank K. Sobchak (eds), *The U.S. Army in the Iraq War*, vol. 2 (Carlisle: Strategic Studies Institute and U.S. Army War College Press, 2019), 67.

104. Rayburn and Sobchak, *U.S. Army in the Iraq War*, vol. 1, 498.

105. Bremer, *My Year in Iraq*, 34, 360, 366.

106. Osman, *Sectarianism in Iraq*, 131.

107. Ibid., 132–133; Marr and al-Marashi, *The Modern History of Iraq*, 224–225.

108. Nicolas Pelham, "Allawi reaches out to purged Ba'athists," *Financial Times*, 29 June 2004; Iyad Allawi, "Give us back our dignity," *Independent on Sunday*, 27 June 2004.

109. Interview with Ali Allawi, London, 1 October 2015. See also, Ali Muhammad al-Shamrani, *Sira' al-'Addad: al-Mu'arada al-'Iraqiyya ba'd Harb al-Khalij* [*The Conflict of Counters: The Iraqi Opposition after the Gulf War*] (London: Dar al-Hikma, 2003), 246–247.

110. Cockburn and Cockburn, *Out of the Ashes*, chapter 9.

111. "Iraq's Allawi on Arab tour, deployment of troops, elections, conference," BBC Monitoring Middle East, 31 July 2004.

112. Allawi, *The Occupation of Iraq*, 296.

113. Interview with Raad Alkadiri, Washington, D.C., 29 April 2015.

114. Ma'd Fayyad, "*Wazir al-difa' al-'Iraqi: sanaqul al-radd 'ala-l-irham ila sahat al-duwal allati tad'amuhu*" ["Iraqi minister of defense: we will take the response to terrorism to the countries that back it"], *al-Sharq al-Awsat* (London), 20 July 2004.

115. "Iraqi defence minister warns Iran over sending of spies and saboteurs," Agence France-Presse, 26 July 2004.

116. ICG, *Iran in Iraq*, 1, 3.

117. Hashim, *Insurgency and Counter-Insurgency*, 71.

118. A particularly notable example of the divide between the secular Shi'a and Shi'a Islamists was the Allawi government's attempt to quell the Sadrist uprising of August 2004. See, Allawi, *The Occupation of Iraq*, 321; and Cockburn, *Muqtada al-Sadr*, 162.

119. Gordon and Trainor, *The Endgame*, 142.

120. Allawi, *The Occupation of Iraq*, 343.

121. Anthony Shadid, "Iraq's Shiite Clergy Push To Get Out The Vote," *Washington Post*, 7 December 2004.

122. Allawi, *The Occupation of Iraq*, 338–339; Marr and al-Marashi, *The Modern History of Iraq*, 226.

123. "Alleged Zarqawi tape vows to fight Iraq vote," Reuters, 23 January 2005.

124. Hashim, *Insurgency and Counter-Insurgency*, 48.

125. "Iraq's spy chief accuses Iranian embassy of killing agents," Agence France-Presse, 14 October 2004.

126. Quoted in Annia Ciezadlo, "Intrigue, power plays as Iraq campaign season starts; Some are concerned about Iranian influence in process," *Christian Science Monitor*, 16 December 2004.

127. Quoted in Robin Wright and Peter Baker, "Iraq, Jordan See Threat To Election From Iran; Leaders Warn Against Forming Religious State," *Washington Post*, 8 December 2004.

128. Allawi, *The Occupation of Iraq*, 308.

129. Telephone interview with Raad Alkadiri, 13 October 2015.

130. Allawi, *The Occupation of Iraq*, 307; ICG, *Iran in Iraq*, 6.

131. Robin Wright and Peter Baker, "Iraq, Jordan See Threat To Election From Iran; Leaders Warn Against Forming Religious State," *Washington Post*, 8 December 2004.

132. 04AMMAN10191_a, "King Abdullah's Meeting with CoDel Kolbe," 27 December 2004 (WikiLeaks); 04AMMAN10245_a, "King Optimistic on West Bank, 'More Nervous' on Iraq After January 'Crossroads,'" 29 December 2004 (WikiLeaks).

133. "Jordan foreign minister warns of Iranian-Shi'i 'axis' of Iraq, Syria, Lebanon," BBC Monitoring Middle East, 2 January 2005; Bassam al-Baddarin, "*Qiyam nidham dini 'Shi'i bi-nakha Farisiyya' fi-l-'Iraq*

yaʿni tashkil mihwar maʿa Suriyya wa Lubnan" ["Rise of a religious Shiʿi regime 'with a Persian flavor' in Iraq means the formation of an axis with Syria and Lebanon"], *al-Quds al-ʿArabi* (London), 31 December 2004.

134. See, Osman, *Sectarianism in Iraq*, 143.
135. "New Iraq government to be sworn in 13 weeks after polls," Agence France-Presse, 3 May 2005.
136. Telephone interview with a former American diplomat, 8 September 2015. See also 06RIYADH9078_a, "APHSCT Townsend's November 15 Meeting with Saudi King Abdullah," 13 December 2006 (WikiLeaks), which notes that in a conversation with a U.S. official, "The King estimated that four to five million Iranians had infiltrated into Iraq over the years and suspected that there are some areas in Iraq where Persians are posing as Iraqis."
137. Telephone interview with a former American diplomat, 8 September 2015.
138. Telephone interview with a senior Bush administration official, 15 July 2015.
139. Interview with a Saudi foreign policy adviser, London, 8 August 2018.
140. 08JEDDAH361_a, "Saudi FM and NSC Head Discuss Intel Cooperation, Iraq, Iran, Palestinians and Pakistan," 25 August 2008 (WikiLeaks); 08RIYADH767_a, "S/I Satterfield Brief to Saudis on Iraq Developments," 14 May 2008 (WikiLeaks).
141. Telephone interview with a former American diplomat, 8 September 2015.
142. "Minister says Jordan protecting Iraq's Arabism by opposing Iraq's interference," BBC Monitoring Middle East, 2 January 2005.
143. Interview with Marwan Muasher, Beirut, 11 September 2015.
144. Interview with Jamal Khashoggi, Washington, D.C., 24 April 2018.
145. Interview with a Saudi royal family insider, London, 17 August 2018.
146. Osman, *Sectarianism in Iraq*, 150.
147. Gordon and Trainor, *The Endgame*, 139–140, 187; also interview with a Lebanese reporter, Middlesbrough, 12 April 2016.
148. "Line-up of the new Iraqi government of Ibrahim Jaafari," Agence France-Presse, 3 May 2005; and "Iraq fills crucial cabinet post," BBC

News, 8 May 2005, http://news.bbc.co.uk/1/hi/world/middle_east/
4527685.stm, retrieved 10 November 2016.

149. Allawi, *The Occupation of Iraq*, 394.

150. Anthony Cordesman and Emma R. Davies, *Iraq's Insurgency and the Road to Civil Conflict*, vol. 1 (Westport: Praeger Security International, 2008), 82; Dodge, *Iraq*, 125.

151. Tripp, *A History of Iraq*, 297.

152. Osman, *Sectarianism in Iraq*, 237; and Haddad, *Sectarianism in Iraq*, 166–172.

153. "Iraqi PM secures Kuwait aid pledge," Agence France-Presse, 19 June 2005; 05BAGHDAD4908_a, "PM Discusses Prison Inspections, Visit to Saudi Arabia, Border Closures, Incident at Umm Qasr," 8 December 2005 (WikiLeaks).

154. "Iran FM makes landmark visit to Iraq," Agence France-Presse, 17 May 2005.

155. "Iraq to launch military, anti-terror cooperation with Iran," Agence France-Presse, 7 July 2005.

156. Ibid.

157. Gareth Smyth, "Iraqi delegation cements ties with Iran," *Financial Times*, 19 July 2005.

158. Cordesman and Davies, *Iraq's Insurgency*, vol. 1, 150.

159. Oliver Poole, "Nerves Stretched to Breaking Point as Baghdad Clings to Normal Life," *Daily Telegraph*, 20 July 2005; Toby Dodge, *Iraq: From War to a New Authoritarianism* (Abingdon: Routledge for the International Institute for Strategic Studies, 2012), 58.

160. Dodge, *Iraq: From War to a New Authoritarianism*, 63.

161. Kagan, *The Surge*, 6.

162. Steve Negus, "Iraq Sunni blame police and Shia for killings," *Financial Times*, 19 May 2005.

163. Dodge, *Iraq: From War to a New Authoritarianism*, 58.

164. Ibid., 60; Dodge, *Iraq's Future*, 23.

165. Steve Negus, "Iraqi Sunni blame police and Shia for killings," *Financial Times*, 19 May 2005.

166. Gordon and Trainor, *The Endgame*, 185.

167. John F. Burns, "Torture Alleged at Ministry Site Outside Baghdad," *New York Times*, 16 November 2005.

168. ICG, *Unmaking Iraq: A Constitutional Process Gone Awry*, Middle East Briefing No. 19 (26 September 2005), 8–9.

169. Ibid., 9.

170. "Iraqi Constitution Angers Sunnis," Associated Press, 28 August 2005; "Arab League chief 'deeply disturbed' by Iraq constitution," Agence France-Presse, 25 August 2005.

171. Allawi, *The Occupation of Iraq*, 415–417.

172. Telephone interview with a former American diplomat, 21 May 2005; interview with Mowaffaq al-Rubaie, London, 10 December 2015.

173. "Arabs plan to hold pan-Iraqi reconciliation conference, Iraq apologizes to Saudi minister," Associated Press, 3 October 2005.

174. Ibid.

175. Interview with Jamal Khashoggi, Washington, D.C., 24 April 2018; interview with a Saudi royal family insider, London, 17 August 2018.

176. 06RIYADH7_a, "Ambassador Khalilzad Seeks Post-Iraqi Elections Support From Saudi Leaders," 2 January 2006 (WikiLeaks).

177. 06JEDDAH450_a, "Ambassador Khalilzad Meets with Saudi Crown Prince and King," 5 July 2006 (WikiLeaks).

178. Bob Woodward, *The War Within: A Secret White House History, 2006–2008* (New York: Simon & Schuster Paperbacks, 2008), 347. This exchange was also recounted to me in a telephone interview with a former American diplomat, 30 November 2015. For a similar exchange, see also 06JEDDAH450_a, "Ambassador Khalilzad Meets with Saudi Crown Prince and King," 5 July 2006 (WikiLeaks).

179. Abd al-Wahhab al-Qasab, "*al-'Iraq wa-l-Sa'udiyya: Inshighalat al-Hadir*" ["Iraq and Saudi Arabia: Present Concerns"], *Ara hawla-l-Khalij*, Issue 7 (2005).

180. Jamil al-Hujailan, "al-Sa'udiyya wa 'Arubat al-'Iraq" ["Saudi Arabia and the Arabism of Iraq"], *al-Sharq al-Awsat* (London), 29 November 2005.

181. Ibid.

3. KING ABDULLAH AND NURI AL-MALIKI

1. Marr and al-Marashi, *The Modern History of Iraq*, 235.

2. Ibid., 235.

3. Allawi, *The Occupation of Iraq*, 439; Gordon and Trainor, *The Endgame*, 143, 147, 184; Zalmay Khalilzad, *The Envoy: From Kabul to the White House, My Journey Through a Turbulent World* (New York: St. Martin's Press, 2016), 259.

4. Gordon and Trainor, *The Endgame*, 195.

5. Ellen Knickmeyer and Bassam Sebti, "Toll in Iraq's Deadly Surge: 1,300," *Washington Post*, 28 February 2006.

6. Dodge, *Iraq: From War to a New Authoritarianism*, 58.

7. Gordon and Trainor, *The Endgame*, 192; Khalilzad, *The Envoy*, 260–261.

8. Khalilzad, *The Envoy*, 261.

9. Gordon and Trainor, *The Endgame*, 196.

10. Khalilzad, *The Envoy*, 263–264.

11. 06RIYADH7_a, "Ambassador Khalilzad Seeks Post-Iraqi Elections Support From Saudi Leaders," 2 January 2006 (WikiLeaks).

12. Khalilzad, *The Envoy*, 262; Gordon and Trainor, *The Endgame*, 196.

13. Khalilzad, *The Envoy*, 262.

14. 06BAGHDAD402_a, "Shia Islamist PM Contenders: No Perfect Candidate," 10 February 2006 (Wikileaks).

15. Interview with Zalmay Khalilzad, Washington, D.C., 13 May 2015.

16. Telephone interview with Ryan Crocker, 5 June 2015.

17. "Iraqi premier on protests, Syria, relations with Turkey," BBC Monitoring Middle East, 11 February 2013.

18. Telephone interview with Ryan Crocker, 5 June 2015.

19. Interview with Zalmay Khalilzad, Washington, D.C., 13 May 2015; Ned Parker and Raheem Salman, "Notes from the Underground: The Rise of Nouri al-Maliki," *World Policy*, 20 February 2012, https://worldpolicy.org/2012/02/20/notes-from-the-underground-the-rise-of-nour-al-maliki/, retrieved 25 March 2019.

20. Parker and Salman, "Notes from the Underground."

21. Interview with Lebanese reporter, Beirut, 6 March 2015.

22. Telephone interview with former British diplomat, 14 April 2015.

23. Parker and Salman, "Notes from the Underground."

24. Interview with Ali Allawi, London, 1 October 2015.

25. 06BAGHDAD402_a, "Shia Islamist PM Contenders: No Perfect Candidate," 10 February 2006 (WikiLeaks).

26. Ibid.; Parker and Salman, "Notes from the Underground."

27. Dodge, *Iraq: From War to a New Authoritarianism*, 53.

28. Anthony Shadid, "In Iraq, Political Ambiguity; Old Alliances Shift after January Vote," *Washington Post*, 4 April 2009.

29. Telephone interview with a former American diplomat, 8 September 2015.

30. See "List of Iraqi Cabinet Members," Associated Press, 20 May 2006.

31. Dodge, *Iraq: From War to a New Authoritarianism*, 125.

32. Kagan, *The Surge*, 3.

33. ICG, *Iraq's Civil War, the Sadrists and the Surge*, Middle East Report No. 72, 7 February 2008, 3.

34. Dodge, *Iraq: From War to a New Authoritarianism*, 59.

35. Allawi, *Occupation of Iraq*, 446.

36. "Iraqi PM orders release of 2,500 detainees," Agence France-Presse, 6 June 2006; Nouri al-Maliki, "Our Strategy for a Democratic Iraq," *Washington Post*, 9 June 2006.

37. Hamza Hendawi, "Iraq premier boasts early successes, but security breakthrough still uncertain," Associated Press, 17 June 2006.

38. "Iraq PM offers 'olive branch' to rebels," Agence France-Presse, 25 June 2006.

39. Telephone interviews with a former American diplomat, 8 September 2015 and 30 November 2015.

40. Interview with an Iraqi diplomat, Washington, D.C., 17 August 2015.

41. Interview with Sami al-Askari, London, 14 January 2016.

42. Interview with a Saudi royal family insider, London, 17 August 2018.

43. Written exchange with Nuri al-Maliki, June 2020; exchange mediated by Sami al-Askari.

44. Interview with Sami al-Askari, London, 14 January 2016.

45. 06BAGHDAD2175_a, "Prime Minister Ready to Launch National Reconciliation Proposal," 25 June 2006 (WikiLeaks).

46. 06BAGHDAD2363_a, "VP Hashimi Discusses Maliki Visit to Saudi Arabia," 5 July 2006, (WikiLeaks).

47. 06BAGHDAD2581_a, "Talabani: Iranian Update and Seeking Political Support for Baghdad Security," 19 July 2006 (WikiLeaks).

48. 06JEDDAH449_a, "Ambassador Khalilzad Discusses Iran, Detainees and Iraqi Reconciliation Plan with Saudi Foreign Minister," 5 July 2006 (WikiLeaks).

49. Khalilzad, *The Envoy*, 273.

50. 06JEDDAH450_a, "Ambassador Khalilzad Meets with Saudi Crown Prince and King," 5 July 2006 (WikiLeaks).

51. Interview with Zalmay Khalilzad, Washington D.C., 13 May 2015.

52. 06JEDDAH450_a, "Ambassador Khalilzad Meets with Saudi Crown Prince and King," 5 July 2006 (WikiLeaks).

53. "Iraq PM in Saudi Arabia to discuss peace plan," Agence France-Presse, 1 July 2006.

54. "Iraq PM wins Saudi backing for peace efforts," Agence France-Presse, 1 July 2006.

55. Written exchange with Nuri al-Maliki, June 2020; exchange mediated by Sami al-Askari.

56. Khalilzad, *The Envoy*, 273.

57. 06BAGHDAD2401_a, "Prime Minister Pleased with Visits to Saudi Arabia, Kuwait, and UAE," 9 July 2006 (WikiLeaks).

58. Ibid.

59. The embassy source was Harb al-Zuhair, a Saudi businessman with Iraqi family connections who, according to the cable, was close to the royal family; 06RIYADH5322_a, "Iraqi Prime Minister Visits Kingdom on First Trip Abroad," 5 July 2006.

60. Interview with James Jeffrey, Washington, D.C., 11 May 2015. Jeffrey was in Saudi Arabia as part of a U.S. delegation in August 2006, which is confirmed by a U.S. diplomatic cable made available by WikiLeaks; see 06RIYADH6440_a, "Country Clearance Approval for Visit," 13 August 2006 (WikiLeaks).

61. 09RIYADH447_a, "Counterterrorism Adviser Brennan's Meeting with Saudi King Abdullah," 22 March 2009 (WikiLeaks); see also 08RIYADH1034_a, "Sen. Kerry in Saudi—Iran, Iraq and Oil," 6 July 2008 (WikiLeaks); 08RIYADH649_a, "Saudi King Abdullah and Senior Princes on Saudi Policy toward Iraq," 20 April 2008 (WikiLeaks).

62. 09RIYADH447_a, "Counterterrorism Adviser Brennan's Meeting with Saudi King Abdullah," 22 March 2009 (WikiLeaks).

63. Telephone interview with Ryan Crocker, 5 June 2015.

64. Interview with a former American diplomat, Washington, D.C., 29 July 2015.

65. Telephone interviews with a former American diplomat, 8 September 2015 and 30 November 2015.

66. Interview with Prince Turki al-Faisal, Washington, D.C., 7 November 2018; interview with a Saudi foreign policy adviser, London, 8 August 2018.

67. Interview with a former American diplomat, Washington, D.C., 29 July 2015.

68. Interview with a Saudi foreign policy adviser, London, 8 August 2018.

69. Written exchange with Nuri al-Maliki, June 2020; exchange mediated by Sami al-Askari.

70. Interview with Zalmay Khalilzad, Washington, D.C., 13 May 2015; interview with Sami al-Askari, London, 14 January 2016.

71. "Iraq's premier reaches out to members of Saddam's army for help in curbing violence," Associated Press, 16 December 2006.

72. Interview with Zalmay Khalilzad, Washington, D.C., 13 May 2015.

73. Interview with Sami al-Askari, London, 14 January 2016. Al-Askari said he did not recall precisely when this meeting took place. However, he said the meeting took place prior to a trip he took to Saudi Arabia with Mowaffaq al-Rubaie in the summer of 2008. Therefore, the meeting took place sometime between Maliki's trip to Saudi Arabia in July 2006 and al-Askari's trip to Saudi Arabia in summer 2008.

74. Interview with an American businessman, Washington, D.C., 6 April 2018.

75. 07BAGHDAD567_a, "FM Still Hoping to Bring Ministers to Baghdad; Had Positive Trip to Saudi Arabia," 18 February 2007 (WikiLeaks).

76. Interview with an Iraqi diplomat, Washington, D.C., 17 August 2015.

77. Khalilzad, *The Envoy*, 273.

78. Samir Ubaid, "*Fadiha jadida wa bi-l-watha'iq takshif anna hakim al-'Iraq huwa safir Iran wa anna-l-Maliki sayaqtas min 13 barlamanian*" ["New scandal with documents that reveal that the ruler of Iraq is Iran's ambassador and that Maliki will retaliate against 13 parliamentarians"], *Dunia al-Watan*, 16 March 2007, www.alwatanvoice.com/arabic/content/print/79403.html, retrieved 15 May 2018.

79. Richard Oppel, "U.S. Officials Voice Frustrations with Saudis, Citing Role in Iraq," *New York Times*, 27 July 2007.

80. Interview with Ali AlAhmed, Washington, D.C., 7 May 2018, and email exchange with Ali AlAhmed, 2–3 February 2019.

81. Christopher Hill and James Smith, who were U.S. ambassadors to Iraq and Saudi Arabia, respectively, in the first years of the Obama administration, observed that Saudi leaders made this claim during their tenures. Christopher R. Hill, *Outpost: Life on the Frontlines of American Diplomacy* (New York: Simon & Schuster, 2014), 361; and interview with James Smith, Washington, D.C., 11 June 2015.

82. None of the people I interviewed who had themselves interacted with Abdullah ever questioned the sincerity of Abdullah's claim. Furthermore, I specifically asked two American sources who interacted with Abdullah if he could have made up his claim, and both showed some skepticism based on the emotion with which Abdullah contended Maliki had lied to him. Telephone interview with a former American diplomat, 8 September 2015; telephone interview with a senior Bush administration official, 15 July 2015.

83. Nicholas Blanford, *Killing Mr. Lebanon: The Assassination of Rafik Hariri and Its Impact on the Middle East* (London: I.B. Tauris, 2009), 193.

84. "Israel's Olmert and Hezbollah's Nasrallah both declare victory in Lebanon war," Associated Press, 14 August 2006.

85. "Deal in Lebanon a win for Hezbollah," Associated Press, 21 May 2008.

86. 06JEDDAH450_a, "Ambassador Khalilzad Meets with Saudi Crown Prince and King," 5 July 2006 (WikiLeaks).

87. 06JEDDAH475_a, "Foreign Minister Discusses Tehran Meeting of Iraq Neighbors Conference and Iraq Compact with Ambassador," 12 July 2006 (WikiLeaks).

88. 06RIYADH9078_a, "APHSCT Townsend's November 15 Meeting with Saudi King Abdullah," 13 December 2006 (WikiLeaks).

89. 07BAGHDAD567_a, "FM Still Hoping to Bring Ministers to Baghdad; Had Positive Trip to Saudi Arabia," 18 February 2007 (WikiLeaks).

90. 09RIYADH445_a, "Saudi Intelligence Chief Talks Regional Security with Brennan Delegation," 22 March 2009 (WikiLeaks).

91. 08RIYADH1034_a, "Sen. Kerry in Saudi: Iran, Iraq and Oil," 6 July 2008 (WikiLeaks).

92. Interview with a Saudi foreign policy adviser, London, 8 August 2018.

93. This assessment is based on a thorough investigation of the U.S. diplomatic cables from the U.S. Embassy Riyadh, as well as consultation with Saudi sources such as the Saudi foreign policy adviser and an internal Saudi Foreign Ministry document, al-Fawzan, *al-Tahawwulat fi-l-Siyasat al-Kharijiyya al-Saʿudiyya* (Saudi Cables doc #124421).

94. Irving L. Janis, *Groupthink: Psychological Studies of Policy Decisions and Fiascoes* (Boston: Wadsworth/Cengage Learning, 1982).

95. Richard K. Herrmann, "Perceptions and Image Theory in International Relations," in Huddy, Sears, and Levy, *Oxford Handbook of Political Psychology*, 337.

96. 07RIYADH2461_a, "King Abdullah Snubs Ahmedinejad's Invitation," 11 December 2007 (WikiLeaks); 09RIYADH447_a, "Counterterrorism Adviser Brennan's Meeting with Saudi King Abdullah," 22 March 2009 (WikiLeaks).

97. Telephone interview with Chas Freeman, 16 July 2015.

98. Robert M. Gates, *Duty: Memoirs of a Secretary at War* (New York: Alfred A. Knopf, 2014), 185; 07RIYADH2322_a, "Saudi Ambassador to the US on Iran, Sanctions," 20 November 2007; 08RIYADH649_a, "Saudi King Abdullah and Senior Princes on Saudi Policy toward Iraq," 20 April 2008 (WikiLeaks).

99. Interview with Chas Freeman, Washington, D.C., 12 April 2018.

100. 06RIYADH5546_a, "King Expresses Concern about Iranian influence in the Region," 12 July 2006 (WikiLeaks).

101. Ibid.

102. Telephone interview with an Iraqi diplomat, 15 April 2018.

103. "Jordanian premier congratulates Iraqi counterpart on government formation," BBC Monitoring Middle East, 28 April 2005; "Iraqi, Jordanian premiers hold news conference in Baghdad," BBC Monitoring Middle East, 10 September 2005.

104. "Iraqi, Jordanian premiers hold news conference in Baghdad," BBC Monitoring Middle East, 10 September 2005; "Jordanian premier comments on visit to Iraq," BBC Monitoring Middle East, 13 September 2005.

105. Scott Lasensky, "Coming to Terms: Jordan's Embrace of Post-Saddam Iraq," in Henri J. Barkey, Scott B. Lasensky, and Phebe Marr (eds), *Iraq, Its Neighbors, and the United States: Competition, Crisis, and the Reordering of Power* (Washington, D.C.: United States Institute of Peace, 2011).

106. David P. Redlawsk, "A Matter of 'Motivated' Reasoning," in "Barak Obama and the Psychology of the 'Birther' Myth," The Opinion Pages: Room for Debate, *New York Times*, https://www.nytimes.com/roomfordebate/2011/04/21/barack-obama-and-the-psychology-of-the-birther-myth, retrieved 1 March 2018.

107. Redlawsk, "A Matter of 'Motivated' Reasoning."

108. "Crude Oil Prices—70 Year Historical Chart," Macrotrends, https://www.macrotrends.net/1369/crude-oil-price-history-chart, retrieved 27 August 2019; "Saudi Arabia—Data," The World Bank, https://data.worldbank.org/country/saudi-arabia, retrieved 27 August 2019.

109. Leslie Plommer, "Fears Mount For Ailing King Fahd," *Guardian*, 5 December 1995.

110. Interview with a Saudi royal family insider, London, 17 August 2018.

111. See, for instance, Patricia A. Boyle, Lei Yu, Robert S. Wilson, Keith Gamble, Aron S. Buchman, David A. Bennet, "Poor decision making is a consequence of cognitive decline among older persons without Alzheimer's disease or mild cognitive impairment," *PLoS One* 7:8 (August 20, 2012), https://journals.plos.org/plosone/article?id=10.1371/journal.pone.0043647, retrieved 16 August 2019.

112. 08RIYADH1034_a, "Sen. Kerry in Saudi—Iran, Iraq and Oil," 6 July 2008 (WikiLeaks).

113. Interview with a Saudi royal family insider, London, 17 August 2018.

114. 09RIYADH445_a, "Saudi Intelligence Chief Talks Regional Security with Brennan Delegation," 22 March 2009 (WikiLeaks); interview with a Saudi foreign policy adviser, London, 8 August 2018.

115. See, al-Fawzan, *al-Tahawwulat fi-l-Siyasat al-Kharijiyya al-Sa'udiyya* (Saudi Cables doc #124421), 13.

116. Janis, *Groupthink*.

117. Rayburn and Sobchak, *U.S. Army in the Iraq War*, vol. 2, 43–44; Marr and al-Marashi, *The Modern History of Iraq*, 239.

118. Khalilzad, *The Envoy*, 277.

119. Stein, "Building Politics into Psychology," 253.

120. Ramazani, *Revolutionary Iran*, 59.

121. Interview with a Saudi foreign policy adviser, London, 8 August 2018.

122. Frederic M. Wehrey, *Sectarian Politics in the Gulf: From the Iraq War to the Arab Uprisings* (New York: Columbia University Press, 2014), 37.

123. Louër, *Transnational Shia Politics*, 173–174.

124. Interview with Prince Turki, Washington, D.C., 7 November 2018.

125. Jervis, *Perception and Misperception*, 143.

126. Raymond S. Nickerson, "Confirmation Bias: A Ubiquitous Phenomenon in Many Guises," *Review of General Psychology* 2:2 (June 1998): 175–220.

127. Telephone interview with an Iraqi diplomat, 15 April 2018. See, Hasan al-Alawi, *'Abd al-'Aziz al-Tuwaijri: al-Ruh al-Jami'a [Abd al-Aziz al-Tuwaijri: The Universal Soul]* (London: Dar al-Zawra, 2008). See also, *"Hasan 'Alawi yarsud al-ruh al-jami'a … 'Abd al-'Aziz al-Tuwaijri"* ["Hasan Alawi observes the universal soul, Abd al-Aziz al-Tuwaijri"], *al-Riyad*, 18 February 2008, http://www.alriyadh.com/318734, retrieved 3 April 2019.

128. Telephone interview with an Iraqi diplomat, 15 April 2018.

129. Interview with an Saudi royal family insider, London, 17 August 2018.

130. Interview with Ali Allawi, London, 1 October 2015.

131. 05BAGHDAD5065_a, "Preliminary Results Point to Big Shia Alliance Victory; Allawi Faring Poorly," 20 December 2005 (WikiLeaks).

132. 07BAGHDAD941_a, "Talk of New Iraqi Political Party Coalitions," 17 March 2007 (WikiLeaks); 07BAGHDAD1942_a, "Ayad Allawi Rumored to Return, Many in Iraqiyya Unhappy with His Leadership," 12 June 2007 (WikiLeaks); see also 07BAGHDAD828_a, "Iraqiyya Leaders Discuss Withdrawal from GOI," 8 March 2007 (WikiLeaks).

133. Interview with Ghassan Atiyyah, London, 31 October 2015; telephone interview with a former American diplomat, 8 September 2015.

134. 07BAGHDAD1942_a, "Ayad Allawi Rumored to Return, Many in Iraqiyya Unhappy with His Leadership," 12 June 2007 (WikiLeaks); 07BAGHDAD3988_a, "A Year in Review: Ayad Allawi's Iraqiyya

Coalition Threatens Collapse in His Absence," 9 December 2007 (WikiLeaks); 07BAGHDAD3823_a, "Independent CoR Members Says Legislation Delayed by CoR Ineffectiveness, Ayad Allawi Losing Support," 22 November 2007 (WikiLeaks).

135. 07BAGHDAD1942_a, "Ayad Allawi Rumored to Return, Many in Iraqiyya Unhappy with His Leadership," 12 June 2007 (WikiLeaks).

136. Telephone interview with a former American diplomat, 8 September 2015.

137. Interview with a Saudi businessman, London, 17 August 2018.

138. 08BAGHDAD1922_a, "Ayad Allawi Discusses Recent Political Developments," 24 June 2008 (WikiLeaks).

4. SAUDI ARABIA SHUNS IRAQ

1. Wendt, *Social Theory*, 263.

2. Woodward, *The War Within*, 257–258.

3. 06RIYADH9175_a, "MOI Head Says If U.S. Leaves Iraq, Saudi Arabia Will Stand with Sunnis," 26 December 2006 (WikiLeaks).

4. Telephone interview with a former American diplomat, 8 September 2015.

5. Ibid.

6. Interview with a Saudi businessman, London, 17 August 2018.

7. Nawaf Obaid, "Stepping into Iraq," *Washington Post*, 29 November 2006.

8. "Iraqi Sunni spokesman praises Saudi invitation to Shaykh Al-Dari," BBC Monitoring Middle East, 15 October 2006; "Saudi king urges Iraqi Sunni and Shiite clerics to practice patience and serenity," Associated Press, 14 October 2006.

9. Toby Harnden, "We'll arm Sunni insurgents in Iraq, say Saudis," *Daily Telegraph*, 14 December 2006.

10. Marr and al-Marashi, *The Modern History of Iraq*, 241; Rayburn and Sobchak, *U.S. Army in the Iraq War*, vol. 2, 17–32.

11. Telephone interview with a senior Bush administration official, 17 July 2015.

12. Hassan M. Fattah, "U.S. Role Is Called Illegal By Saudi King," *New York Times*, 29 March 2007.

13. Telephone interview with a former American diplomat, 8 September 2015.

14. "*al-Natiq b-ism al-hikuma al-'Iraqiyya: Nurid fath safha jadida ma'a jami' al-duwal al-'Arabiyya*" ["Iraqi government spokesman: We want to open a new page with all the Arab states"] *al-Sharq al-Awsat* (London), 19 April 2007.

15. Telephone interview with Ryan Crocker, 5 June 2015.

16. Woodward, *War Within*, 347–348; see also, "Cheney Embarks on Mission to Middle East," Associated Press, 9 May 2007. This exchange between Abdullah and Cheney was also communicated to me by a former American diplomat. Telephone interview with a former American diplomat, 30 November 2015.

17. Telephone interview with a senior Bush administration official, 17 July 2015. In fact, Abdullah himself later told an Obama administration official that he "had refused former President Bush's entreaties that he meet with Maliki." See 09RIYADH447_a, "Counterterrorism Adviser Brennan's Meeting with Saudi King Abdullah," 22 March 2009 (WikiLeaks).

18. Interview with Prince Turki al-Faisal, Washington, D.C., 7 November 2018.

19. 07BAGHDAD831_a, "Ambassador and PM: Neighbors Conference, Saudi Arabia, Kurdistan Trip," 8 March 2007 (WikiLeaks).

20. Ibid.

21. 07BAGHDAD1467_a, "Scenesetter: Iraq on the Eve of Sharm Al Shaykh Conferences," 30 April 2007 (WikiLeaks).

22. 07BAGHDAD1236_a, "CG's April 5 Meeting with the PM," 10 April 2007 (WikiLeaks).

23. Written exchange with Nuri al-Maliki, June 2020; exchange mediated by Sami al-Askari. During this period, Bush and Maliki had regular meetings, usually via video conference. In our written exchange, Maliki explained to me that Bush, prior to his attempt to compel Abdullah to engage, had expressed confidence that he would be able to persuade the Saudi king. However, Maliki observed to me that in their next meeting, following Bush's attempt, Bush admitted that he had been unsuccessful, despite staying up with Abdullah till midnight. Maliki

said that Bush called Abdullah "an old man whose mind is in a cor-
ner." Mowaffaq Al-Rubaie, then the Iraqi national security adviser who
attended Bush and Maliki's video conferences, similarly recalled that
Bush called Abdullah "an old man with ossified ideas." Interview by
FaceTime with Mowaffaq Al-Rubaie, 21 May 2020.

24. Telephone interview with Ryan Crocker, 5 June 2015.

25. Written exchange with Nuri al-Maliki, June 2020; exchange mediated
by Sami al-Askari.

26. Interview with Sami al-Askari, London, 14 January 2016.

27. 09BAGHDAD2230_a, "CODEL McCain Meeting with Iraqi President
Talabani," 17 August 2009 (WikiLeaks).

28. 10BAGHDAD243_a, "VP Hashemi Reviews De-Ba'athification Issue,
Regional Relations with A/S Feltman," 31 January 2010 (WikiLeaks).

29. Rayburn and Sobchak, *U.S. Army in the Iraq War*, vol. 1, 529–530.

30. Ibid.

31. 10BAGHDAD243_a, "VP Hashemi Reviews De-Ba'athification Issue,
Regional Relations with A/S Feltman," 31 January 2010 (WikiLeaks).

32. 07BAGHDAD1666_a, "Maliki Says Neighbors and JAM Are Serious
Threats," 22 May 2007 (WikiLeaks). Al-Maliki reiterated this concern
in mid-June. See 07BAGHDAD2021_a, "Deputy Secretary Emphasizes
Legislative Priorities with Maliki," 19 June 2007 (WikiLeaks).

33. David Ignatius, "Cheney and the Saudis," *Washington Post*, 9 May 2007.

34. "Sunni Cabinet ministers suspend participation in Cabinet meetings,"
Associated Press, 29 June 2007.

35. "In a bold power play, Iraq's largest Sunni bloc suspends Cabinet membership," Associated Press, 25 July 2007.

36. "Iraqi political crisis grows as more ministers boycott Cabinet,"
Associated Press, 6 August 2007.

37. Zalmay Khalilzad, "Why the United Nations Belongs in Iraq," *New
York Times*, 20 July 2007.

38. Helene Cooper, "U.S. Officials Voice Frustrations with Saudis," *New
York Times*, 27 July 2007.

39. 07BAGHDAD2514_a, "PM Maliki: We Will Not Let Tawafuq Stop
the Political Process," 30 July 2007 (WikiLeaks).

40. 08RIYADH649_a, "Saudi King Abdullah and Senior Princes on Saudi
Policy toward Iraq," 20 April 2008 (WikiLeaks).

41. 07BAGHDAD567_a, "FM Still Hoping to Bring Ministers to Baghdad; Had Positive Trip to Saudi Arabia," 18 February 2007 (WikiLeaks).

42. Ibid.

43. 07BAGHDAD3849_a, "Talabani Briefs Ambassador on Tour of Arab States," 26 November 2007 (WikiLeaks).

44. "Saudi Arabia promises to consider reopening embassy in Iraq," Associated Press, 1 August 2007.

45. 07RIYADH1710_a, "Saudi Delegation to Baghdad Requests Logistical Support," 14 August 2007 (WikiLeaks).

46. Ibid.

47. "Saudi diplomatic mission arrives in Iraq to 'study' re-opening embassy," BBC Monitoring Middle East, 29 August 2007.

48. 08RIYADH649_a, "Saudi King Abdullah and Senior Princes on Saudi Policy toward Iraq," 20 April 2008 (WikiLeaks).

49. 08RIYADH708_a, "Saudis on Assisting Iraq," 1 May 2008 (WikiLeaks).

50. Ibid.; and 08RIYADH767_a, "S/I Satterfield Brief to Saudis on Iraq Developments," 14 May 2008 (WikiLeaks).

51. 08RIYADH1205_a, "Saudi MFA Official on Iraq," 6 August 2008 (WikiLeaks).

52. Telephone interview with Ryan Crocker, 5 June 2015.

53. Interview with an American businessman, Washington, D.C., 6 April 2018.

54. Ibid.

55. Iraq Body Count—Database, https://www.iraqbodycount.org/database/, retrieved 26 June 2016.

56. Kagan, *The Surge*, 178; Rayburn and Sobchak, *U.S. Army in the Iraq War*, vol. 2, 66, 222.

57. Rayburn and Sobchak, *U.S. Army in the Iraq War*, vol. 2, 223.

58. ICG, *Iraq's Civil War*, 6, 9; Rayburn and Sobchak, *U.S. Army in the Iraq War*, vol. 2, 223.

59. Rayburn and Sobchak, *U.S. Army in the Iraq War*, vol. 2, 229.

60. Ibid., 231.

61. ICG, *Iraq's Civil War*, 17.

62. Ibid., 17; and Marr and al-Marashi, *The Modern History of Iraq*, 244; Rayburn and Sobchak, *U.S. Army in the Iraq War*, vol. 2, 274–276.

63. Gordon and Trainor, *The Endgame*, 465; Michael Knights and Ed Williams, *The Calm before the Storm: The British Experience in Southern Iraq*, Washington Institute for Near East Policy, Policy Focus #66, February 2007, 1.

64. Rayburn and Sobchak, *U.S. Army in the Iraq War*, vol. 2, 355.

65. Multi-National Corps–Iraq, "IO Support to Basra PIC: Mission Analysis," 30 November 2007, quoted in Gordon and Trainor, *The Endgame*, 468; see also, Rayburn and Sobchak, *U.S. Army in the Iraq War*, vol. 2, 355.

66. Rayburn and Sobchak, *U.S. Army in the Iraq War*, vol. 2, 356.

67. Gordon and Trainor, *The Endgame*, 469–470.

68. ICG, *Iraq after the Surge II: The Need for a New Political Strategy*, Middle East Report No. 75 (30 April 2008), 15–16; Dodge, *Iraq: From War to a New Authoritarianism*, 159; Gordon and Trainor, *The Endgame*, 473.

69. Telephone interview with a former American diplomat, 8 September 2015.

70. Interview via FaceTime with Mowaffaq Al-Rubaie, 21 May 2020.

71. "Iraqi prime minister vows to fight militias in Basra to the end," Associated Press, 27 March 2008.

72. "Fighting in Basra as Shiite gunmen take to streets of Baghdad, other cities," Associated Press, 25 March 2008.

73. "Shiite cleric al-Sadr pulls fighters off streets; Iraqi government welcomes move," Associated Press, 30 March 2008.

74. Marr and al-Marashi, *The Modern History of Iraq*, 254–255.

75. Rayburn and Sobchak, *U.S. Army in the Iraq War*, Vol. 2, 368, 374.

76. "Iraqi PM al-Maliki sets 4 conditions for stopping crackdown against Shiite militias," Associated Press, 25 April 2008.

77. Marr and al-Marashi, *The Modern History of Iraq*, 255.

78. Rayburn and Sobchak, *U.S. Army in the Iraq War*, Vol. 2, 379.

79. Ibid., 364.

80. Hamza Hendawi, "Analysis: Iraq's al-Maliki wins rare Kurdish, Sunni support in militia crackdown," Associated Press, 6 April 2008.

81. Ibid.; Dean Yates, "ANALYSIS: Iraq PM boosted by backing for militia purge," Reuters, 6 April 2008.

82. "Iraqi Islamic Party leader interviewed on government formation, other issues," BBC Monitoring Middle East, 7 July 2008.

83. "Iraq PM rejects 'policies of interference' at neighbours' talks opening session," BBC Monitoring Middle East, 22 April 2008.

84. "Iraqi prime minister interviewed on security, political situation," BBC Monitoring Middle East, 27 April 2008.

85. 08BAGHDAD1483_a, "Maliki Demands Halt to Iranian and Syrian Interference," 12 May 2008 (WikiLeaks).

86. 08BAGHDAD1784_A, "PM Maliki Recounts His June 7–9 Visit to Tehran," 14 June 2008 (WikiLeaks).

87. 08BAGHDAD1708_a, "VP Adel on Iran's View of SFA and Iranian Meddling in Iraq, 5 June 2008 (WikiLeaks).

88. Gordon and Trainor, *The Endgame*, 455–456.

89. Rayburn and Sobchak, *U.S. Army in the Iraq War*, vol. 2, 380–381.

90. 08BAGHDAD486_a, "Zebari Pessimistic about Kosovo Recognition; Downbeat about SFA Preparations," 20 February 2008 (WikiLeaks); see also 08BAGHDAD921_a, "NSA Rubaie on Upcoming Diplomatic Outreach," 26 March 2008 (WikiLeaks); 08BAGHDAD1256_a, "Hashemi: Olive Branch to Maliki Tentatively Bearing Fruit," 23 April 2008 (WikiLeaks).

91. Turki al-Sahil, *"Mowaffaq al-Rubaie: sallamna al-Riyad 6 Sa'udiyyin qabl yawmain"* ["Mowaffaq al-Rubaie: We handed Riyadh 6 Saudis two days ago"], *al-Sharq al-Awsat* (London), 27 March 2008.

92. 08BAGHDAD1198_a, "The Ambassador's and General Petraeus' April 14 Meeting with PM Maliki," 17 April 2008 (WikiLeaks).

93. Ibid.

94. "Jordanian paper urges Arabs to support 'pro-Arab Shi'i revolution' in Iraq," BBC Monitoring Middle East, 24 April 2008.

95. "UAE foreign minister, Iraqi counterpart address news conference," BBC Monitoring Middle East, 6 June 2008.

96. 08BAGHDAD1734_a, "FM Abdullah bin Zayed: 'I'm Thrilled to be Here,'" 8 June 2008 (WikiLeaks).

97. "King reiterates Jordan's support for Iraq's security, consolidating ties," BBC Monitoring Middle East, 11 August 2008.

98. "Jordan, Iraq issue joint statement at end of Prime Minister Nuri al-Maliki's visit," BBC Monitoring Middle East, 14 June 2008.

99. "Iraqi, Lebanese premiers hold news conference on Baghdad visit, talks," BBC Monitoring Middle East, 21 August 2008.

100. "Official says 'many' countries to open embassies in Baghdad; Al-Iraqiyah update," BBC Monitoring Middle East, 8 September 2008; "UK troops' mission in Basra in 2009 will be training, supervision, Iraq roundup," BBC Monitoring Middle East, 17 October 2008; "Iraqi leader receives Kuwait envoy credentials," BBC Monitoring Middle East, 23 October 2008.

101. "Iraqi PM receives Egyptian ministers," BBC Monitoring Middle East, 6 October 2008.

102. "Egypt names first envoy to Iraq since 2005 killing," Agence France-Presse, 16 June 2009.

103. "Iraqi, Palestinian presidents hold joint news conference in Baghdad," BBC Monitoring Middle East, 6 April 2009.

104. "Iraqi foreign minister discusses ties with Arab countries," BBC Monitoring Middle East, 17 August 2008.

105. "UAE university professor views foreign minister's Iraq visit," BBC Monitoring Middle East, 5 June 2008.

106. "The Iraqi Upturn; Don't look now, but the U.S.-backed government and army may be winning the war," *Washington Post*, 1 June 2008.

107. Dunia Frontier Consultants, *Private Foreign Investment in Iraq*, November 2009, 2, 12, http://www.iier.org/i/uploadedfiles/publication/real/1365985820_011109IIERForeignInvestmentDunia4B.pdf, retrieved 16 November 2016.

108. Lindsay Carroll and Muthanna Edan, "There and back again: Egyptian workers remember their time in Iraq," *Egypt Independent*, 21 March 2013.

109. "Egyptian industry stages fair on Iraqi reconstruction," Agence France-Presse, 7 March 2004.

110. For instance, setting up a trade council and joint economic committee in 2004. "Iraqi, Egyptian businessmen set up trade council," Reuters, 8 March 2004; and "Egyptian-Iraqi higher committee formed to support joint cooperation," BBC Monitoring Middle East, 21 July 2004.

111. Interview with a Lebanese politician, Beirut, 10 September 2015.

112. Dunia Frontier Consultants, *Private Foreign Investment in Iraq*, 8.

113. Ibid., 8.

114. ICG, *Reshuffling the Cards? (II): Syria's New Hand*, Middle East Report No. 93, 16 December 2009, 7–8.

115. 09BAGHDAD171_a, "FM Zebari on Kuwait Summit—Sharp Divisions on Gaza, but New Level of Respect for Iraq," 23 January 2009 (WikiLeaks).

116. "Iraqi foreign minister on election, Obama pledges, ties with Turkey, Iran," BBC Monitoring Middle East, 31 January 2009.

117. 09BAGHDAD3316_a, "NEA A/S Feltman's Meeting with President Talabani," 23 December 2009 (WikiLeaks).

118. Interview with a Lebanese politician, Beirut, 10 September 2015.

119. "Lebanese MP Al-Hariri visits Iraq, meets top leaders," BBC Monitoring Middle East, 18 July 2008; 08BAGHDAD2298_a, "Hariri Visit Furthers Opening to Arab Neighbors, Snubs Tehran," 23 July 2008 (WikiLeaks).

120. "Lebanon's MP al-Hariri Meets Shi'i Figures Al-Sistani, Al-Hakim," BBC Monitoring Middle East, 17 July 2008; 08BAGHDAD2298_a, "Hariri Visit Furthers Opening to Arab Neighbors, Snubs Tehran," 23 July 2008 (WikiLeaks); and telephone interview with Ryan Crocker, 5 June 2015.

121. Telephone interview with Ryan Crocker, 5 June 2015.

122. Written exchange with Nuri al-Maliki, June 2020; exchange mediated by Sami al-Askari.

123. "Iraqi government spokesman comments on Lebanese MP Al-Hariri's visit; update," BBC Monitoring Middle East, 17 July 2008.

124. Telephone interview with Ryan Crocker, 5 June 2015.

125. 08BAGHDAD2298_a, "Hariri Visit Furthers Opening to Arab Neighbors, Snubs Tehran," 23 July 2008 (WikiLeaks).

126. 09CAIRO1349_a, "General Petraeus' Meeting with EGIS Chief Soliman," 14 July 2009 (WikiLeaks).

127. 08BAGHDAD1518_a, "Barham Salih on SFA/SOFA, Jordan Trip, Talabani's Health," 15 May 2008 (WikiLeaks).

128. 09RIYADH947_a, "Scenesetter for Centcom Commander Petraeus' July 21–22 Visit to Saudi Arabia," 20 July 2009 (WikiLeaks).

129. 09BAGHDAD938_a, "FM Zebari on Proposed April 26 GCC3 Meeting in Baghdad," 6 April 2009 (WikiLeaks).

130. 09BAGHDAD1408_a, "Ambassador, CG and PM Discuss Diyala, UK and NATO Security Agreements, PM Visit to DC," 30 May 2009 (WikiLeaks).

131. 09BAGHDAD1431_a, "Iraq-Saudi Arabia: No Rapprochement in Sight," 1 June 2009 (WikiLeaks); see also, "Al-Maliki criticizes 'Saudi stances on Iraq'; US troops kill 'two terrorists,'" BBC Monitoring Middle East, 28 May 2009.

132. "Iraqi PM criticizes Saudi 'negative stance'; political, security update 29 May," BBC Monitoring Middle East, 29 May 2009.

133. "Saudi interior minister rejects Iraqi accusations on border control," BBC Monitoring Middle East, 31 May 2009.

134. Interview with Sami al-Askari, London, 14 January 2016; and interview with Mowaffaq Al-Rubaie, London, 10 December 2015.

135. "Iraq MP says Saudi call for tighter border control 'astonishing'; update 30 May," BBC Monitoring Middle East, 31 May 2009.

5. IRAQ'S 2010 PARLIAMENTARY ELECTIONS

1. Merton, *Social Theory*, 423.

2. Madon, Willard, Guyll, and Scherr, "Self-Fulfilling Prophecies," 1.

3. 09BAGHDAD2230_a, "CODEL McCain Meeting with Iraqi President Talabani," 17 August 2009 (WikiLeaks).

4. Ibid.; 09BAGHDAD2108_a, "FM Zebari Urges More Supportive USG Stance on Chapter VII Issues; Details Ashraf Situation," 5 August 2009 (WikiLeaks); 09BAGHDAD2239_a, "Iraqi National Security Advisor on PM's Trip to Syria, Iranian and Saudi Influence," 18 August 2009 (WikiLeaks).

5. 08RIYADH1668_a, "Saud Al Faisal on Pakistan, Iraq, Lebanon, Palestinian Unity, and Iran," 8 November 2008 (WikiLeaks).

6. Written exchange with Nuri al-Maliki, June 2020; exchange mediated by Sami al-Askari.

7. Marr and al-Marashi, *The Modern History of Iraq*, 261.

8. "Al-Maliki delivers live speech on Iraqi TV, urges strong central government," BBC Monitoring Middle East, 11 November 2008.

9. Marr and al-Marashi, *The Modern History of Iraq*, 256; ICG, *Iraq's Provincial Elections: The Stakes*, Middle East Report No. 82 (27 January 2009), 17.

10. "Iraq to reject US deal without pullout timetable," Agence France-Presse, 8 July 2008; Marr and al-Marashi, *The Modern History of Iraq*, 257–260.

11. "Parliament's approval of pact 'great national achievement'—Iraqi premier," BBC Monitoring Middle East, 28 November 2008; Marr and al-Marashi, *The Modern History of Iraq*, 260.

12. Amit R. Paley, "In Iraq's Provincial Elections, Main Issue Is Maliki Himself," *Washington Post*, 17 January 2009; 08BAGHDAD4018_a, "'The Ax Is Already In The Head': Rural Baghdad Optimistic about Elections, Fears Iran," 23 December 2008 (WikiLeaks); Zaid Al-Ali, *The Struggle for Iraq's Future: How Corruption, Incompetence and Sectarianism Have Undermined Democracy* (New Haven: Yale University Press, 2014).

13. 08BAGHDAD4018_a, "'The Ax is Already in the Head': Rural Baghdad Optimistic about Elections, Fears Iran," 23 December 2008 (WikiLeaks).

14. "Glance at final results from Iraqi provincial elections," Associated Press, 19 February 2009.

15. Ibid.

16. Anthony Shadid, "New Alliances In Iraq Cross Sectarian Lines," *Washington Post*, 20 March 2009; "Glance at final results from Iraqi provincial elections," Associated Press, 19 February 2009.

17. Anthony Shadid, "In Iraq, Political Ambiguity; Old Alliances Shift After January Vote," *Washington Post*, 4 April 2009; Anthony Shadid, "New Alliances In Iraq Cross Sectarian Lines," *Washington Post*, 20 March 2009.

18. Waleed Ibrahim, "Iraq's ISCI wants to mend tattered Shi'ite alliance," Reuters, 13 May 2009.

19. Anthony Shadid, "New Alliances in Iraq Cross Sectarian Lines," *Washington Post*, 20 March 2009.

20. 09BAGHDAD2239_a, "Iraqi National Security Advisor on PM's Trip to Syria, Iranian and Saudi Influence," 18 August 2009 (WikiLeaks);

09BAGHDAD2230_a, "CODEL McCain Meeting with Iraqi President Talabani," 17 August 2009 (WikiLeaks); 09BAGHDAD1950_a, "AMB, CG and PM Discuss Upcoming Visit, Syria and NATO," 19 July 2009 (WikiLeaks).

21. 09BAGHDAD2455_a, "PM Maliki Advisor on Syria, Arab–Kurd Talks, Election Coalitions, and Regional Interference in Iraqi Political Process," 11 September 2009 (WikiLeaks).

22. Telephone interview with a senior Bush administration official, 17 July 2005.

23. Parker and Salman, "Notes from the Underground."

24. "Iraqi prime minister addresses Bani-Isa tribes' general conference," BBC Monitoring Middle East, 2 March 2009; "Iraqi PM addresses Al-Anbar official, tribal chiefs, citizens on domestic issue," BBC Monitoring Middle East, 7 July 2009.

25. 09BAGHDAD2671_a, "Prominent Sunni Sheikh to Announce Coalition; Expresses Willingness to Join PM Maliki," 5 October 2009 (WikiLeaks).

26. Anthony Shadid, "In Iraq, Political Ambiguity," *Washington Post*, 20 March 2009.

27. "Glance at final results from Iraqi provincial elections," Associated Press, 19 February 2009.

28. Hamza Hendawi, "Iraq's changing politics: US-backed Sunni clan chief seeks partnership with Shiite premier," Associated Press, 3 April 2009.

29. Ibid.

30. Tim Cocks, "ANALYSIS: Iraq–U.S. pact leaves PM Maliki stronger than ever," Reuters, 28 November 2008.

31. Hamza Hendawi, ""Iraq's changing politics: US-backed Sunni clan chief seeks partnership with Shiite premier,"Associated Press, 3 April 2009; interview with Sterling Jensen, Cambridge, 2 August 2018.

32. "Iraqi PM meets US defence secretary; new political bloc formed; update 28 Jul," BBC Monitoring Middle East, 29 July 2009.

33. Al-Ali, *Struggle for Iraq's Future*, 123; 09BAGHDAD2245_a, "Da'wa Party Conference Stresses National Unity and Sovereignty While a Da'wa-ISCI Coalition Tenuous," 18 August 2009 (WikiLeaks).

34. Ammar Karim, "Iraq PM set to break with Shiite coalition in January

polls," Agence France-Presse, 13 August 2009; 09BAGHDAD2245_a, "Da'wa Party Conference Stresses National Unity and Sovereignty While a Da'wa-ISCI Coalition Tenuous," 18 August 2009 (WikiLeaks).

35. Ammar Karim, "Iraq PM set to break with Shiite coalition in January polls," Agence France-Presse, 13 August 2009.

36. "Iraqi PM rejects 'sectarianism'; Al-Qa'idah members arrested; roundup," BBC Monitoring Middle East, 25 January 2009.

37. "Iraqi PM urges opposition, Ba'thists to join political process," BBC Monitoring Middle East, 10 March 2009; "Iraqi PM, defence minister address Al-Ubayd tribe conference on reconciliation," BBC Monitoring Middle East, 12 March 2009.

38. "Iraqi PM addresses Al-Anbar officials, tribal chiefs, citizens on domestic issue," BBC Monitoring Middle East, 7 July 2009.

39. Ibid.

40. The adviser was Abd al-Muhsin al-Tuwaijri, assistant deputy commander of the Saudi Arabian National Guard and son of Abd al-Aziz al-Tuwaijri. 10RIYADH221_a, "Saudi-Iraqi Relations: Riyadh Back in the Game?," 23 February 2010 (WikiLeaks).

41. Interview with a Saudi royal family insider, London, 17 August 2018.

42. "Iraqi PM Al-Maliki says 'foreign countries' behind recent Baghdad bombings," BBC Monitoring Middle East, 14 December 2009.

43. In terms of statistics, in 2008, 856 Iraqi civilians had been killed on average each month, in comparison to 2,170 in 2007 and 2,454 in 2006; the monthly civilian death count reached a post-invasion low of 372 in January 2009, but then rose to 563 that June. Iraq Body Count—Database, https://www.iraqbodycount.org/database/, retrieved 10 August 2016. See also, "June is deadliest month for Iraqis this year," Associated Press, 1 July 2009.

44. 09BAGHDAD2561_a, "The Great Game in Mesopotamia: Iraq and Its Neighbors, Part II," 24 September 2009 (WikiLeaks); 09BAGHDAD 2239_a, "Iraqi National Security Advisor on PM's Trip to Syria, Iranian and Saudi Influence," 18 August (WikiLeaks).

45. 09BAGHDAD1408_a, "Ambassador, CG and PM Discuss Diyala, UK and NATO Security Agreements, PM Visit to DC," 30 May 2009 (WikiLeaks); "Iraqis accuse Sunni states of meddling before polls," Reuters, 18 August 2009.

46. Cordesman and Davies, *Iraq's Insurgency* vol. 1, 55, 211; and Rayburn and Sobchak (eds), *U.S. Army in the Iraq War*, vol. 1, 416–417.

47. 09BAGHDAD2108_a, "FM Zebari Urges More Supportive USG Stance on Chapter VII Issues; Details Ashraf Situation," 5 August 2009 (WikiLeaks). On the deteriorating security situation in Nineveh at this time, see ICG, *Iraq's New Battlefront: The Struggle over Nineveh*, Middle East Report No. 90 (28 September 2009).

48. "Iraqi prime minister asks Syria to hand over people accused of insurgent links," Associated Press, 18 August 2009.

49. 09BAGHDAD2239_a, "Iraqi National Security Advisor on PM's Trip to Syria, Iranian and Saudi Influence," 18 August 2009 (WikiLeaks).

50. "Maliki says Syrian secret services met Iraqi extremists," Agence France-Presse, 3 September 2009.

51. Interview with Sami al-Askari, London, 14 January 2016.

52. "Incidents: Iraq Body Count," https://www.iraqbodycount.org/database/incidents/page477, retrieved 11 July 2017; "Qaeda claims Baghdad bombings that killed 95," Agence France-Presse, 26 August 2009.

53. "Al-Qaida emerges as main suspect in Iraq bombings," Associated Press, 20 August 2009.

54. Timothy Williams, "Deadliest Bombs Since '07 Shatter Iraqi Complexes," *New York Times*, 26 October 2009.

55. "Wave of coordinated attacks strike government sites in Baghdad, killing at least 127," Associated Press, 8 December 2009.

56. Interview with a former senior U.S. military commander, Washington, D.C., 22 June 2015.

57. Jane Arraf, "Baghdad governor: Sunni MPs may be arrested for bombing," *Christian Science Monitor*, 23 August 2009.

58. Interview with Hamid al-Bayati, Wayne, NJ, 10 October 2015; Telephone interview with a former American diplomat, 26 June 2015; "Al-Sharqiyah: Zebari accuses Neighbouring states of 'interfering' in Iraq," BBC Monitoring Middle East, 23 August 2009.

59. "Iraq recalls envoy to Syria after truck bombings," Agence France-Presse, 25 August 2009.

60. 09BAGHDAD2270_a, "FM Zebari Provides Message of Reassurance, Insists Attackers Had Outside Support," 21 August 2009 (WikiLeaks).

61. "Iraqi security forces on high alert after Baghdad blasts," Agence France-Presse, 26 October 2009.

62. "Iraq bombers backed by groups in Syria, Saudi: senior cop," Agence France-Presse, 9 December 2009.

63. 09BAGHDAD2504_a, "Iraqi FM Urges P-5 Ambassadors for Support of GOI's UN Move," 16 September 2009 (WikiLeaks).

64. 09BAGHDAD2562_a, "The Great Game in Mesopotamia: Iraq and Its Neighbors, Part I," 24 September 2009 (WikiLeaks).

65. Ibid.

66. 09BAGHDAD2270_a, "FM Zebari Provides Message of Reassurance, Insists Attackers Had Outside Support," 21 August 2009.

67. Wehrey et al, *Saudi-Iranian Relations*, 78; ICG, *Engaging Syria? U.S. Constraints and Opportunities*, Middle East Report No. 83 (11 February 2009), 19.

68. "Arabic article examines Syrian stand on Riyadh ties, Lebanon solution," BBC Monitoring Middle East, 5 March 2007; Walid Shuqair, *"Dimashq ta'tabir Lubnan madkhalan li-tatwir al-musalaha al-Suriyya al-Sa'udiyya"* ["Damascus considers Lebanon a gateway to develop Syrian–Saudi reconciliation"], *al-Hayat* (London), 1 April 2007; ICG, *Reshuffling the Cards? (II)*, 6. Indicating the depth of Saudi hostility to the Assad regime at this time, King Abdullah publicly hosted prominent Syrian dissident Rif'at al-Assad in October 2007, and Saudi Foreign Minister Saud al-Faisal called upon the Arab League to place sanctions on Syria during the 2008 Arab summit in Damascus; "Saudi king's meeting with Rif'at al-Asad reportedly angers Syrians," BBC Monitoring Middle East, 12 October 2007; "Saudi FM slams Syria as Arab summit opens in Damascus, calls for sanctions," Associated Press, 29 March 2008.

69. "Syria Surprised by Saudi Reconciliation: Sources," *Asharq al-Awsat* (English), 22 January 2009.

70. "King Abdullah hosts Assad for bilateral meeting in Saudi Arabia," *Daily Star* (Lebanon), 25 September 2009; Roueida Mabardi, "Saudi, Syria urge Lebanon unity government: SANA," Agence France-Presse, 8 October 2009; "Syrian president, Saudi king discuss bilateral ties, regional developments," BBC Monitoring Middle East, 14 January 2010.

71. 10BAGHDAD119_a, "Senior MFA Official Reviews Iraq's Relations with Neighbors," 18 January 2010 (WikiLeaks).

72. Rita Daou, "Hariri ends landmark Syria visit with call to rebuild ties," Agence France-Presse, 20 December 2009; Rana Moussaoui, "Hariri visit seen as turning point in Lebanon–Syria ties," Agence France-Presse, 21 December 2009; "Jumblatt hails Hariri visit as result of Saudi–Syria thaw," *Daily Star* (Lebanon, 22 December 2009; Michael Young, "Why the Lebanese feel so switched off," *Daily Star* (Lebanon), 24 December 2009.

73. Patrick Worsnip, "Iraq PM asks for UN inquiry into Baghdad bombings," Reuters, 4 September 2009; "UN says special envoy to visit Iraq after Baghdad blasts," Agence France-Presse, 31 October 2009.

74. 09BAGHDAD2504_a, "Iraqi FM Urges P-5 Ambassadors for Support of GOI's UN Move," 16 September 2009.

75. Interview with Hamid al-Bayati, Wayne, NJ, 10 October 2015.

76. 09BAGHDAD2363_a, "FM Zebari on GOI Pursuit of UN Criminal Inquiry, Iranian/Turkish Mediation on Syria," 2 September 2009 (WikiLeaks).

77. 09BAGHDAD2569_a, "Prime Minister Accuses Iran of Trying to Destabilize Iraq," 24 September 2009 (WikiLeaks).

78. Ibid.; 09BAGHDAD2245_a, "Daʿwa Party Conference Stresses National Unity and Sovereignty While a Daʿwa–ISCI Coalition Tenuous," 18 August 2009 (WikiLeaks); see also 09BAGHDAD2455_a, "PM Maliki Advisor on Syria, Arab–Kurd Talks, Election Coalitions, and Regional Interference in Iraqi Political Process," 11 September 2009 (WikiLeaks); and 09BAGHDAD2562_a, "The Great Game in Mesopotamia: Iraq and Its Neighbors, Part I," 24 September 2009 (WikiLeaks).

79. 09BAGHDAD1950_a, "Amb, CG, and PM Discuss Upcoming Visit, Syria and NATO," 19 July 2009 (WikiLeaks).

80. 09BAGHDAD2569_a, "Prime Minister Accuses Iran of Trying to Destabilize Iraq," 24 September 2009 (WikiLeaks).

81. 09BAGHDAD2441_a, "PM Maliki, CODEL Levin Discuss Foreign Interference in Iraq, August 19 Bombings," 10 September 2009 (WikiLeaks); see also 09BAGHDAD2455_a, "PM Maliki Adviser on

Syria, Arab–Kurd Talks, Election Coalitions, and Regional Interference in Iraqi Political Process," 11 September 2009 (WikiLeaks).

82. 09BAGHDAD2108_a, "FM Zebari Urges More Supportive USG Stance on Chapter VII Issues; Details Ashraf Situation," 5 August 2009 (WikiLeaks); 09BAGHDAD2230_a, "CODEL McCain Meeting with Iraqi President Talabani," 17 August 2009 (WikiLeaks); "Iraqi President Talabani interviewed on sidelines of UN General Assembly," BBC Monitoring Middle East, 1 October 2009.

83. 10BAGHDAD36_a, "Vice President Abd al-Mahdi's January 12–14 Visit to Washington," 6 January 2010 (WikiLeaks).

84. 09BAGHDAD2444_a, "Sunni Political Parties Fractured Despite Heightened Electoral Participation," 10 September 2009 (WikiLeaks); 09BAGHDAD3314_a, "NEA A/S Feltman's Meeting with President Talabani," 23 December 2009 (WikiLeaks); 10BAGHDAD350_a, "South Baghdad: On the Eve of U.S. Military Reduction, the Former 'Triangle of Death' at a Crossroads," 10 February 2010 (WikiLeaks).

85. "Iraqi awakening, salvation councils contemplating electoral coalitions; roundup," BBC Monitoring Middle East, 27 July 2009; "Iraqi PM meets US defence secretary; new political bloc formed; update 28 Jul," BBC Monitoring Middle East, 29 July 2009; Anthony Shadid, "Maliki's tactics stun friends and foes," *Financial Times*, 31 July 2009; Anthony Shadid and Nada Bakri, "In Sign of Times, Alliances Shift Ahead of Iraqi Elections," *Washington Post*, 30 September 2009.

86. Qassim Abdul-Zahra, "Iraq's Shiite prime minister announces election alliance with Sunnis who fought insurgents," Associated Press, 1 October 2009.

87. Osman, *Sectarianism in Iraq*, 147–148.

88. Written exchange with Nuri al-Maliki, June 2020; exchange mediated by Sami al-Askari.

89. "Iraq political roundup; Da'wa Party, Islamic party leaders debate alliances," BBC Monitoring Middle East, 10 October 2009.

90. Interview with Saudi businessman, London, 17 August 2018; see also 08BAGHDAD3569_a, "Sheikh Claims Iraqi Tribes Asking Saudis for Support," 12 November 2008 (WikiLeaks).

91. "ANALYSIS: Trouble in former Qaeda heartland bodes ill for Iraq," Reuters, 23 August 2009.

92. "Al-Sharqiyah TV rounds up political, security developments in Iraq," BBC Monitoring Middle East, 1 November 2009.

93. "Iraqi political leaders to form new electoral coalition; security roundup," BBC Monitoring Middle East, 25 May 2009.

94. ICG, *Iraq's Uncertain Future: Elections and Beyond*, Middle East Report No. 94 (25 February 2010), 31.

95. "Arrest warrant for MP seen as part of 'hot electoral battle' in Iraq; update," BBC Monitoring Middle East, 24 October 2009.

96. Interview with Ghassan Atiyyah, London, 31 October 2015.

97. Ibid.

98. Ibid.; also interview with Ali Allawi, London, 1 October 2015.

99. Interview with Lebanese reporter, Beirut, 6 March 2015.

100. Osman, *Sectarianism in Iraq*, 147–148.

101. Ahmet Davutoglu, "Turkey's Mediation: Critical Reflections From the Field," *Middle East Policy* 20:1 (Spring 2013), 84; Aaron Stein, *Turkey's New Foreign Policy: Davutoglu, the AKP and the Pursuit of Regional Order*, Whitehall Paper 83 (Abingdon: Routledge Journals for the Royal United Services Institute for Defence and Security Studies, 2014), 23.

102. Emma Sky, *The Unraveling: High Hopes and Missed Opportunities in Iraq* (New York: Public Affairs, 2015), 319–320; ICG, *Déjà Vu All Over Again? Iraq's Escalating Political Crisis*, Middle East Report No. 126 (30 July 2012), 12f. See also, Stein, *Turkey's New Foreign Policy*, 25; and Henri J. Barkey, "A Transformed Relationship: Turkey and Iraq," in Barkey, Lasensky, and Marr (eds), *Iraq, Its Neighbors, and the United States*, 59–60.

103. *"al-Saʿudiyya tahtafil bi-l-Quds … wa-l-malik yusallim Erdogan jaʾizat ʿkhidmat al-Islam"* ["Saudi Arabia celebrates Jerusalem, and the king awards Erdogan the 'Service to Islam' award"], *al-Sharq al-Awsat*, 10 March 2010; *"Khadim al-haramaini al-sharifaini yaʿqid ijtimaʿan maʿa al-Daktur Ayad ʿAllawi"* ["The Guardian of the Two Holy Mosques concludes a meeting with Dr. Ayad Allawi"], *al-Sharq al-Awsat*, 21 February 2010. See also, "Iraqi former PM Allawi meets Saudi king ahead of polls," Reuters, 20 February 2010; 10RIYADH 221_a, "Saudi-Iraqi Relations: Riyadh Back in the Game?," 23 February 2010 (WikiLeaks).

104. Kim Gamel and Qassim Abdul-Zahra, "Shiite groups form new alliance excluding Iraq's PM in major shake-up ahead of January vote," Associated Press, 25 August 2009.

104. 09BAGHDAD2569_a, "Prime Minister Accuses Iran of Trying to Destabilize Iraq," 24 September 2009 (WikiLeaks).

105. Ibid.

106. Telephone interview with Raad Alkadiri, 24 September 2015; email correspondence with Raad Alkadiri, 24 September 2015. For a similar assessment, see Al-Ali, *Struggle for Iraq's Future*, 123.

107. "Maliki throws all-or-nothing hat into election: analysts," Agence France-Presse, 31 August 2009.

108. "Maliki 'certain' of Iraq poll victory," Agence France-Presse, 3 March 2010.

109. See, for instance, "Iraqi PM addresses conference on announcement of State of Law coalition," BBC Monitoring Middle East, 2 October 2009; "Iraqi PM highlights danger of reigniting 'sectarianism,'" BBC Monitoring Middle East, 3 October 2009; "Iraqi PM addresses first constituent conference of Baghdad tribes," BBC Monitoring Middle East, 8 January 2010.

110. ICG, *Iraq's Uncertain Future*, 12.

111. "Al-Iraqiyah TV carries 'confessions' of alleged mastermind of 19 Aug blasts," BBC Monitoring Middle East, 24 August 2019; "Iraq airs confessions of suspects in huge bombings," Agence France-Presse, 22 November 2009.

112. "Iraqi PM addresses media on elections law, security issue, Ba'th Party," BBC Monitoring Middle East, 13 November 2009. See also, for instance, "Iraqi PM addresses tribal chiefs on security, terrorism, reconciliation," BBC Monitoring Middle East, 15 November 2009; "UPDATE 2: Iraq's Maliki blasts foreign support for bombings," Reuters, 9 December 2009.

113. "Iraq PM ramps up attacks on Baathists before vote," Associated Press, 22 November 2009.

114. ICG, *Iraq's Uncertain Future*, 27–28.

115. Ibid., 29.

116. Ibid., 28–29; Sky, *The Unraveling*, 314.

117. "Iraqi premier calls for applying fully justice law," BBC Monitoring Middle East, 17 January 2010.

118. Telephone interview with Christopher Hill, 13 July 2015.

119. ICG, *Iraq's Uncertain Future*, 31.

120. Email correspondence with Raad Alkadiri, 24 September 2015.

121. Ibid.

122. "A look at seat distribution in Iraq's parliament according to complete vote returns," Associated Press, 26 March 2010.

123. "Allawi narrowly wins Iraq election, Maliki rejects result," Agence France-Presse, 26 March 2010.

124. "Iraq PM Maliki calls for vote recount: statement," Agence France-Presse, 21 March 2010; Gordon and Trainor, *The Endgame*, 618.

125. Gordon and Trainor, *The Endgame*, 618.

126. "Allawi blames USA, Iran for failure to gain Iraqi premier post," BBC Monitoring Middle East, 30 November 2010; "Iraqi MP criticizes Allawi's remarks against PM," BBC Monitoring Middle East, 11 June 2011; "Ex-Iraqi premier calls for early elections, raps Iranian interference," BBC Monitoring Middle East, 15 September 2011.

127. See, for instance, Marc Lemieux and Shamiran Mako, "Political Parties, Elections and the Transformation of Iraqi Politics Since 2003," in Benjamin Isakhan, Shamiran Mako, and Fadi Dawood (eds), *State and Society in Iraq: Citizenship under Occupation, Dictatorship and Democratisation* (London: I.B. Tauris, 2017), 250.

128. "Iran reportedly actively pursuing Al-Maliki's reelection," BBC Monitoring Middle East, 22 September 2010; "Al-Hakim's party threatens to leave Iraqi bloc over Iranian pressure on Al-Sadr," BBC Monitoring Middle East, 30 September 2010. The first report is from Al-Sharqiya TV, and the second from *al-Sharq al-Awsat*.

129. See, for instance, Dodge, *Iraq: From War to a New Authoritarianism*, 188.

130. Written exchange with Nuri al-Maliki, June 2020; exchange mediated by Sami al-Askari. Iraq political observer Raad Alkadiri also conveyed to me that Maliki appeared to genuinely believe that the election had been stolen from him as a result of foreign interference. Email correspondence with Raad Alkadiri, 24 September 2015.

131. Interview with former American diplomat, Washington, D.C., 26 May 2015; telephone interview with Christopher Hill, 13 July 2015; interview with Lebanese reporter, Middlesbrough, 12 April 2016.

132. Interview with Sami al-Askari, London, 14 January 2016.

133. 09BAGHDAD2455_a, "PM Maliki Advisor on Syria, Arab-Kurd Talks, Election Coalitions, and Regional Interference in Iraqi Political Process," 11 September 2009 (WikiLeaks).

134. Marr and al-Marashi, *The Modern History of Iraq*, 272.

135. "Iraqi National Alliance, State of Law Coalition to merge 'this week': paper," BBC Monitoring Middle East, 4 May 2010.

136. Mustafa Zain, "*al-Intikhabat wa-l-sira' 'ala-l-'Iraq*" ["The Elections and the Struggle for Iraq"], *al-Hayat* (London), 15 March 2010; telephone interview with Christopher Hill, 13 July 2015; interview with former American diplomat, Washington, D.C., 4 June 2015.

137. 'Uday Hatim, "*al-Ahzab al-shi'iyya taltaqi fi Iran thaniyyatan*" ["The Shi'a parties meet in Iran again"], *al-Hayat* (London), 3 May 2010; "Pan-Arab paper views talks on selecting new Iraqi prime minister, proposals," BBC Monitoring Middle East, 24 May 2010.

138. "Iraq's Sadrists say Maliki can remain as PM," AFP, 15 May 2010.

139. See, Abd al-Wahid Tu'ma, "*Safqa tadman li-l-Sadr tanfidh shurutihi muqabil ta'yid al-Maliki*" ["Deal guarantees Sadr his conditions in exchange for supporting al-Maliki"], *al-Hayat* (London), 16 July 2010; Abd al-Wahid Tu'ma, "*Ra'is al-hukuma iltaqa mas'ulin 'Iraniyyin fi Bairut*" ["The prime minister met with Iranian officials in Beirut"], *al-Hayat* (London), 14 July 2010; "Iraqi forces accomplish 'intelligence milestone' in Baghdad," BBC Monitoring Middle East, 30 August 2010; "Hardline Sadrists throw support behind Iraqi PM, with hopes of taking over after US leaves," Associated Press, 1 October 2010.

140. Interview with James Jeffrey, Washington, D.C., 11 May 2015; "Kurdish negotiator says deal is close on pact to keep PM al-Maliki as Iraq leader," Associated Press, 8 October 2010.

141. See "Iraqi premier, Kurdistan president give news conference," BBC Monitoring Middle East, 9 August 2010; "Kurdish negotiator says deal is close on pact to keep PM al-Maliki as Iraq leader," Associated Press, 8 October 2010.

142. "Allawi blames USA, Iran for failure to gain Iraqi premier post," BBC Monitoring Middle East, 30 November 2010. See also, "Iraqi MP criticizes Allawi's remarks against PM," BBC Monitoring Middle East, 11 June 2011; "Ex-Iraqi premier calls for early elections, raps Iranian interference," BBC Monitoring Middle East, 15 September 2011.

143. On 16 July, it was reported that Maliki was refusing to concede on some of Muqtada's demands; three days later, Muqtada met with Allawi, and the next day Muqtada issued a statement praising concessions made by Iraqiyya and calling upon State of Law also "to make concessions to serve the public interest." See, Abd al-Wahid Tu'ma, "Safqa tadman li-l-Sadr tanfidh shurutihi muqabil ta'yid al-Maliki" ["Deal guarantees Sadr his conditions in exchange for supporting al-Maliki"], al-Hayat (London), 16 July 2010; "Allawi seeks Sadr's support to become Iraqi PM," Reuters, 19 July 2010; "Website says Muqtada al-Sadr says meeting with Allawi positive, fruitful," BBC Monitoring Middle East, 20 July 2010.

144. Interview with Raad Alkadiri, Washington, D.C., 29 April 2015.

145. Al-Ali, The Struggle for Iraq's Future, 157.

146. "Iraqi Al-Sadr Trend supports national partnership government; roundup," BBC Monitoring Middle East, 4 April 2010; "Iraqi president arrives in Saudi Arabia," BBC Monitoring Middle East, 11 April 2010; "Saudi king receives Iraqi Shi'i party leader Ammar al-Hakim," BBC Monitoring Middle East, 14 April 2010; "Iraqi Kurdistan president start official visit to Saudi Arabia to Saudi Arabia 12 Apr: roundup," BBC Monitoring Middle East, 12 April 2010.

147. Paul Handley, "Maliki 'hijacking' Iraqi elections: top Saudi prince," Agence France-Presse, 15 May 2010.

148. Interview with Prince Turki al-Faisal, Washington, D.C., 7 November 2018.

149. "Saudi invites Iraq politicians to Riyadh for talks," Agence France-Presse, 30 October 2010.

150. "Iraq's Allawi, Al-Hakim discuss Saudi king's initiative," BBC Monitoring Middle East, 11 November 2010.

151. Ibid.; "Allawi blames USA, Iran for failure to gain Iraqi premier post," BBC Monitoring Middle East, 30 November 2010.

6. SAUDI ARABIA AND IRAQ AFTER THE ARAB SPRING

1. Jasir al-Jasir, *"Khutat al-nizam al-Safawi fi Iran li-tadmir duwal al-khalij"* ["The Plans of the Safavid regime in Iran to destroy the Gulf states"], *al-Jazira*, 12 March 2011, http://www.al-jazirah.com/2011/20110312du10.htm, retrieved 22 July 2020; Jasir al-Jasir, *"Khutat al-nizam al-Safawi li-tadmir duwal al-khalij"* ["The Plans of the Safavid regime to destroy the Gulf states"], *al-Jazira*, 13 March 2011, https://www.ncr-iran.org/ar/اخبار-مقالات-سيده ر/12077, retrieved 22 July 2020; Jasir al-Jasir, *"Khutat al-nizam al-Safawi li-tadmir al-duwal al-'Arabiyya—Misr—3"* ["The Plans of the Safavid regime to destroy the Arab states—Egypt—3"], *al-Jazira*, 14 March 2011, https://www.ncr-iran.org/ar/اخبار-مقالات-سيده ر/12083, retrieved 22 July 2020; Jasir al-Jasir, *"Khutat al-nizam al-Safawi li-tadmir al-duwal al-'Arabiyya 4—istighlal shabab wa Aqbat Misr"* ["The Plans of the Safavid regime to destroy the Arab states 4—exploiting the youth and Copts of Egypt"], *al-Jazira*, 15 March 2011, https://www.ncr-iran.org/ar/اخبار-مقالات-سيده ر/12092, retrieved 22 July 2020; Jasir al-Jasir, *"Khutat al-nizam al-Safawi li-tadmir al-duwal al-'Arabiyya"* ["The Plans of the Safavid regime to destroy the Arab states"], *al-Jazira*, 16 March 2011, https://www.ncr-iran.org/ar/اخبار-مقالات-سيده ر/12100, retrieved 22 July 2020. For a report in English on this series of articles, see "Saudi paper reveals Iranian document on plans to destroy, control Arab states," BBC Monitoring Middle East, 23 March 2011.

2. Jasir al-Jasir, *"Khutat al-nizam al-Safawi fi Iran li-tadmir duwal al-khalij"* ["The Plans of the Safavid regime in Iran to destroy the Gulf states"], *al-Jazira*, 12 March 2011, http://www.al-jazirah.com/2011/20110312du10.htm, retrieved 22 July 2020.

3. Jasir al-Jasir, *"Khutat al-nizam al-Safawi li-tadmir al-duwal al-'Arabiyya 4—istighlal shabab wa Aqbat Misr"* ["The Plans of the Safavid regime to destroy the Arab states 4—exploiting the youth and Copts of Egypt"], *al-Jazira*, 15 March 2011, https://www.ncr-iran.org/ar/خبار-مقالات-سيده ر/12092, retrieved 22 July 2020.

4. See, Madawi Al-Rasheed, "Sectarianism as Counter-Revolution: Saudi Responses to the Arab Spring," in Hashemi and Postel (eds),

Sectarianization. It should also be pointed out that this series of articles appeared at a critical moment. The first article was published a day following a publicized "Day of Rage" in the kingdom, and the Saudi intervention in Bahrain took place on the day the third article was published.

5. Jasir al-Jasir, "*Khutat al-nizam al-Safawi li-tadmir al-duwal al-'Arabiyya*" ["The Plans of the Safavid regime to destroy the Arab states"], *al-Jazira*, 16 March 2011, https://www.ncr-iran.org/ar/اخبار-مقالات-رسیده/12100, retrieved 22 July 2020.

6. Mashari al-Dhayidi, "*Iran wa-l-Ikhwan … wa-l-manzil al-khashin*" ["Iran and the Brotherhood, and the rough house"], *al-Sharq al-Awsat*, 29 November 2011.

7. 08RIYADH1034_a, "Sen. Kery in Saudi—Iran, Iraq and Oil," 6 July 2008 (WikiLeaks).

8. Adam Entous, Nour Malas, and Margaret Coker, "A Veteran Saudi Power Player Works To Build Support to Topple Assad," *Wall Street Journal*, 25 August 2013.

9. Ibid.

10. Interview with a Saudi royal family insider, London, 17 August 2018.

11. Skype interview with Sajad Jiyad, 5 June 2020.

12. Written exchange with Nuri al-Maliki, June 2020; exchange mediated by Sami al-Askari.

13. "*Khilaf tarikhi baina-l-Maliki wa-l-malik 'Abdullah … a'jaz Bush (sha-hid)*" ["The historical dispute between al-Maliki and King Abdullah … Bush was unable (Watch)"], Arabi21, 31 October 2017, https://arabi21.com/story/1045533/خلاف-تاریخي-بین-المالكي-و الملك-عبد-الله-أعجز-بوش-شاهد, retrieved 16 June 2020.

14. Ibid.; Written exchange with Nuri al-Maliki, June 2020; exchange mediated by Sami al-Askari.

15. Interview with a Saudi royal family insider, London, 17 August 2018.

16. "Bahrain showdown divides Iraqis on sectarian lines," Reuters, 15 March 2011; "Iraq Shiite authority condemns Bahrain crackdown," Agence France-Presse, 16 March 2011; Anwar Faruqi, "Fellow Shiites rally behind Bahrain protestors," Agence France-Presse, 16 March 2011; Muhanad Mohammed, "Biggest Iraqi Shi'ite rally against Saudis in

Bahrain," Reuters, 18 March 2011; "Iraqi Shi'ites want Saudis to withdraw from Bahrain," Reuters, 23 April 2011.

17. "Iran seeks to raise trade with Iraq to $10 bln this year," Reuters, 6 July 2011; "Iraqi premier hails visit by Iranian delegation as 'new starting point,'" BBC Monitoring Middle East, 6 July 2011.

18. Skype interview with Sajad Jiyad, 5 June 2020.

19. Sammy Ketz, "Iraq's Shiites grudgingly back Syria's Baath," Agence France-Presse, 25 April 2011.

20. Rania El Gamal, "ANALYSIS: Iraqi Shi'ites fear fallout of Syria turbulence," Reuters, 28 September 2011.

21. Ibid.

22. Ibid.

23. "*Khilaf tarikhi baina-l-Maliki wa-l-malik 'Abdullah ... a'jaz Bush (shahid)*" ["The historical dispute between al-Maliki and King Abdullah ... Bush was unable (Watch)"], 'Arabi21, 31 October 2017, https://arabi21.com/story/1045533/عبد‮-‬الملك‮-‬و‮-‬المالكي‮-‬بين‮-‬تاريخي‮-‬خلاف‮-‬شاهد‬ بوش‮-‬أعجز‮-‬الله, retrieved 16 June 2020.

24. Mapping Militant Organizations, "Asa'ib Ahl al-Haq," Stanford University (July 2008), https://cisac.fsi.stanford.edu/mappingmilitants/profiles/asaib-ahl-al-haq, retrieved 30 July 2020.

25. Adam Schreck and Qassim Abdul-Zahra, "Iraqi militia's plan to lay down arms and join politics could boost Iran's role," Associated Press, 6 January 2012.

26. Mapping Militant Organizations, "Asa'ib Ahl al-Haq," Stanford University (July 2008), https://cisac.fsi.stanford.edu/mappingmilitants/profiles/asaib-ahl-al-haq, retrieved 30 July 2020.

27. Ned Parker, "U.S. official: Iraq continues to allow Iranian overflights to Syria," *Los Angeles Times*, 27 February 2013; "Iraqi efforts to block Iranian overflights 'not enough': U.S. official," Reuters, 5 February 2014.

28. Marr and al-Marashi, *The Modern History of Iraq*, 274–275.

29. Ibid., 281.

30. Laith Hammoudi, "Iraq's Maliki lashes out at Sunni province seeking autonomy," McClatchy, 31 October 2011.

31. Salam Faraj, "Iraq PM moves to oust deputy as US forces leave," Agence France-Presse, 18 December 2011.

32. Rania El Gamal, "FEATURE: U.S. pullout leaves Iraq fragile, divided," Reuters, 18 December 2011; Muʿid Fayyad, *"Naʾib raʾis al-wuzaraʾ al-ʿIraqi: Iran musaitira ʿala kul umur al-balad … wa-l-hukuma al-haliyya tashakkalat wa baqiyya bi-qarariha"* ["Iraqi deputy prime minister: Iran is in control of all the affairs of state, and the current government was formed and remains by its decision"], *al-Sharq al-Awsat*, 23 February 2012.

33. "Turkey becoming 'hostile state': Iraq PM," Agence France-Presse, 20 April 2012.

34. Aaron Stein and Philipp C. Bleek, "Turkish–Iranian Relations: From 'Friends with Benefits' to 'It's Complicated,'" *Insight Turkey* 14:4 (2012): 142; Stein, *Turkey's New Foreign Policy*, 25.

35. "Iraq hails improving Saudi security ties," 29 February 2012, AhramOnline, http://english.ahram.org.eg/NewsContent/2/8/35725/World/Region/Iraq-hails-improving-Saudi-security-ties.aspx, retrieved 6 November 2020.

36. Alice Fordham, "Iraq, Saudi Arabia show signs of improved relations after years of strain," *Washington Post*, 4 March 2012, https://www.washingtonpost.com/world/middle_east/iraq-and-saudi-arabia-show-signs-of-improved-relations-after-years-of-strain/2012/03/04/gIQAXnxBrR_story.html, retrieved 6 November 2020; Muhammad Talib al-Ahmadi, *"ʿUkaz taʿbur khutut al-nar wa tatajannab al-tafjirat wa tuhawir raʾis al-wuzaraʾ al-ʿIraqi"* ["*Okaz* crosses the lines of fire and avoids explosions and talks with the Iraqi prime minister,"], *Okaz*, 29 February 2012, https://www.okaz.com.sa/article/457948.

37. Iyad Abu Shaqra, *"Kif tahawwalat Suriya min 'laʿib' ila 'malʿab'?"* ["How did Syria transform from a 'player" to a 'playing field'?"], *al-Sharq al-Awsat*, 26 March 2012.

38. Hamza Hendawi and Lara Jakes, "Arab leaders stay away from Baghdad summit," *Christian Science Monitor*, 29 March 2012, https://www.csmonitor.com/World/Latest-News-Wires/2012/0329/Arab-leaders-stay-away-from-Baghdad-summit, retrieved 6 November 2020.

39. "Iraq PM warns Sunni protestors, makes small concession," Reuters, 1 January 2013.

40. Patrick Markey, "ANALYSIS: Sunni discontent and Syria fears feed Iraqi unrest," Reuters, 29 January 2013.

41. Based on conversations with multiple Iraqi Shi'a sources between 2015 and 2020; ICG, "Make or Break: Iraq's Sunnis and the State," Middle East Report No. 144 (14 August 2013), 13–14.

42. Sinan Salaheddin, "As Sunni violence spirals, some Shiites issue call to arms and Iraqi government seeks US help," Associated Press, 29 October 2013; Iraq Body Count—Database, https://www.iraqbodycount.org/database/, retrieved 5 August 2020.

43. Based on conversations with multiple Iraqi Shi'a sources between 2015 and 2020.

44. "Qatar, Saudi Arabia accused of supporting violence in Iraq; roundup," BBC Monitoring Middle East, 30 October 2012; Karin Laub, "Iraq PM says Syrian-style revolt 'will not happen' in his country, despite mounting protests," Associated Press, 2 February 2013; Suadad al-Salhy and Sylvia Westall, "INSIGHT: Iraqis hesitate on the edge of chaos," Reuters, 19 September 2013.

45. Ana Swanson, "How the Islamic State makes its money," *Washington Post*, 18 November 2015.

46. Ian Bremmer, "The Top 5 Countries Where ISIS Gets Its Foreign Recruits," *Time*, 14 April 2017, https://time.com/4739488/isis-iraq-syria-tunisia-saudi-arabia-russia/, retrieved 18 November 2020; Haytham Mouzahem, "Saudi Wahhabi Sheikh Calls On Iraq's Jihadists to Kill Shiites," Al-Monitor, 28 April 2013, https://www.al-monitor.com/pulse/originals/2013/04/wahhabi-sheikh-fatwa-iraq-kill-shiites-children-women.html, retrieved 12 March 2021.

47. Adam Schreck, "Fresh clashes between Sunnis and security forces in Iraq prompt fears of wider struggle," Associated Press, 24 April 2013.

48. Prashant Rao, "Iraq cabinet unveils sweeping reform of Saddam law," Agence France-Presse, 7 April 2013.

49. "Iraqi Prime Minister Al-Maliki speaks on desire to mend ties with Saudi Arabia," BBC Monitoring Middle East, 6 May 2013.

50. "Maliki announced his readiness to visit Saudi Arabia to end the differences," National Iraqi News Agency, 7 November 2013.

51. "Iran, Syria, reportedly 'angry' at Kuwait's positive role in Saudi-Iraq ties," BBC Monitoring Middle East, 12 November 2013.

52. Written exchange with Nuri al-Maliki, June 2020; exchange mediated by Sami al-Askari.

53. Angus McDowall and Suadad al-Salhy, "UPDATE 5: Iraq militia says fires mortar bombs at Saudi as warning," Reuters, 21 November 2013; "Iraqi Shiite group claims firing mortar rounds into Saudi Arabian border area over insults," Associated Press, 22 November 2013; "Iraq Shiite Jaish al-Mukhtar sends 'warning message' to Saudi Arabia," Middle East Online, 21 November 2013, https://middle-east-online.com/en/iraq-shiite-jaish-al-mukhtar-sends-'warning-message'-saudi-arabia, retrieved 17 November 2020.

54. "Nuri al-Maliki: *'al-Saʻudiyya wa Qatar tuqaddimani daʻman ghair mahdud li-l-irhabiyyin fi-l-ʻIraq wa Suriya'*" ["Nuri al-Maliki: 'Saudi Arabia and Qatar are providing unlimited support to the terrorists in Iraq and Syria'"], France24, 8 March 2014, https://www.france24.com/ar/20140308-العراق-المالكي-طائفية-أمن-إرهاب, retrieved 17 June 2020.

55. Aya Batrawy and Matthew Lee, "Gulf nations struggle with Iraq militant blowback," Associated Press, 18 June 2014.

56. "US senators accuse Iraq's Maliki of 'sectarian' agenda," Agence France-Presse, 30 October 2013; Missy Ryan, "ANALYSIS: U.S. fears grow about Iraq, but response remains limited," Reuters, 7 January 2014.

57. Skype interview with Sajad Jiyad, 5 June 2020.

58. Ahmed Rasheed, "EXCLUSIVE: Iraq signs deal to buy arms, ammunition from Iran-document," Reuters, 24 February 2014.

59. *"Al-Maliki yuhajim al-Saʻudiyya min Iran: ma al-maniʻ min taqdim al-musaʻada li-l-Asad?"* ["Al-Maliki attacks Saudi Arabia from Iran: What is the objection to providing assistance to Assad?"], CNN Arabic, 3 January 2017, https://arabic.cnn.com/middleeast/2017/01/03/iraq-isis-nuri-maliki, retrieved 17 June 2020.

60. "Iran sent 'small numbers' of operatives into Iraq: US," Agence France-Presse, 20 June 2014; Qassim Abdul-Zahra and Hamza Hendawi, "Iranian commanders on front line of Iraq's fight," Associated Press, 17 July 2014.

61. Qassim Abdul-Zahra and Vivian Salama, "Iraq: al-Maliki rejects Iran's urging to step down," Associated Press, 23 July 2014; Sameer N. Yacoub and Vivian Salama, "Iraq's top Shiite cleric urges peaceful transition," Associated Press, 1 August 2014.

62. "Glad to be rid of Maliki, Saudi Arabia congratulates new Iraq PM," Reuters, 12 August 2014.

63. "Saudi Arabia invites Iraq's Abadi to visit in big sign of thaw," Reuters, 23 March 2015.

64. FaceTime interview with a former American diplomat, 22 February 2021; Skype interview with Sajad Jiyad, 5 June 2020.

65. FaceTime interview with a former American diplomat, 22 February 2021.

66. "Saudi, Iraqi leaders hold landmark talks," Al-Arabiya, 11 November 2014; "Iraq seeks KSA help to return to Arab fold," Arab News, 21 November 2014.

67. FaceTime interview with a former American diplomat, 22 February 2021.

68. Email exchange with Douglas Silliman, 18 February 2021.

69. "Saudi foreign minister optimistic about overcoming Mideast challenges," *Arab News*, 16 February 2017.

70. FaceTime interview with a former American diplomat, 22 February 2021.

71. Ibid.; Telephone interview with Douglas Silliman, 18 June 2020.

72. "Iraq PM criticises Saudi envoy's 'unacceptable' remarks," BBC Middle East Monitoring, 7 September 2016; FaceTime interview with a former American diplomat, 22 February 2021.

73. Ben Kesling, "Iraq Asks Saudi Arabia to Recall Ambassador Who Criticized Shiite Militias," Dow Jones Newswires, 28 August 2016.

74. FaceTime interview with a former American diplomat, 22 February 2021.

75. Omar Sattar, "Iraq's PM concludes tightrope regional tour," Al-Monitor, 23 June 2017, https://www.al-monitor.com/pulse/originals/2017/06/iraq-saudi-iran-kuwait-is-mosul-abadi.html, retrieved 9 March 2021; "'I valued King Salman's friendship,' tweets Iraqi PM on Saudi visit," Al Arabiya, 22 October 2017.

76. Sattar, "Iraq's PM concludes tightrope regional tour."

77. "As relations thaw, Saudi Arabia and Iraq pledge cooperation against IS," Reuters, 22 October 2017.

78. Maher Chmaytelli, "UPDATE 3: Saudi oil minister makes high profile Iraq visit, calls for economic cooperation," Reuters, 21 October 2017; Saudi Arabia and Iraq to re-open border crossing after 27 years,"

Reuters, 15 August 2017; "Saudi airline launches flights to Iraq after 25 years," BBC Monitoring Middle East, 12 October 2017.

79. "A Conversation with Adel al-Jubeir," Council on Foreign Relations, 26 September 2018, https://www.cfr.org/event/conversation-adel-al-jubeir, retrieved 10 March 2021.

80. Telephone interview with an American diplomat, 18 February 2021.

81. David Arminas, "Saudi re-opens Jadeedah Arar crossing," World Highways, 4 December 2020, https://www.worldhighways.com/wh9/news/saudi-re-opens-jadeedah-arar-crossing.

82. Vivian Nereim, "Saudi Arabia to Contribute $3 Billion to Iraq Investment Fund," Bloomberg, 31 March 2021, https://www.bloomberg.com/news/articles/2021-03-31/iraqi-prime-minister-says-turning-new-page-with-saudi-arabia, retrieved 12 April 2021.

83. Telephone interview with an American diplomat, 18 February 2021.

84. Telephone interview with an American diplomat, 25 February 2021.

85. Telephone interview with an American diplomat, 18 February 2021.

86. Ibid.

87. Hamdan al-Shehri, "Saudi Arabia and Iraq's gateway to prosperity," *Arab News*, 20 November 2020.

88. Hassan Al Mustafa, "Saudi-Iraqi relations: A regional safety net," Al Arabiya, 9 April 2017, https://english.alarabiya.net/views/news/middle-east/2017/04/09/Saudi-Iraqi-relations-A-regional-safety-net, retrieved, 10 March 2021; "Iraqi PM Abadi heads to Saudi Arabia at start of MidEast tour," Reuters, 19 June 2017.

89. "Iraq PM hails Iran's role in defeating terrorism," BBC Monitoring Middle East, 7 April 2019.

90. Telephone interview with an American diplomat, 18 February 2021; Suadad al-Salhy, "How Iraq's Kadhimi used Iran visit to stake a claim for sovereignty," Middle East Eye, 25 July 2020, https://www.middleeasteye.net/news/iraq-iran-kadhimi-trip-stake-claim-sovereignty, retrieved 10 March 2021.

91. Hassan al-Mustafa, "Kadhimi deepens cooperation with Saudi Arabia, UAE in Gulf tour," Al-Monitor, 8 April 2021, https://www.al-monitor.com/originals/2021/04/kadhimi-deepens-cooperation-saudi-arabia-uae-gulf-tour, retrieved 12 April 2021; Andrew England, "Saudi

and Iranian officials hold talks to patch up relations," *Financial Times*, 18 April 2021.

92. FaceTime interview with Sajad Jiyad, 26 February 2021.

93. Haddad, *Understanding "Sectarianism,"* chapter 7.

CONCLUSION: A PROPHECY FULFILLED

1. See, for instance, Tim Arango, "Iran Dominates in Iraq after U.S. 'Handed the Country Over,'" *New York Times*, 15 July 2017; Garrett Nada, "Part 1: Iran's Role in Iraq," Wilson Center, 26 April 2018; https://www.wilsoncenter.org/article/part-1-irans-role-iraq, retrieved 1 September 2020.

2. Dexter Filkins, "In Extremists' Iraq Rise, America's Legacy,"*New Yorker*, 11 June 2014, https://www.newyorker.com/news/news-desk/in-extremists-iraq-rise-americas-legacy, retrieved 31 August 2020.

3. Tim Arango, "Maliki's Bid to Keep Power in Iraq Seems to Collapse," *New York Times*, 12 August 2014; Nour Malas, "Iraqi Leader Maliki Loses Backing of Shiite Figure and Iran for New Term," *Wall Street Journal*, 22 July 2014.

4. Alex Vatanka, "Iran's Moment of Truth with Maliki," Middle East Institute, 24 June 2014, https://www.mei.edu/publications/irans-moment-truth-maliki, retrieved 1 September 2020; Mina Aldroubi, "Iraq's former PM Nouri Al Maliki 'not welcome' in new government," *National*, 14 June 2018. See also, Dov S. Zakheim, "Iraq's riots threaten Iran's plan for Middle East dominance," *Hill*, 9 December 2019, https://thehill.com/opinion/international/473606-iraqs-riots-threaten-irans-plan-for-middle-east-dominance, retrieved 1 September 2020.

5. See, for instance, Frederic Wehrey et al, *Saudi-Iranian Relations since the Fall of Saddam* (Santa Monica: RAND Corporation, 2009), xii; Neil Partrick, "Saudi Arabia and Iran," in Neil Patrick (ed.), *Saudi Arabian Foreign Policy: Conflict and Cooperation* (London: I.B. Tauris, 2016), 117; René Rieger, *Saudi Arabian Foreign Relations: Diplomacy and Mediation in Conflict Resolution* (Abingdon: Routledge, 2016), 54.

6. Trevor Johnston et al, *Could the Houthis be the Next Hizballah?: Iranian Proxy Development and the Future of the Houthi Movement* (Santa Monica: RAND Corporation, 2020), 8.

7. Thomas L. Friedman, "A Geopolitical Earthquake Just Hit the Mideast," *New York Times*, 13 August 2020.

8. Eric Edelman and Ray Takeyh, "The Next Iranian Revolution: Why Washington Should Seek Regime Change in Tehran," *Foreign Affairs* (May/June 2020), https://www.foreignaffairs.com/articles/middle-east/2020-04-13/next-iranian-revolution, retrieved 10 November 2020.

BIBLIOGRAPHY

Government Sources

United States:

Foreign Relations of the United States, 1969–1976, Vol. XXVII, Iran; Iraq, 1973–1976, Office of the Historian, Department of State.

National Archives, General Records of the Department of State, Central Foreign Policy Files.

U.S. Diplomatic Cables released by WikiLeaks.
Embassy Amman, selected cables 2004.
Embassy Baghdad, selected cables 2005–2010.
Embassy Cairo, selected cables 2009.
Embassy Riyadh, selected cables 1985–2010.
Consulate Basrah, selected cables 2008.
Consulate General Jeddah, selected cables 2006–2008.

Saudi Arabia:

The Saudi Cables released by WikiLeaks, selected documents 2006–2012.

Interviews

Ali AlAhmed, Saudi political activist, Washington, D.C., 7 May 2018.
Raad Alkadiri, policy adviser to UK Special Representative's Office,

BIBLIOGRAPHY

Baghdad (2003–2004), senior policy adviser, UK Embassy, Baghdad (2006–2007), Washington, D.C., 29 April 2015, 27 May 2015; by telephone, 24 September 2015, 13 October 2015; by email September 2015.

Ali Allawi, scholar and Iraqi minister of trade and defense (2003–2004), minister of finance (2005–2006, 2020–), London, 1 October 2015.

Sami al-Askari, Iraqi parliamentarian, London, 16 January 2016; by WhatsApp, 28 May 2020.

Ghassan Atiyyah, scholar and director of the Iraq Foundation for Development and Democracy, London, 31 October 2015.

Hamid al-Bayati, SCIRI spokesman (1990s), deputy foreign minister of Iraq (2003–2005), permanent representative of Iraq to the United Nations (2006–2013), Wayne, New Jersey, 10 October 2015.

L. Paul Bremer, III, presidential envoy to Iraq and administrator of the Coalition Provisional Authority (2003–2004), by telephone, 4 August 2015; by email, December 2015.

Eliot Cohen, counsellor, U.S. Department of State (2007–2009), Washington, D.C., 5 May 2015.

Ryan Crocker, U.S. ambassador to Iraq (2007–2009), by telephone, 5 June 2015.

Eric Edelman, U.S. under-secretary of defense for policy (2005–2009), Washington, D.C., 7 May 2015.

Prince Turki al-Faisal, Saudi ambassador to the U.S. (2005–2007), Saudi ambassador to the UK (2003–2005), director of General Intelligence (1979–2001), Washington, D.C., 7 November 2018.

Wyche Fowler, U.S. ambassador to Saudi Arabia (1996–2001), by telephone, 10 August 2015.

Samir Frangieh, Lebanese politician, Beirut, 12 March 2015.

Chas W. Freeman, Jr, U.S. ambassador to Saudi Arabia (1989–1992), by Skype, 16 July 2015, 12 November 2015; Washington, D.C., 12 April 2018.

Edward Gnehm, U.S. ambassador to Jordan (2001–2004), Washington, D.C., 10 June 2015.

Christopher Hill, U.S. ambassador to Iraq (2009–2010), by telephone, 13 July 2015.

James Jeffrey, U.S. chargé d'affaires in Iraq (2005), deputy national security adviser (2007–2008), U.S. ambassador to Iraq (2010–2012), Washington, D.C., 11 May 2015, 26 May 2015, 4 June 2015.

Sterling Jensen, Arabic interpreter and cultural adviser to Multi-National Force–Iraq based in Anbar and Nineveh (2006–2008), Cambridge, 2 August 2018; by telephone, 12 May 2020.

Sajad Jiyad, Iraq political analyst, by Skype, 5 June 2020, 26 February 2021.

Robert Jordan, U.S. ambassador to Saudi Arabia (2001–2003), by telephone 30 April 2015, 6 January 2016; Dallas, Texas, 15 June 2015.

Zalmay Khalilzad, U.S. ambassador to Iraq (2005–2007), Washington D.C., 13 May 2015; by telephone 29 June 2015.

Hilal Khashan, professor of political studies, American University of Beirut, Beirut, 26 February 2015.

Jamal Khashoggi, former editor-in-chief of *al-Watan* (Abha), *Arab News* (Riyadh), former media adviser to Prince Turki al-Faisal, Washington, D.C., 24 April 2018.

Lt. Gen. Douglas Lute (ret.), U.S. assistant to the president and deputy national security adviser for Iraq and Afghanistan (2007–2009), by telephone, 1 July 2015.

Nuri al-Maliki, prime minister of Iraq (2006–2014), by email and WhatsApp, June 2020; written exchange mediated by Sami al-Askari.

Marwan Muasher, Jordanian foreign minister (2002–2004), Jordanian deputy prime minister (2004–2005), Beirut, 11 September 2015.

Ronald Neumann, U.S. political adviser in Iraq (2004–2005), Washington, D.C., 26 May 2015.

Sir Derek Plumbly, UK ambassador to Saudi Arabia (2000–2003), London, 6 November 2015.

Francis Ricciardone, U.S. special coordinator for the Transition of Iraq (1999–2001), email correspondence, 8 October 2015.

Mowaffaq al-Rubaie, Iraqi national security adviser (2003–2009), London, 10 December 2015; by FaceTime, 21 May 2020.

Douglas Silliman, U.S. ambassador to Iraq (2016–2019), by telephone, 18 June 2020.

James Smith, U.S. ambassador to Saudi Arabia (2009–2013), Washington, D.C., 11 June 2015.

BIBLIOGRAPHY

Samir Sumaidaie, Iraqi Governing Council member (2003–2004), Iraqi permanent representative to the United Nations (2004–2006), Iraqi ambassador to the United States (2006–2011), by telephone, 10 July 2015, 15 July 2015.

Tariq Tell, assistant professor of political science, American University of Beirut, Beirut, 10 March 2015.

David Welch, U.S. ambassador to Egypt (2001–2005), assistant secretary of state for Near East affairs (2005–2008), by telephone, 19 April 2016.

Joseph Westphal, U.S. ambassador to Saudi Arabia (2014–2017), by FaceTime, 12 February 2021.

American businessman, Washington, D.C., 6 April 2018.

American diplomat, by telephone, 17 February 2021.

Clinton administration official, by telephone, 27 October 2015.

Former American diplomat, by telephone, 21 May 2015.

Former American diplomat, by telephone, 26 June 2015.

Former American diplomat, by telephone, 22 July 2015.

Former American diplomat, by telephone, 31 July 2015.

Former American diplomat, by telephone, 8 September 2015, 30 November 2015.

Former American diplomat, by telephone, 18 February 2021.

Former American diplomat, by FaceTime, 22 February 2021.

Former senior U.S. military commander, Washington, D.C., 22 June 2015.

Former senior U.S. military commander, by telephone, 18 February 2016.

Former British diplomat, by telephone, 14 April 2015.

Former British diplomat, London, 15 April 2015.

Former British diplomat, London, 9 November 2015.

Former British diplomat, London, 2 December 2015.

Iraqi diplomat, Washington, D.C., 29 April 2015.

Iraqi diplomat, Washington, D.C., 17 August 2015; by telephone, 15 April 2018.

Iraqi diplomat, Washington, D.C., 5 June 2020.

Iraqi Shiʿa Islamist, London, 4 November 2015.

Lebanese columnist, Beirut, 4 March 2015.

Lebanese columnist, Beirut, 9 March 2015.

Lebanese columnist, Beirut, 18 March 2015.

BIBLIOGRAPHY

Lebanese politician, Beirut, 10 September 2015.

Lebanese reporter, Beirut, 6 March 2015.

Lebanese reporter, Middlesbrough, 12 April 2016.

Saudi businessman, London, 17 August 2018.

Saudi foreign policy adviser, London, 8 August 2018.

Senior Bush administration official, by telephone, 17 July 2015.

Senior Bush administration official, by telephone, 15 July 2015.

Books, Articles, and Reports

Aarts, Paul and Gerd Nonneman (eds). *Saudi Arabia in the Balance: Political Economy, Society, Foreign Affairs* (New York: New York University Press, 2005).

Abdo, Geneive. *The New Sectarianism: The Arab Uprisings and the Rebirth of the Shi'a–Sunni Divide*, Brookings, Analysis Paper Number 29 (April 2013).

Agha, Hussein J. and Ahmad S. Khalidi. *Syria and Iran: Rivalry and Cooperation* (London: Pinter Publishers for the Royal Institute of International Affairs, 1995).

al-Alawi, Hasan. *al-Ta'thirat al-Turkiyya fi-l-Mashru' al-Qawmi al-'Arabi fi-l-'Iraq* [*Turkish Influences in the Arab Nationalist Project in Iraq*] (London: Dar al-Zawra, 1988).

'Abd al-'Aziz al-Tuwaijri: al-Ruh al-Jami'a [*Abd al-Aziz al-Tuwaijri: The Universal Soul*] (London: Dar al-Zawra, 2008).

Al-Ali, Zaid. *The Struggle for Iraq's Future: How Corruption, Incompetence and Sectarianism Have Undermined Democracy* (New Haven: Yale University Press, 2014).

Allawi, Ali A. *The Occupation of Iraq: Winning the War, Losing the Peace* (New Haven: Yale University Press, 2007).

Allison, Graham T. "Conceptual Models and the Cuban Missile Crisis." *The American Political Science Review* 63:3 (September 1969): pp. 689–718.

Essence of Decision: Explaining the Cuban Missile Crisis (Boston: Little, Brown, 1971).

Allison, Graham T. and Morton H. Halperin. "Bureaucratic Politics: A Paradigm and Some Policy Implications," in Raymond Tanter and

BIBLIOGRAPHY

Richard H. Ullman (eds), *Theory and Policy in International Relations* (Princeton: Princeton University Press, 1972).

Alsultan, Fahad M. and Pedram Saeid. *The Development of Saudi-Iranian Relations since the 1990s: Between Conflict and Accommodation* (London: Routledge, 2017).

Alvandi, Roham. *Nixon, Kissinger, and the Shah: The United States and Iran in the Cold War* (Oxford: Oxford University Press, 2014).

Amos, John W. "The Iran–Iraq War," in Robert G. Darius, John W. Amos, and Ralph H. Magnus (eds), *Gulf Security into the 1980s: Perpetual and Strategic Dimensions* (Palo Alto: Hoover Institution Press, 1984).

Ansari, Ali M. *Iran under Ahmadinejad: The Politics of Confrontation*, Adelphi Paper 393 (Abingdon: Routledge, 2007).

Arjomand, Said Amir. *The Turban for the Crown: The Islamic Revolution in Iran* (Oxford: Oxford University Press, 1988).

Art, Robert J. "Bureaucratic Politics and American Foreign Policy: A Critique." *Policy Sciences* 4:4 (December 1973): pp. 467–490.

El Azhary, M.S. (ed.). *The Iran-Iraq War: An Historical, Economic, and Political Analysis* (London: Croom Helm, 1984).

Bacevich, Andrew J. and Efraim Inbar (eds). *The Gulf War of 1991 Reconsidered* (London: Frank Cass, 2003).

Baker, James A, III, with Thomas M. Defrank. *The Politics of Diplomacy: Revolution, War and Peace 1989–1992* (New York: G.P. Putnam's Sons, 1995).

Baker, James A., III, Lee H. Hamilton, Lawrence S. Eagleburger, Vernon E. Jordan, Jr, Edwin Meese III, Sandra Day O'Connor, Leon E. Panetta, William J. Perrty, Charles S. Robb, Leon E. Panetta, William J. Perry, Charles S. Robb, and Alan K. Simpson. *The Iraq Study Group Report: The Way Forward, A New Approach* (New York: Vintage Books, 2006).

Baram, Amatzia. *Culture, History and Ideology in the Formation of Ba'thist Iraq, 1968–89* (Houndmills: Macmillan in association with St. Antony's College, Oxford, 1991).

Bar-Joseph, Uri. "The hubris of initial victory," in Clive Jones and Sergio Catignani (eds), *Israel and Hizbollah: An Asymmetric Conflict in Historical and Comparative Perspective* (London: Routledge, 2010).

BIBLIOGRAPHY

Barkey, Henri J. "A Transformed Relationship: Turkey and Iraq," in Henri J. Barkey, Scott B. Lasensky, and Phebe Marr (eds), *Iraq, Its Neighbors, and the United States: Competition, Crisis, and the Reordering of Power* (Washington, D.C.: United States Institute of Peace, 2011).

Barkey, Henri J. and Scott B. Lasensky and Phebe Marr (eds). *Iraq, Its Neighbors, and the United States: Competition, Crisis, and the Reordering of Power* (Washington, D.C.: United States Institute of Peace, 2011).

Barnett, Michael N. "Identity and Alliances in the Middle East," in Peter J. Katzenstein (ed.), *The Culture of National Security: Norms and Identity in World Politics* (New York: Columbia University Press, 1996).

Dialogues in Arab Politics: Negotiations in Regional Order (New York: Columbia University Press, 1998).

Batatu, Hanna. *The Old Social Classes and the Revolutionary Movements of Iraq: A Study of Iraq's Old Landed and Commercial Classes and of its Communists, Ba'thists, and Free Officers* (Princeton: Princeton University Press, 1978).

Bauer, Raymond A. "Problems of Perception and the Relations between the United States and Soviet Union." *The Journal of Conflict Resolution* 5:3 (September 1961): pp. 223–229.

Al-Bayati, Hamid. *From Dictatorship to Democracy: An Insider's Account of the Iraqi Opposition to Saddam* (Philadelphia: University of Pennsylvania Press, 2011).

Bengio, Ofra and Meir Litvak (eds). *The Sunna and Shi'a in History: Division and Ecumenism in the Muslim Middle East* (New York: Palgrave Macmillan, 2011).

Bin Sultan, Khaled, with Patrick Seale. *Desert Warrior: A Personal View of the Gulf War by the Joint Forces Commander* (London: HarperCollins Publishers, 1995).

Blanford, Nicholas. *Killing Mr. Lebanon: The Assassination of Rafik Hariri and Its Impact on the Middle East* (London: I.B. Tauris, 2009).

Warriors of God: Inside Hezbollah's Thirty-Year Struggle against Israel (New York: Random House, 2011).

Bonin, Richard. *Arrows of the Night: Ahmad Chalabi and the Selling of the Iraq War* (New York: Anchor Books, 2011).

Boyle, P.A., L. Yu, R.S. Wilson, K. Gamble, A.S. Buchman, and D.A.,

Bennet. "Poor decision making is a consequence of cognitive decline among older persons without Alzheimer's disease or mild cognitive impairment," *PLoS One* 7:8 (2012), https://journals.plos.org/plosone/article?id=10.1371/journal.pone.0043647, retrieved 16 August 2019.

Brand, Laurie A. *Jordan's Inter-Arab Relations: The Political Economy of Alliance Making* (New York: Columbia University Press, 1994).

Bremer, L. Paul, III with Malcolm McConnell. *My Year in Iraq: The Struggle to Build a Future of Hope* (New York: Simon & Schuster, 2006).

Brewer, Marilynn B. "The Social Self: On Being the Same and Different at the Same Time." *Personality and Social Psychology Bulletin* 17:5 (October 1991): pp. 475–482.

Brewer, Marilynn B. and Wendi Gardner. "Who is the 'We'? Levels of Collective Identity and Self Representations." *Journal of Personality and Social Psychology* 71:1 (1996): pp. 83–93.

Brunner, Rainer. "Sunnis and Shiites in Modern Islam: Politics, Rapprochement and the Role of Al-Azhar," in Brigitte Maréchal and Sami Zemni (eds), *The Dynamics of Sunni-Shia Relationships: Doctrine, Transnationalism, Intellectuals and the Media* (London: Hurst, 2013).

Bush, George W. "Remarks on the Future of Iraq," 26 February 2003, in *Selected Speeches of President George W. Bush, 2001–2008*, 168, https://georgewbush-whitehouse.archives.gov/infocus/bushrecord/documents/Selected_Speeches_George_W_Bush.pdf, retrieved 31 October 2016.

Bush, George and Brent Scowcroft. *A World Transformed* (New York: Vintage, 1999).

Byman, Daniel L. "Regional Consequences of Internal Turmoil in Iraq," in Mehran Kamrava (ed.), *The International Politics of the Persian Gulf* (Syracuse: Syracuse University Press, 2011).

Byman, Daniel L. and Kenneth M. Pollack. "Let Us Now Praise Great Men: Bringing the Statesman Back In." *International Security* 25:4 (Spring 2001): pp. 107–146.

Cheney, Dick, with Liz Cheney. *In My Time: A Personal and Political Memoir* (New York: Threshold Editions, 2011).

Chubin, Shahram. "Iran and the War," in Efraim Karsh (ed.), *The Iran–Iraq War: Impact and Implications* (Basingstoke: Macmillan in association with The Jaffee Center for Strategic Studies, 1989).

BIBLIOGRAPHY

Chubin, Shahram and Charles Tripp. *Iran and Iraq at War* (London: I.B. Tauris, 1988).

Iran-Saudi Arabia Relations and Regional Order: Iran and Saudi Arabia in the balance of power in the Gulf, Adelphi Paper 304 (Oxford: Oxford University Press for the International Instittue for Strategic Studies, 1996).

Chubin, Shahram and Sepehr Zabih. *The Foreign Relations of Iran: A Developing State in a Zone of Great-Power Conflict* (Berkeley: University of California Press, 1974).

Cleveland, William L. *The Making of an Arab Nationalist: Ottomanism and Arabism in the Life and Thought of Satiʿ Al-Husri* (Princeton: Princeton University Press, 1971).

Cockburn, Andrew and Patrick Cockburn. *Out of the Ashes: The Resurrection of Saddam Hussein* (New York: HarperCollins, 1999).

Cockburn, Patrick. *The Occupation: War and Resistance in Iraq* (London: Verso, 2007).

Muqtada al-Sadr and the Battle for the Future of Iraq (New York: Scribner, 2008).

The Rise of Islamic State: ISIS and the New Sunni Revolution (London: Verso, 2015).

Cohen, Raymond. *Threat Perception in International Crisis* (Madison: University of Wisconsin Press, 1979).

Cole, Juan R.I. and Nikki R. Keddie (eds). *Shiʿism and Social Protest* (New Haven: Yale University Press, 1986).

Cordesman, Anthony and Emma R. Davies. *Iraq's Insurgency and the Road to Civil Conflict*, 2 vols. (Westport: Praeger Security International, 2008).

Cordesman, Anthony and Nawaf Obaid. *National Security in Saudi Arabia: Threats, Responses, and Challenges* (Westport: Praeger Security International, 2005).

Cottam, Richard W. *Foreign Policy Motivation: A General Theory and a Case Study* (Pittsburgh: University of Pittsburgh Press, 1977).

Daalder, Ivo H. and James M. Lindsay. *America Unbound: The Bush Revolution in Foreign Policy* (Hoboken: Wiley, 2005).

Darius, Robert G., John W. Amos, and Ralph H. Magnus (eds). *Gulf*

BIBLIOGRAPHY

Security into the 1980s: Perpetual and Strategic Dimensions (Palo Alto: Hoover Institution Press, 1984).

Darwich, May. *Threat and Alliances in the Middle East: Saudi and Syrian Policies in a Turbulent Region* (Cambridge: Cambridge University Press, 2019).

Davis, Eric. *Memories of State: Politics, History, and Collective Identity in Modern Iraq* (Berkeley: University of California Press, 2005).

Davutoglu, Ahmet. "Turkey's Mediation: Critical Reflections from the Field." *Middle East Policy* 20:1 (Spring 2013): pp. 83–90.

Dawisha, Adeed. "Saudi Arabia's Search for Security," in Charles Tripp (ed.), *Regional Security in the Middle East* (Aldershot: Gower for The International Institute for Strategic Studies, 1984).

"Arab Regimes: Legitimacy and Foreign Policy," in Adeed Dawisha and I. William Zartman (eds), *Beyond Coercion: The Durability of the Arab State* (London: Croom Helm, 1988).

Arab Nationalism in the Twentieth Century: From Triumph to Despair (Princeton: Princeton University Press, 2003).

Iraq: A Political History from Independence to Occupation (Princeton: Princeton University Press, 2009).

Dawisha, Adeed (ed.). *Islam in Foreign Policy* (Cambridge: Cambridge University Press in association with The Royal Institute of International Affairs, 1983).

Dawisha, Adeed and I. William Zartman (eds). *Beyond Coercion: The Durability of the Arab State* (London: Croom Helm, 1988).

Dodge, Toby. *Inventing Iraq: The Failure of Nation Building and a History Denied* (London: Hurst, 2003).

Iraq's Future: The Aftermath of Regime Change, Adelphi Paper 372 (Oxford: Routledge for The International Institute for Strategic Studies, 2005).

Iraq: From War to a New Authoritarianism (Abingdon: Routledge for the International Institute for Strategic Studies, 2012).

Duelfer, Charles A. *Hide and Seek: The Search for Truth in Iraq* (New York: Public Affairs, 2009).

Duelfer, Charles A. and Stephen Benedict Dyson. "Chronic Misperception and International Conflict: The U.S.-Iraq Experience." *International Security* 36:1 (Summer 2011): pp. 73–100.

BIBLIOGRAPHY

Dunia Frontier Consultants. *Private Foreign Investment in Iraq* (November 2009), http://www.iier.org/i/uploadedfiles/publication/real/136598582 0_011109IIERForeignInvestmentDunia4B.pdf, retrieved 16 November 2016.

Edelman, Eric and Ray Takeyh. "The Next Iranian Revolution: Why Washington Should Seek Regime Change in Tehran." *Foreign Affairs*, May/June 2020, https://www.foreignaffairs.com/articles/middle-east/2020–04–13/next-iranian-revolution, retrieved 10 November 2020.

Ehteshami, Anoushiravan. *After Khomeini: The Iranian Second Republic* (London: Routledge, 1995).

Ehteshami, Anoushiravan and Raymond A. Hinnebusch. *Syria and Iran: Middle Powers in a Penetrated Regional System* (London: Routledge, 1997).

Elmadani, Abdullah. *Indo-Saudi Relations 1947–1997: Domestic Concerns and Foreign Relations*, PhD thesis (Exeter University, 2004).

Farouk-Sluglett, Marion and Peter Sluglett. *Iraq Since 1958: From Revolution to Dictatorship*, third edition (London: I.B. Tauris, 2001).

Fawn, Rick and Raymond Hinnebusch (eds). *The Iraq War: Causes and Consequences* (Boulder: Lynne Rienner, 2006).

Fierke, Karin M. and Knud Erik Jørgensen (eds). *Constructing International Relations: The Next Generation* (Armonk: M.E. Sharpe, 2011).

Filkins, Dexter. "In Extremists' Iraq Rise, America's Legacy." *New Yorker*, 11 June 2014, https://www.newyorker.com/news/news-desk/in-extremists-iraq-rise-americas-legacy, retrieved 31 August 2020.

Finlay, David J., Ole R. Holsti, and Richard R. Fagen. *Enemies in Politics* (Chicago: Rand McNally & Company, 1967).

Fisher, Ronald J., Herbert C. Kelman, and Susan Allen Nan. "Conflict Analysis and Resolution," in Leonie Huddy, David O. Sears, and Jack S. Levy (eds), *The Oxford Handbook of Political Psychology* (Oxford: Oxford University Press, 2013).

Fiske, Susan T. and Shelley E. Taylor. *Social Cognition: From Brains to Culture*, third edition (London: Sage, 2017).

Franzosi, Roberto. "The Press as a Source of Socio-Historical Data: Issues in the Methodology of Data Collection from Newspapers." *History Methods: A Journal of Quantitative and Interdisciplinary History* 20:1 (1987): pp. 5–16.

BIBLIOGRAPHY

Freedman, Lawrence and Efraim Karsh. *The Gulf Conflict, 1990–1991* (London: Faber and Faber, 1994).

Freeh, Louis J. *My FBI: Bringing Down the Mafia, Investigating Bill Clinton, and Fighting the War on Terror* (New York: St. Martin's Griffin, 2005).

Freeman, Chas W., Jr. *America's Misadventures in the Middle East* (Charlottesville: Just World Books, 2010).

Friedman, Thomas L. "A Geopolitical Earthquake Just Hit the Mideast." *New York Times*, 13 August 2020, https://www.nytimes.com/2020/08/13/opinion/israel-uae.html, retrieved 31 August 2020.

Fuller, Graham E. and Rend Rahim Francke. *The Arab Shiʿa: The Forgotten Muslims* (New York: St. Martin's Press, 2001).

Furtig, Henner. *Iran's Rivalry with Saudi Arabia between the Gulf Wars* (Reading: Ithaca Press, 2002).

Ganji, Babak. *A Shiʿi Enclave? Iranian Policy Towards Iraq*, Middle East Series 06/09 (London: Conflict Studies Research Centre, March 2006).

Gates, Robert M. *Duty: Memoirs of a Secretary at War* (New York: Alfred A. Knopf, 2014).

Gause, F. Gregory, III. *Saudi–Yemeni Relations: Domestic Structures and Foreign Influence* (New York: Columbia University Press, 1990).

Oil Monarchies: Domestic and Security Challenges in the Arab Gulf States (New York: Council on Foreign Relations Press, 1994).

"Balancing What? Threat Perception and Alliance Choice in the Gulf." *Security Studies* 13:2 (2003): pp. 273–305.

"Saudi Arabia: Iraq, Iran, the Regional Power Balance, and the Sectarian Question." *Strategic Insights*, VI:2, March 2007, https://core.ac.uk/download/pdf/36704532.pdf, retrieved 5 December 2016.

The International Relations of the Persian Gulf (Cambridge: Cambridge University Press, 2010).

"Saudi Arabia's Regional Security Strategy," in Mehran Kamrava (ed.), *The International Politics of the Persian Gulf* (Syracuse: Syracuse University Press, 2011).

"The Foreign Policy of Saudi Arabia," in Raymond Hinnebusch and Anoushiravan Ehteshami (eds), *The Foreign Policies of Middle East States*, second edition (Boulder: Lynne Rienner Publishers, 2014).

BIBLIOGRAPHY

Beyond Sectarianism: The New Middle East Cold War, Brookings Doha Center Analysis Paper, Number 11 (July 2014).

Glaser, Charles L. *Rational Theory of International Politics* (Princeton: Princeton University Press, 2010).

Glosemeyer, Iris. "Checks, Balances and Transformation in the Saudi Political System," in Paul Aarts and Gerd Nonneman (eds), *Saudi Arabia in the Balance: Political Economy, Society, Foreign Affairs* (New York: New York University Press, 2005).

Goodarzi, Jubin M. *Syria and Iran: Diplomatic Alliance and Power Politics in the Middle East* (London: Tauris Academic Studies, 2009).

Gordon, Michael R. and General Bernard E. Trainor. *The Endgame: The Inside Story of the Struggle for Iraq, from George W. Bush to Barack Obama* (New York: Pantheon, 2012).

Haas, Mark L. *The Ideological Origins of Great Power Politics, 1789–1989* (Ithaca: Cornell University Press, 2005).

Haddad, Fanar. *Sectarianism in Iraq: Antagonistic Visions of Unity* (London: Hurst, 2011).

"Sectarian Relations Before 'Sectarianization' in Pre-2003 Iraq," in Nader Hashemi and Danny Postel (eds), *Sectarianization: Mapping the New Politics of the Middle East* (New York: Oxford University Press, 2017).

Understanding "Sectarianism": Sunni-Shi'a Relations in the Modern Arab World (New York: Oxford University Press, 2020).

Hagan, Joe D., Philip P. Everts, Haruhiro Fukui, and John D. Stempel. "Foreign Policy by Coalition: Deadlock, Compromise, and Anarchy." *International Studies Review* 3:2 (Summer 2001), pp. 169–216.

Halperin, Morton H., Priscilla A. Clapp, and Arnold Kanter. *Bureaucratic Politics and Foreign Policy*, second edition (Washington, D.C.: The Brookings Institution, 2006).

Hanson, Victor Davis. "Our Enemies, the Saudis," *Commentary*, 1 July 2002, https://www.commentarymagazine.com/articles/our-enemies-the-saudis/, retrieved 31 October 2016.

Hashim, Ahmed S. *Insurgency and Counter-Insurgency in Iraq* (Ithaca: Cornell University Press, 2006).

Hashemi, Nader and Danny Postel (eds). *Sectarianization: Mapping the New Politics of the Middle East* (Oxford: Oxford University Press, 2017).

BIBLIOGRAPHY

Hermann, Charles, Janice Gross Stein, Bengt Sundelius, and Stephen G. Walker. "Resolve, Accept, or Avoid: Effects of Group Conflict on Foreign Policy Decisions." *International Studies Review* 3:2 (Summer 2001): pp. 133–168.

Hermann, Margaret G. "How Decision Units Shape Foreign Policy: A Theoretical Framework." *International Studies Review* 3:2 (Summer 2001): pp. 47–81.

Hermann, Margaret G., Thomas Preston, Bahgat Korany, and Timothy M. Shaw. "Who Leads Matters: The Effects of Powerful Individuals." *International Studies Review* 3:2 (Summer 2001): pp. 83–131.

Herring, Eric and Glen Rangwala. *Iraq in Fragments: The Occupation and Its Legacy* (Ithaca: Cornell University Press, 2006).

Herrmann, Richard K. "Perceptions and Image Theory in International Relations," in Leonie Huddy, David O. Sears, and Jack S. Levy (eds), *The Oxford Handbook of Political Psychology* (Oxford: Oxford University Press, 2013).

Hertog, Steffen. *Princes, Brokers, and Bureaucrats: Oil and the State in Saudi Arabia* (Ithaca: Cornell University Press, 2010).

bin Hethlain, Naif. *Saudi Arabia and the US since 1962: Allies in Conflict* (London: Saqi, 2010).

Hill, Christopher R. *Outpost: Life on the Frontlines of American Diplomacy* (New York: Simon & Schuster, 2014).

Hilsman, Roger, Laura Gaughran, and Patricia A. Weitsman. *The Politics of Policy Making in Defense and Foreign Affairs: Conceptual Models and Bureaucratic Politics*, third edition (Englewood Cliffs: Prentice Hall, 1993).

Hinnebusch, Raymond. *The International Politics of the Middle East* (Manchester: Manchester University Press, 2003).

"The Sectarian Surge in the Middle East and the Dynamics of the Regional States-System." *Tidsskrift for Islamforskning* 13:1 (2019): 25–61.

Hinnebusch, Raymond and Anoushiravan Ehteshami (eds). *The Foreign Policies of Middle East States*, second edition (Boulder: Lynne Rienner, 2014).

Hirst, David. *Beware of Small States: Lebanon, Battleground of the Middle East* (New York: Nation Books, 2010).

BIBLIOGRAPHY

Holden, David, and Richard Johns. *The House of Saud* (London: Sidgwick and Jackson, 1981).

Holsti, Ole R. "The Belief System and National Images: A Case Study." *Journal of Conflict Resolution* 6:3 (September 1962): pp. 244–252.

Hopf, Ted. *Reconstructing the Cold War: The Early Years, 1945–1958* (Oxford: Oxford University Press, 2012).

Houghton, David Patrick. "Reinvigorating the Study of Foreign Policy Decision Making: Toward a Constructivist Approach." *Foreign Policy Analysis* 3 (2007): pp. 24–45.

"The Role of Self-Fulfilling and Self-Negating Prophecies in International Relations." *International Studies Review* 11:3 (September 2009): pp. 552–584.

Hovland, Carl I., Irving L. Janis, and Harold H. Kelley. *Communication and Persuasion: Psychological Studies of Opinion Change* (New Haven: Yale University Press, 1953).

Huddy, Leonie, David O. Sears, and Jack S. Levy (eds). *The Oxford Handbook of Political Psychology*, second edition (Oxford: Oxford University Press, 2013).

Ibrahim, Fouad. *The Shi'is of Saudi of Saudi Arabia* (London: Saqi, 2006).

Indyk, Martin. *Innocent Abroad: An Intimate Account of American Diplomacy in the Middle East* (New York: Simon & Schuster, 2009).

International Crisis Group. *Iraq's Transition: On a Knife Edge*, Middle East Report No. 27 (27 April 2004).

Iraq: Allaying Turkey's Fears over Kurdish Ambitions, Middle East Report No. 35 (26 January 2005).

Iran in Iraq: How Much Influence?, Middle East Report No. 38 (21 March 2005).

Syria after Lebanon, Lebanon after Syria, Middle East Report No. 39 (12 April 2005).

Iraq: Don't Rush the Constitution, Middle East Report No. 42 (8 June 2005).

Unmaking Iraq: A Constitutional Process Gone Awry, Middle East Briefing No. 19 (26 September 2005).

In Their Own Words: Reading the Iraqi Insurgency, Middle East Report No. 50 (15 February 2006).

BIBLIOGRAPHY

The Next Iraqi War? Sectarianism and Civil Conflict, Middle East Report No. 52 (27 February 2006).

Iraq's Muqtada al-Sadr: Spoiler or Stabiliser?, Middle East Report No. 55 (11 July 2006).

Where Is Iraq Heading? Lessons from Basra, Middle East Report No. 67 (25 June 2007).

Shiite Politics in Iraq: The Role of the Supreme Council, Middle East Report No. 70 (15 November 2007).

Iraq's Civil War, the Sadrists and the Surge, Middle East Report No. 72 (7 February 2008).

Iraq after the Surge I: The New Sunni Landscape, Middle East Report No. 74 (30 April 2008).

Iraq after the Surge II: The Need for a New Political Strategy, Middle East Report No. 75 (30 April 2008).

Engaging Syria? Lessons from the French Experience, Middle East Briefing No. 27 (15 January 2009).

Iraq's Provincial Elections: The Stakes, Middle East Report No. 82 (27 January 2009).

Engaging Syria? U.S. Constraints and Opportunities, Middle East Report No. 83 (11 February 2009).

Iraq's New Battlefront: The Struggle over Nineveh, Middle East Report No. 90 (28 September 2009).

Reshuffling the Cards? (I): Syria's Evolving Strategy, Middle East Report No. 92 (14 December 2009).

Reshuffling the Cards? (II): Syria's New Hand, Middle East Report No. 93 (16 December 2009).

Iraq's Uncertain Future: Elections and Beyond, Middle East Report No. 94 (25 February 2010).

Loose Ends: Iraq's Security Forces between U.S. Drawdown and Withdrawal, Middle East Report No. 99 (26 October 2010).

Trial by Fire: The Politics of the Special Tribunal for Lebanon, Middle East Report No. 100 (2 December 2010).

Iraq's Secular Opposition: The Rise and Decline of Al-Iraqiya, Middle East Report No. 127 (31 July 2012).

Déjà Vu All Over Again? Iraq's Escalating Political Crisis, Middle East Report No. 126 (30 July 2012).

BIBLIOGRAPHY

Make or Break: Iraq's Sunnis and the State, Middle East Report No. 144 (14 August 2013).

The International Institute for Strategic Studies. *The Military Balance, 1970–1971* (London: The International Institute for Strategic Studies, 1970).

The Military Balance, 1977–1978 (London: The International Institute for Strategic Studies, 1977).

The Military Balance, 1990–1991 (London: The International Institute for Strategic Studies, 1990).

The Military Balance, 1993–1994 (London: Brassey's, 1993).

Isakhan, Benjamin. "The Road to the 'Islamic State': State-Society Relations after the US Withdrawal from Iraq," in Benjamin Isakhan, Shamiran Mako, and Fadi Dawood (eds), *State and Society in Iraq: Citizenship under Occupation, Dictatorship and Democratisation* (London: I.B. Tauris, 2017).

Isakhan, Benjamin (ed.). *The Legacy of Iraq: From the 2003 War to the "Islamic State"* (Edinburgh: Edinburgh University Press, 2015).

Isakhan, Benjamin, Shamiran Mako, and Fadi Dawood (eds). *State and Society in Iraq: Citizenship under Occupation, Dictatorship and Democratisation* (London: I.B. Tauris, 2017).

Jabar, Faleh A. *The Shi'ite Movement in Iraq* (London: Saqi, 2003).

Postconflict Iraq: A Race for Stability, Reconstruction, and Legitimacy, United States Institute of Peace, Special Report 120 (May 2004).

Janis, Irving L. *Groupthink: Psychological Studies of Policy Decisions and Fiascoes* (Boston: Wadsworth/Cengage Learning, 1982).

Jansen, G. H. "The Attitudes of the Arab Governments," in M.S. El Azhary (ed.), *The Iran–Iraq War: An Historical, Economic, and Political Analysis* (London: Croom Helm, 1984).

Jervis, Robert. "Perceiving and Coping with Threat," in Robert Jervis, Richard Ned Lebow, and Janice Gross Stein (eds), *Psychology and Deterrence* (Baltimore: The Johns Hopkins University Press, 1985).

American Foreign Policy in a New Era (New York: Routledge, 2005).

Why Intelligence Fails: Lessons from the Iranian Revolution and the Iraq War (Ithaca: Cornell University Press, 2010).

"Do Leaders Matter and How Would We Know?" *Security Studies* 22:2 (2013): pp. 153–179.

Perception and Misperception in International Politics, second edition (Princeton: Princeton University Press, 2017).

Jervis, Robert, Richard Ned Lebow, and Janice Gross Stein (eds). *Psychology and Deterrence* (Baltimore: The Johns Hopkins University Press, 1985).

Johnson, Rob. *The Iran–Iraq War* (New York: Palgrave Macmillan, 2010).

Johnston, Trevor, Matthew Lane, Abigail Casey, Heather J. Williams, Ashley L. Rhoades, James Sladden, Nathan Vest, Jordan R. Reimer, and Ryan Haberman. *Could the Houthis Be the Next Hizballah? Iranian Proxy Development in Yemen and the Future of the Houthi Movement* (Santa Clara: RAND Corporation, 2020).

Jones, Clive and Sergio Catignani (eds). *Israel and Hizbollah: An Asymmetric Conflict in Historical and Comparative Perspective* (London: Routledge, 2010).

Jones, Toby C. "Rebellion on the Saudi Periphery: Modernity, Marginalization, and the Shi'a Uprising of 1979." *International Journal of Middle East Studies* 38:2 (May 2006), pp. 213–233.

Desert Kingdom: How Oil and Water Forged Modern Saudi Arabia (Cambridge: Harvard University Press, 2010).

"Saudi-Iraq Relations: Devolving Chaos or Acrimonious Stability?" in Henri J. Barkey, Scott B. Lasensky, and Phebe Marr (eds), *Iraq, Its Neighbors, and the United States: Competition, Crisis, and the Reordering of Power* (Washington, D.C.: United States Institute of Peace, 2011).

Jordan, Robert W., with Steve Fiffer. *Desert Diplomat: Inside Saudi Arabia Following 9/11* (Lincoln: Potomac Books, 2015).

Kagan, Kimberly. *The Surge: A Military History* (New York: Encounter Books, 2009).

Kamrava, Mehran (ed.). *The International Politics of the Persian Gulf* (Syracuse: Syracuse University Press, 2012).

Karsh, Efraim. "Military Power and Foreign Policy Goals: The Iran-Iraq War Revisited." *International Affairs*, 64:1 (Winter 1987–1988): pp. 83–95.

The Iran–Iraq War, 1980–1988 (Oxford: Osprey Publishing Ltd., 2002).

BIBLIOGRAPHY

Karsh, Efraim (ed.). *The Iran–Iraq War: Impact and Implications* (Basingstoke: Macmillan in association with The Jaffee Center for Strategic Studies, 1989).

Karsh, Efraim and Inari Rautsi. *Saddam Hussein: A Political Biography* (New York: Grove Press, 1991).

Katzenstein, Peter J. (ed.). *The Culture of National Security: Norms and Identity in World Politics* (New York: Columbia University Press, 1996).

Kechichian, Joseph A. *Succession in Saudi Arabia* (New York: Palgrave, 2001).

Keddie, Nikki R. *Roots of Revolution: An Interpretative History of Modern Iran* (New Haven: Yale University Press, 1981).

Kelman, Herbert C. (ed.). *International Behavior: A Social-Psychological Analysis* (New York: Holt, Reinhart and Winston, 1965).

Kerr, Malcolm H. *The Arab Cold War: Gamal Abd al-Nasir and His Rivals, 1958–1970*, third edition (Oxford: Oxford University Press for The Royal Institute of International Affairs, 1971).

Keynoush, Banafsheh. *Saudi Arabia and Iran: Friends or Foes?* (London: Palgrave Macmillan, 2016).

Khadduri, Majid. *Independent Iraq 1932–1958: A Study in Iraqi Politics*, second edition (London: Oxford University Press for The Royal Institute of International Affairs, 1960).

Republican 'Iraq: A Study in 'Iraqi Politics since the Revolution of 1958 (London: Oxford University Press, 1969).

Socialist Iraq: A Study in Iraqi Politics since 1968 (Washington, D.C.: Middle East Institute, 1978).

The Gulf War: The Origins and Implications of the Iraq–Iran Conflict (Oxford: Oxford University Press, 1988).

Khalilzad, Zalmay. *The Envoy: From Kabul to the White House, My Journey through a Turbulent World* (New York: St. Martin's Press, 2016).

Khalilzad, Zalmay M. and Paul Wolfowitz. "Overthrow Him," *Weekly Standard*, 1 December 1997, http://www.weeklystandard.com/overthrow-him/article/10022, retrieved 21 October 2016.

Khong, Yuen Foong. *Analogies at War: Korea, Munich, Dien Bien Phu, and the Vietnam Decisions of 1965* (Princeton: Princeton University Press, 1992).

BIBLIOGRAPHY

Knights, Michael and Ed Williams. *The Calm before the Storm: The British Experience in Southern Iraq*, Washington Institute for Near East Policy, Policy Focus #66 (February 2007).

Korany, Bahgat, "Defending the Faith amid Change: The Foreign Policy of Saudi Arabia," in Bahgat Korany and Ali E. Dessouki (eds), *The Foreign Policies of Arab States: The Challenge of Change*, second edition (Boulder: Westview Press, 1991).

Korany, Bahgat and Ali E. Dessouki. *The Foreign Policies of Arab States: The Challenge of Change*, second edition (Boulder: Westview Press, 1991).

Kostiner, Joseph. "Shi'i Unrest in the Gulf," in Martin Kramer (ed.), *Shi'ism, Resistance, and Revolution* (Boulder: Westview Press, 1987).

Kramer, Martin (ed.). *Shi'ism, Resistance, and Revolution* (Boulder: Westview Press, 1987).

Kraochwil, Friedrich V. "Constructivism as an Approach to Inter-disciplinary Study," in Karin M. Fierke and Knud Erik Jørgensen (eds), *Constructing International Relations: The Next Generation* (Armonk: M.E. Sharpe, 2001).

Kydd, Andrew H. "Trust, Reassurance, and Cooperation." *International Organization* 54:2 (Spring 2000): pp. 325–357.

——— *Trust and Mistrust in International Relations* (Princeton: Princeton University Press, 2005).

Laitin, David D. *Identity in Formation: The Russian Speaking Populations of the Near Abroad* (Ithaca: Cornell University Press, 1998).

Larson, Deborah Welch. *The Origins of Containment: A Psychological Explanation* (Princeton: Princeton University Press, 1985).

Lasensky, Scott B. "Coming to Terms: Jordan's Embrace of Post-Saddam Iraq," in Henri J. Barkey, Scott B. Lasensky, and Phebe Marr (eds), *Iraq, Its Neighbors, and the United States: Competition, Crisis, and the Reordering of Power* (Washington, D.C.: United States Institute of Peace, 2011).

Lawson, Fred H. (ed.). *Demystifying Syria* (London: Saqi in association with The London Middle East Institute, 2009).

Lazarus, Richard S. *Psychological Stress and the Coping Process* (New York: McGraw-Hill, 1966).

BIBLIOGRAPHY

Lebow, Richard Ned and Janice Gross Stein. *We All Lost the Cold War* (Princeton: Princeton University Press, 1994).

Lemieux, Marc and Shamiran Mako. "Political Parties, Elections and the Transformation of Iraqi Politics Since 2003," in Benjamin Isakhan, Shamiran Mako and Fadi Dawood (eds), *State and Society in Iraq: Citizenship under Occupation, Dictatorship and Democratisation* (London: I.B. Tauris, 2017).

Levy, Jack S. "Psychology and Foreign Policy," in David O. Sears, Leonie Huddy, and Robert Jervis (eds), *The Oxford Handbook of Political Psychology* (Oxford: Oxford University Press, 2003).

"Psychology and Foreign Policy Decision-Making," in Leonie Huddy, David O. Sears, and Jack S. Levy (eds), *The Oxford Handbook of Political Psychology*, second edition (Oxford: Oxford University Press, 2013).

Litwak, Robert S. "The Soviet Union and the Iran–Iraq War," in Efraim Karsh (ed.), *The Iran-Iraq War: Impact and Implications* (Basingstoke: Macmillan in association with The Jaffee Center for Strategic Studies, 1989).

Longrigg, Stephen Hemsley. *'Iraq, 1900 to 1950: A Political, Social, and Economic History* (London: Oxford University Press, 1953).

Louër, Laurence. *Transnational Shia Politics: Religious and Political Networks in the Gulf* (London: Hurst in association with the Centre d'Etudes et de Recherches Internationales, 2008).

Louër, Laurence. Trans. John King. *Shiism and Politics in the Middle East* (New York: Columbia University Press, 2012).

Louër, Laurence. Trans. Ethan Rundell. *Sunnis and Shi'a: A Political History of Discord* (Princeton: Princeton University Press, 2020).

Lowenthal, Abraham F. *The Dominican Intervention* (Cambridge: Harvard University Press, 1972).

Luciani, Giacomo and Hazem Beblawi. *The Rentier State* (London: Croom Helm, 1987).

Luizard, Pierre-Jean. *La Formation de l'Irak contemporain: Le rôle politique des ulémas chiites à la fin de la domination ottoman et au moment de la construction de l'Etat irakien* [*The Formation of Contemporary Iraq: The Political Role of the Shi'a 'Ulama' at the End of the Ottoman Domination*

BIBLIOGRAPHY

and at the Moment of the Construction of the Iraqi State] (Paris: Edition du Centre national de la recherche scientifique, 1991).

Lukitz, Liora. *Iraq: The Search for National Identity* (London: Frank Cass, 1995).

Mabon, Simon. *Saudi Arabia and Iran: Soft Power Rivalry in the Middle East* (London: I.B. Tauris, 2013).

Mackie, Diane M., Leila T. Worth, and Arlene G. Asuncion. "Processing of Persuasive In-Group Messages." *Journal of Personality and Social Psychology* 58:5 (1990): pp. 812–822.

Madon, Stephanie, Jennifer Willard, Max Guyll, and Kyle C. Scherr. "Self-Fulfilling Prophecies: Mechanisms, Power, and Links to Social Problems." *Social and Personality Psychology Compass* 5:8 (2011): pp. 578–590.

al-Mani', Salih. *"al-'Alaqat al-Sa'udiyya al-'Iraqiyya fi A'qab Ihtilal al-'Iraq"* ["Saudi–Iraq Relations in the Wake of the Occupation of Iraq"], *Ara hawla-l-Khalij*, Issue 7 (2005).

Mann, James. *Rise of the Vulcans: The History of Bush's War Cabinet* (New York: Viking, 2004).

Mapping Militant Organizations. "Asa'ib Ahl al-Haq." Stanford University. Last modified July 2018. https://cisac.fsi.stanford.edu/mappingmilitants/profiles/asaib-ahl-al-haq, retrieved 30 July 2020.

Maréchal, Brigitte and Sami Zemni (eds). *The Dynamics of Sunni-Shia Relationships: Doctrine, Transnationalism, Intellectuals and the Media* (London: Hurst, 2013).

Marr, Phebe and Ibrahim al-Marashi. *The Modern History of Iraq*, fourth edition (Boulder: Westview Press, 2017).

Marr, Phebe and Sam Parker. "The New Iraq: The Post-2003 Upheavals and Regional Aftershocks," in Henri J. Barkey, Scott B. Lasensky, and Phebe Marr (eds), *Iraq, Its Neighbors, and the United States: Competition, Crisis, and the Reordering of Power* (Washington, D.C.: United States Institute of Peace, 2011).

Marschall, Christin. *Iran's Persian Gulf Policy: From Khomeini to Khatami* (London: Routledge, 2003).

Mason, Robert. *Foreign Policy in Iran and Saudi Arabia: Economics and Diplomacy in the Middle East* (London: I.B. Tauris, 2015).

Matthiesen, Toby. *The Other Saudis: Shiism, Dissent and Sectarianism* (Cambridge: Cambridge University Press, 2015).

McDermott, Rose. *Political Psychology in International Relations* (Ann Arbor: The University of Michigan Press, 2004).

McNaugher, Thomas L. "Walking Tightropes in the Gulf," in Efraim Karsh (ed.), *The Iran–Iraq War: Impact and Implications* (Basingstoke: Macmillan in association with The Jaffee Center for Strategic Studies, 1989).

Mearsheimer, John J. *The Tragedy of Great Power Politics* (New York: W.W. Norton & Company, 2011).

Merton, Robert K. *Social Theory and Social Structure*, second edition (Glencoe: The Free Press, 1957).

Morgenthau, Hans J. Revised by Kenneth W. Thompson and W. David Clinton. *Politics among Nations: The Struggle for Power and Peace*, seventh edition (Boston: McGraw Hill, 2005).

Murphy, Dan. "New Iraqi leader cuts a strong figure," *Christian Science Monitor*, 20 July 2004, https://www.csmonitor.com/2004/0720/p01s03-woiq.html, retrieved 6 September 2017.

Mylroie, Laurie. *Regional Security After Empire: Saudi Arabia and the Gulf*, PhD thesis (Harvard University, 1985).

A Study in Revenge: Saddam Hussein's Unfinished War Against America (Washington, D.C.: AEI Press, 2000).

Nada, Garrett. "Part 1: Iran's Role in Iraq." Wilson Center, 26 April 2018, https://www.wilsoncenter.org/article/part-1-irans-role-iraq, retrieved 1 September 2020.

Nakash, Yitzhak. *The Shi'is of Iraq* (Princeton: Princeton University Press, 1994).

Reaching for Power: The Shi'a in the Modern Arab World (Princeton: Princeton University Press, 2006).

Neustadt, Richard E. and Ernest R. May. *Thinking in Time: The Uses of History for Decisionmakers* (New York: The Free Press, 1986).

Niblock, Tim. *Saudi Arabia: Power, Legitimacy and Survival* (London: Routledge, 2006).

Niblock, Tim (ed.). *Iraq: The Contemporary State* (New York: St. Martin's Press, 1982).

Nickerson, Raymond S. "Confirmation Bias: A Ubiquitous Phenomenon in Many Guises." *Review of General Psychology* 2:2 (June 1998): pp. 175–220.

Nisbett, Richard and Less Ross. *Human Inference: Strategies and Short-comings of Social Judgment* (Englewood Cliffs: Prentice-Hall, Inc., 1980).

Nonneman, Gerd. *Iraq, the Gulf States & the War: A Changing Relationship, 1980–1986 and beyond* (London: Ithaca Press, 1986).

"The Gulf States and the Iran–Iraq War: Pattern Shifts and Continuities" in Lawrence G. Potter and Gary G. Sick (eds), *Iran, Iraq, and the Legacies of War* (New York: Palgrave Macmillan, 2004).

"Determinants and Patterns of Saudi Foreign Policy: 'Omnibalancing' and 'Relative Autonomy' in Multiple Environments," in Paul Aarts and Gerd Nonneman (eds), *Saudi Arabia in the Balance: Political Economy, Society, Foreign Affairs* (New York: New York University Press, 2005).

Obaid, Nawaf and Anthony Cordesman. *Saudi Militants in Iraq: Assessment and Kingdom's Response*, Center for Strategic and International Studies (19 September 2005).

O'Ballance, Edgar. *The Gulf War* (London: Brassey's Defence Publishers, 1988).

Olson, Robert. "Turkey's Relations with the Gulf Cooperation Council from 2003 to 2007: New Paradigms?" *Mediterranean Quarterly* 19: 3 (summer 2008): pp. 68–87.

Onuf, Nicholas. *World of Our Making: Rules and Rule in Social Theory and International Relations* (Columbia: University of South Carolina Press, 1989).

Osman, Khalil F. *Sectarianism in Iraq: The Making of State and Nation since 1920* (London: Routledge, 2015).

Palmer, Michael A. *Guardians of the Gulf: A History of America's Expanding Role in the Persian Gulf, 1833–1992* (New York: Free Press, 1992).

Parker, Ned and Raheem Salman. "Notes from the Underground: The Rise of Nouri al-Maliki." *World Policy*, 20 February 2012, https//world-policy.org/2012/02/20/notes-from-the-underground-the-rise-of-nouri-al-maliki/, retrieved 25 March 2019.

Partrick, Neil. "Domestic Factors and Foreign Policy" in Neil Partrick (ed.), *Saudi Arabian Foreign Policy: Conflict and Cooperation* (London: I.B. Tauris, 2016).

"Saudi Arabia and Iran," in Neil Partrick (ed.), *Saudi Arabian Foreign Policy: Conflict and Cooperation* (London: I.B. Tauris, 2016).

"Saudi Arabia and Iraq," in Neil Partrick (ed.), *Saudi Arabian Foreign Policy: Conflict and Cooperation* (London: I.B. Tauris, 2016).

Partrick, Neil (ed.). *Saudi Arabian Foreign Policy: Conflict and Cooperation* (London: I.B. Tauris, 2016).

Perks, Robert and Alistair Thomson (eds). *The Oral History Reader*, third edition (London: Routledge, 2016).

Peterson, J.E. *Saudi Arabia and the Illusion of Security*, Adelphi Paper 348 (Oxford: Oxford University Press for The International Institute for Strategic Studies, 2002).

Pollack, Kenneth M. "Ties that Bind: The United States, Iraq, and the Neighbors," in Henri J. Barkey, Scott B. Lasensky, and Phebe Marr (eds), *Iraq, Its Neighbors, and the United States: Competition, Crisis, and the Reordering of Power* (Washington, D.C.: United States Institute of Peace, 2011).

"Something Is Rotten in the State of Iraq," *National Interest*, No. 115 (September/October 2011), pp. 59–68.

"Reading Machiavelli in Iraq," *National Interest*, No. 122 (November/December 2012), pp. 8–19.

Potter, Laurence G. (ed.). *Sectarian Politics in the Persian Gulf* (New York: Oxford University Press, 2014).

Powell, Colin with Joseph E. Persico. *My American Journey* (New York: Ballantine Books, 1996).

Prados, Alfred B. "Jordan: U.S. Relations and Bilateral Issues," CRS Issue Brief for Congress, Congressional Research Service, 26 April 2006, p. ii, available at http://www.fas.org/sgp/crs/mideast/IB93085.pdf, retrieved 4 June 2016.

Preuschaft, Menno. "Islam and Identity in Foreign Policy," in Neil Partrick (ed.), *Saudi Arabian Foreign Policy: Conflict and Cooperation* (London: I.B. Tauris, 2016).

Pruitt, Dean G. "Definition of the Situation as a Determinant of International Action," in Herbert C. Kelman (ed.), *International Behavior: A*

BIBLIOGRAPHY

Social-Psychological Analysis (New York: Holt, Reinhart and Winston, 1965).

al-Qasab, Abd al-Wahhab. *"al-'Iraq wa-l-Sa'udiyya: Inshighalat al-Hadir"* ["Iraq and Saudi Arabia: Present Concerns"], *Ara hawla-l-Khalij*, Issue 7 (2005).

Quandt, William B. *Saudi Arabia in the 1980s: Foreign Policy, Security, and Oil* (Washington, D.C.: Brookings Institution, 1981).

Ramazani, R.K. *Iran's Foreign Policy, 1941–1973* (Charlottesville: University Press of Virginia, 1975).

Revolutionary Iran: Challenge and Response in the Middle East (Baltimore: Johns Hopkins University Press, 1986).

Independence without Freedom: Iran's Foreign Policy (Charlottesville: University of Virginia Press, 2013).

"Iran's Export of the Revolution: Its Politics, Ends, and Means," in R.K. Ramazani, *Independence without Freedom: Iran's Foreign Policy* (Charlottesville: University of Virginia Press, 2013).

"Shiism in the Persian Gulf," in R.K. Ramazani, *Independence without Freedom: Iran's Foreign Policy* (Charlottesville: University of Virginia Press, 2013).

Al-Rasheed, Madawi. "Circles of Power: Royals and Society in Saudi Arabia," in Paul Aarts and Gerd Nonneman (eds), *Saudi Arabia in the Balance: Political Economy, Society, Foreign Affairs* (New York: New York University Press, 2005).

"Saudi Arabia: The Challenge of the US Invasion of Iraq," in Rick Fawn and Raymond Hinnebusch (eds), *The Iraq War: Causes and Consequences* (Boulder: Lynne Rienner, 2006).

A History of Saudi Arabia, second edition (Cambridge: Cambridge University Press, 2010).

"Sectarianism as Counter-Revolution: Saudi Responses to the Arab Spring," in Nader Hashemi and Danny Postel (eds), *Sectarianization: Mapping the New Politics of the Middle East* (Oxford: Oxford University Press, 2017).

Rayburn, Colonel Joel E. and Colonel Frank K. Sobchak (eds). *The U.S. Army in the Iraq War*, 2 vols. (Carlisle: Strategic Studies Institute and U.S. Army War College Press, 2019).

BIBLIOGRAPHY

Redlawsk, David P. "A Matter of 'Motivated' Reasoning," in "Barack Obama and the Psychology of the 'Birther' Myth," The Opinion Pages: Room for Debate, *New York Times*, 21 April 2011, https://www.nytimes.com/roomfordebate/2011/04/21/barack-obama-and-the-psychology-of-the-birther-myth, retrieved 1 March 2018.

Ricks, Thomas E. *Fiasco: The American Military Adventure in Iraq* (New York: Penguin Press, 2006).

Riedel, Bruce and Bilal Y. Saab. "Al Qaeda's Third Front: Saudi Arabia," *Washington Quarterly* 31:2 (Spring 2008): pp. 33–46.

Rieger, René. *Saudi Arabian Foreign Relations: Diplomacy and Mediation in Conflict Resolution* (Abingdon: Routledge, 2016).

Risse-Kappen, Thomas. "Democratic Peace—Warlike Democracies? A Social Constructivist Interpretation of the Liberal Argument." *European Journal of International Relations* 1:4 (1995): pp. 491–517.

Ritchie, Nick and Paul Rogers. *The Political Road to War with Iraq: Bush, 9/11 and the Drive to Overthrow Saddam* (London: Routledge, 2007).

Rokeach, Milton. *The Open and Closed Mind: Investigations into the Nature of Belief Systems and Personality Systems* (New York: Basic Books, 1960).

Rosati, Jerel A. "Developing a Systematic Decision-Making Framework: Bureaucratic Politics in Perspective." *World Politics* 33:2 (January 1981): 234–252.

Rousseau, David L. *Identifying Threats and Threatening Identities: The Social Construction of Realism and Liberalism* (Stanford: Stanford University Press, 2006).

Rubin, Barry. "The Gulf States and the Iran-Iraq War," in Efraim Karsh (ed.), *The Iran–Iraq War: Impact and Implications* (Basingstoke: Macmillan in association with The Jaffee Center for Strategic Studies, 1989).

Safran, Nadav. *Saudi Arabia: The Ceaseless Quest for Security* (Ithaca: Cornell University Press, 1988).

Salama, Ghassan. *al-Siyasa al-kharijiyya al-Sa'udiyya mundhu 'am 1945: Dirasa fi-l-'alaqat al-duwaliyya* [*Saudi Foreign Policy since 1945: A Study in International Relations*] (Beirut: Ma'had al-Inma' al-'Arabi, 1980).

Salloukh, Bassel F. "The Sectarianization of Geopolitics in the Middle East," in Nader Hashemi and Danny Postel (eds), *Sectarianization:*

BIBLIOGRAPHY

Mapping the New Politics of the Middle East (Oxford: Oxford University Press, 2017).

Salmoni, Barak A., Bryce Loidolt, Madeleine Wells. *Regime and Periphery in Northern Yemen: The Huthi Phenomenon* (Santa Clara: RAND Corporation, 2010).

Samore, Gary Samuel. *Royal Family Politics in Saudi Arabia (1953–1982)*, PhD thesis (Harvard University, 1983).

Sassoon, Joseph. *Saddam Hussein's Ba'th Party: Inside an Authoritarian Regime* (Cambridge: Cambridge University Press, 2012).

al-Saud, Faisal bin Salman. *Iran, Saudi Arabia and the Gulf: Power Politics in Transition* (London: I.B. Tauris, 2003).

Schenker, David. *Dancing with Saddam: The Strategic Tango of Jordanian–Iraqi Relations* (Washington, D.C.: Washington Institute for Near East Policy, 2003).

Seale, Patrick. *The Struggle for Syria: A Study of Post-War Arab Politics 1945–1958* (London: Oxford University Press, 1965).

Seale, Patrick and Maureen McConville. *Asad of Syria: The Struggle for the Middle East*, second edition (Berkeley: University of California Press, 1995).

Sears, David O., Leonie Huddy, and Robert Jervis (eds). *The Oxford Handbook of Political Psychology* (Oxford: Oxford University Press, 2003).

al-Shamrani, Ali Muhammad. *Sira' al-'addad: al-Mu'arada al-'Iraqiyya ba'd harb al-Khalij* [*The Conflict of Counters: The Iraqi Opposition after the Gulf War*] (London: Dar al-Hikma, 2003).

Shannon, Vaughn P. and Paul A. Kowert (eds). *Psychology and Constructivism in International Relations: An Ideational Alliance* (Ann Arbor: The University of Michigan Press, 2012).

Shapiro, Michael J., and G. Matthew Bonham. "Cognitive Process and Foreign Policy Decision-Making." *International Studies Quarterly* 17:2 (June 1973): pp. 147–174.

Shimko, Keith L. *Images and Arms Control: Perceptions of the Soviet Union in the Reagan Administration* (Ann Arbor: The University of Michigan Press, 1991).

Sky, Emma. *The Unravelling: High Hopes and Missed Opportunities in Iraq* (New York: Public Affairs, 2015).

BIBLIOGRAPHY

Sluglett, Peter. *Britain in Iraq: Contriving King and Country* (London: I.B. Tauris, 2007).

Snyder, Mark, Elizabeth Decker Tanke, and Ellen Berscheid. "Social Perception and Interpersonal Behavior: On the Self-Fulfilling Nature of Social Stereotypes." *Journal of Personality and Social Psychology* 35:9 (1977): pp. 656–666.

Snyder, Richard C., H.W. Bruck, and Burton Sapin (eds). *Foreign Policy Decision-Making: An Approach to International Politics* (New York: Free Press, 1962).

Spiegel, Steven L. *The Other Arab-Israeli Conflict* (Chicago: The University of Chicago Press, 1985).

Stein, Aaron. *Turkey's New Foreign Policy: Davutoglu, the AKP and the Pursuit of Regional Order*, White Hall Paper 83 (Abingdon: Routledge Journals for the Royal United Services Institute for Defence and Security Studies, 2014).

Stein, Aaron and Philipp C. Bleek. "Turkish-Iranian Relations: From 'Friends with Benefits' to 'It's Complicated.'" *Insight Turkey* 14:4 (2012): 137–150.

Stein, Janice Gross. "Building Politics into Psychology: The Misperception of Threat." *Political Psychology* 9:2 (June 1988): pp. 245–271.

"Reassurance in International Conflict Management." *Political Science Quarterly* 106:3 (Autumn 1991): pp. 431–451.

"Threat Perception in International Relations," in Leonie Huddy, David O. Sears, and Jack S. Levy (eds), *The Oxford Handbook of Political Psychology*, second edition (Oxford: Oxford University Press, 2013).

Steinbruner, John D. *The Cybernetic Theory of Decision: New Dimensions of Political Analysis* (Princeton: Princeton University Press, 1974).

Stenslie, Stig. *Regime Stability in Saudi Arabia: The Challenge of Succession* (London: Routledge, 2012).

Sunayama, Sonoko. *Syria and Saudi Arabia: Collaboration and Conflicts in the Oil Era* (London: Tauris Academic Studies, 2007).

Tanter, Raymond and Richard H. Ullman (eds). *Theory and Policy in International Relations* (Princeton: Princeton University Press, 1972).

Tetlock, Philip E. *Expert Political Judgment: How Good Is It? How Can We Know?* (Princeton: Princeton University Press, 2005).

BIBLIOGRAPHY

Thomas, William and Dorothy Swain Thomas. *The Child in America* (New York: Knopf, 1928).

Transfeld, Mareike. "Iran's Small Hand in Yemen," Carnegie Endowment for International Peace, 14 February 2017, https://carnegieendowment. org/sada/67988, retrieved 30 August 2019.

Treviño, Rusty. "Is Iran an Offensives Realist or Defensive Realist? A Theoretical Reflection on Iranian Motives for Creating Instability." *Journal of Strategic Security* 6:3 (Fall 2013): pp. 382–392.

Tripp, Charles. *A History of Iraq*, third edition (Cambridge: Cambridge University Press, 2007).

Tripp, Charles (ed.). *Regional Security in the Middle East* (Aldershot: Gower for The International Institute for Strategic Studies, 1984).

Ubaid, Samir. "*Fadiha jadida wa bi-l-watha'iq takshif anna hakim al-'Iraq huwa safir Iran wa anna-l-Maliki sayaqtas min 13 barlamanian*" ["New scandal with documents that reveal that the ruler of Iraq is Iran's ambassador and that al-Maliki will retaliate against 13 parliamentarians"]. *Dunia al-Watan*, 16 March 2007, https://www.alwatanvoice.com/arabic/content/print/79403.html, retrieved 15 May 2018.

United States Department of Defense. *Measuring Stability and Security in Iraq*, Report to Congress (November 2006).

Measuring Stability and Security in Iraq, Report to Congress (March 2007).

Measuring Stability and Security in Iraq, Report to Congress (June 2007).

Measuring Stability and Security in Iraq, Report to Congress (September 2007).

Measuring Stability and Security in Iraq, Report to Congress (December 2007).

Measuring Stability and Security in Iraq, Report to Congress (March 2008).

Measuring Stability and Security in Iraq, Report to Congress (June 2008).

Measuring Stability and Security in Iraq, Report to Congress (September 2008).

Measuring Stability and Security in Iraq, Report to Congress (December 2008).

BIBLIOGRAPHY

al-Utaibi, Mansur Hasan. *Al-Siyasa al-Iraniyya tujah Duwal Majlis al-Taʿawun al-Khaliji (1979–2000) [Iranian Policy toward the States of the Gulf Cooperation Council (1979–2000)]* (Dubai: Markaz al-Khaliji li-l-Abhath, 2008).

Vassiliev, Alexei. *The History of Saudi Arabia* (New York: New York University Press, 2000).

Vatanka, Alex. "Iran's Moment of Truth with Maliki." Middle East Institute, 24 June 2014, https://www.mei.edu/publications/irans-moment-truth-maliki, retrieved 1 September 2020.

Vertzberger, Yaacov. *The World in their Minds: Information Processing, Cognition, and Perception in Foreign Policy Decisionmaking* (Stanford: Stanford University Press, 1990).

Walt, Stephen M. *The Origins of Alliances* (Ithaca: Cornell University Press, 1987).

Waltz, Kenneth N. *Theory of International Relations* (Reading: Addison-Wesley Publishers, 1979).

Wehrey, Frederic. *Sectarian Politics in the Gulf: From the Iraq War to the Arab Uprisings* (New York: Columbia University Press, 2014).

Wehrey, Frederic (ed.). *Beyond Sunni and Shia: The Roots of Sectarianism in a Changing Middle East* (New York: Oxford University Press, 2017).

Wehrey, Frederic, Theodore W. Karasik, Alireza Nader, Jeremy Ghez, Lydia Hansell, and Robert A. Guffey. *Saudi–Iranian Relations Since the Fall of Saddam: Rivalry, Cooperation, and Implications for U.S. Policy* (Santa Monica: RAND Corporation, 2009).

Wendt, Alexander E. "The agent-structure problem in international relations theory." *International Organization* 41:3 (Summer 1987): pp. 335–370.

"Anarchy is what states make of it: the social construction of power politics." *International Organization* 46:2 (Spring 1992): pp. 391–425.

"Collective Identity Formation and the International State." *The American Political Science Review* 88:2 (June 1994): pp. 384–396.

Social Theory of International Politics (Cambridge: Cambridge University Press, 1999).

Wiley, Joyce N. *The Islamic Movement of Iraqi Shiʿas* (Boulder: Lynne Rienner, 1992).

BIBLIOGRAPHY

Wolfowitz, Paul. "Victory Came Too Easily," *National Interest*, no. 35 (Spring 1994): pp. 87–92.

Woodward, Bob. *Plan of Attack* (New York: Simon & Schuster, 2004).

State of Denial (New York: Simon & Schuster, 2006).

The War Within: A Secret White House History, 2006–2008 (New York: Simon & Schuster, 2008).

Word, Carl O., Mark P. Zanna, and Joel Cooper. "The Nonverbal Mediation of Self-Fulfilling Prophecies in Interracial Interaction." *Journal of Experimental Social Psychology* 10 (1974): pp. 109–120.

Yacoubian, Mona. "Syria and the New Iraq: Between Rivalry and Rapprochement," in Henri J. Barkey, Scott B. Lasensky, and Phebe Marr (eds), *Iraq, Its Neighbors, and the United States: Competition, Crisis, and the Reordering of Power* (Washington, D.C.: United States Institute of Peace, 2011).

Yaphe, Judith S. "Iraq and Its Gulf Arab Neighbors: Avoiding Risks, Seeking Opportunity," in Henri J. Barkey, Scott B. Lasensky, and Phebe Marr (eds), *Iraq, Its Neighbors, and the United States: Competition, Crisis, and the Reordering of Power* (Washington, D.C.: United States Institute of Peace, 2011).

Yarhi-Milo, Keren. *Knowing the Adversary: Leaders, Intelligence, and Assessment of Intentions in International Relations* (Princeton: Princeton University Press, 2014).

Zakheim, Dov S. "Iraq's riots threaten Iran's plan for Middle East dominance." *Hill*, 9 December 2019, https://thehill.com/opinion/international/473606-iraqs-riots-threaten-irans-plan-for-middle-east-dominance, retrieved 1 September 2020.

Websites

Al-Islam.org. "Imam Khomeini's Last Will and Testament," Prologue, www.al-islam.org/imam-khomeini-s-last-will-and-testament/prologue, retrieved 18 November 2015.

Central Intelligence Agency. "The World Factbook—Iraq," https://www.cia.gov/library/publications/the-world-factbook/geos/iz/html, retrieved 21 January 2018.

Gallup News, "Iraq—Historical Gallup Trends," http://www.gallup.com/poll/1633/iraq.aspx, retrieved 5 June 2016.

BIBLIOGRAPHY

icausalties.org. "Iraq Coalition Casualties: Fatalities by Year and Month," http://icasualties.org/iraq/ByMonth.aspx, retrieved on 21 April 2016.

The Independent High Electoral Commission (Iraq). *"Asma' al-fa'izin fi-l-intikhabat al-ula—al-jam'iyya al-wataniyya wa majalis al-muhafazat"* ["Names of the Winners in the First Elections for the National Assembly and Provincial Councils"], http://www.ihec.iq/ftpar/election2004/other/name2.pdf, retrieved 10 July 2017.

"Asma' a'da' majlis al-nuwab al-muntakhabin fi intikhabat majlis al-nuwab" [Names of the Elected Members of the Council of Representatives in the Council of Representatives Elections"], http://www.ihec.iq/ftpar/regulation2005/other/The_names_of_the_members_of_the_House_of_Representatives_ar.pdf, retrieved 10 July 2017.

"Nata'ij intikhabat majlis al-nuwab al-'Iraqi 2010" ["2010 Council of Representatives Election Results"], http://www.ihec.iq/ar/result.html, retrieved 10 July 2017.

Iraq Body Count. "Database," https://www.iraqbodycount.org/database/, retrieved 26 June 2016.

"Incidents," https://www.iraqbodycount.org/database/incidents/page477, retrieved 11 July 2017.

Iraq Watch. "Open Letter to the President," Project for a New American Century, 19 February 1998, http://www.iraqwatch.org/perspectives/rumsfeld-openletter.htm, retrieved 18 February 2016.

Macrotrends. "Crude Oil Prices—70 Year Historical Chart," http://www.macrotrends.net/1369/crude-oil-price-history-chart, retrieved 27 August 2019.

Musings on Iraq. "Columbia University Charts Sectarian Cleansing of Baghdad," http://musingsoniraq.blogspot.co.uk/2009/11/blog-post.html, retrieved 11 April 2017.

National Council of Resistance of Iran. Jasir al-Jasir, *"Khutat al-nizam al-Safawi li-tadmir duwal al-khalij"* ["The Plans of the Safavid regime to destroy the Gulf states"], *al-Jazira*, 13 March 2011, https://www.ncr-iran.org/ar/اخبار-مقالات-سيده/12077, retrieved 22 July 2020.

Jasir al-Jasir, *"Khutat al-nizam al-Safawi li-tadmir al-duwal al-'Arabiyya—Misr—3"* ["The Plans of the Safavid regime to destroy the Arab states—Egypt—3"], *al-Jazira*, 14 March 2011, https://www.ncr-iran. org/ar/اخبار-مقالات-رسيده/12083, retrieved 22 July 2020.

Jasir al-Jasir, "*Khutat al-nizam al-Safawi li-tadmir al-duwal al-'Arabiyya 4—istighlal shabab wa Aqbat Misr*" ["The Plans of the Safavid regime to destroy the Arab states 4—exploiting the youth and Copts of Egypt"], *al-Jazira*, 15 March 2011, https://www.ncr-iran.org/ رسيده-مقالات-اخبار/12092, retrieved 22 July 2020.

Jasir al-Jasir, "*Khutat al-nizam al-Safawi li-tadmir al-duwal al-'Arabiyya*" ["The Plans of the Safavid regime to destroy the Arab states"], *al-Jazira*, 16 March 2011, https://www.ncr-iran.org/اخبار-مقالات-رسيده/ 12092, retrieved 22 July 2020.

Republic of Iraq, Ministry of Interior. "Iraqi Constitution," http://www. iraqinationality.gov.iq/attach/iraqi_constitution.pdf, retrieved 15 August 2016.

Ronald Reagan Oral History Project. "Interview with Caspar Weinberger," 19 November 2002, pp. 28–29. https://www.millercenter.org/the-presidency/presidential-oral-histories/caspar-weinberger-oral-history-secretary-defense, retrieved 21 February 2019.

United Nations High Commissioner for Refugees. "Iraqis in Jordan: Their Numbers and Characteristics," p. 3, http://www.unhcr.org/47626a232. pdf, retrieved 4 June 2016.

United Nations Security Council. "Resolution 687 of 3 April 1991," https://documents-dds-ny.un.org/doc/RESOLUTION/GEN/NR0/ 596/23/IMG/NR059623.pdf?OpenElement, retrieved 19 October 2016.

"Resolution 1441 of 8 November 2002," http://www.un.org/en/ga/ search/view_doc.asp?symbol=S/RES/1441(2002), retrieved 1 November 2016.

"Resolution 1559 of 2 September 2004," http://www.un.org/en/ga/ search/view_doc.asp?symbol=S/RES/1559(2004), retrieved 14 July 2016.

United States Department of Justice. "Unsealed Indictment of Main Suspect in Khobar Towers Bombing, Ahmed Al-Mughassil, et al," https://www.justice.gov/usao-edva/pr/unsealed-indictment-main-sus-pect-khobar-towers-bombing-ahmed-al-mughassil-et-al, retrieved 18 June 2019.

BIBLIOGRAPHY

United States Department of State. "Zarqawi Letter," http://2001–2009. state.gov/p/nea/rls/31694.htm, retrieved 27 April 2016.

World Bank. "The Islamic Republic of Iran." https://data.worldbank.org/country/iran-islamic-rep, retrieved 27 December 2018.

"Iraq." https://data.worldbank.org/country/iraq, retrieved 27 December 2018.

"Saudi Arabia." https://data.worldbank.org/country/saudi-arabia, retrieved 27 December 2018.

INDEX

Note: Page numbers followed by "*n*" refer to notes

INDEX

INDEX

INDEX

INDEX

INDEX

INDEX

INDEX